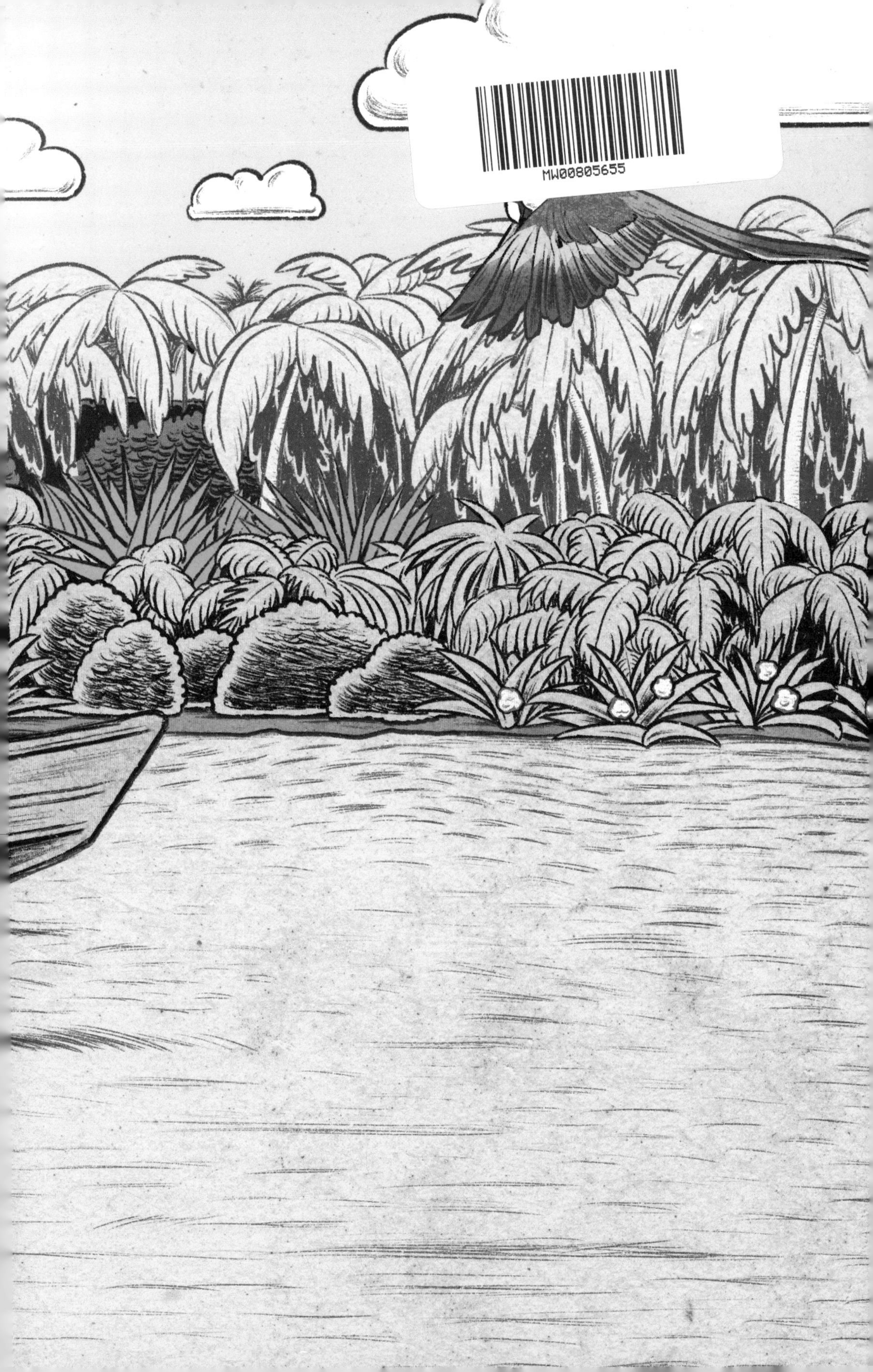

Good.

Good.

FROM THE AMAZON JUNGLE TO SUBURBIA AND BACK

BY FLuX & DAVID GOOD

nbm GRAPHIC NOVELS

Nantier • Beall • Minoustchine

NEW YORK

This book is a work of fiction inspired by actual events.

ISBN 9781681123301
Library of Congress Control Number: 2023952347
© FLuX, David Good, 2024
Printed in China
First printed May 2024

This title is also available wherever e-books are sold (ISBN 9781681123318)

ACKNOWLEDGEMENTS

This book would never have happened if it weren't for so many people. Firstly, I'd like to thank David, who's own coming-of-age & alienation story paralleled my own in many ways (not to mention we grew up not-so-far from each other). Secondly, I want to thank Kenneth Good for writing an incredible work that first sparked my interest in the Yanomami community. Thirdly, I am indebted to Janna Morishima for planting the seed in my brain to reach out to David in the first place. I'd also like to thank Terry Nantier for taking a chance on this book, and Chris Staros & Mark Siegel for their encouragement and help along the way. There are many others here too numerous to mention, including everyone who has inspired me to do what I think is right regardless of what's been done before. Finally, I'd be remiss to not give shout-outs to my wife and two kids for putting up with me sitting in the corner and working on this until the wee hours.

-FLuX

It has been quite the honor working with John Malloy to develop Good. I sincerely appreciate his dedication to seeing this project through to the end. His artistic insight has brought fantastic imagery of my journey in finding myself as an indigenous person and rediscovering my Yanomami heritage. I am forever grateful for Hortensia, who paved the way for me to find my mother in 2011. Though my mother is thousands of miles away, deep in the jungle, with no means of contact, I hope she knows how proud I am to be Yanomami and for learning the 'ways of the rainforest.' Much gratitude to my family and friends who have supported me over the years. For unlimited hugs, kisses, and encouragement, I did not need to go further than my kiddos -Kaleb and Naomi. A special and heartfelt thanks to my Suwa who has shown me love, kindness, and friendship. Suwa ipa ke!

-David Good

"One time I saw a tiny Joshua tree sapling growing not too far from the old tree. I wanted to dig it up and replant it near our house. I told Mom that I would protect it from the wind and water it every day so that it could grow nice and tall and straight. Mom frowned at me. "You'd be destroying what makes it special," she said. "It's the Joshua tree's struggle that gives it its beauty."
- Jeannette Walls, *The Glass Castle*

"In the social jungle of human existence, there is no feeling of being alive without a sense of identity."
- Erik Erikson, psychologist

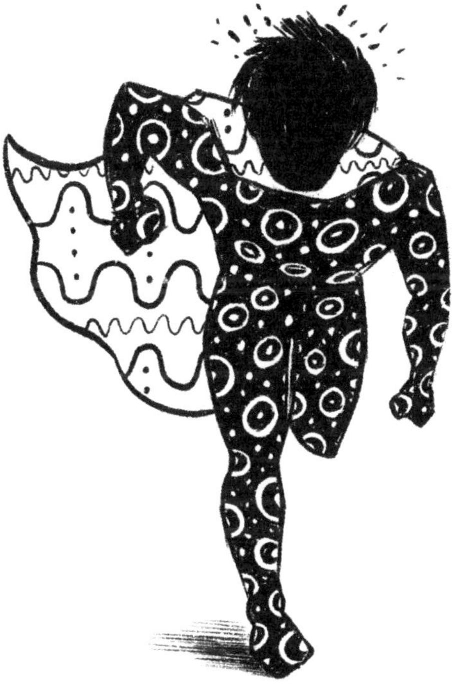

From as far back as I can remember,
I thought I was destined to be a
superhero.

They all had such incredible origin stories... murdered parents...

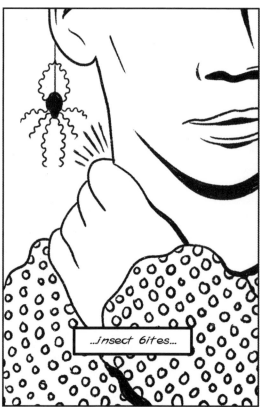

...insect bites...

...alien backgrounds...

...or some crazy chemical spill.

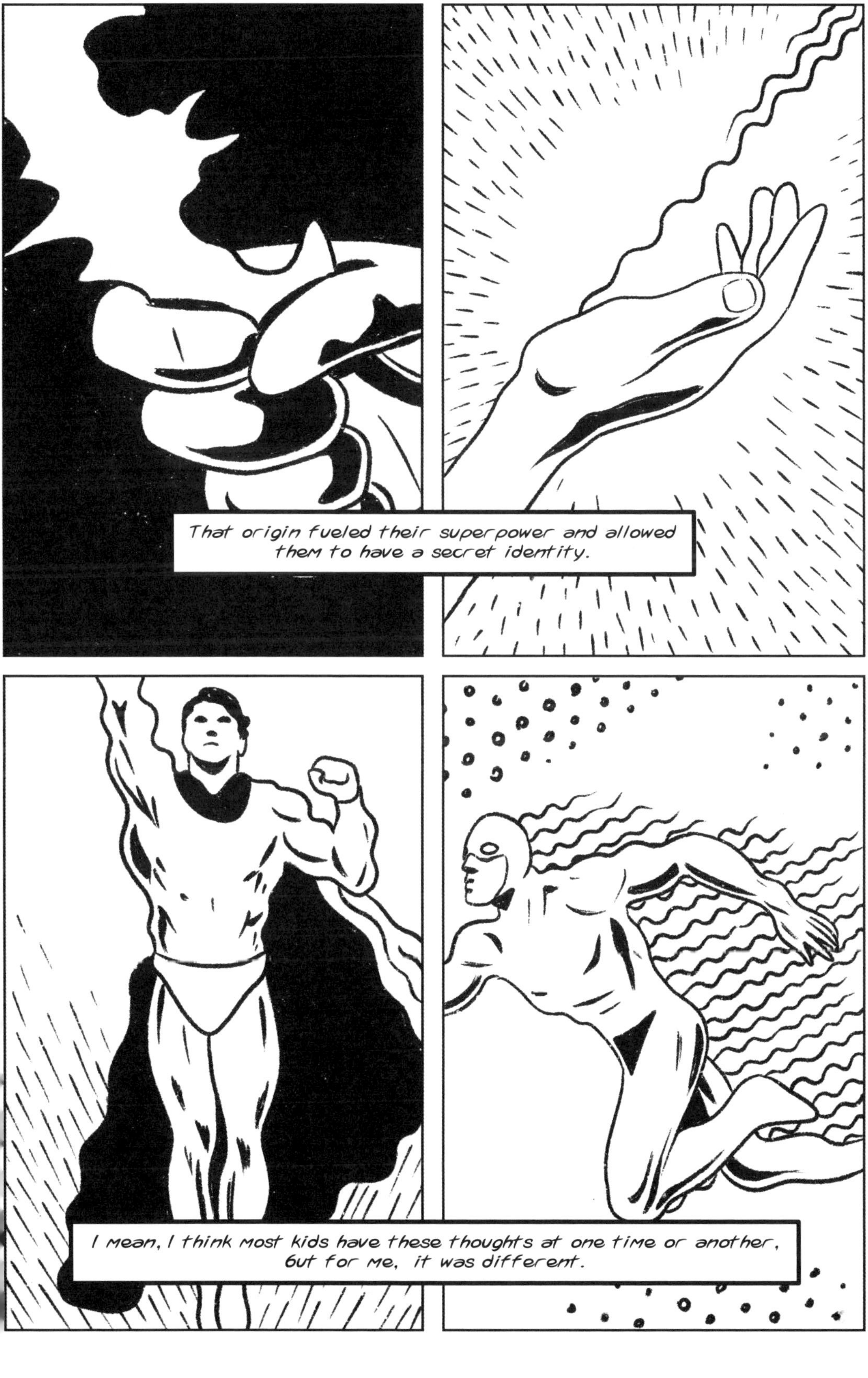
That origin fueled their superpower and allowed them to have a secret identity.
I mean, I think most kids have these thoughts at one time or another, but for me, it was different.

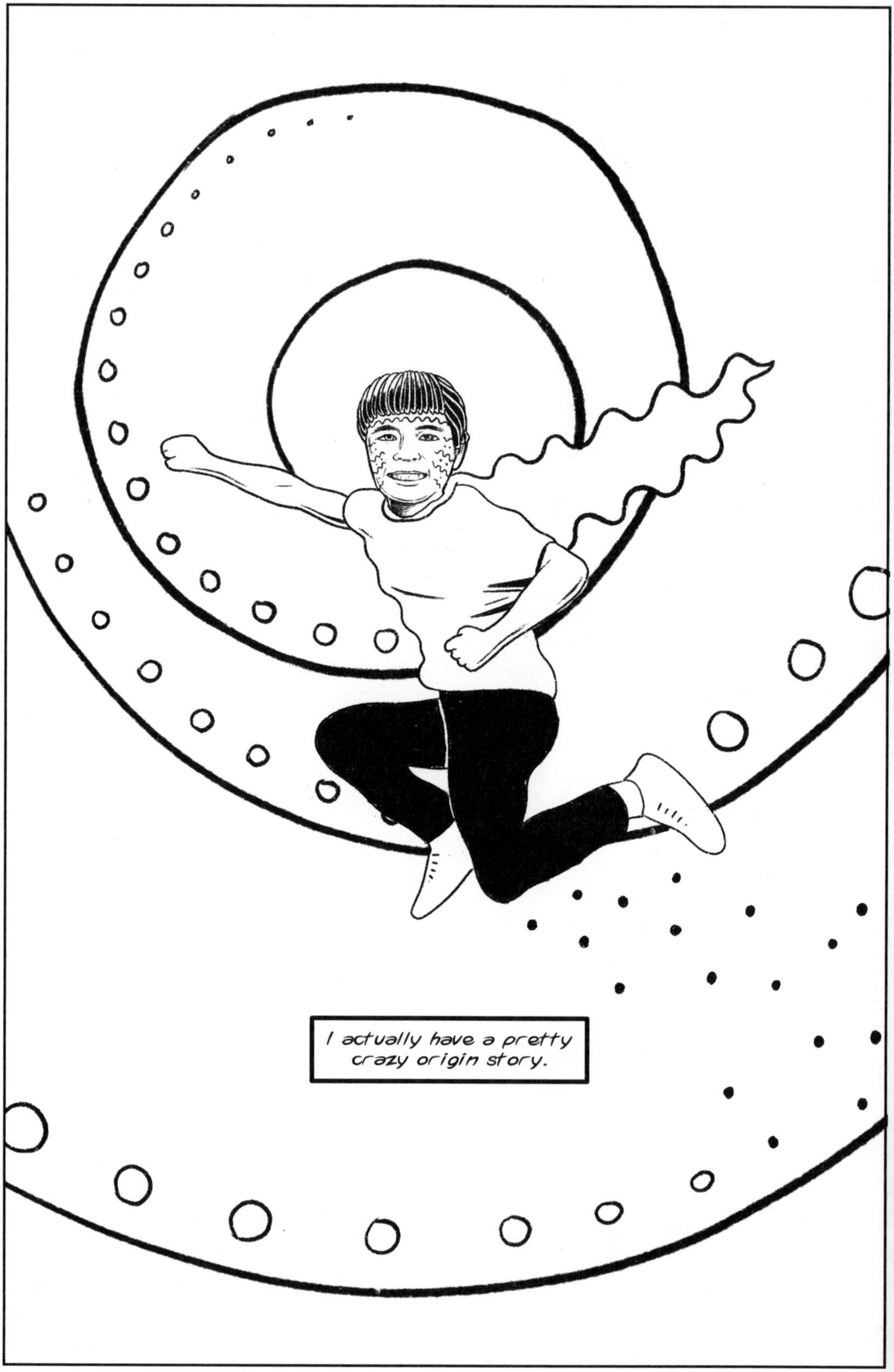
I actually have a pretty crazy origin story.

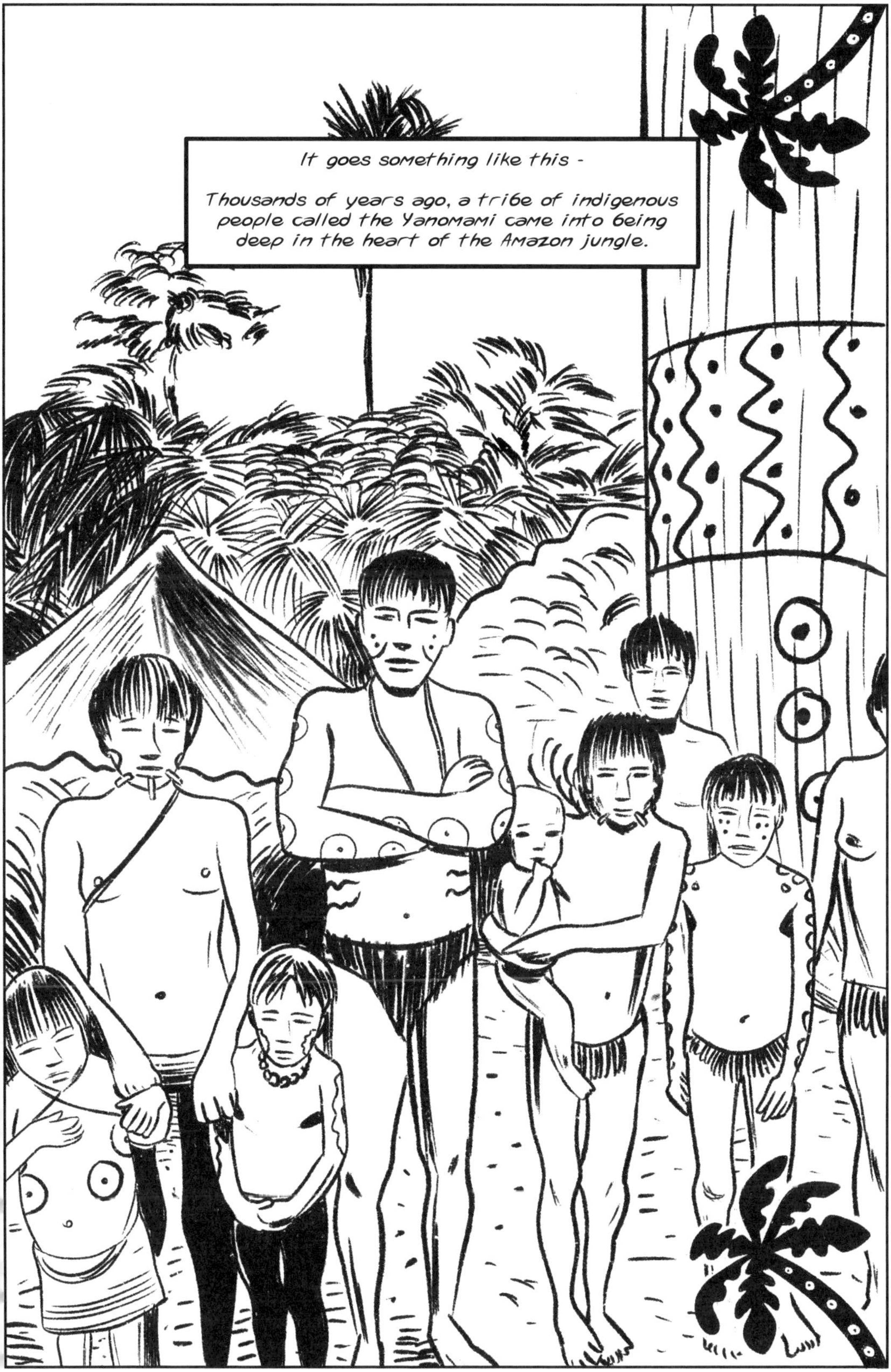
It goes something like this -
Thousands of years ago, a tribe of indigenous people called the Yanomami came into being deep in the heart of the Amazon jungle.

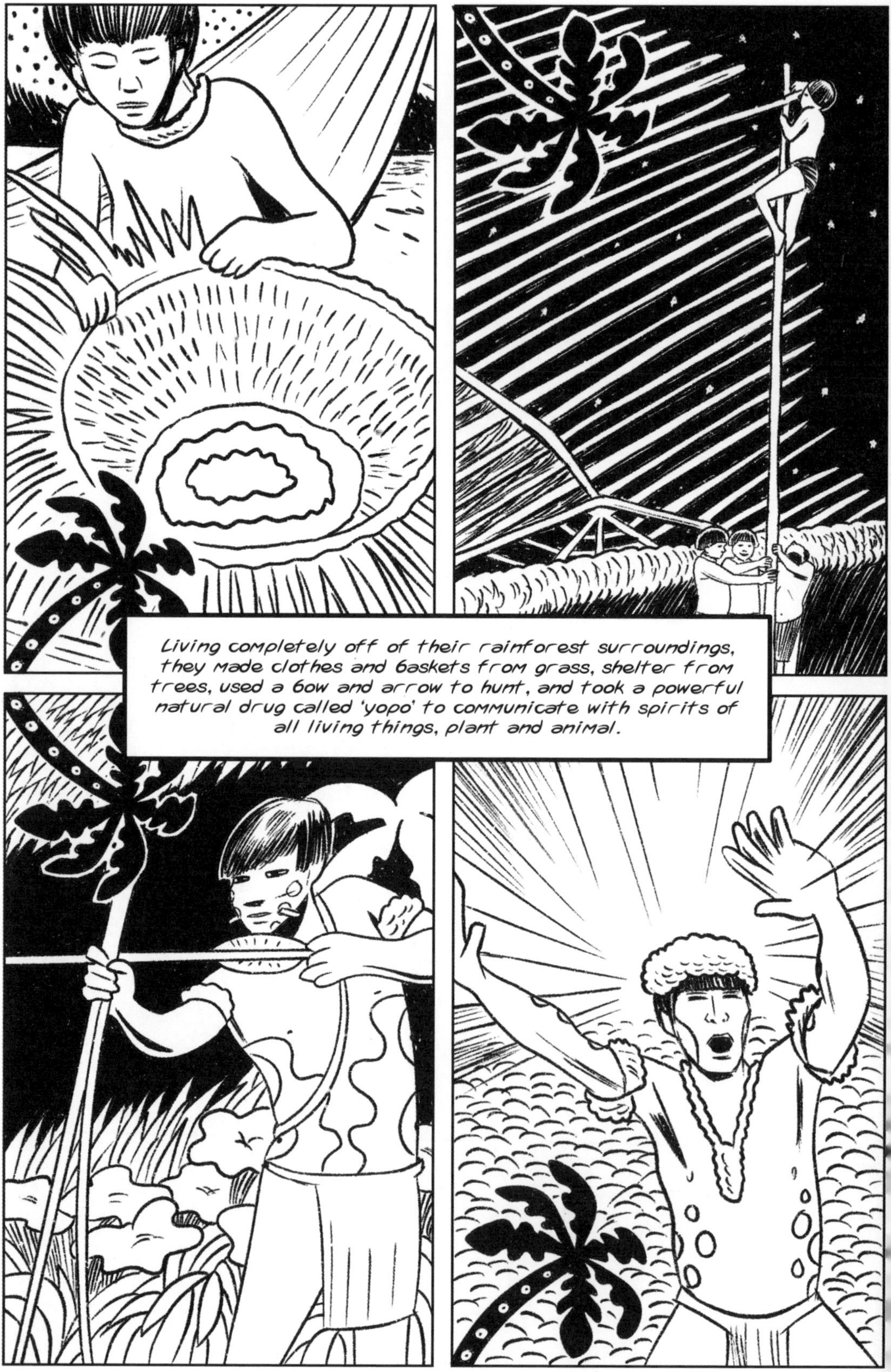
Living completely off of their rainforest surroundings, they made clothes and baskets from grass, shelter from trees, used a bow and arrow to hunt, and took a powerful natural drug called 'yopo' to communicate with spirits of all living things, plant and animal.

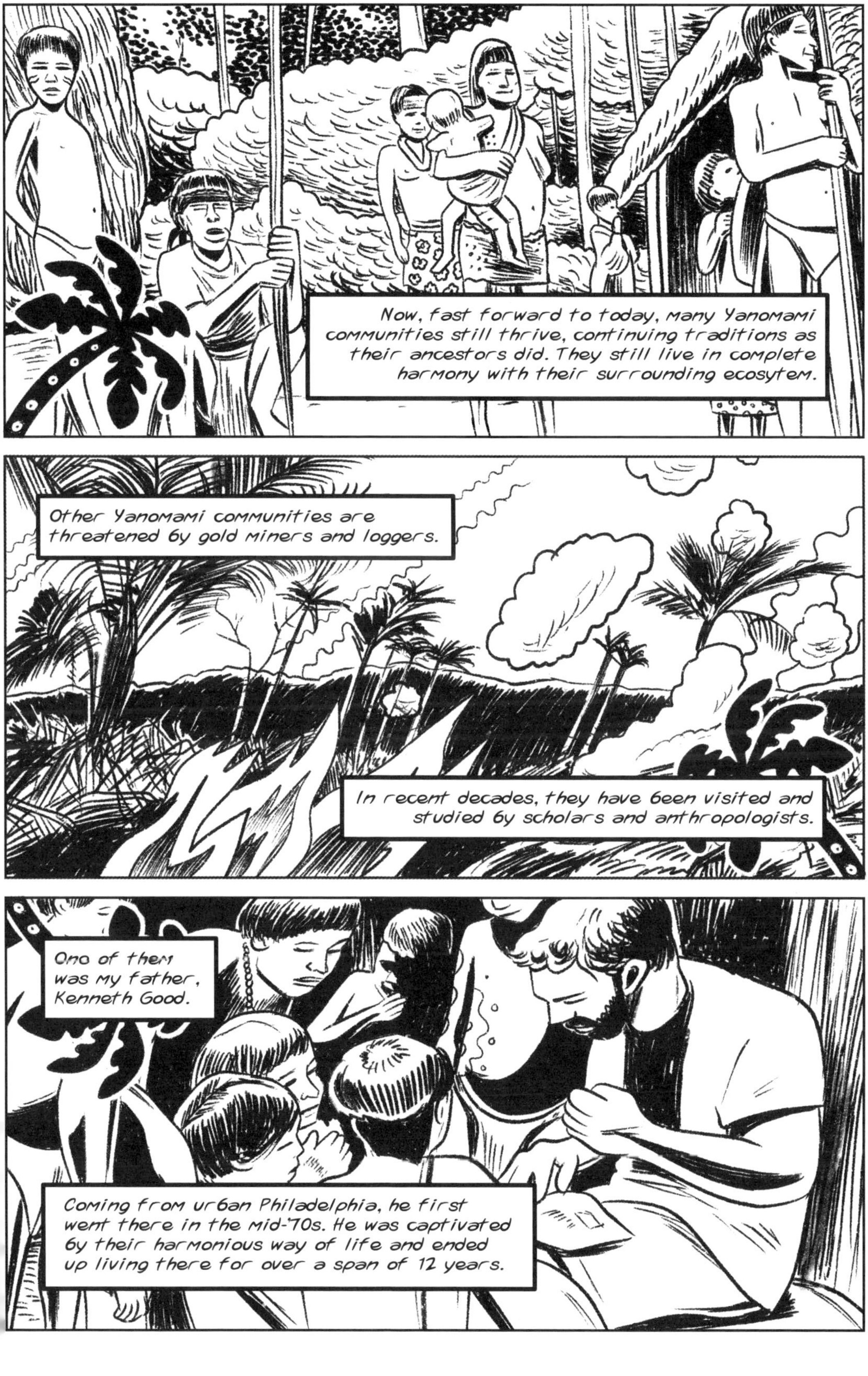
Now, fast forward to today, many Yanomami communities still thrive, continuing traditions as their ancestors did. They still live in complete harmony with their surrounding ecosytem.
Other Yanomami communities are threatened by gold miners and loggers.
In recent decades, they have been visited and studied by scholars and anthropologists.
Ono of them was my father, Kenneth Good.
Coming from urban Philadelphia, he first went there in the mid-'70s. He was captivated by their harmonious way of life and ended up living there for over a span of 12 years.

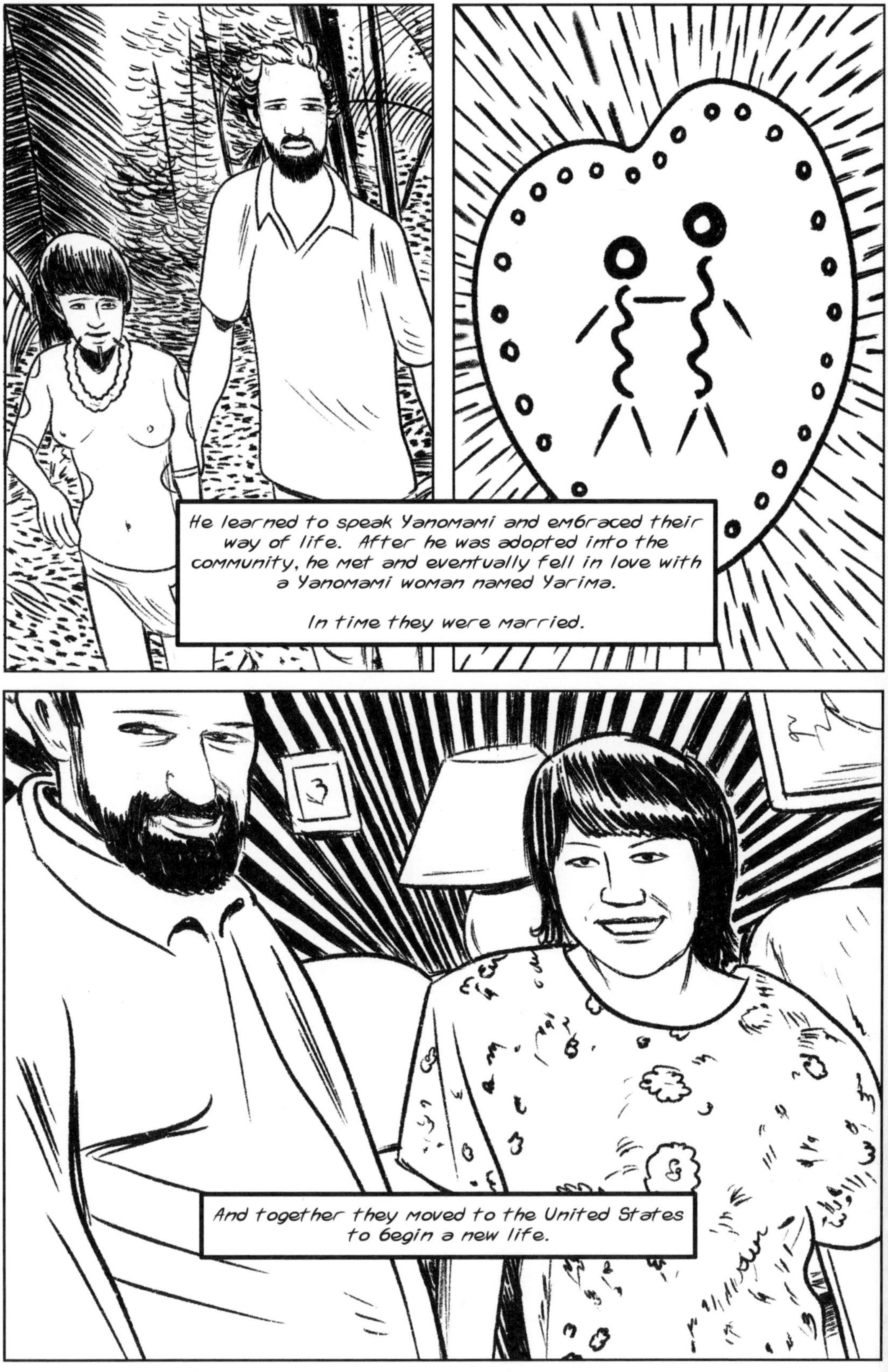
He learned to speak Yanomami and embraced their way of life. After he was adopted into the community, he met and eventually fell in love with a Yanomami woman named Yarima.
In time they were married.
And together they moved to the United States to begin a new life.

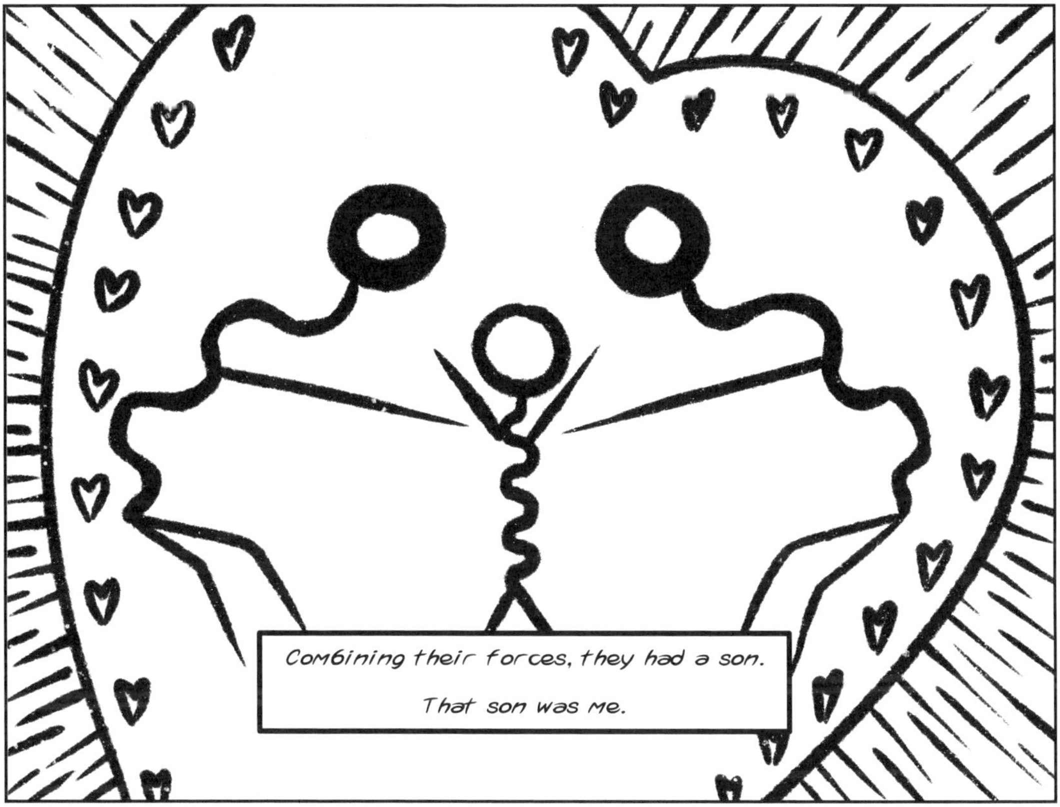
Combining their forces, they had a son.
That son was me.

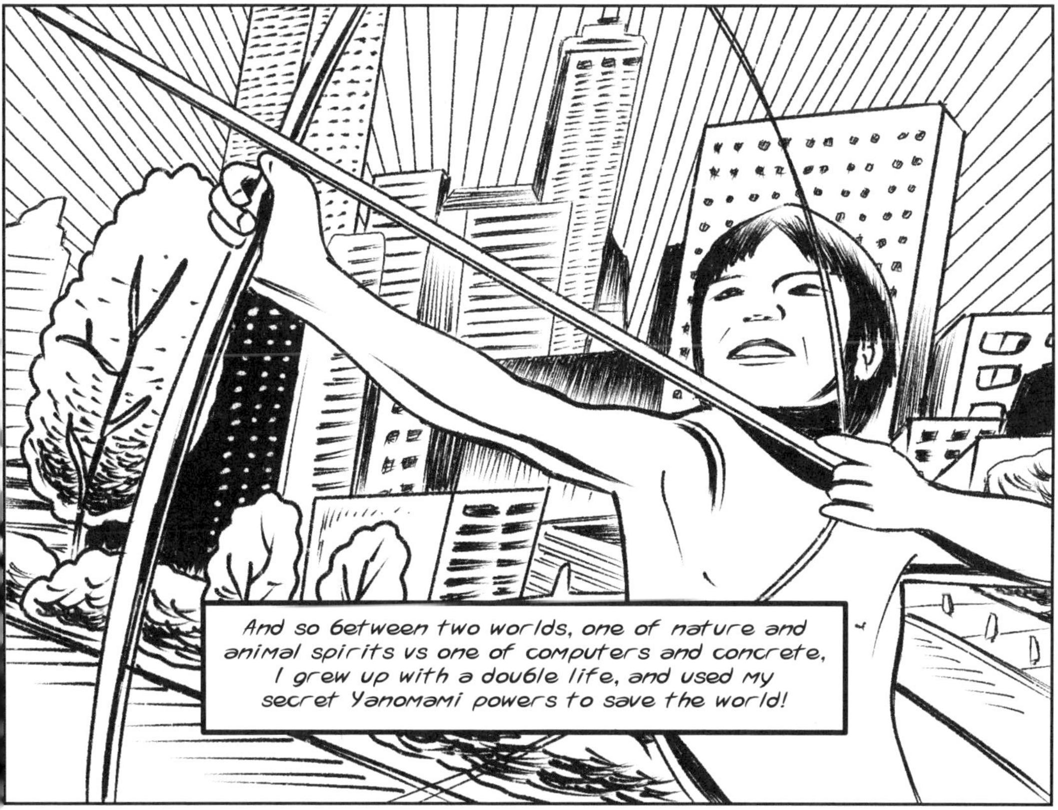
And so between two worlds, one of nature and animal spirits vs one of computers and concrete, I grew up with a double life, and used my secret Yanomami powers to save the world!

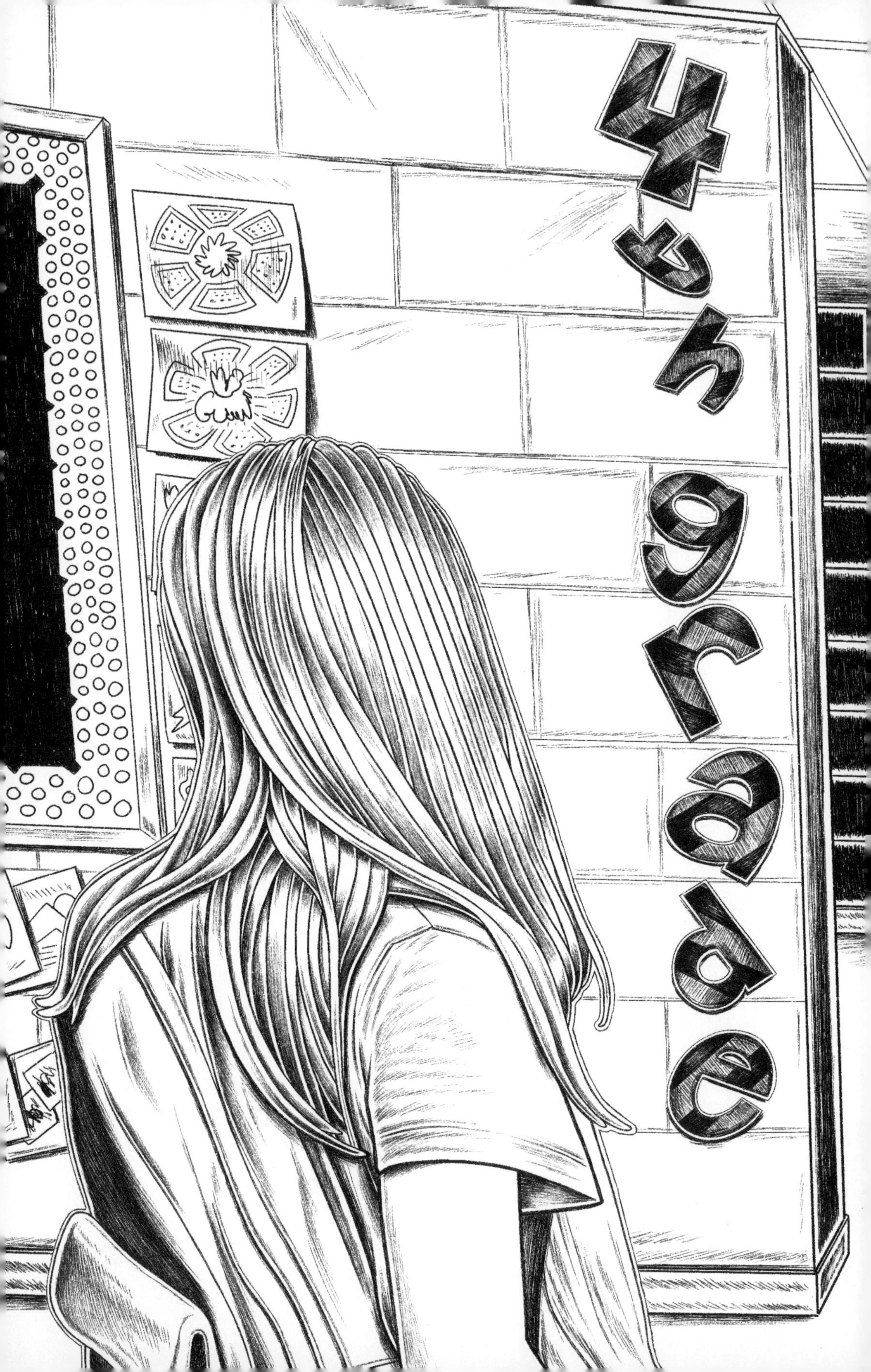
4th grade

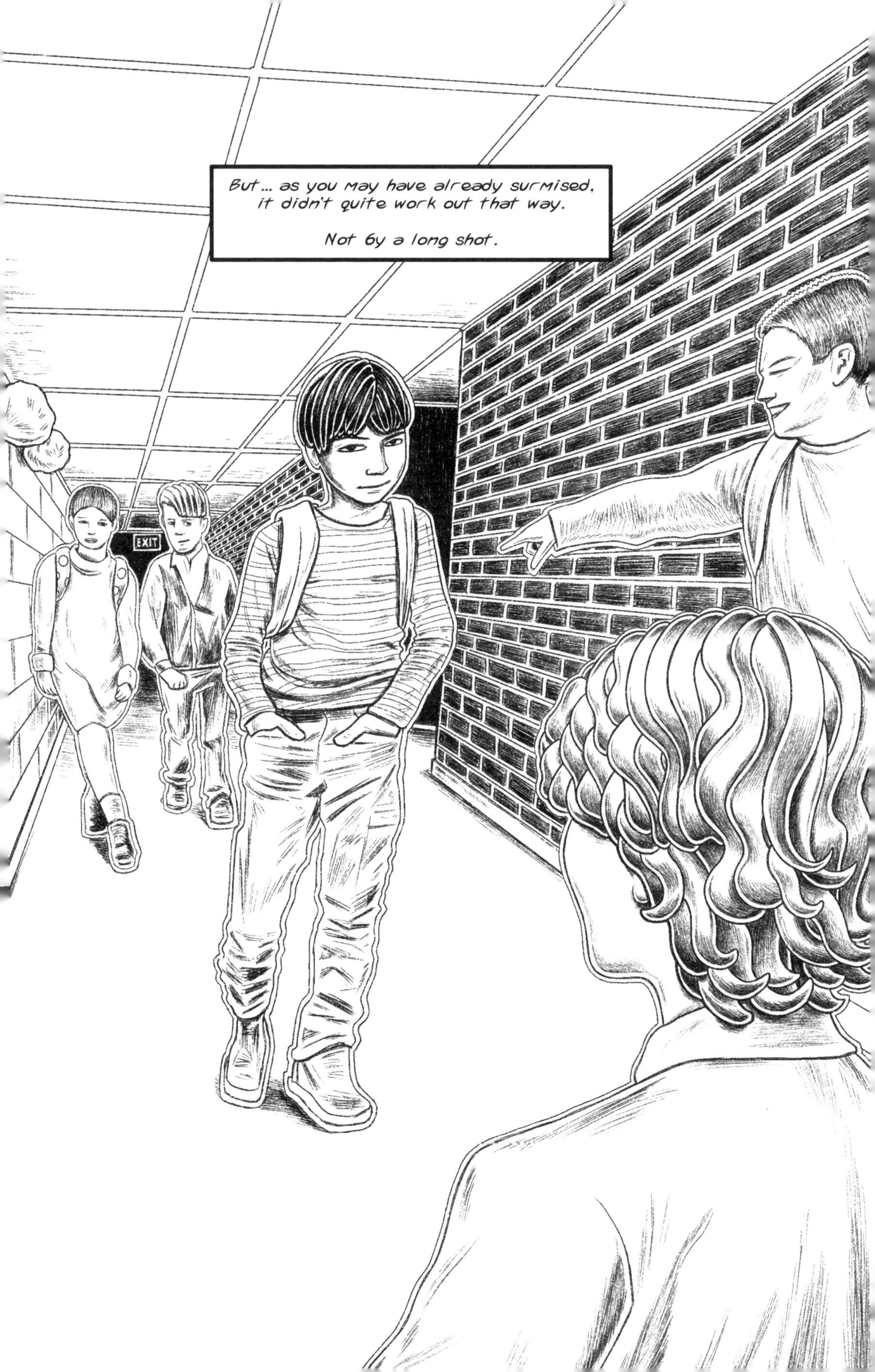
But... as you may have already surmised, it didn't quite work out that way.
Not by a long shot.
EXIT

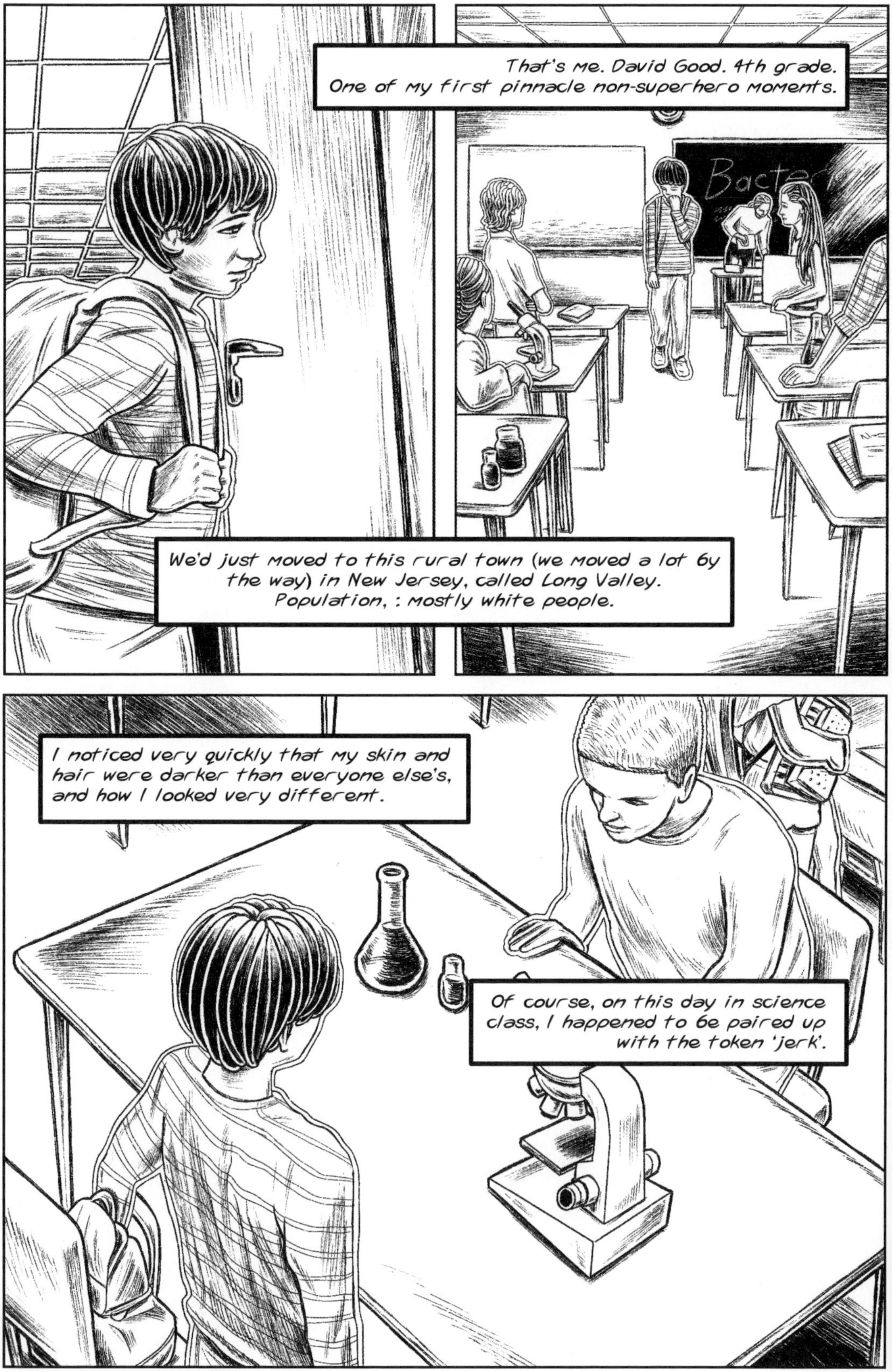
That's me. David Good. 4th grade.
One of my first pinnacle non-superhero moments.
We'd just moved to this rural town (we moved a lot by the way) in New Jersey, called Long Valley.
Population, : mostly white people.
I noticed very quickly that my skin and hair were darker than everyone else's, and how I looked very different.
Of course, on this day in science class, I happened to be paired up with the token 'jerk'.

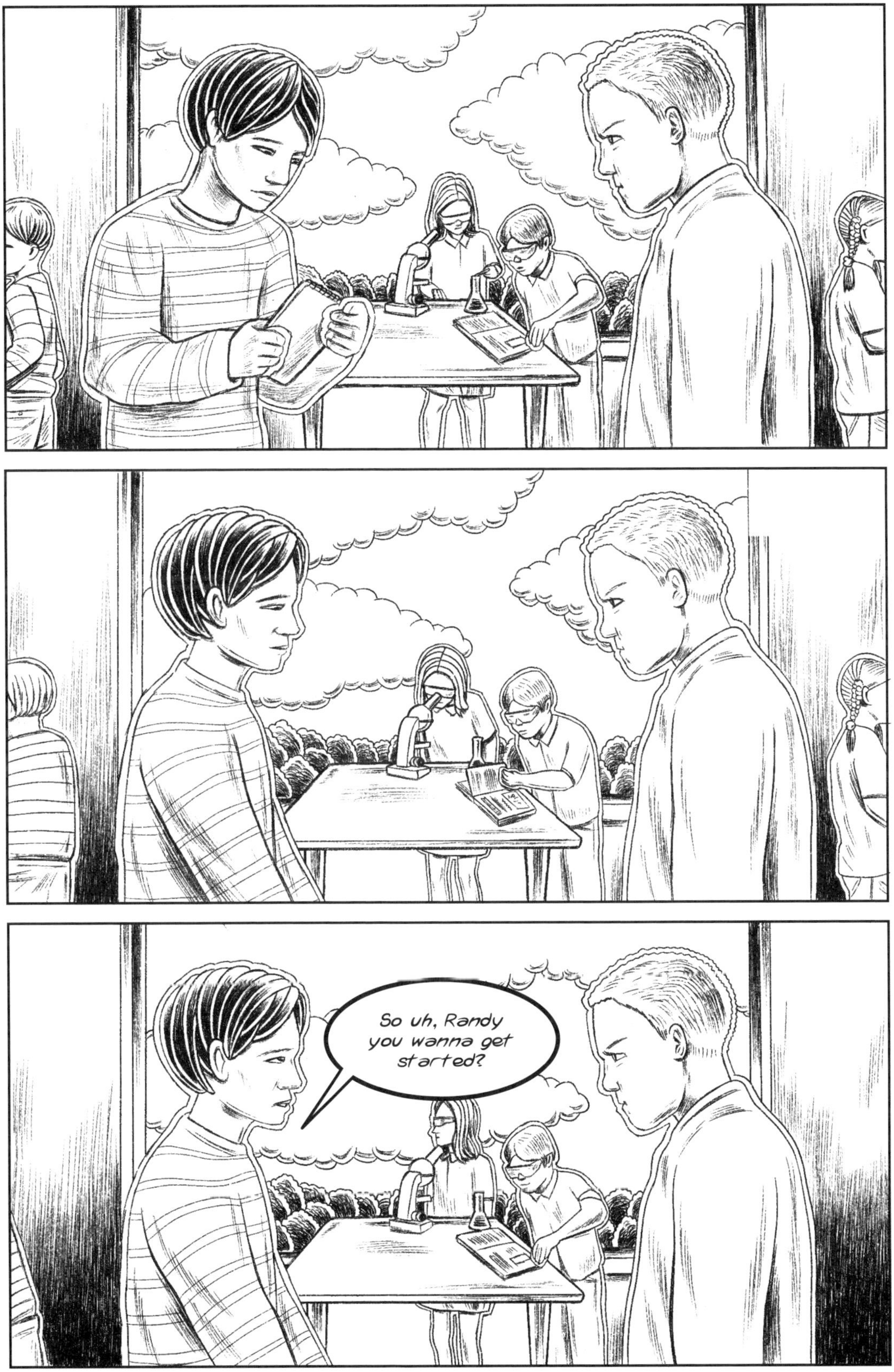
So uh, Randy you wanna get started?

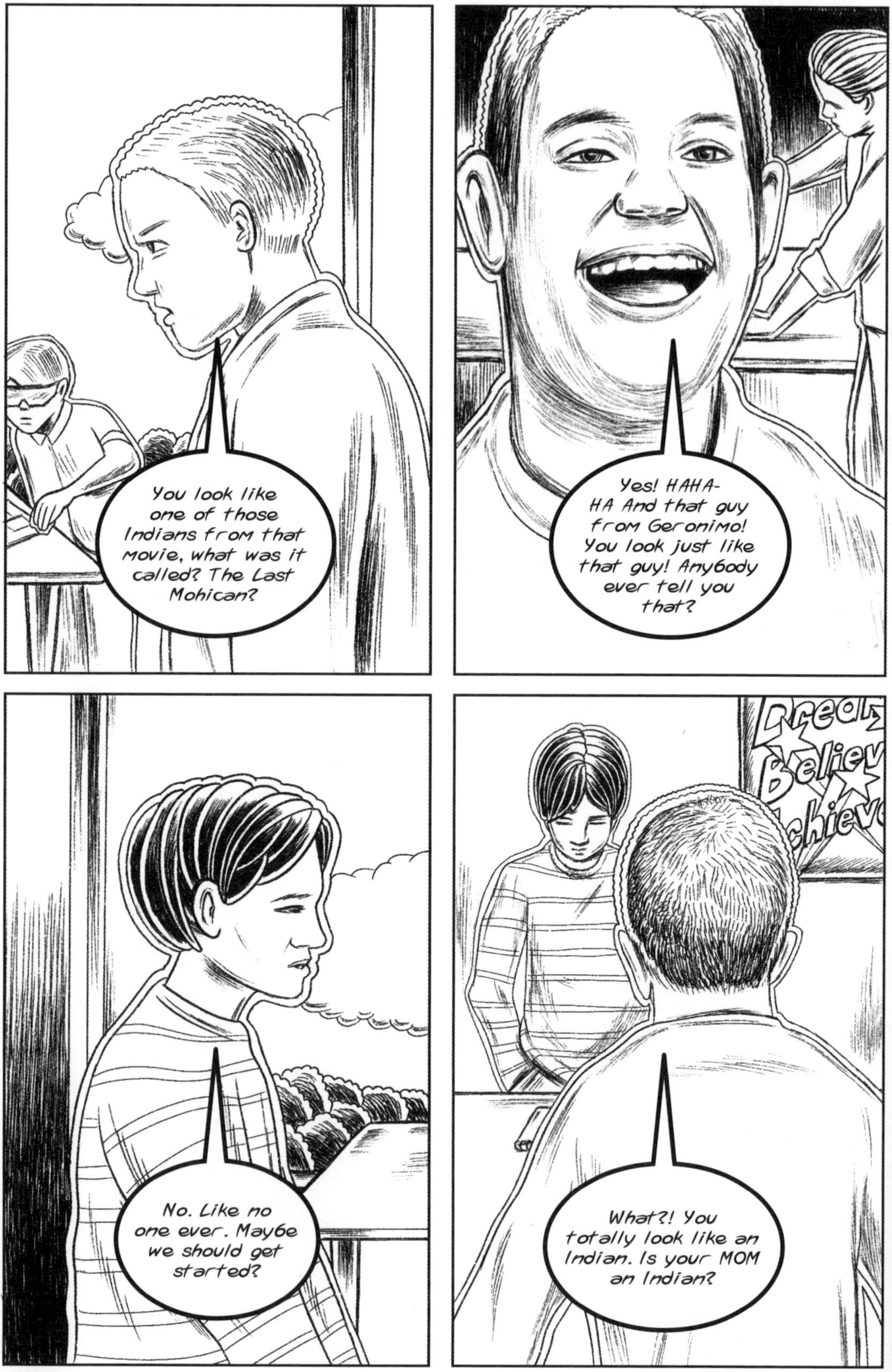
You look like one of those Indians from that movie, what was it called? The Last Mohican?
Yes! HAHA-HA And that guy from Geronimo! You look just like that guy! Anybody ever tell you that?
No. Like no one ever. Maybe we should get started?
What?! You totally look like an Indian. Is your MOM an Indian?

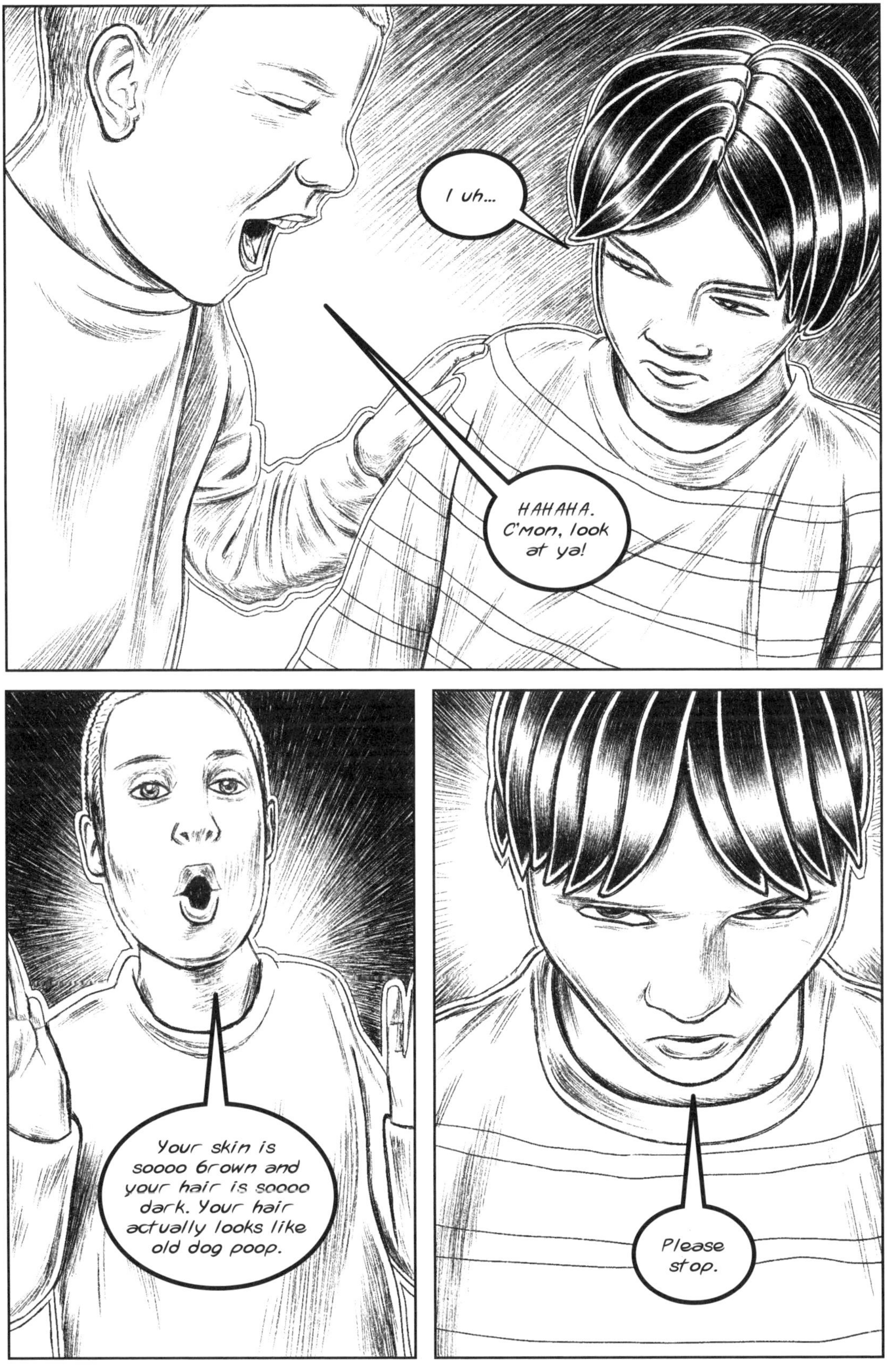
I uh...
HAHAHA. C'mon, look at ya!
Your skin is soooo brown and your hair is soooo dark. Your hair actually looks like old dog poop.
Please stop.

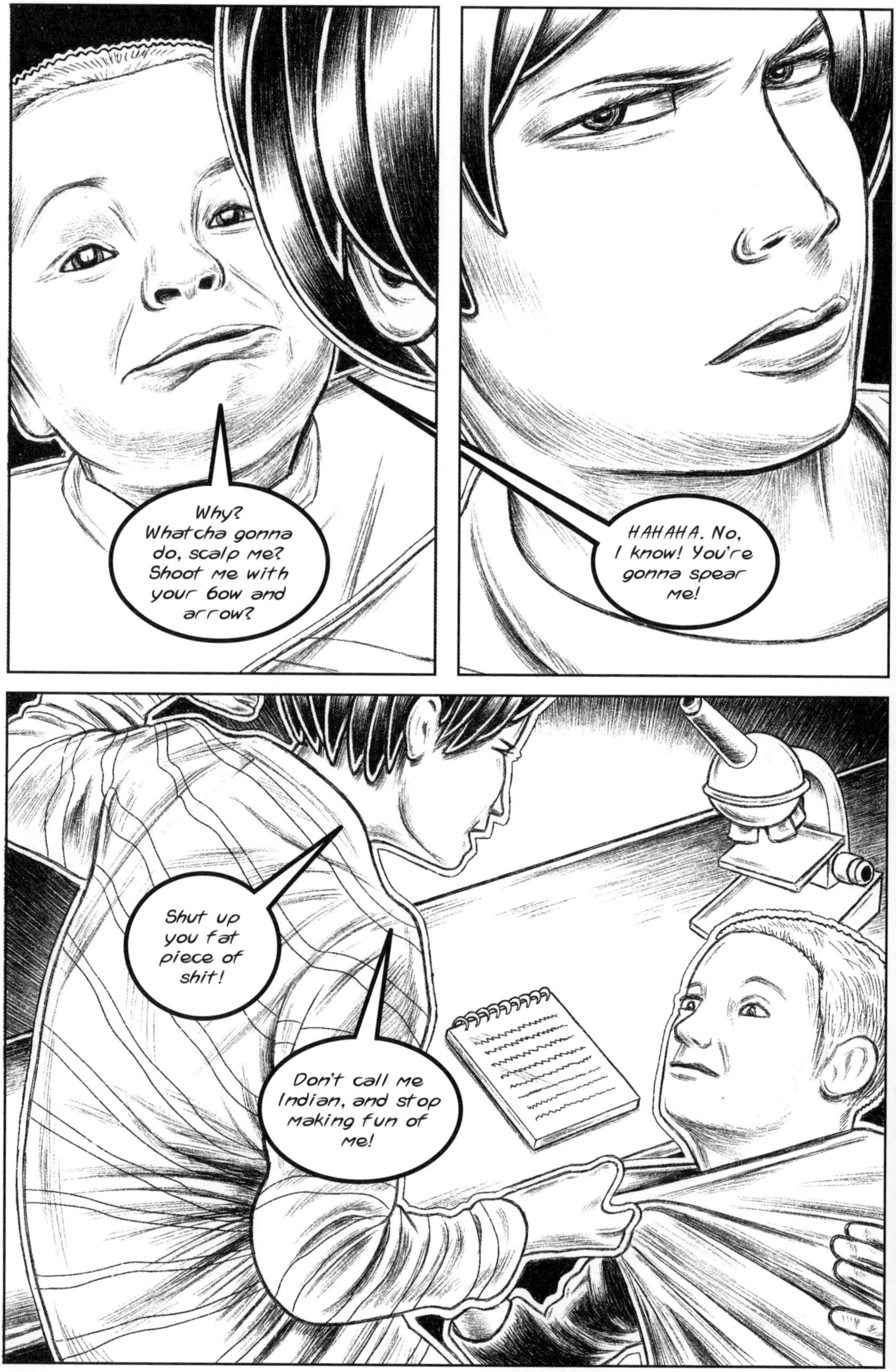
Why? Whatcha gonna do, scalp me? Shoot me with your bow and arrow?
HAHAHA. No, I know! You're gonna spear me!
Shut up you fat piece of shit!
Don't call me Indian, and stop making fun of me!

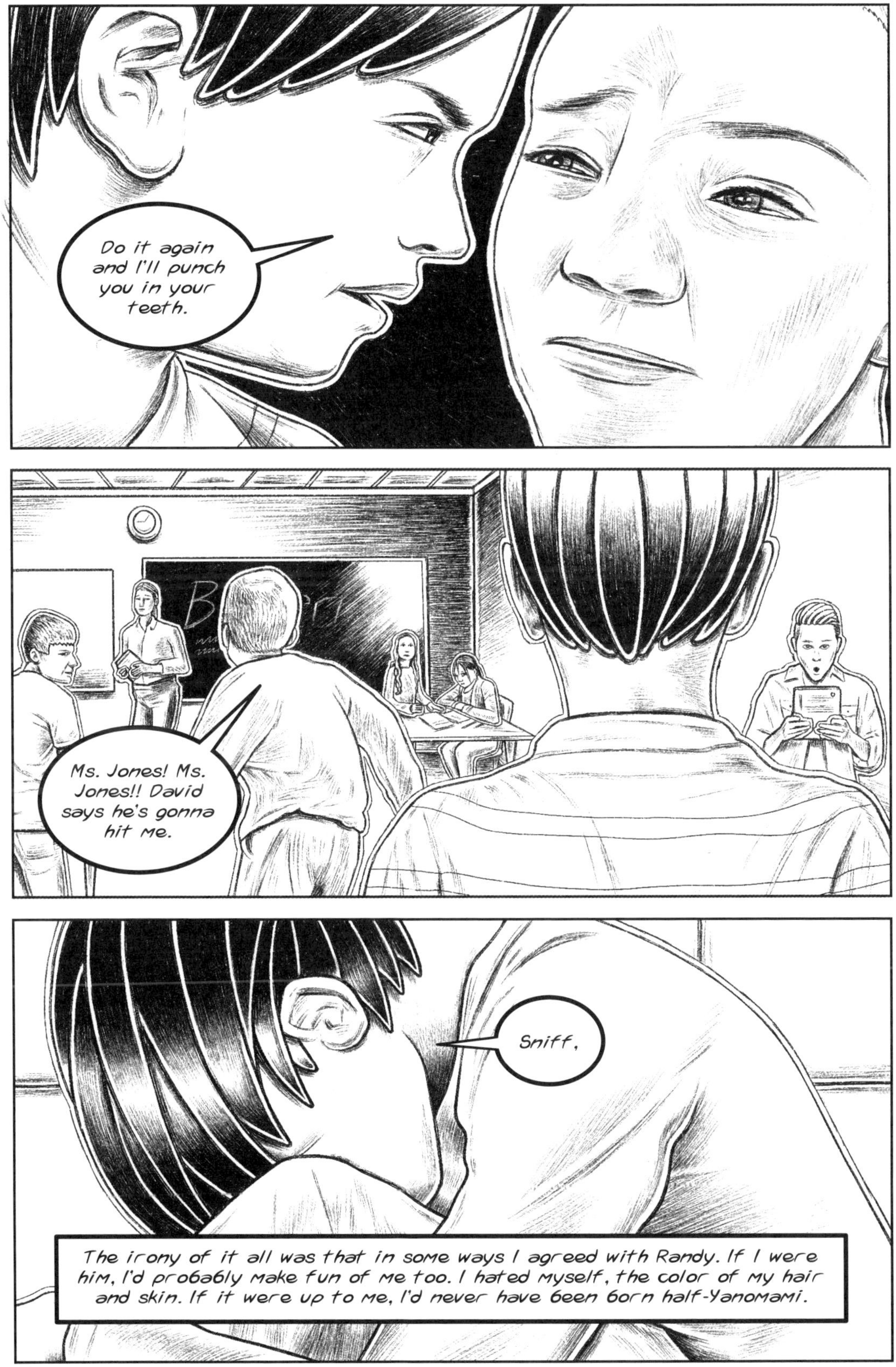
Do it again and I'll punch you in your teeth.
Ms. Jones! Ms. Jones!! David says he's gonna hit me.
Sniff.
The irony of it all was that in some ways I agreed with Randy. If I were him, I'd probably make fun of me too. I hated myself, the color of my hair and skin. If it were up to me, I'd never have been born half-Yanomami.

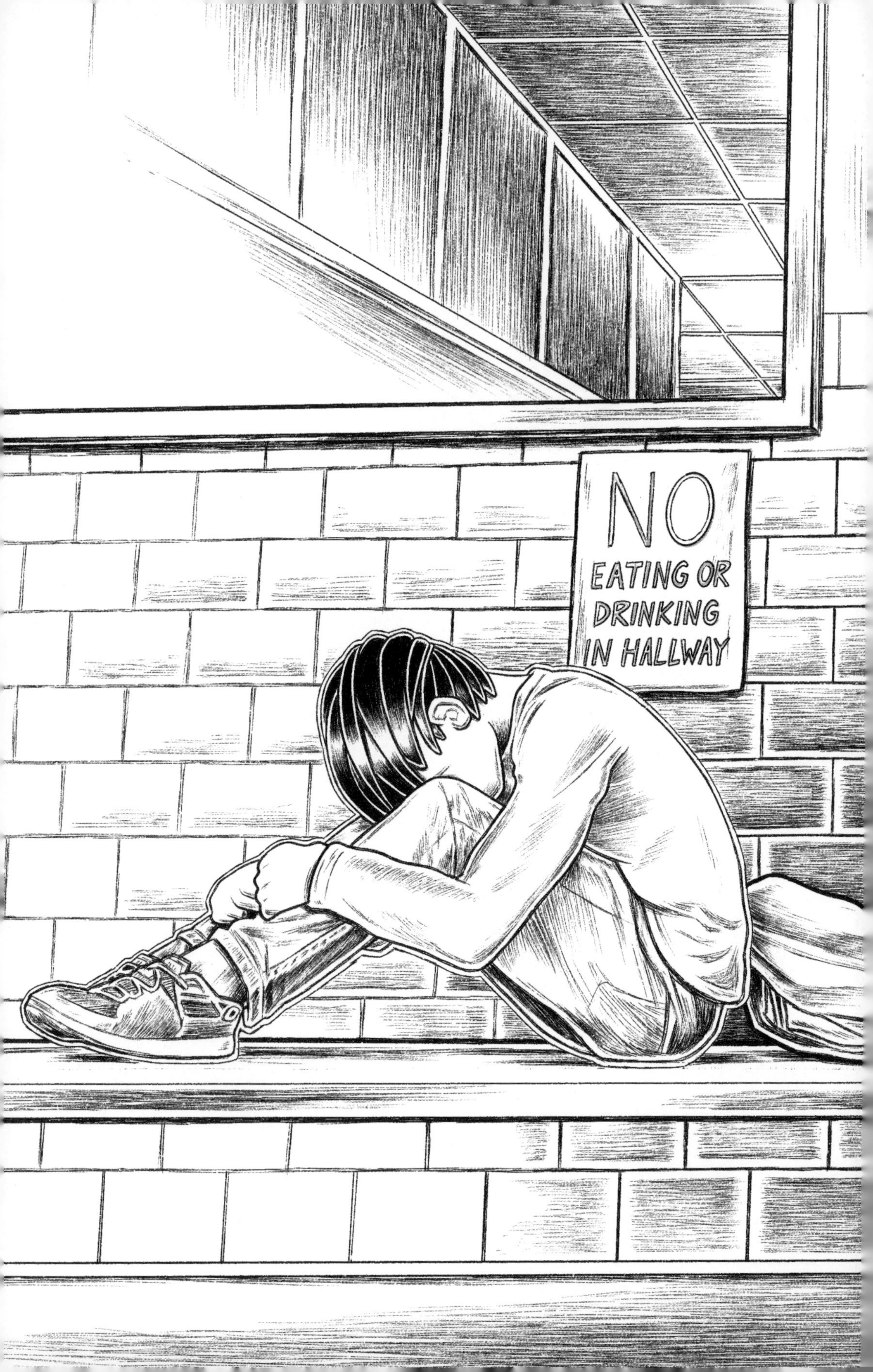
NO
EATING OR
DRINKING
IN HALLWAY

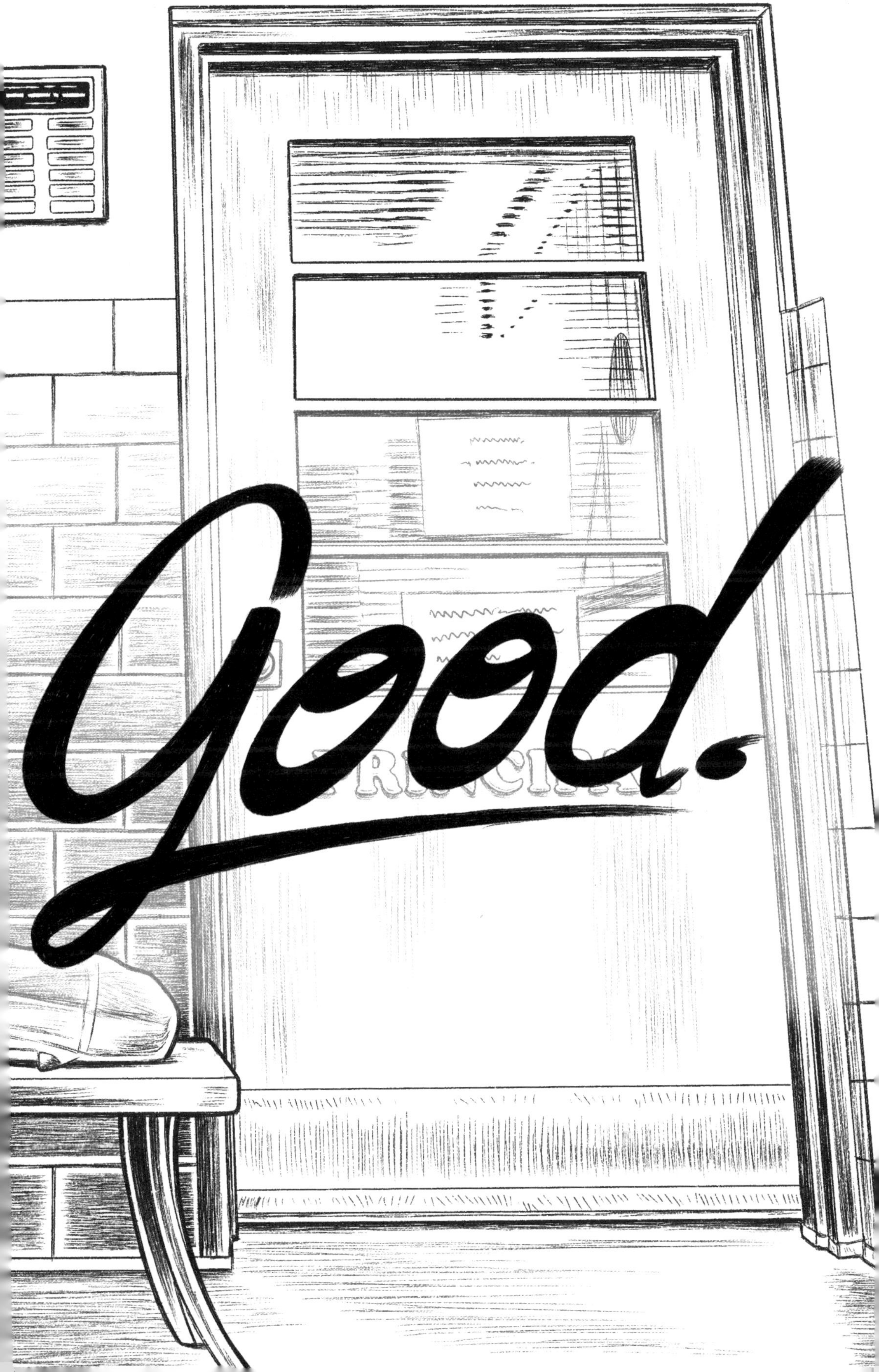
Good.

chapter 1

YARIMA

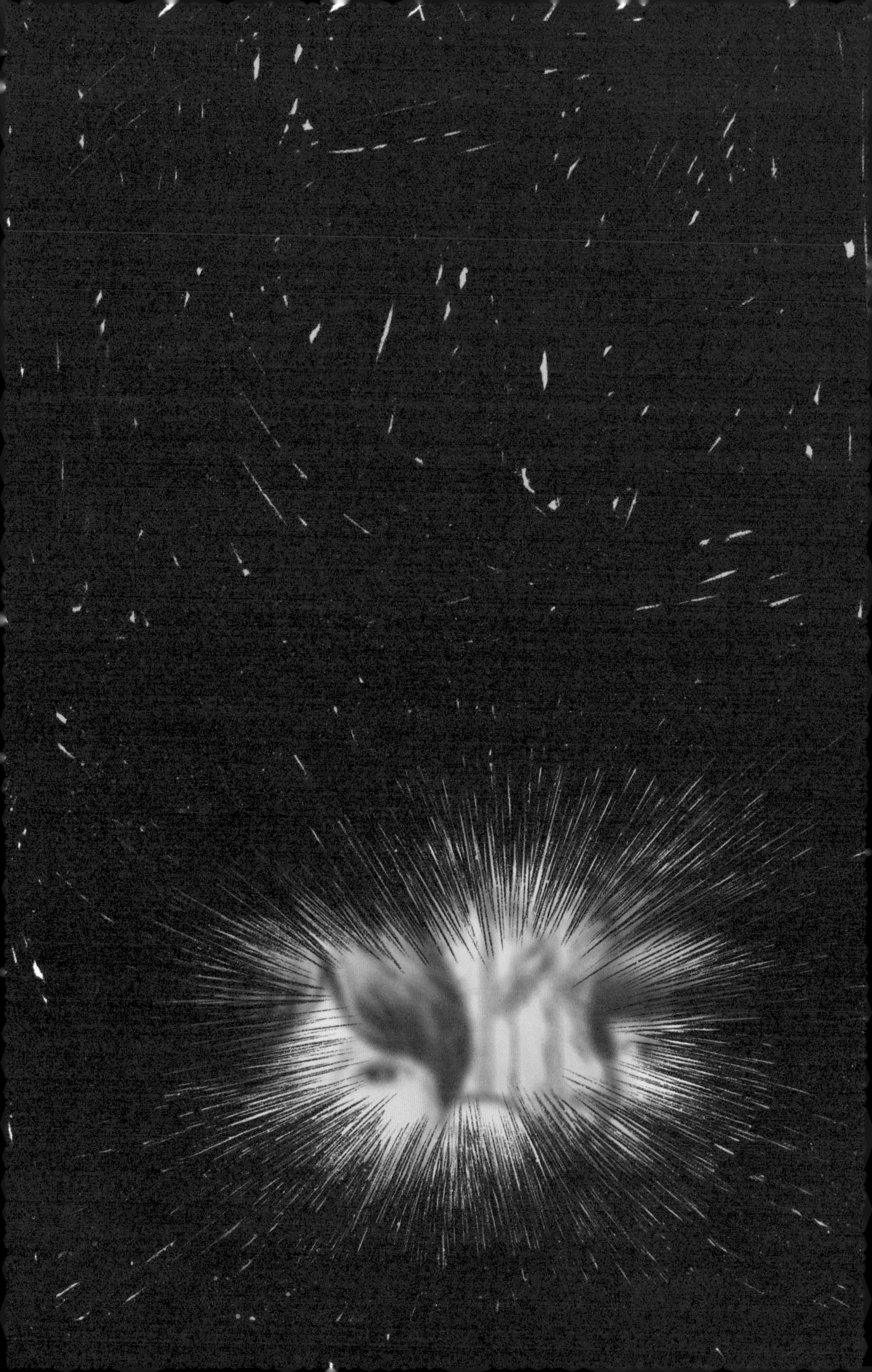

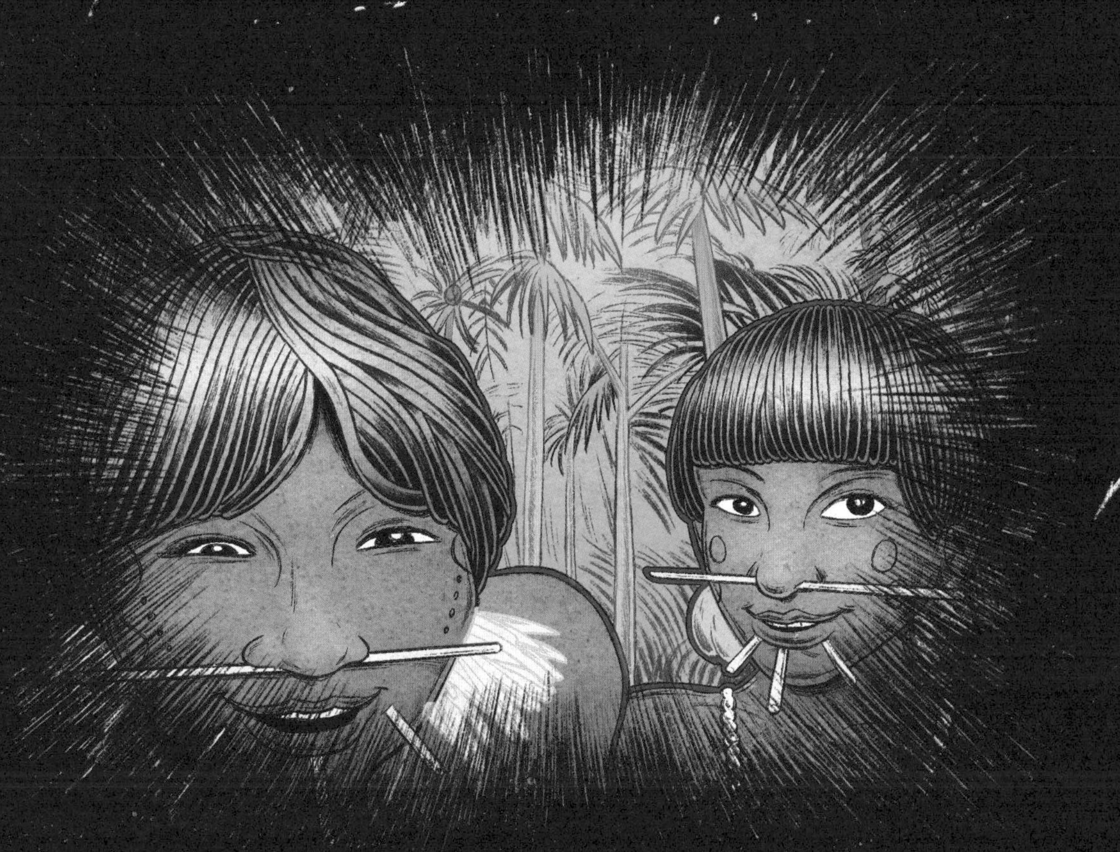

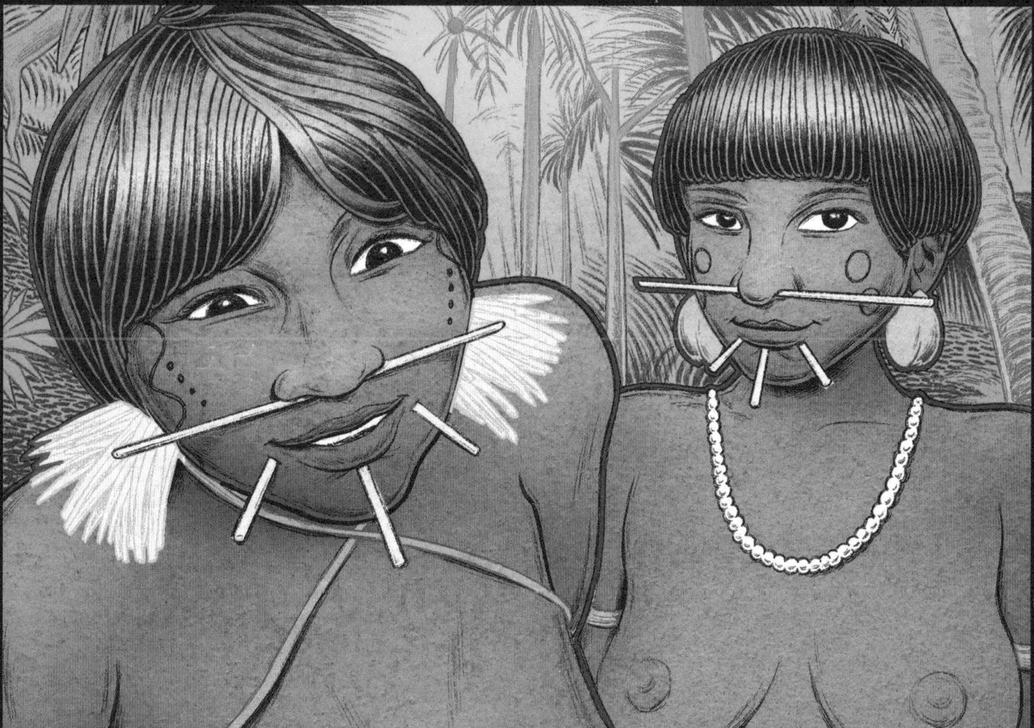

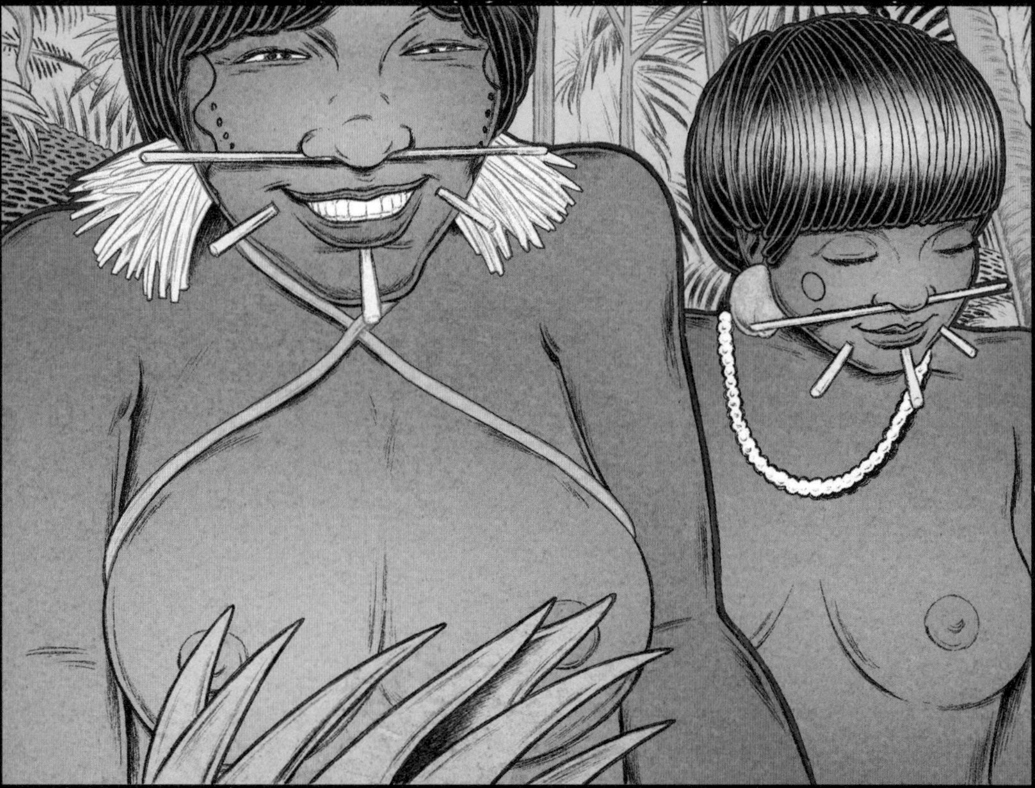
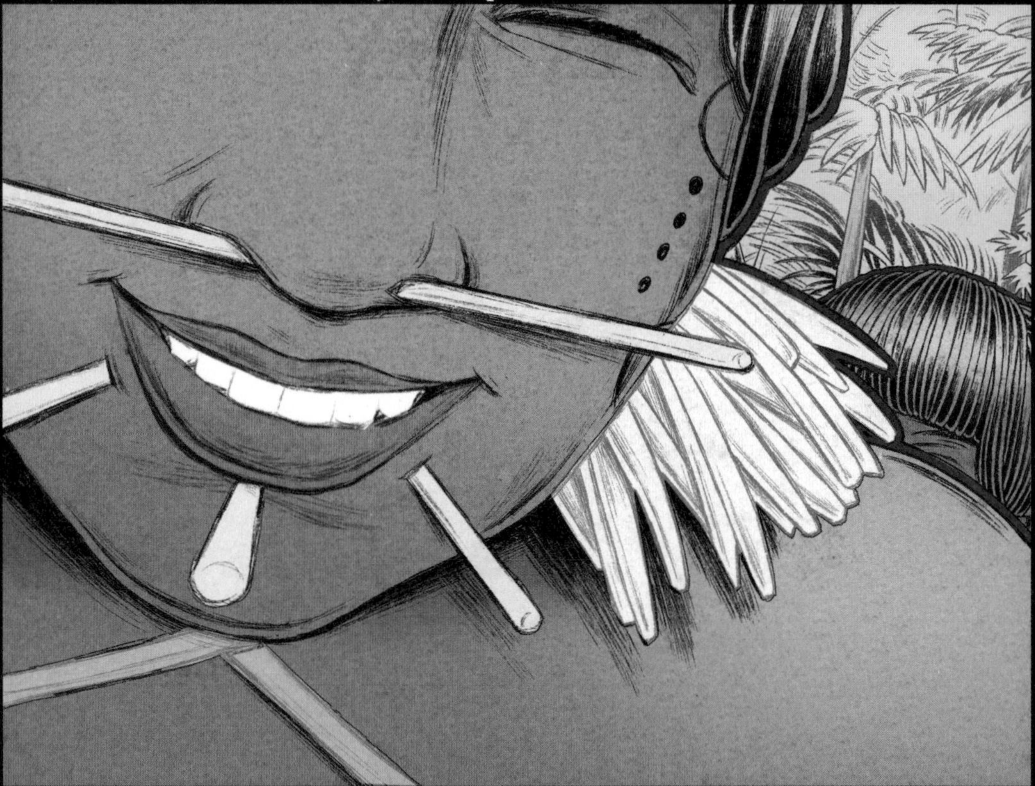

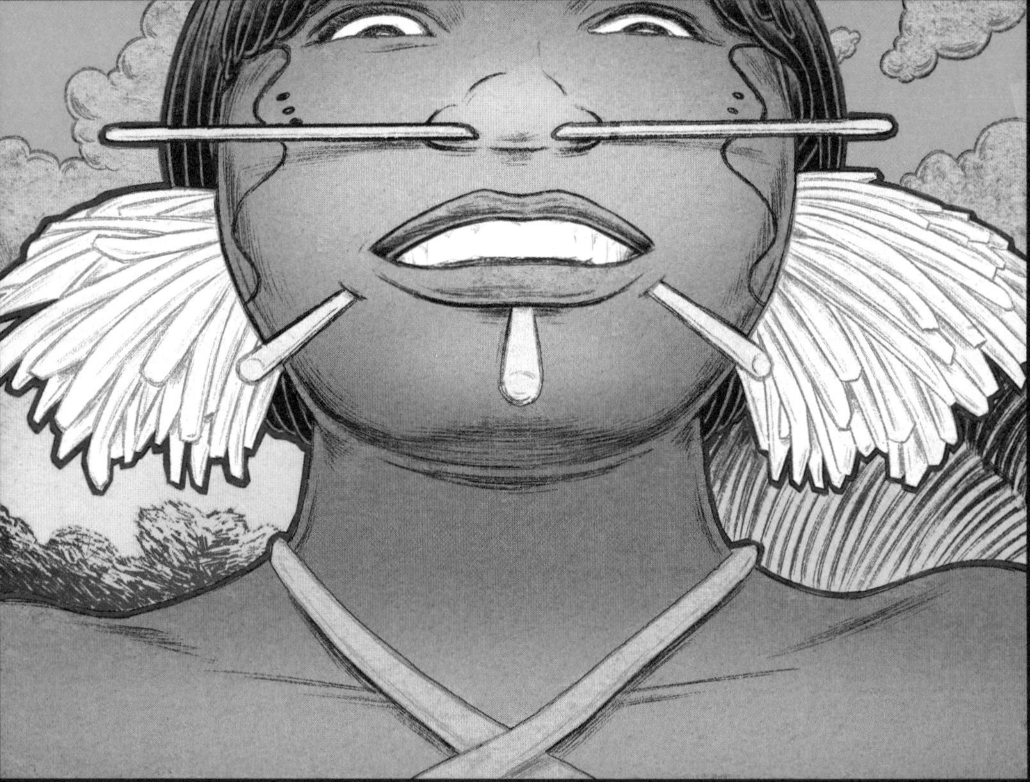
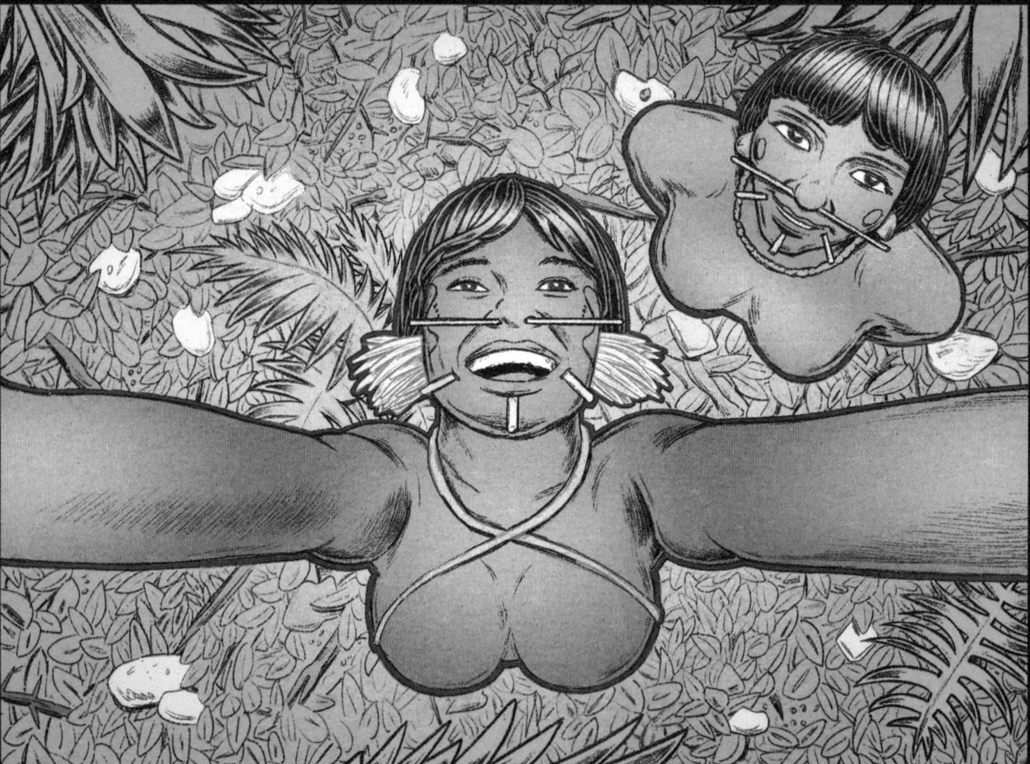

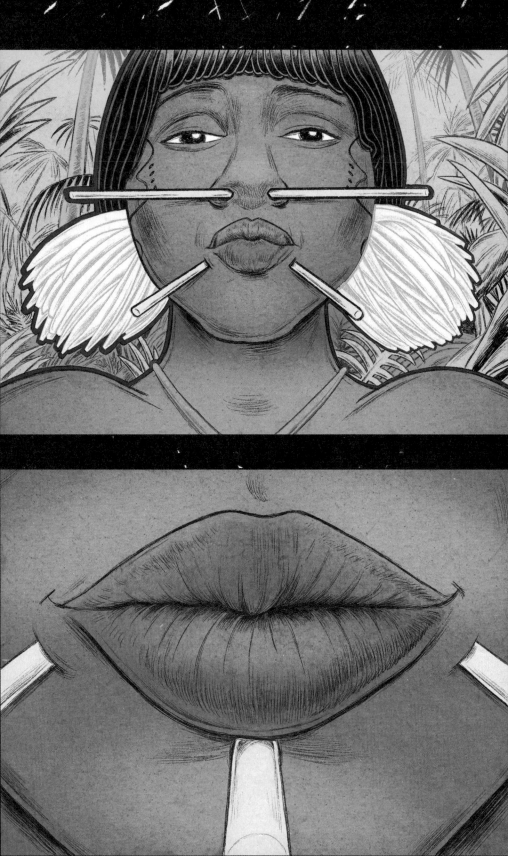

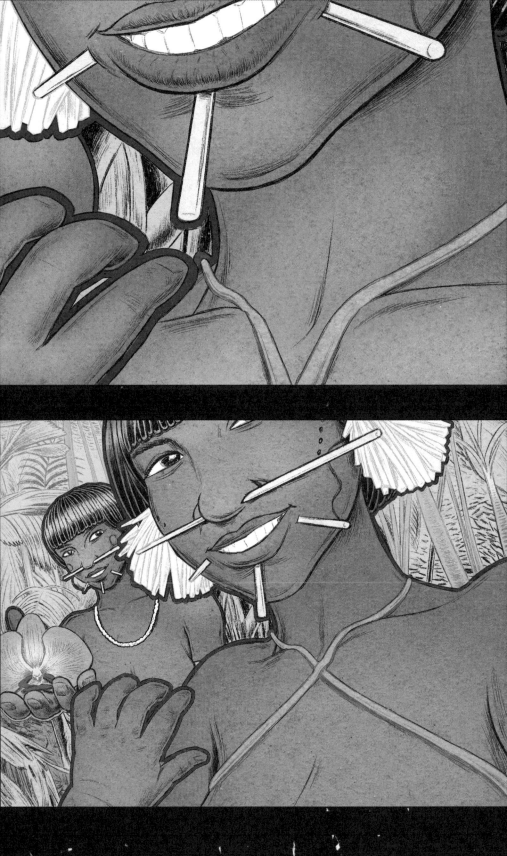

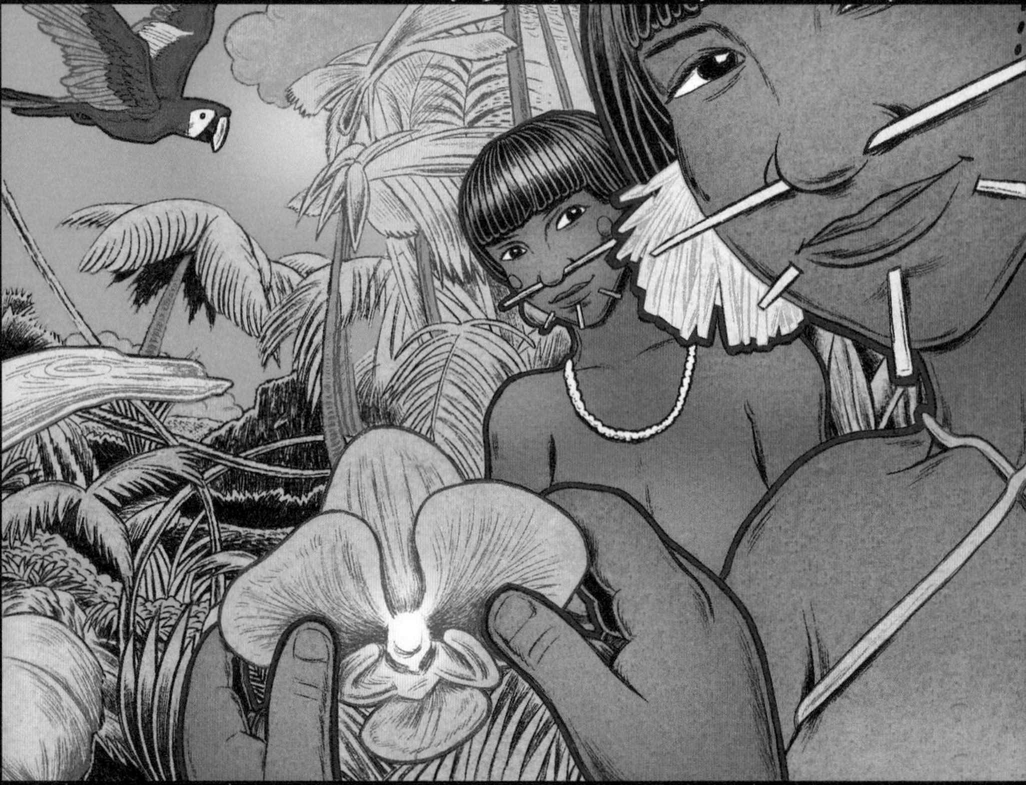

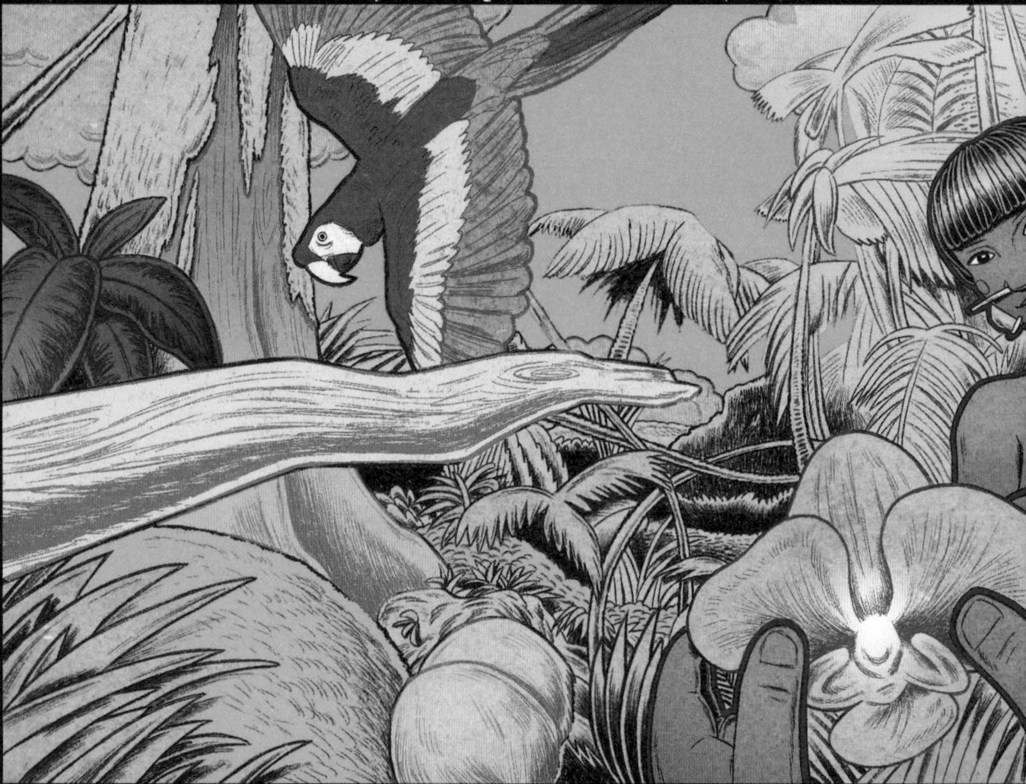

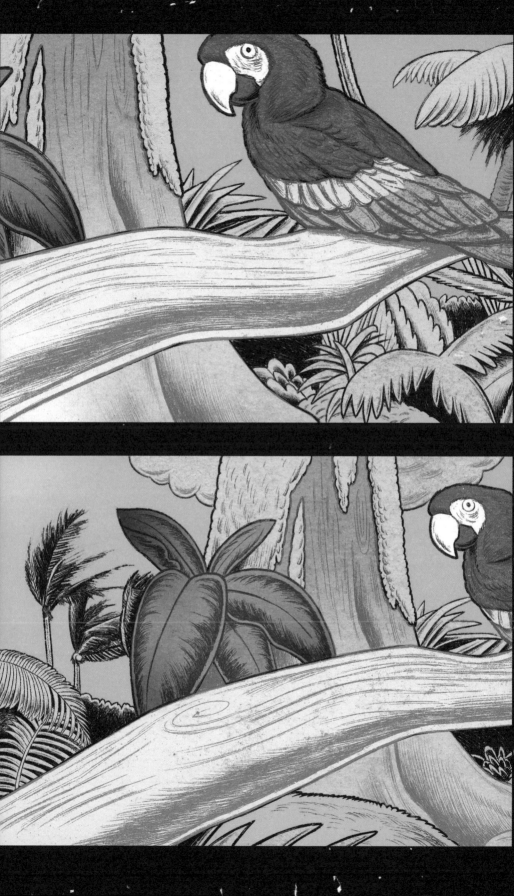

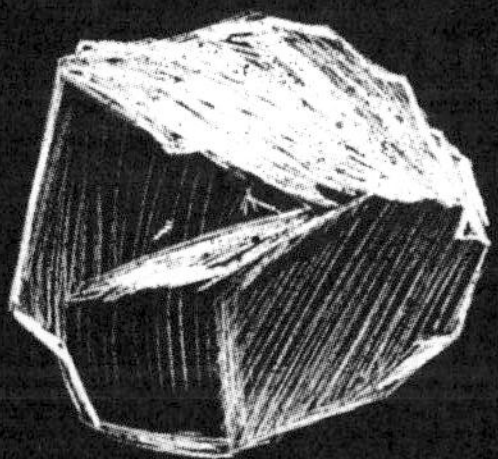

chapter2

DAVID

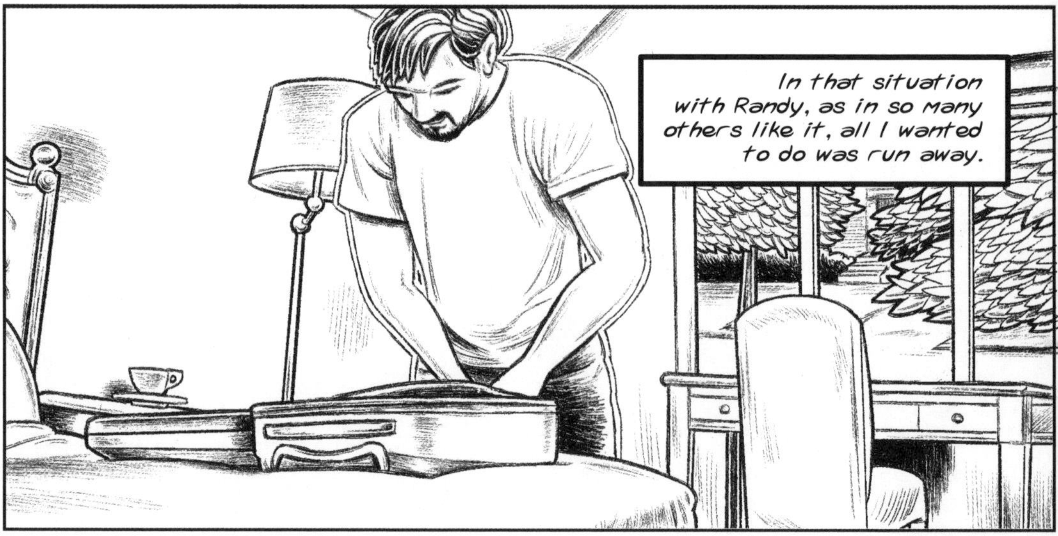
In that situation with Randy, as in so many others like it, all I wanted to do was run away.

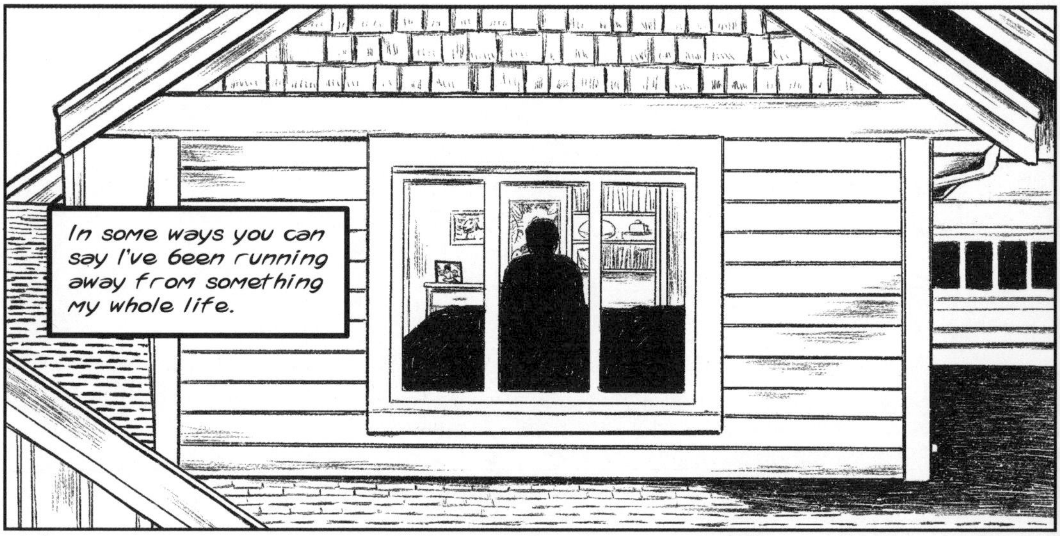
In some ways you can say I've been running away from something my whole life.

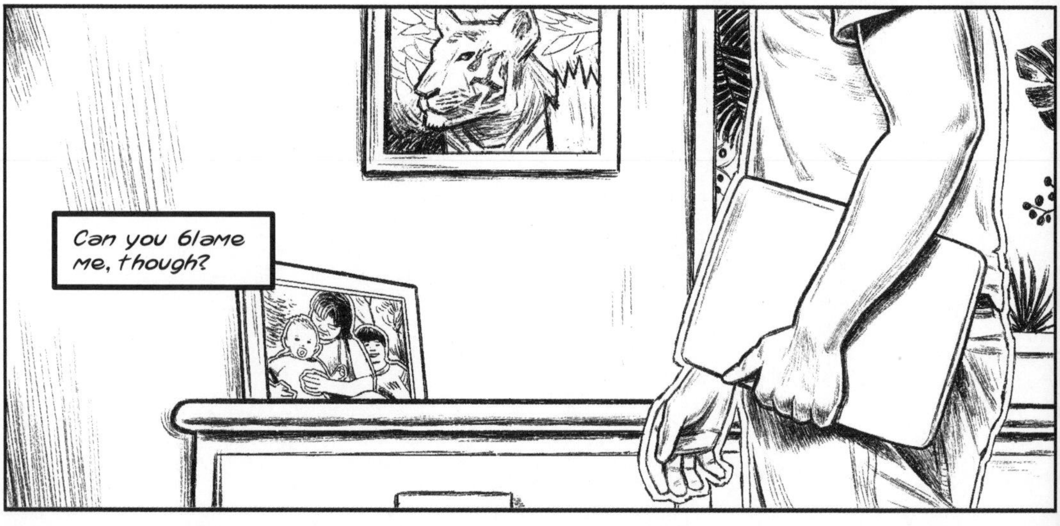
Can you blame me, though?

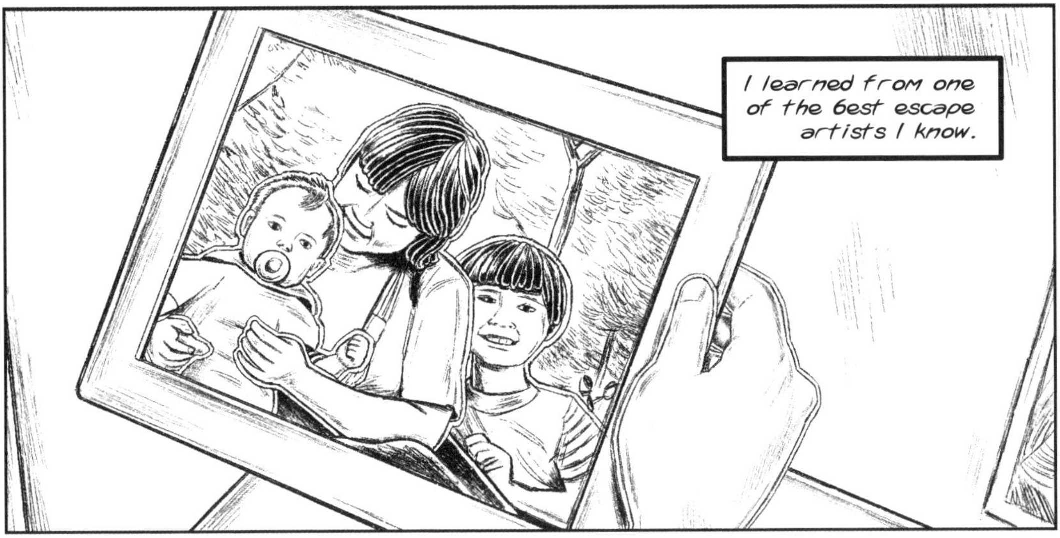
I learned from one of the best escape artists I know.

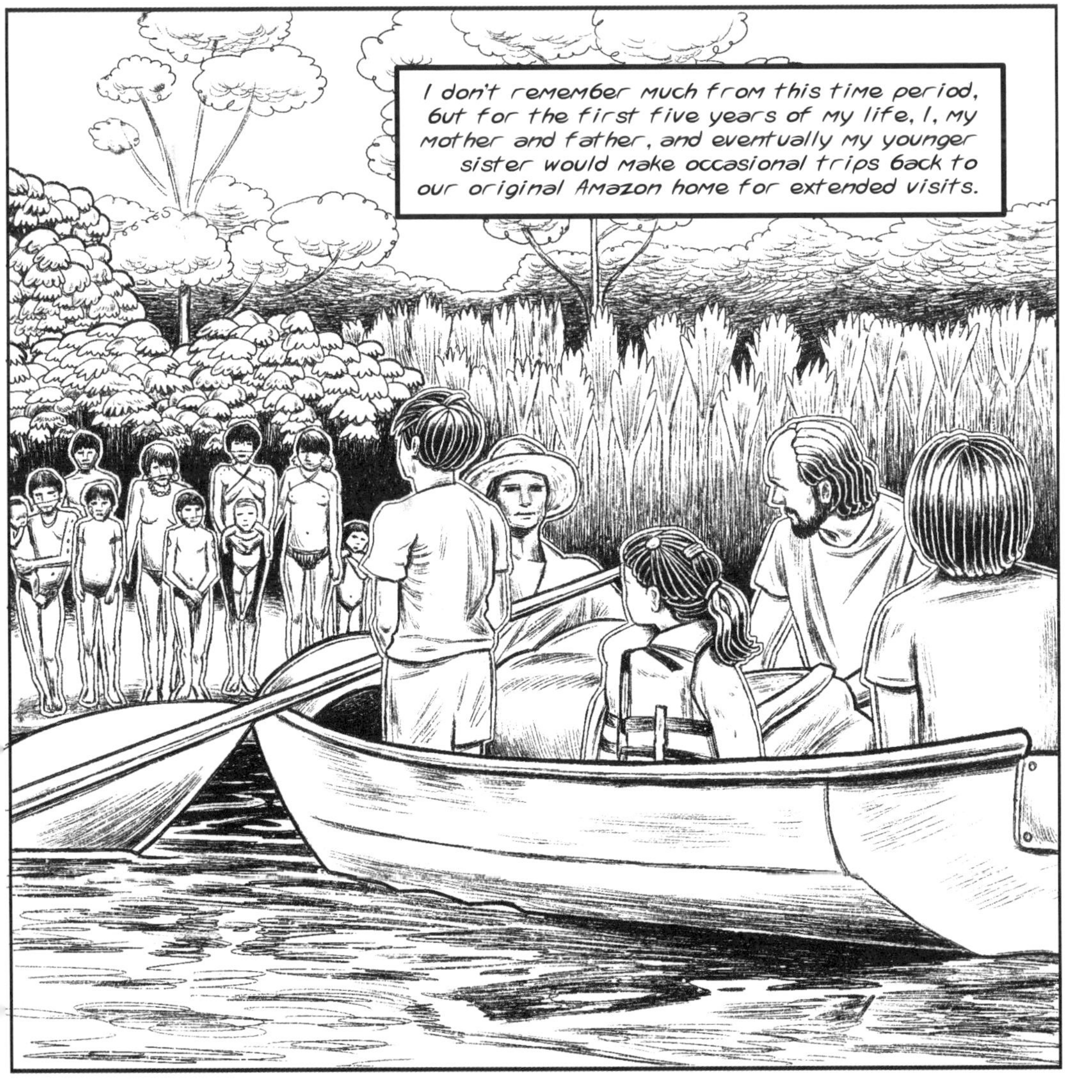
I don't remember much from this time period, but for the first five years of my life, I, my mother and father, and eventually my younger sister would make occasional trips back to our original Amazon home for extended visits.

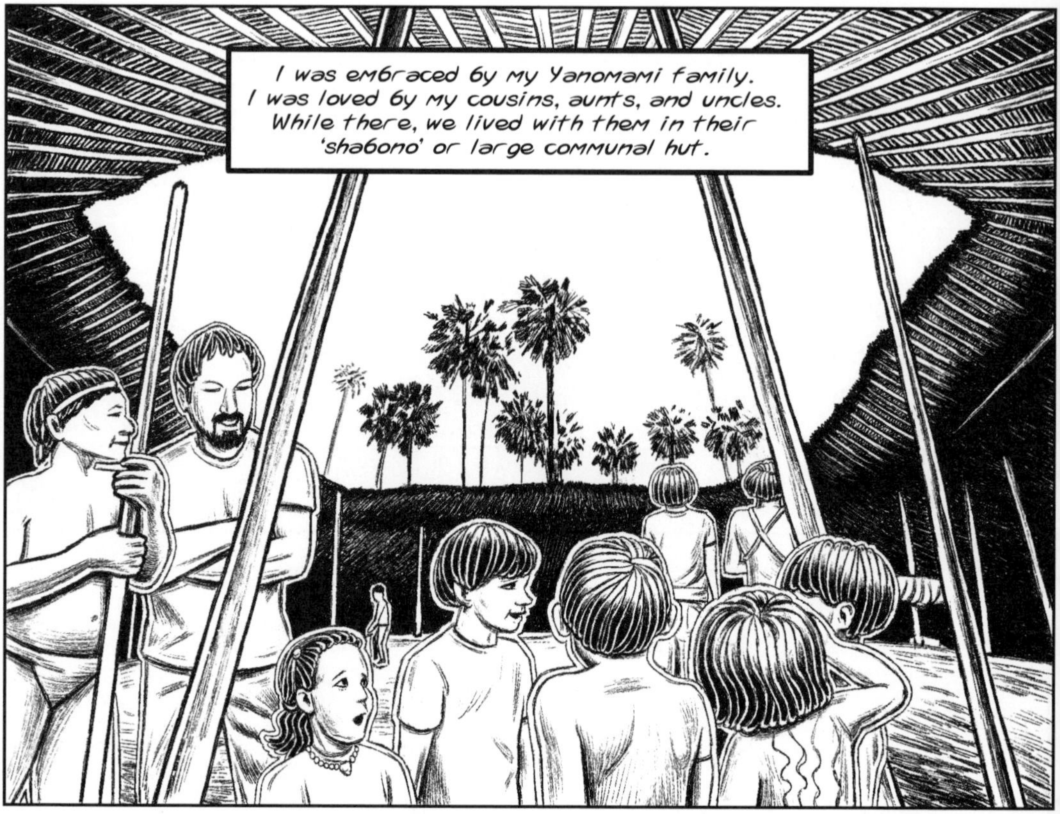
I was embraced by my Yanomami family. I was loved by my cousins, aunts, and uncles. While there, we lived with them in their 'shabono' or large communal hut.

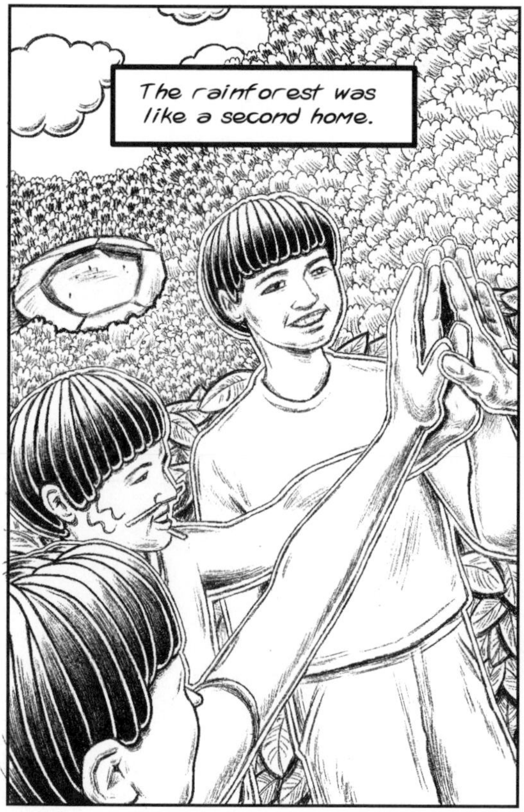
The rainforest was like a second home.

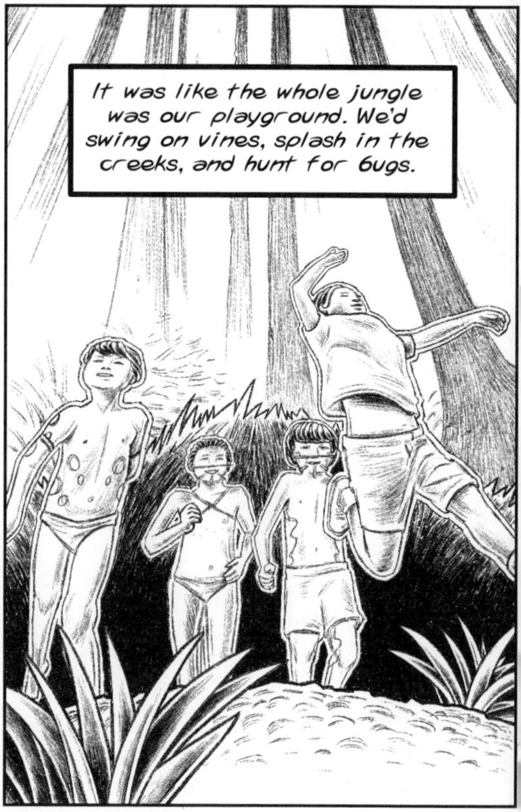
It was like the whole jungle was our playground. We'd swing on vines, splash in the creeks, and hunt for bugs.

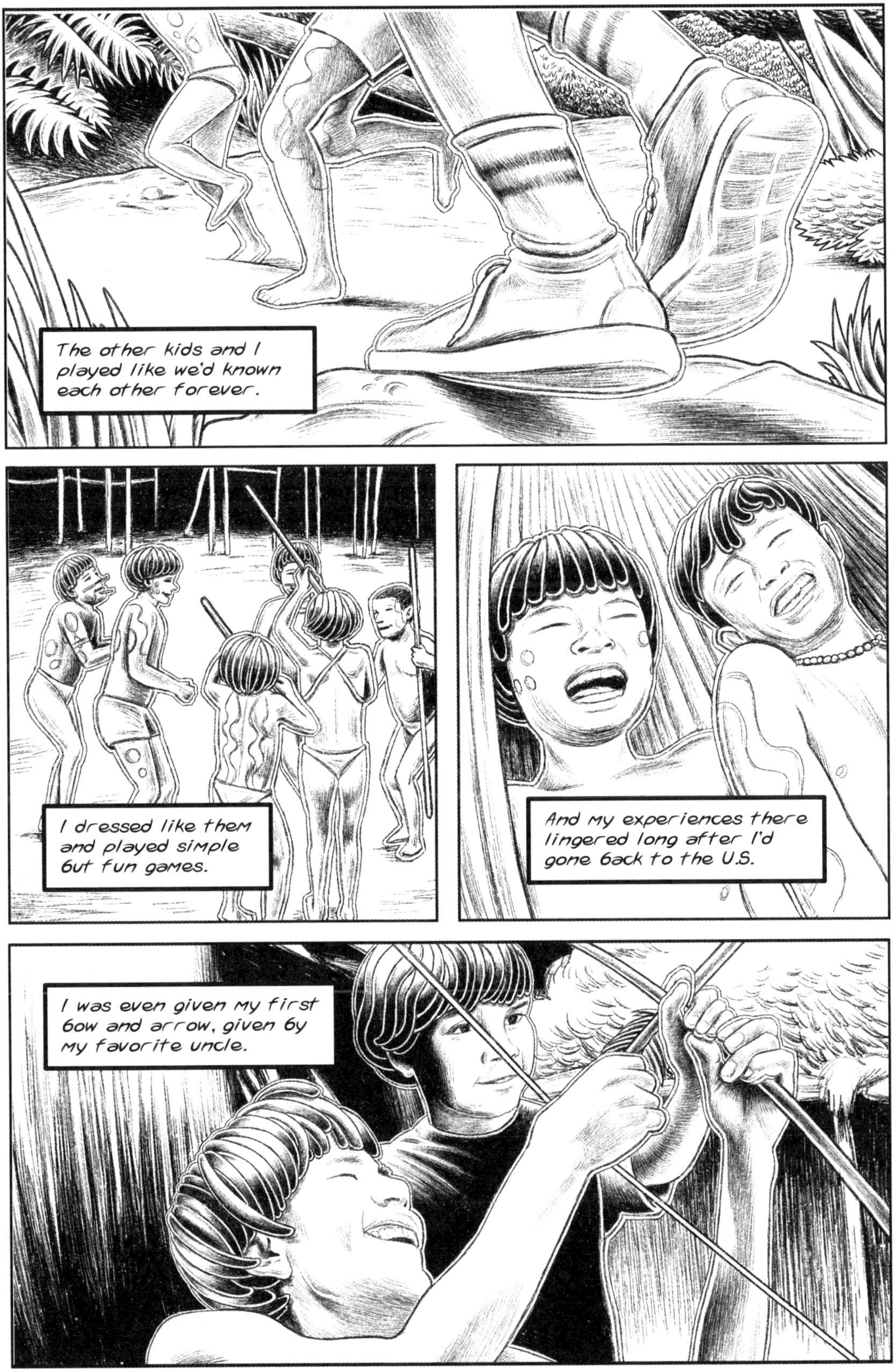
The other kids and I played like we'd known each other forever.
I dressed like them and played simple but fun games.
And my experiences there lingered long after I'd gone back to the U.S.
I was even given my first bow and arrow, given by my favorite uncle.

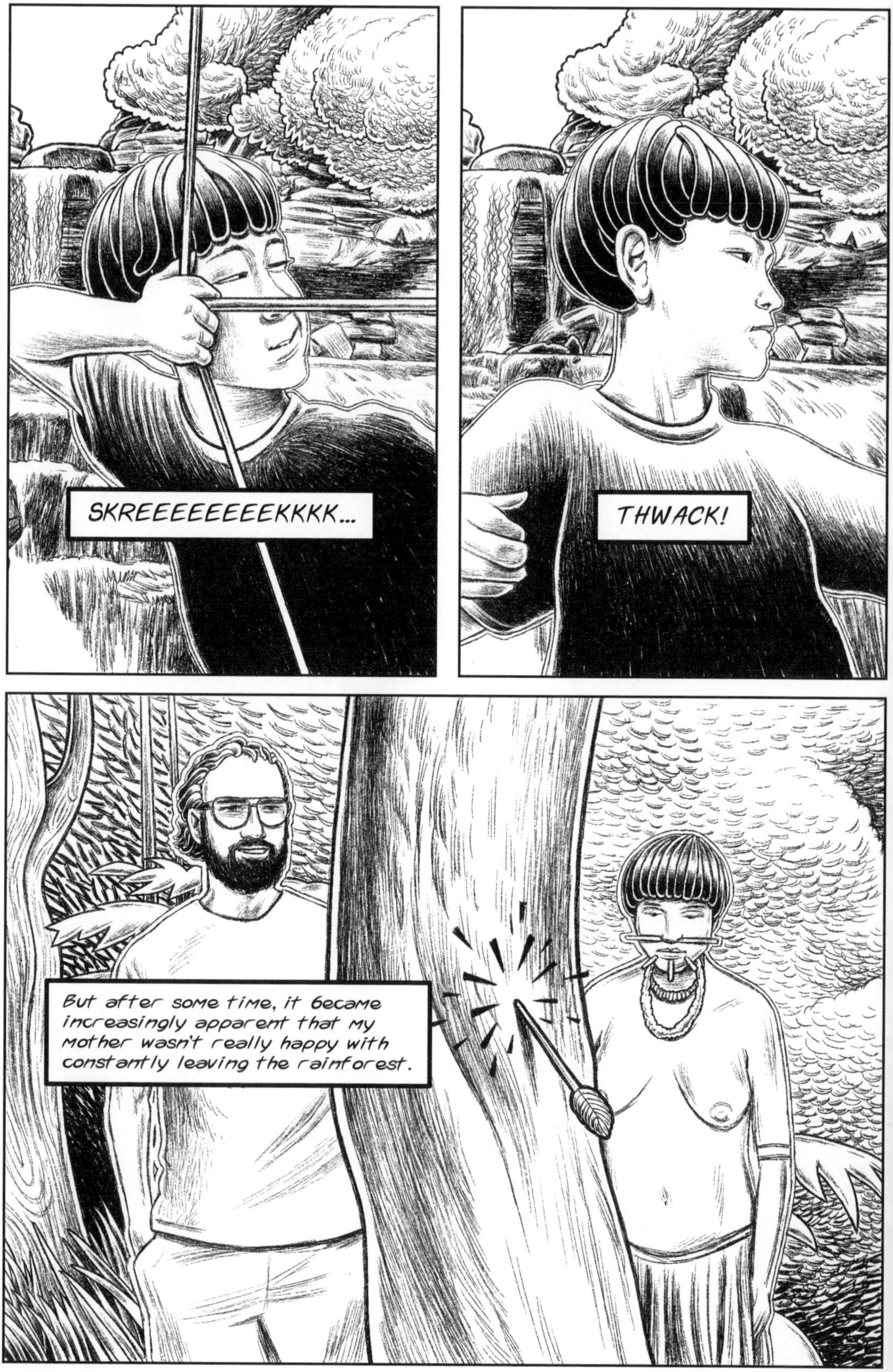
SKREEEEEEEEEKKKK...
THWACK!
But after some time, it became increasingly apparent that my mother wasn't really happy with constantly leaving the rainforest.

She grew more bitter with each return we made to the U.S.

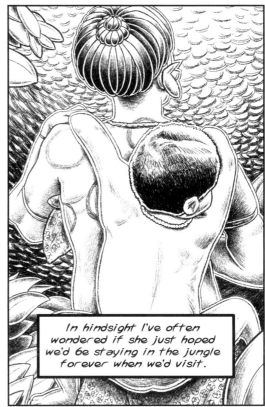

In hindsight I've often wondered if she just hoped we'd be staying in the jungle forever when we'd visit.

By the time my youngest brother was born, she'd decided to stay there with him for an extended period of time.

Oh come on sis. There's no way Santa is real.

Is too!

I remember this took place around Christmastime. My sister and I were staying at our Aunt & Uncle's when my dad left to bring her and my brother back.

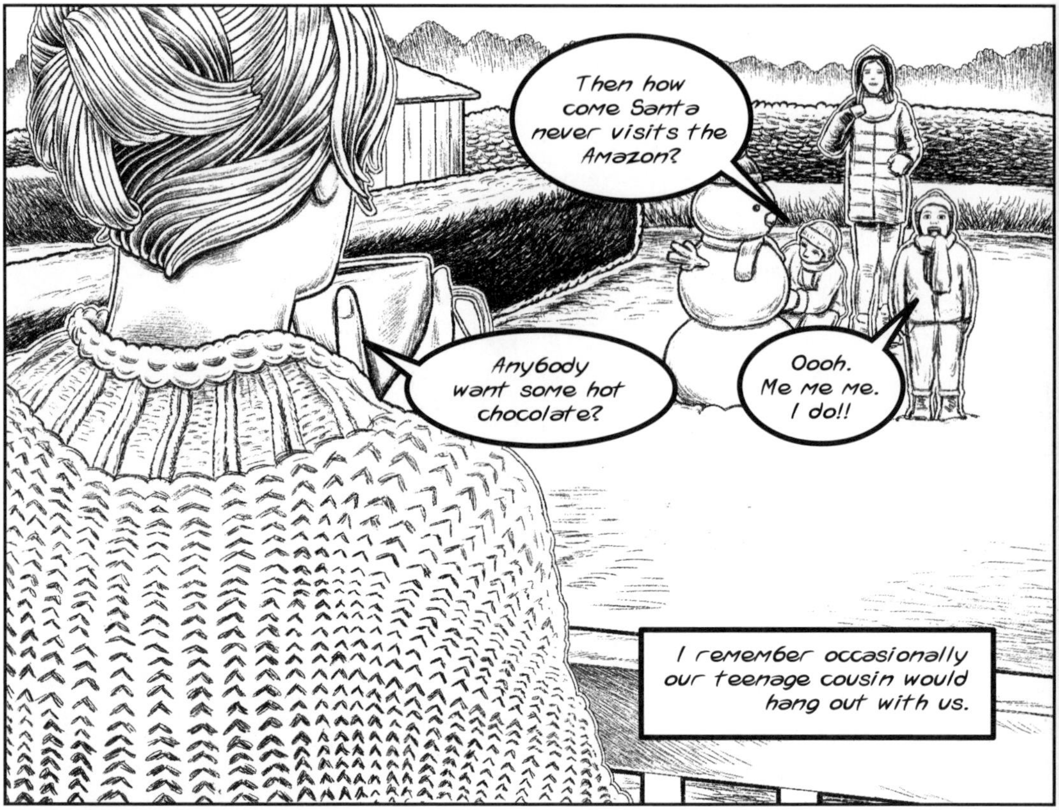
Then how come Santa never visits the Amazon?
Anybody want some hot chocolate?
Oooh. Me me me. I do!!
I remember occasionally our teenage cousin would hang out with us.

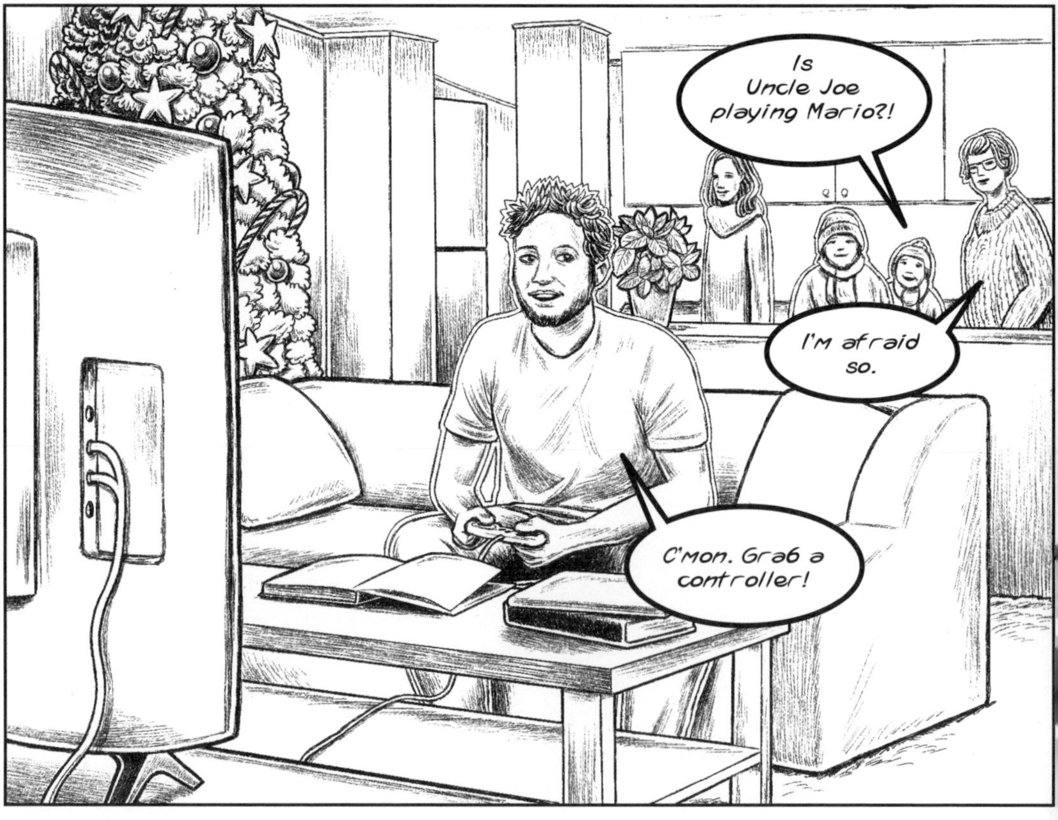
Is Uncle Joe playing Mario?!
I'm afraid so.
C'mon. Grab a controller!

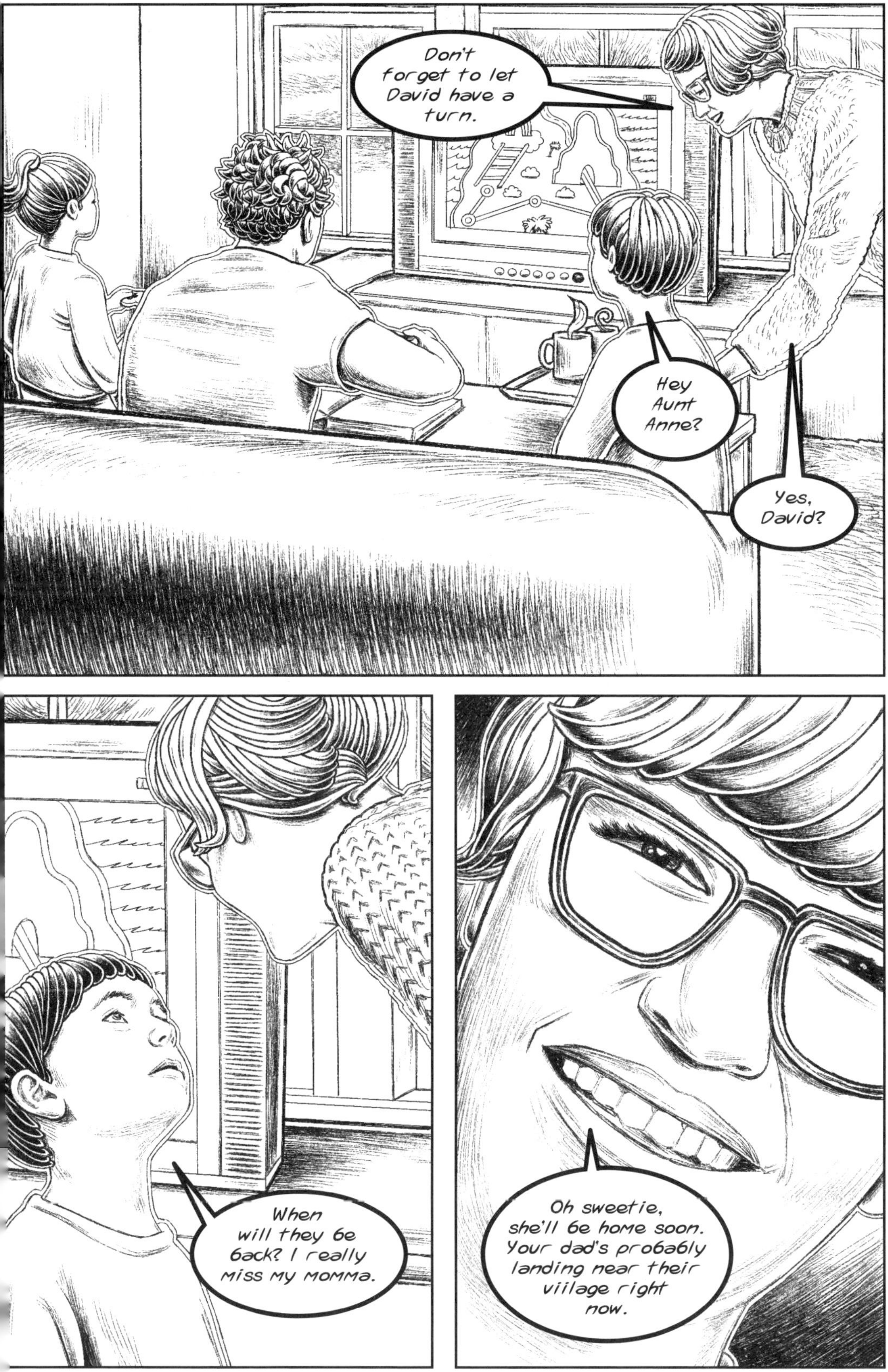
Don't forget to let David have a turn.
Hey Aunt Anne?
Yes, David?
When will they be back? I really miss my momma.
Oh sweetie, she'll be home soon. Your dad's probably landing near their viilage right now.

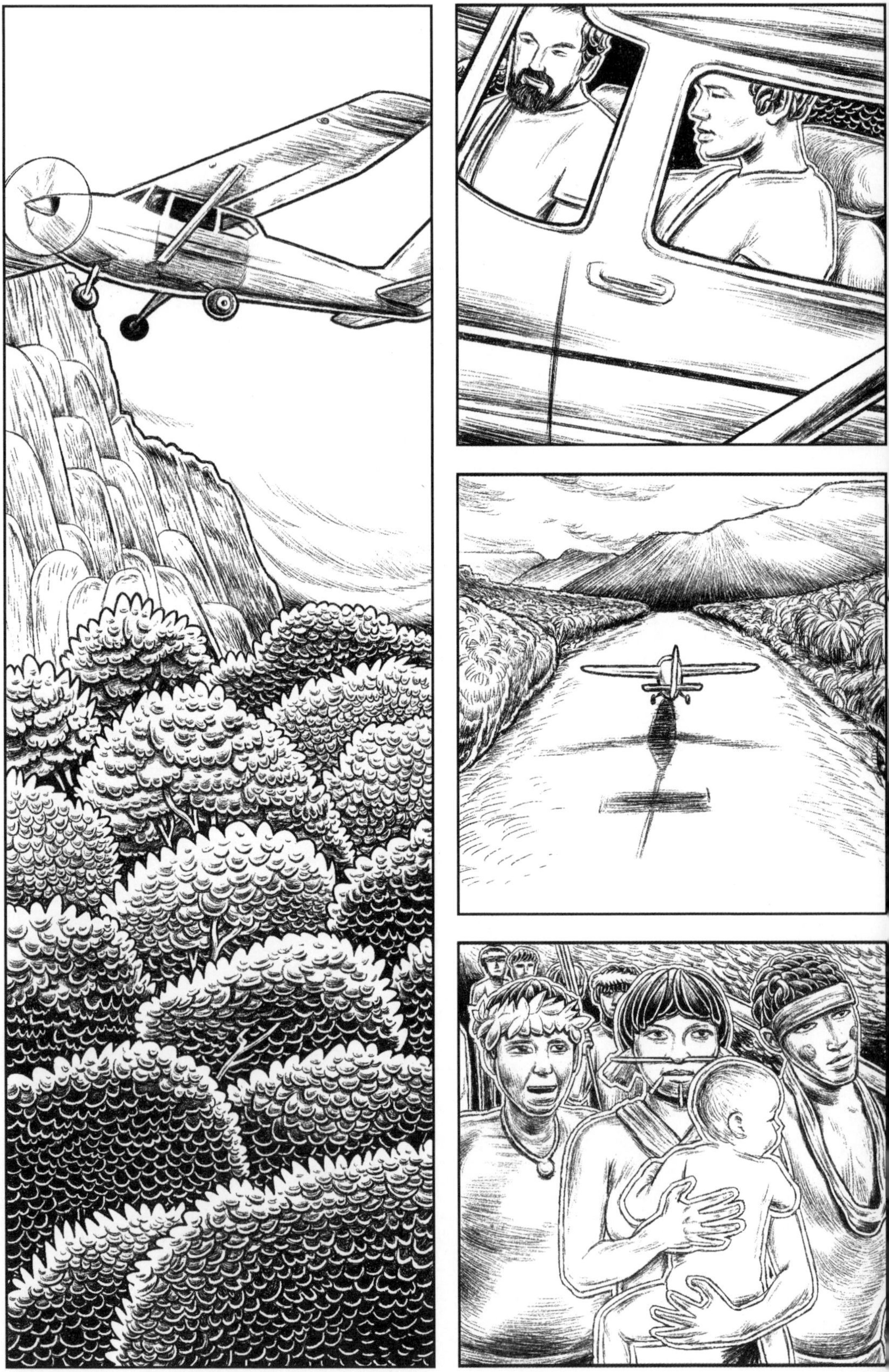

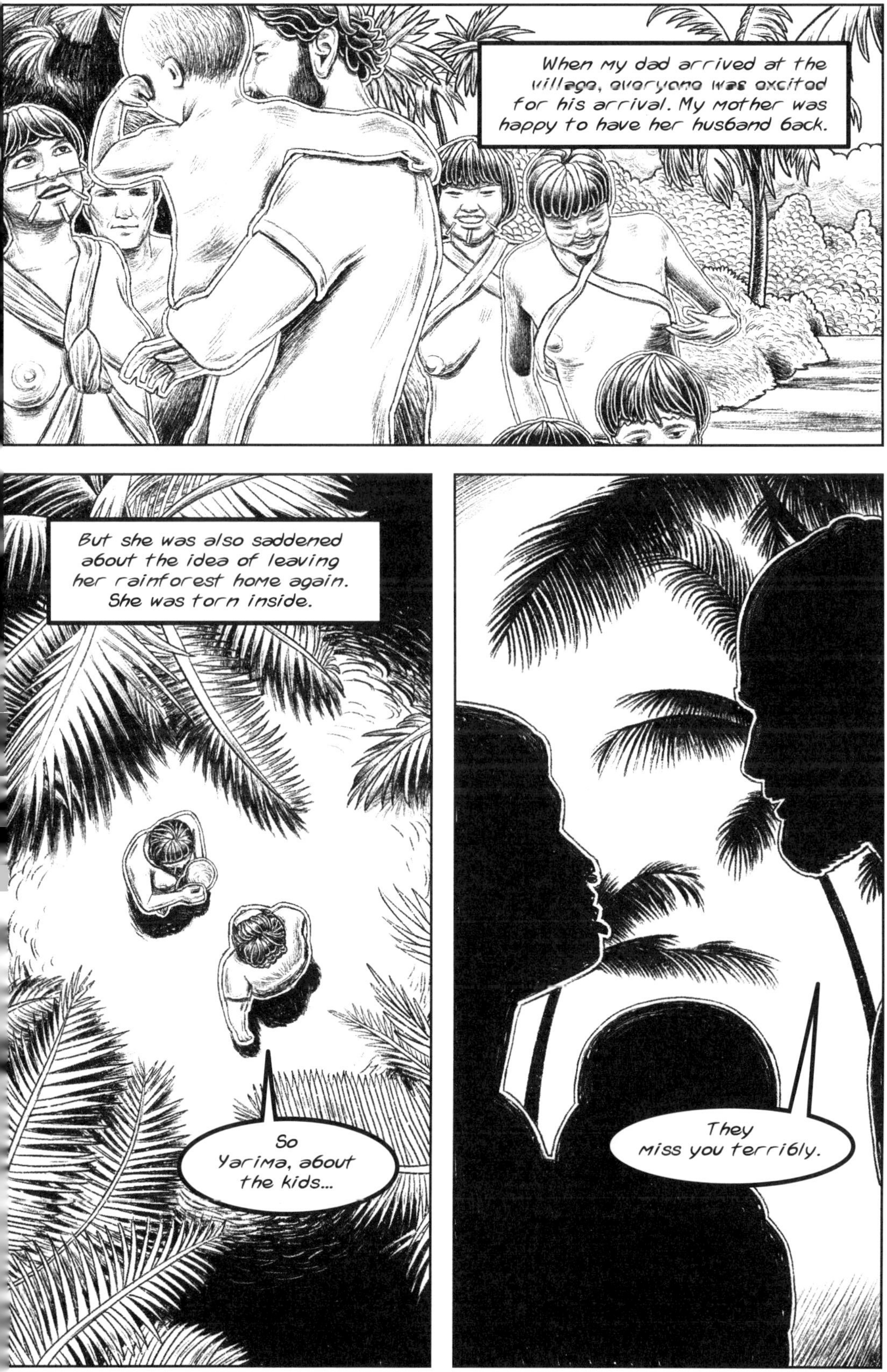
When my dad arrived at the village, everyone was excited for his arrival. My mother was happy to have her husband back.
But she was also saddened about the idea of leaving her rainforest home again. She was torn inside.
So Yarima, about the kids...
They miss you terribly.

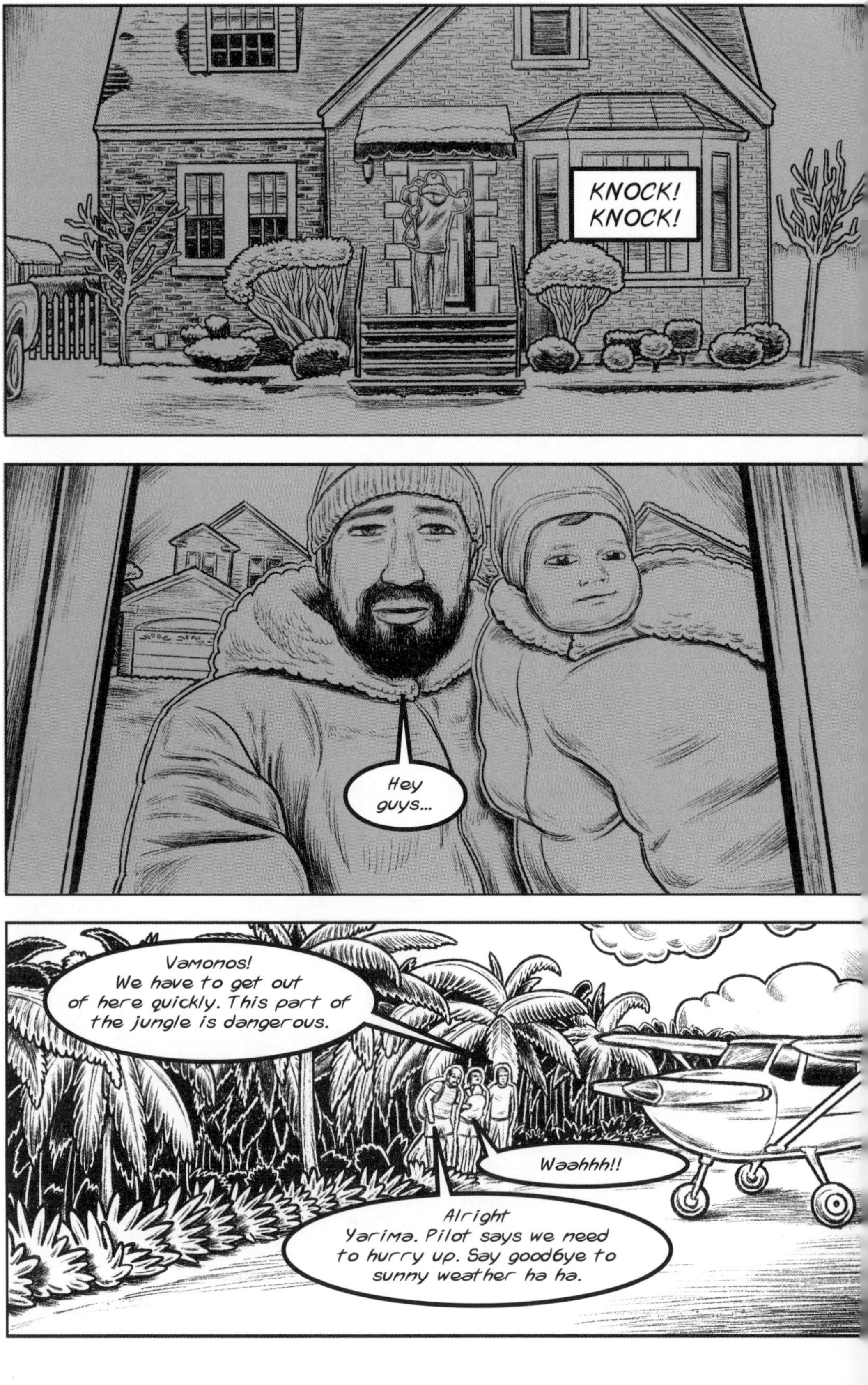
KNOCK! KNOCK!
Hey guys...
Vamonos! We have to get out of here quickly. This part of the jungle is dangerous.
Waahhh!!
Alright Yarima. Pilot says we need to hurry up. Say goodbye to sunny weather ha ha.

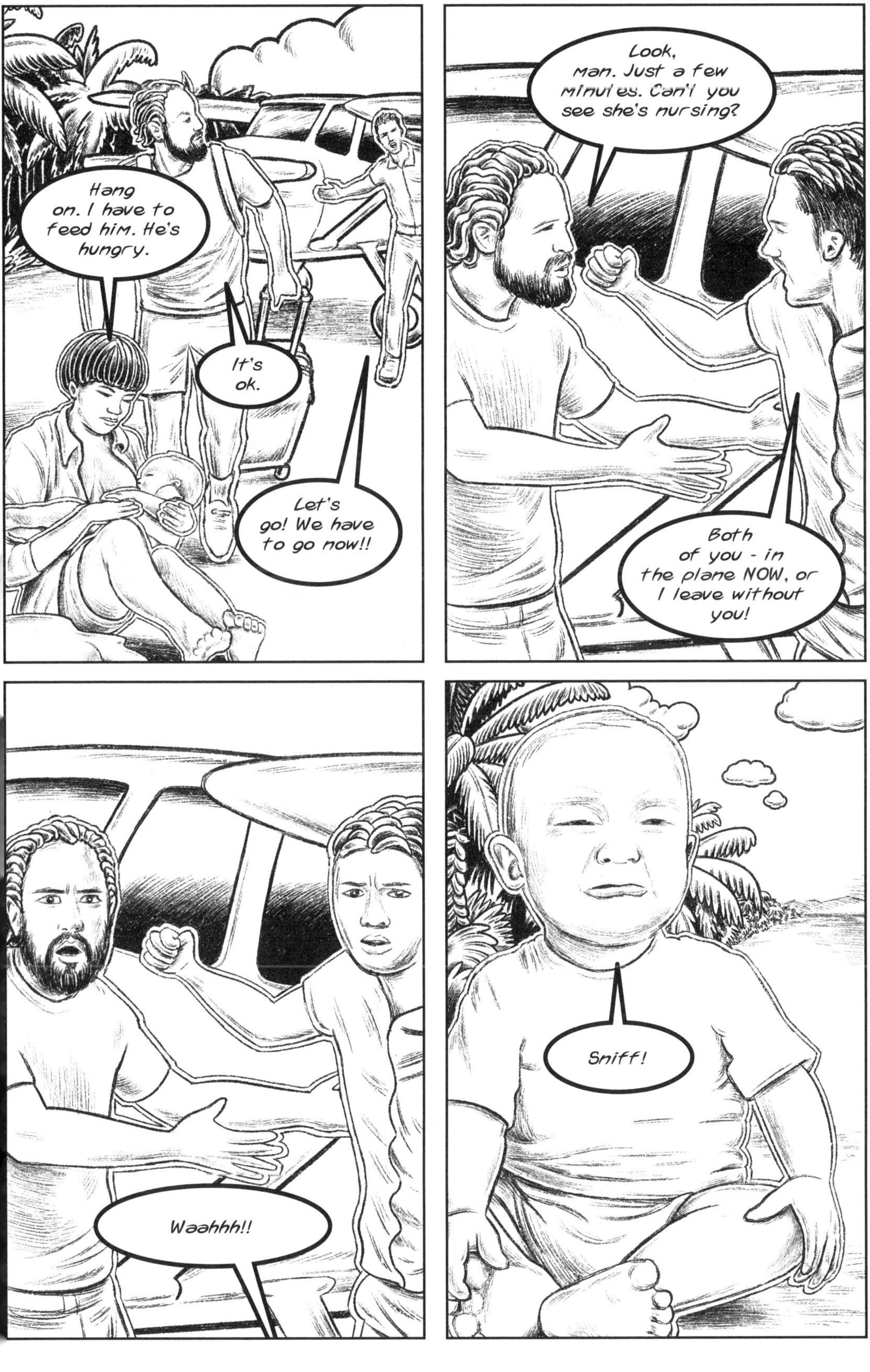
Hang on. I have to feed him. He's hungry.
It's ok.
Let's go! We have to go now!!
Look, man. Just a few minutes. Can't you see she's nursing?
Both of you - in the plane NOW, or I leave without you!
Waahhh!!
Sniff!

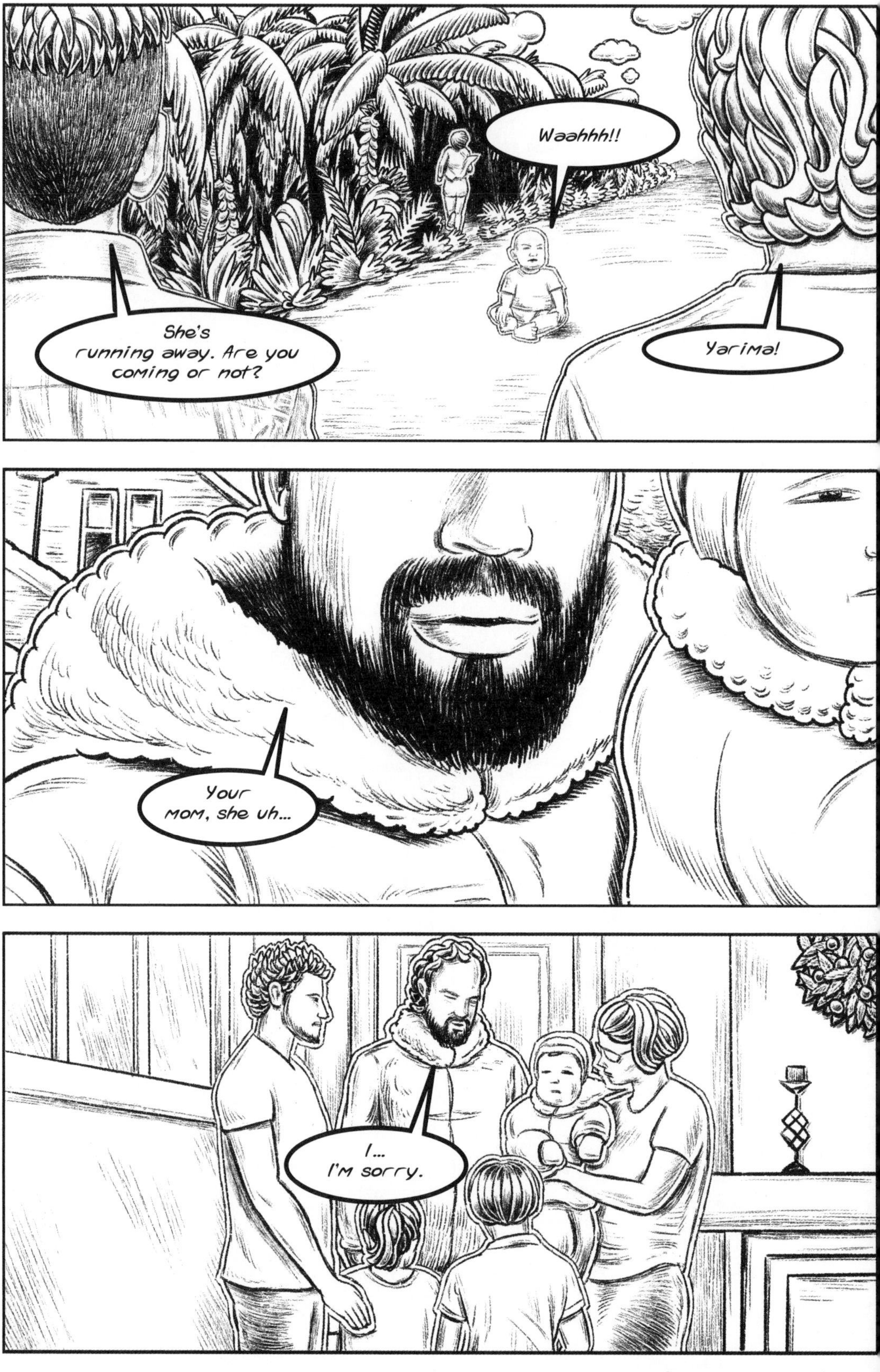
Waahhh!!
She's running away. Are you coming or not?
Yarima!
Your mom, she uh...
I... I'm sorry.

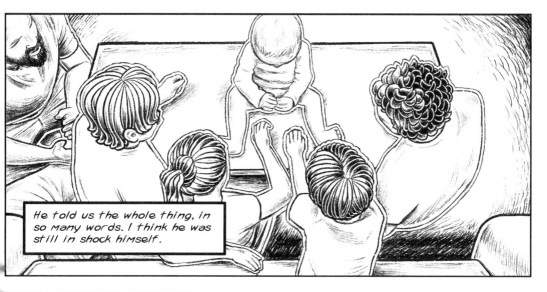

He told us the whole thing, in so many words. I think he was still in shock himself.

He explained more about how he was left with a very difficult choice. Should he have gone after Yarima to try and talk to her? If so, he would have lost the plane ride and been stranded with my baby brother.

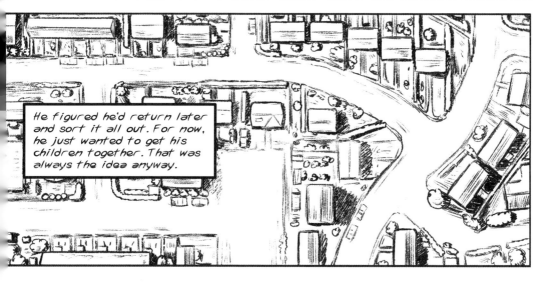

He figured he'd return later and sort it all out. For now, he just wanted to get his children together. That was always the idea anyway.

chapter 3

MIRROR ONE

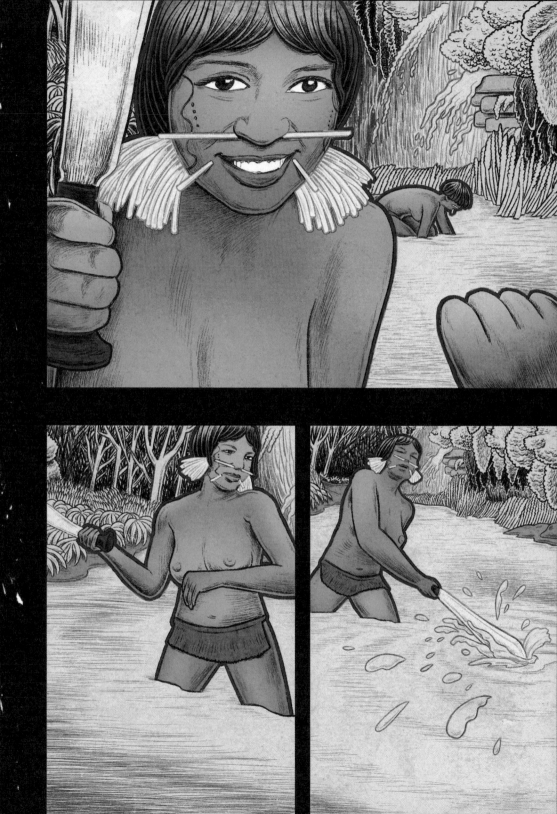

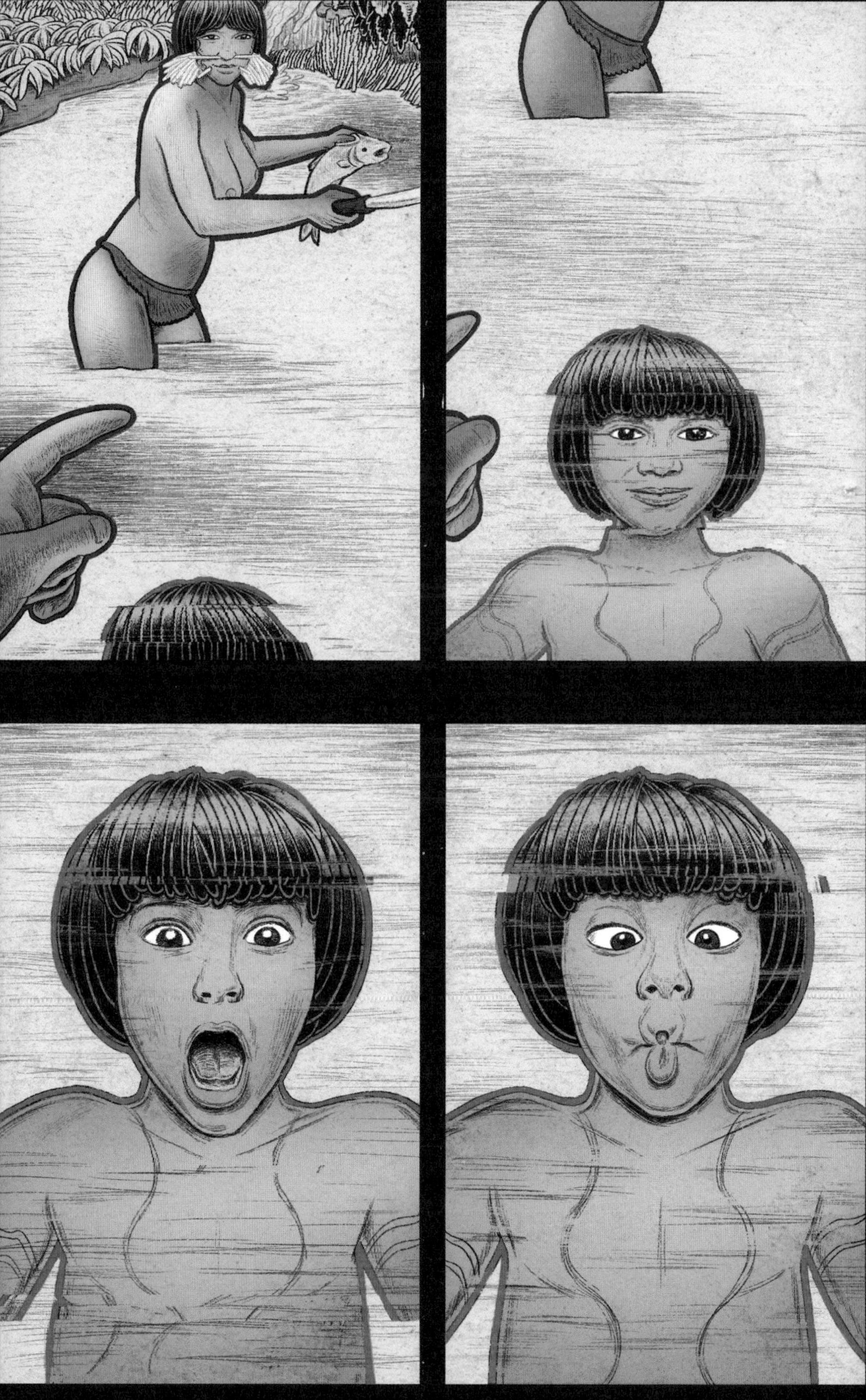

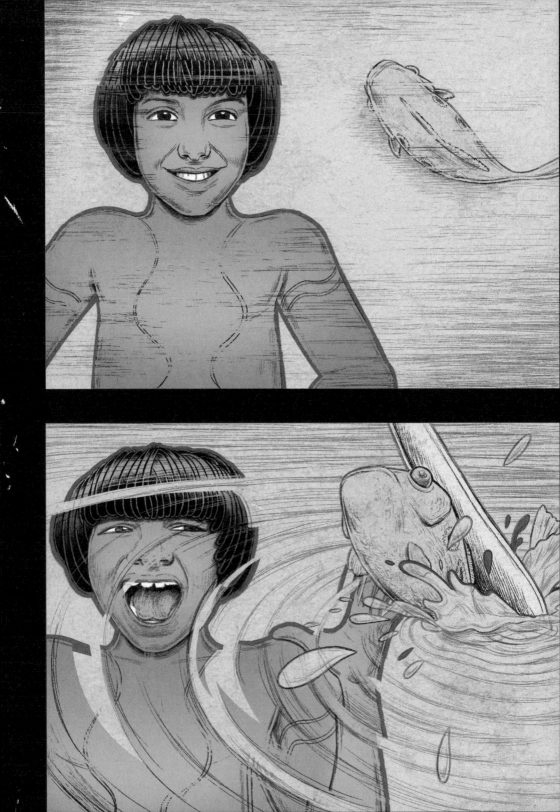

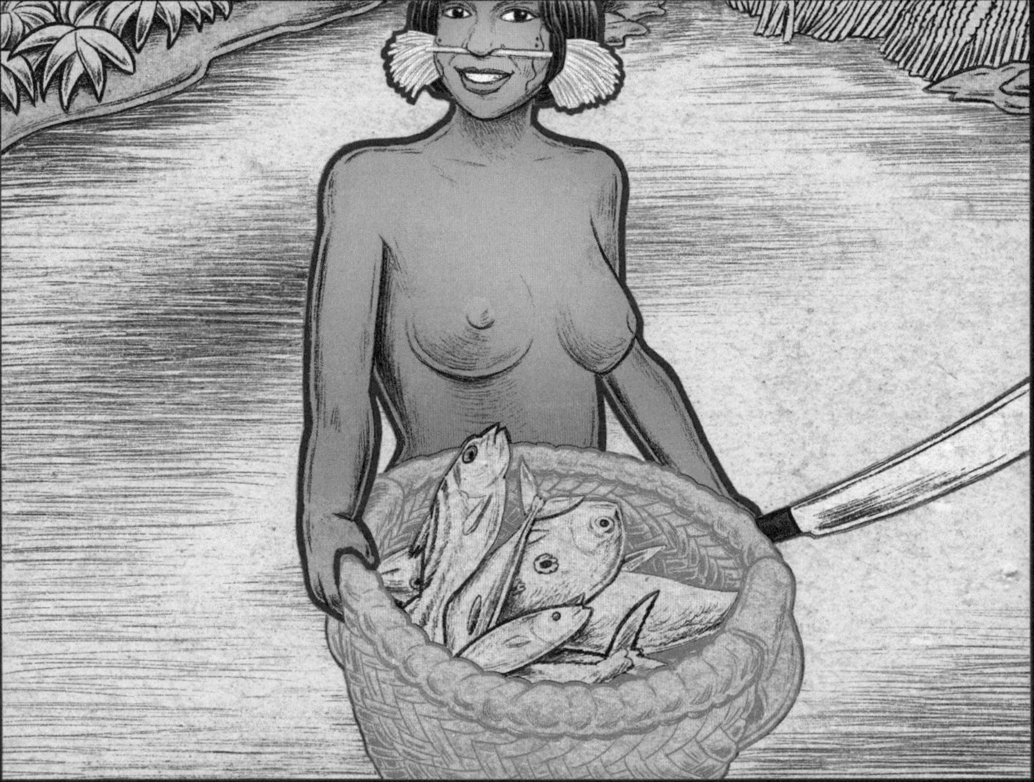

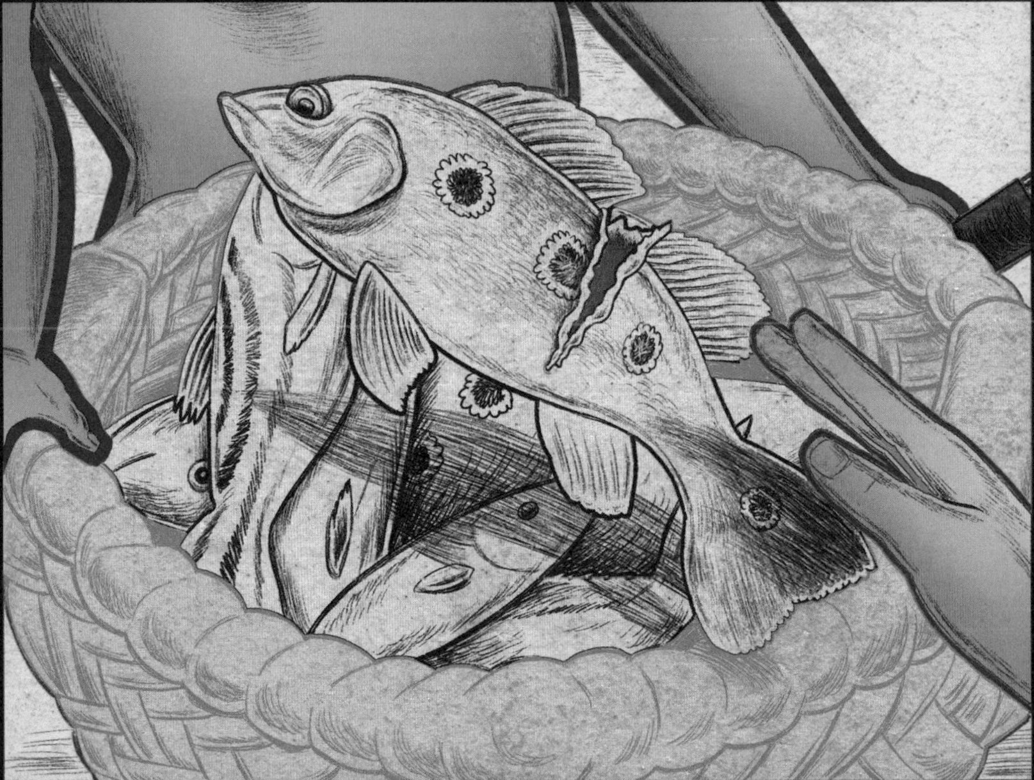

chapter 4

MIRROR TWO

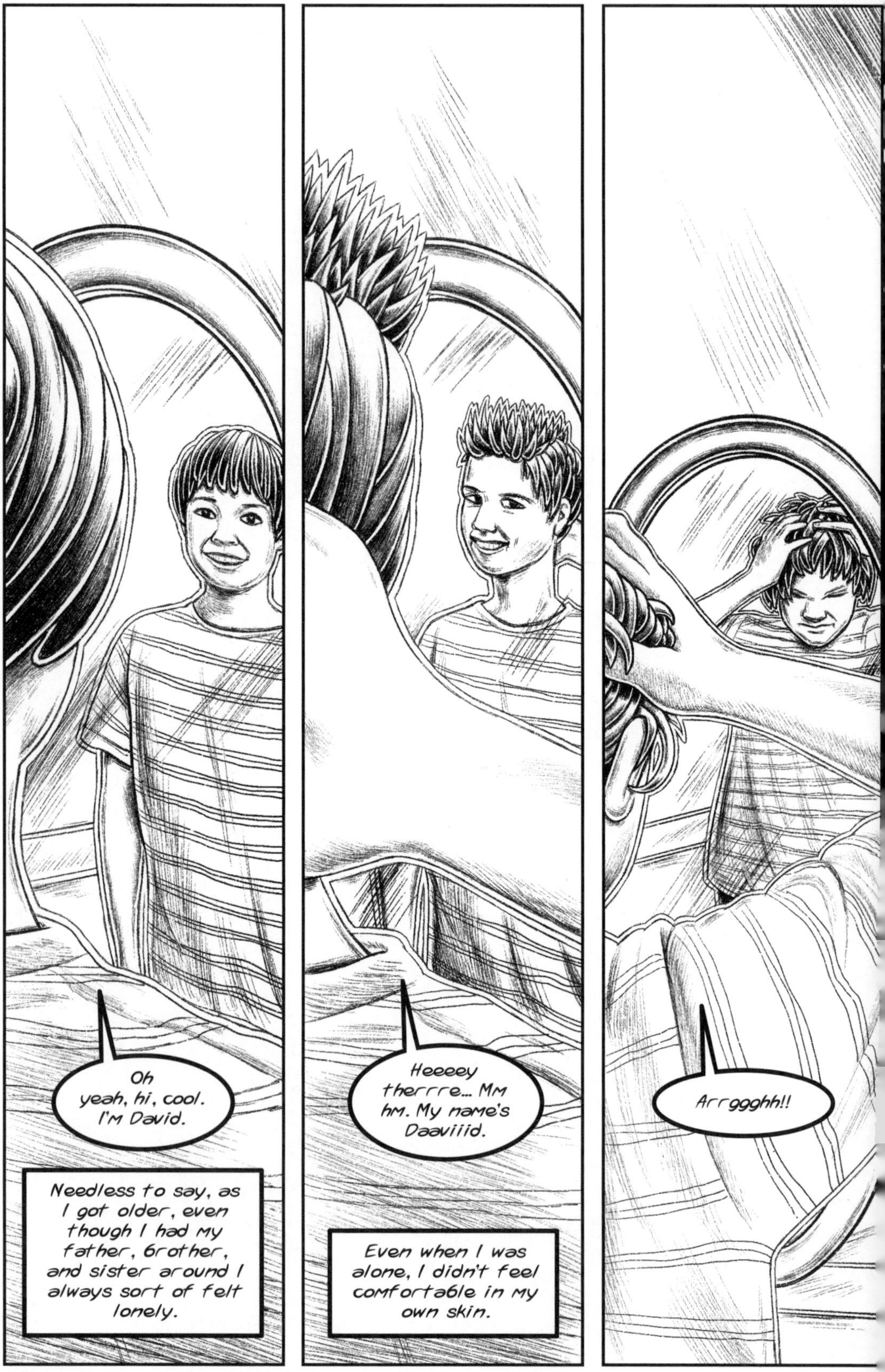
Oh yeah, hi, cool. I'm David.
Needless to say, as I got older, even though I had my father, brother, and sister around I always sort of felt lonely.
Heeeey therrre... Mm hm. My name's Daaviiid.
Even when I was alone, I didn't feel comfortable in my own skin.
Arrggghh!!

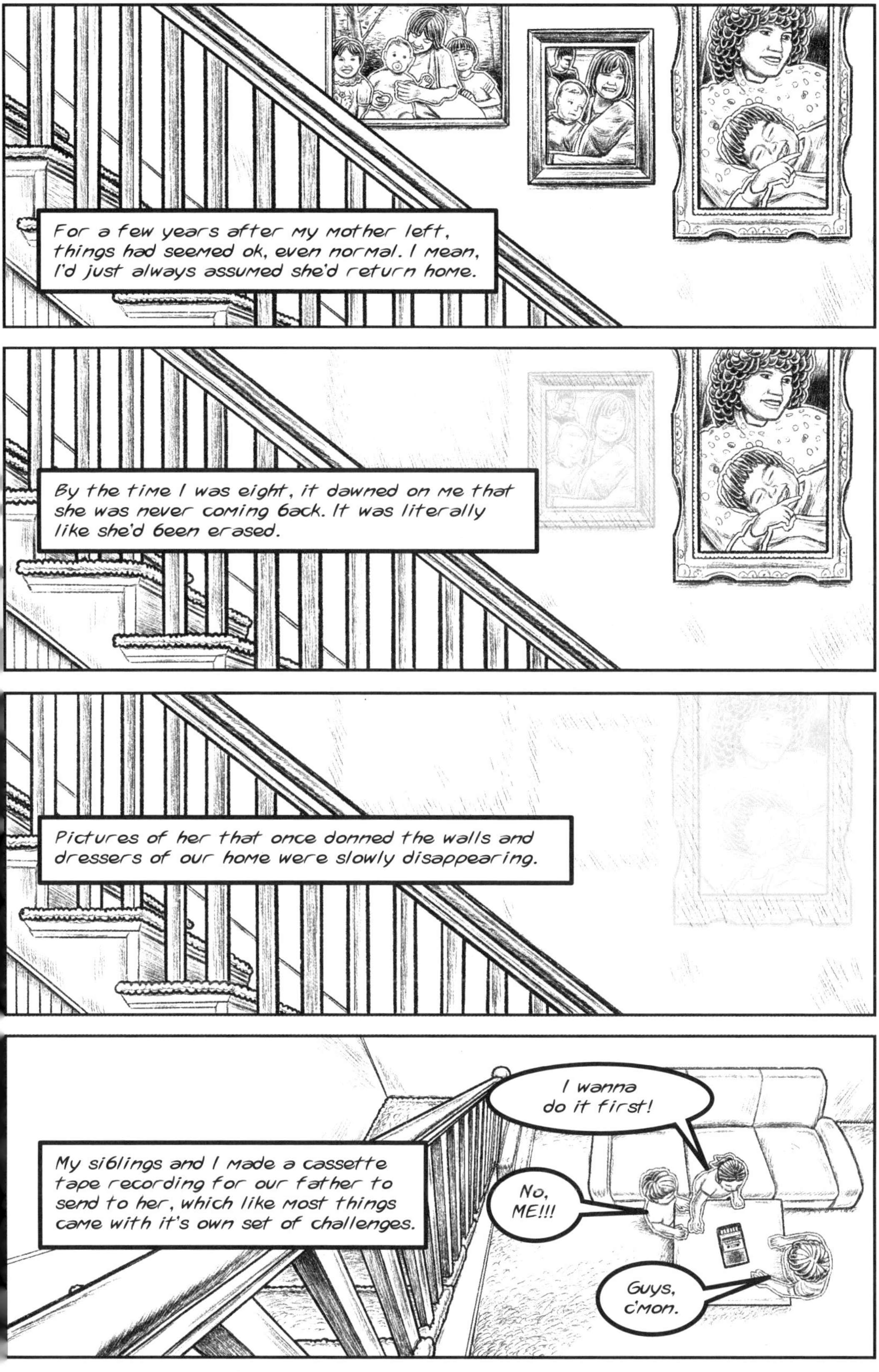

For a few years after my mother left, things had seemed ok, even normal. I mean, I'd just always assumed she'd return home.
By the time I was eight, it dawned on me that she was never coming back. It was literally like she'd been erased.
Pictures of her that once donned the walls and dressers of our home were slowly disappearing.
My siblings and I made a cassette tape recording for our father to send to her, which like most things came with it's own set of challenges.
I wanna do it first!
No, ME!!!
Guys, c'mon.

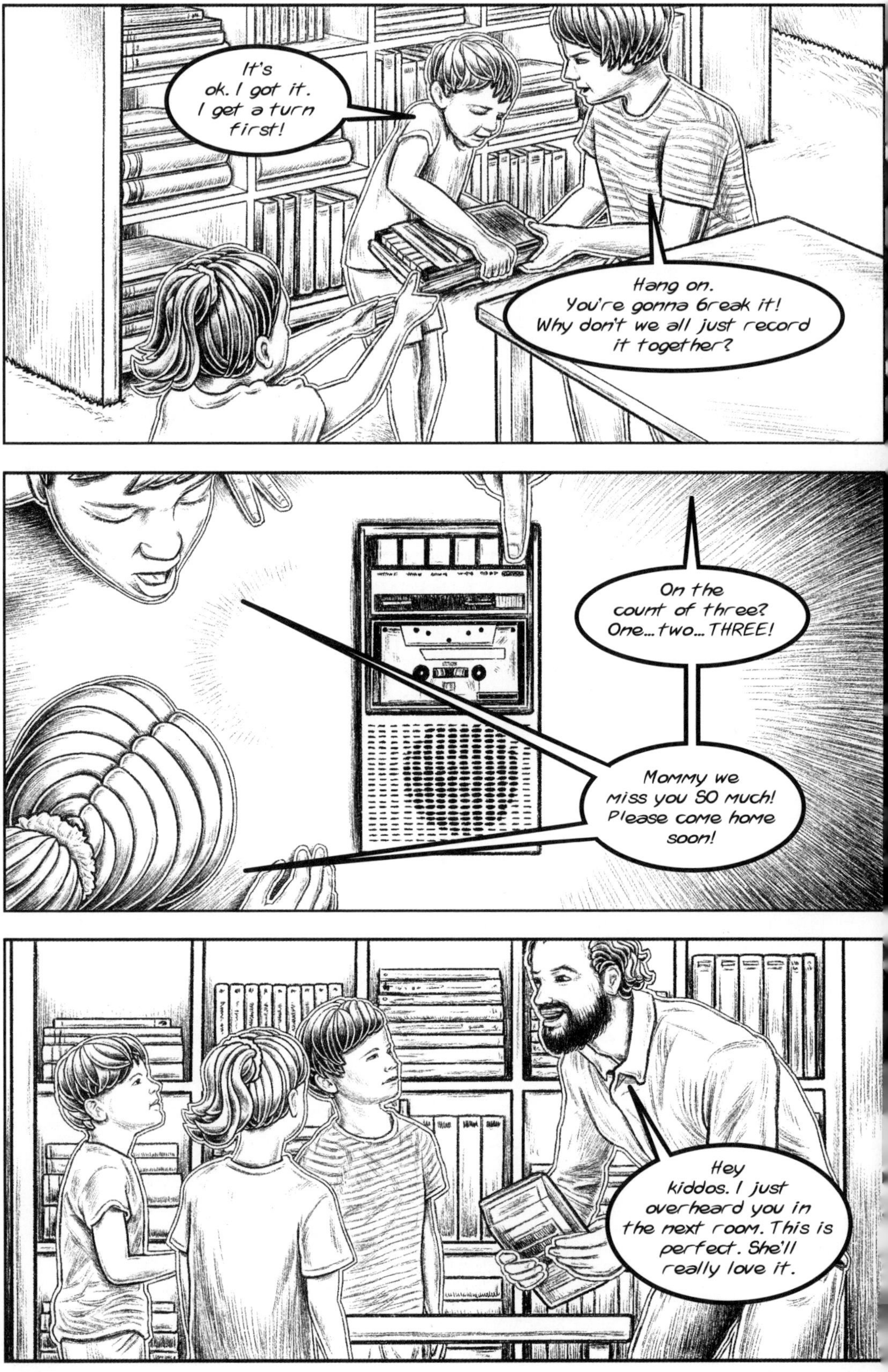
It's ok. I got it. I get a turn first!
Hang on. You're gonna break it! Why don't we all just record it together?
On the count of three? One...two...THREE!
Mommy we miss you SO much! Please come home soon!
Hey kiddos. I just overheard you in the next room. This is perfect. She'll really love it.

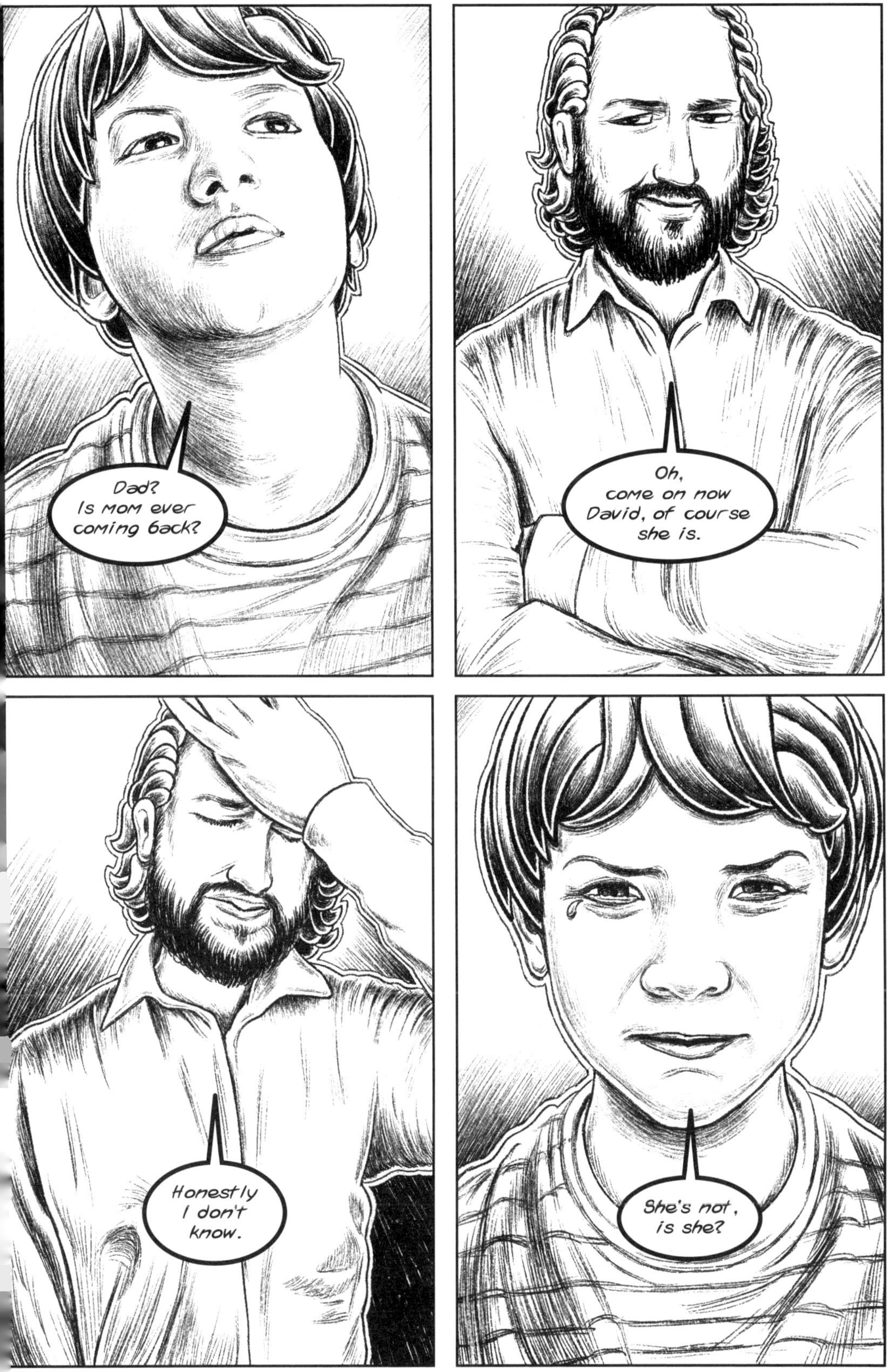
Dad? Is mom ever coming back?
Oh, come on now David, of course she is.
Honestly I don't know.
She's not, is she?

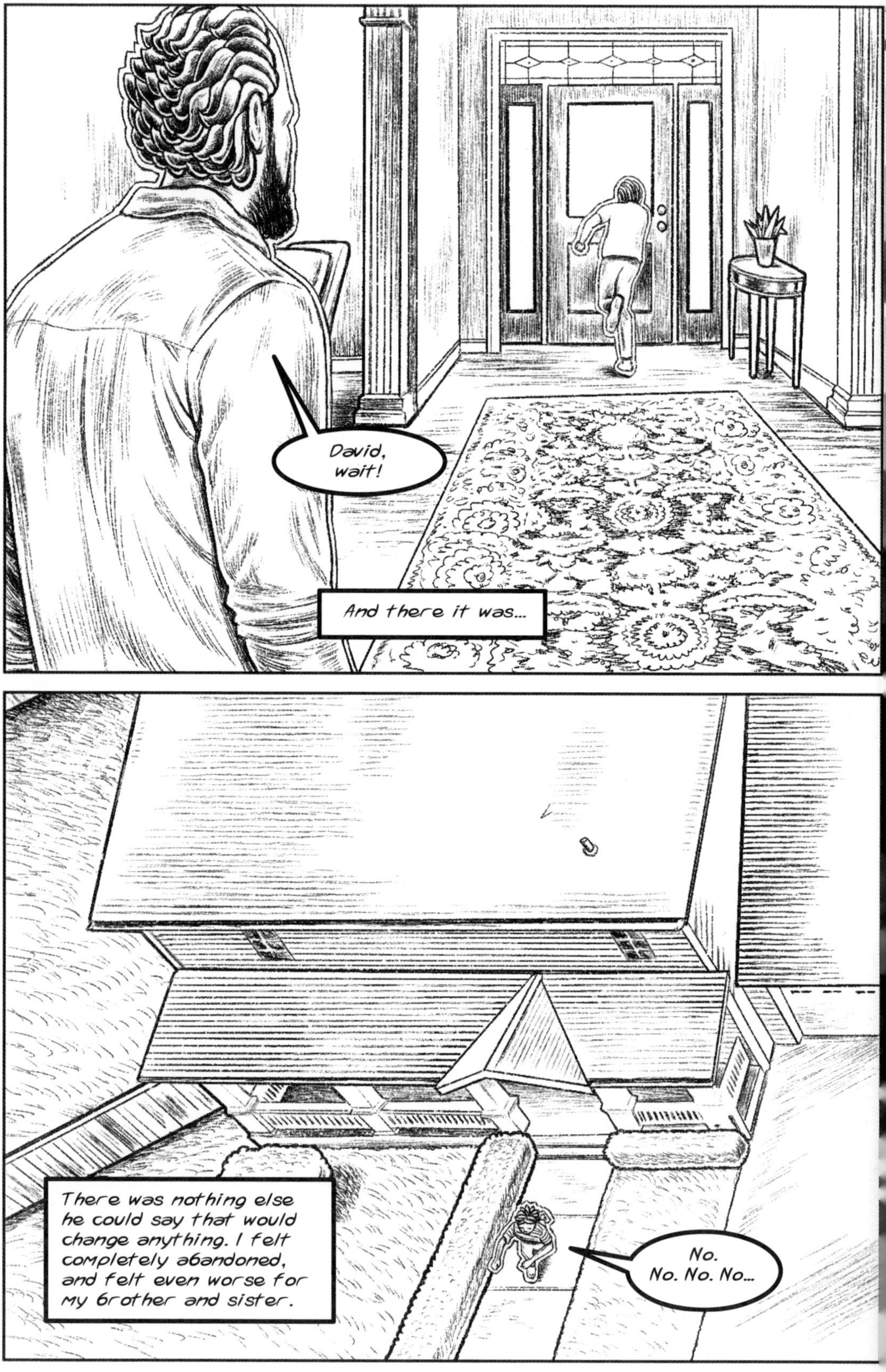
David, wait!
And there it was...
There was nothing else he could say that would change anything. I felt completely abandoned, and felt even worse for my brother and sister.
No. No. No. No...

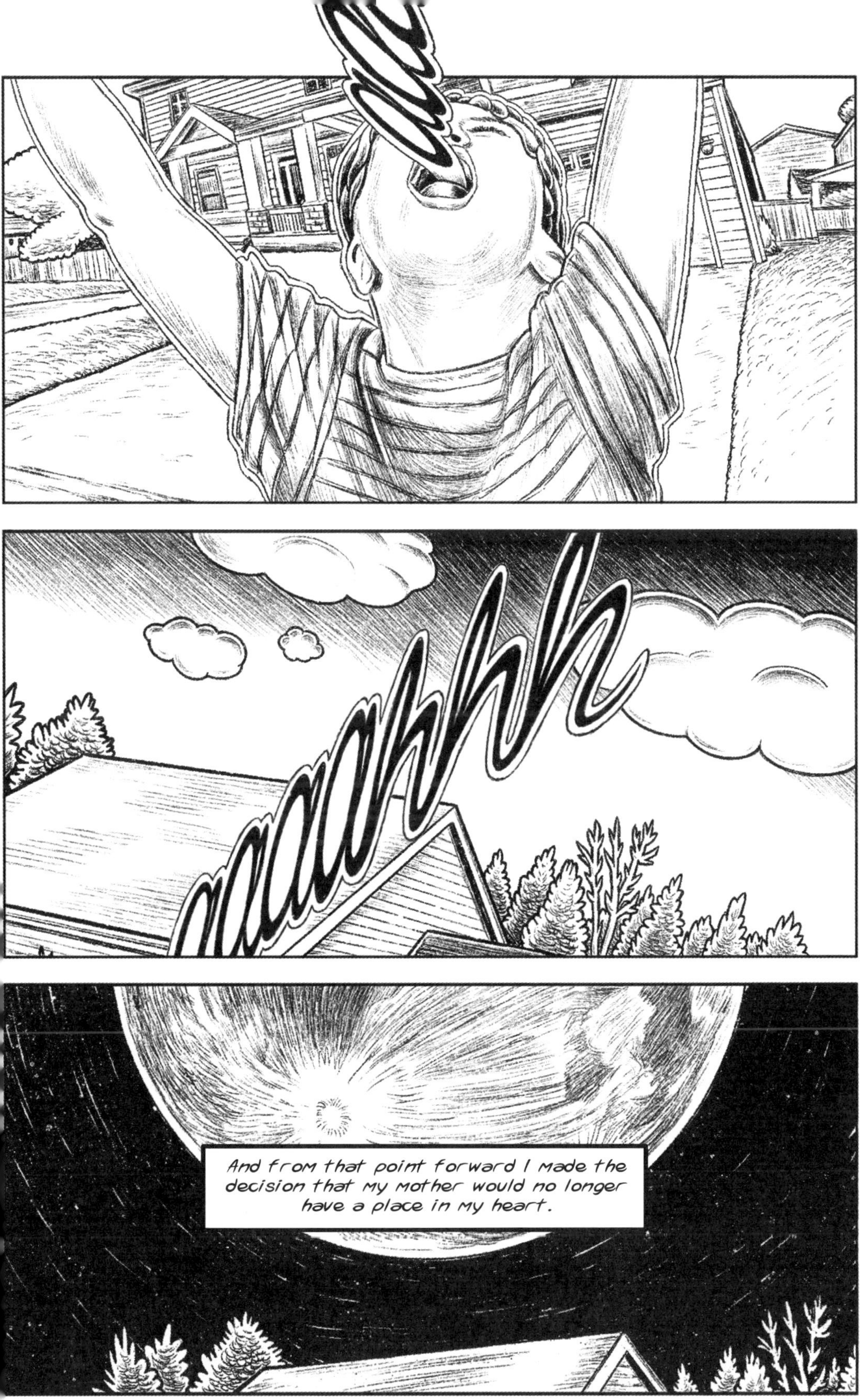
And from that point forward I made the decision that my mother would no longer have a place in my heart.

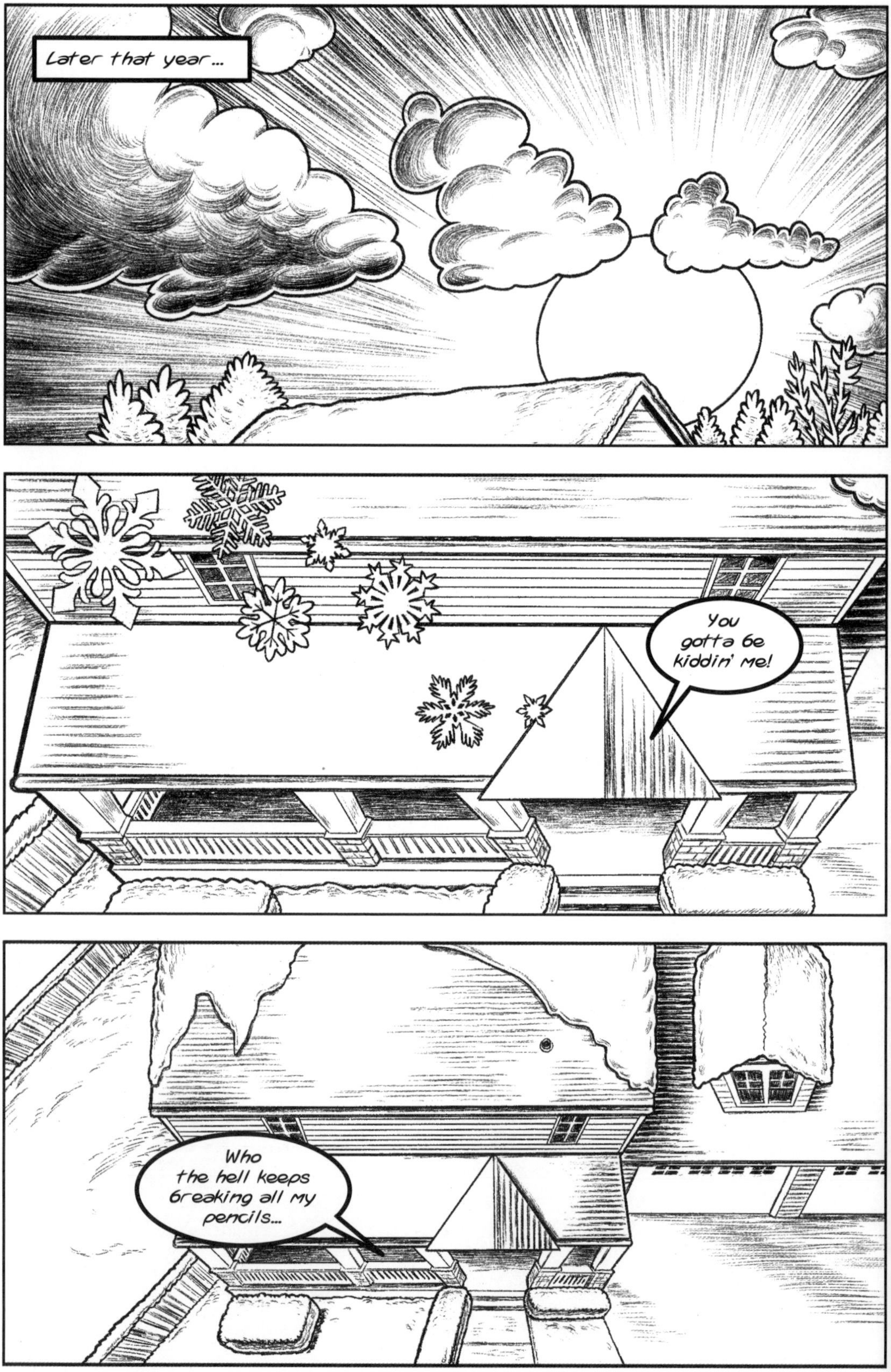
Later that year...
You gotta be kiddin' me!
Who the hell keeps breaking all my pencils...

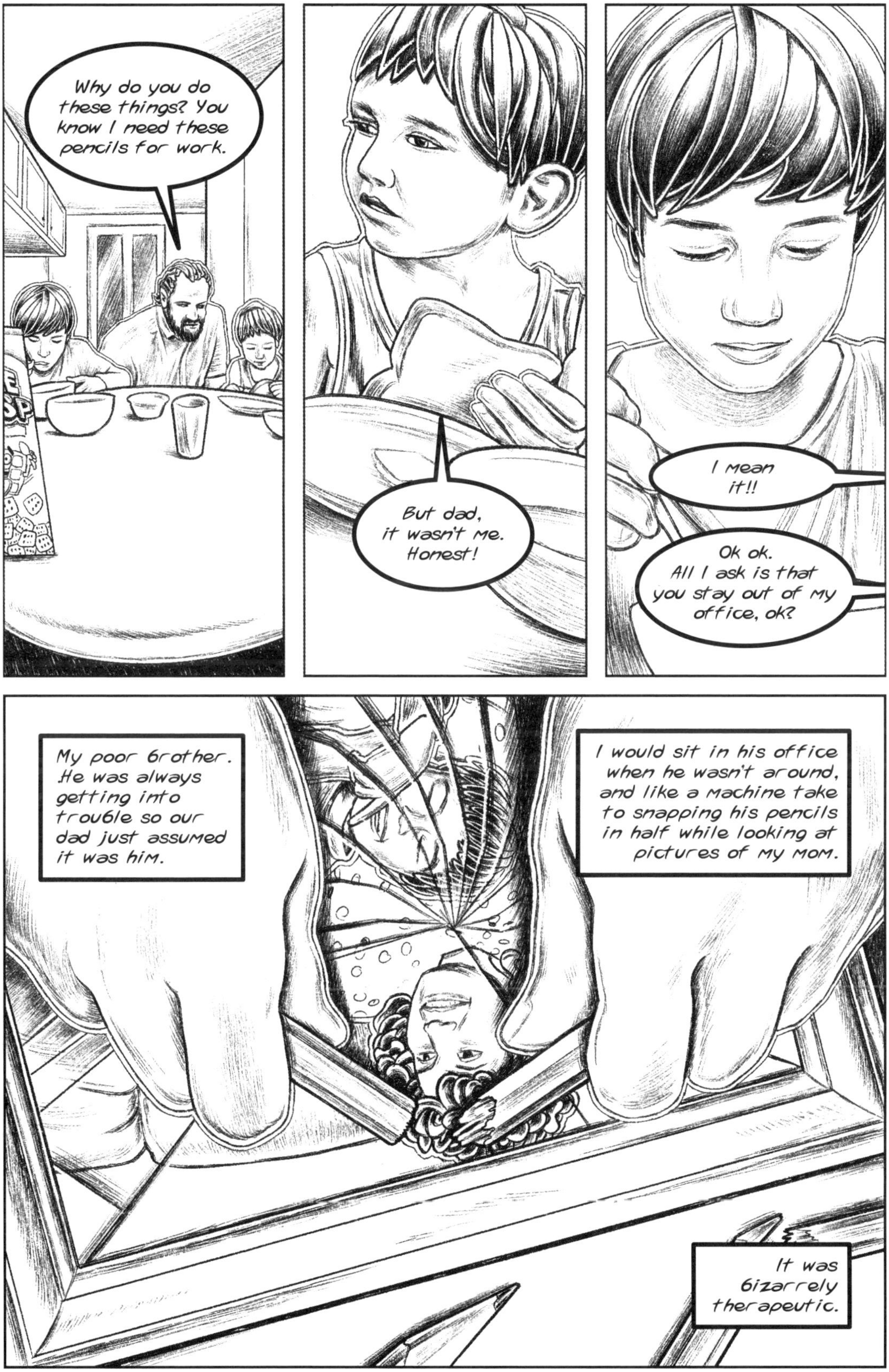
Why do you do these things? You know I need these pencils for work.
But dad, it wasn't me. Honest!
I mean it!!
Ok ok. All I ask is that you stay out of my office, ok?
My poor brother. He was always getting into trouble so our dad just assumed it was him.
I would sit in his office when he wasn't around, and like a machine take to snapping his pencils in half while looking at pictures of my mom.
It was bizarrely therapeutic.

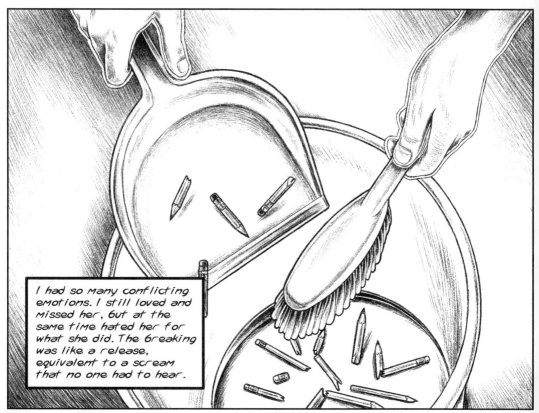

I had so many conflicting emotions. I still loved and missed her, but at the same time hated her for what she did. The breaking was like a release, equivalent to a scream that no one had to hear.

As time went on I continued to try and escape my origin story, maybe as another way of pushing her out of my life, but it always seemed to creep its way back.

Like the time our school took a trip to the American Museum of Natural History in New York.

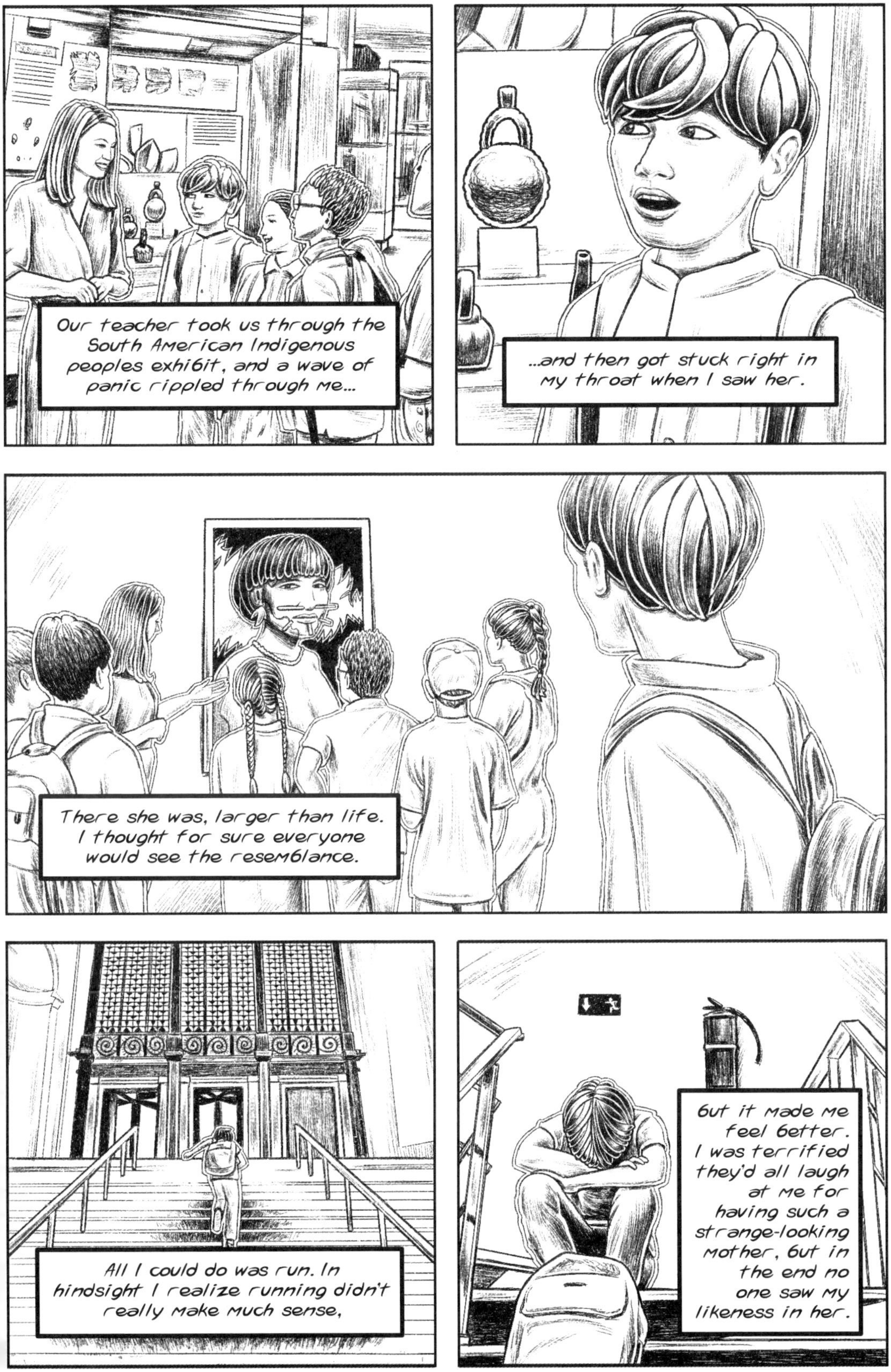

Our teacher took us through the South American Indigenous peoples exhibit, and a wave of panic rippled through me...
...and then got stuck right in my throat when I saw her.
There she was, larger than life. I thought for sure everyone would see the resemblance.
All I could do was run. In hindsight I realize running didn't really make much sense,
but it made me feel better. I was terrified they'd all laugh at me for having such a strange-looking mother, but in the end no one saw my likeness in her.

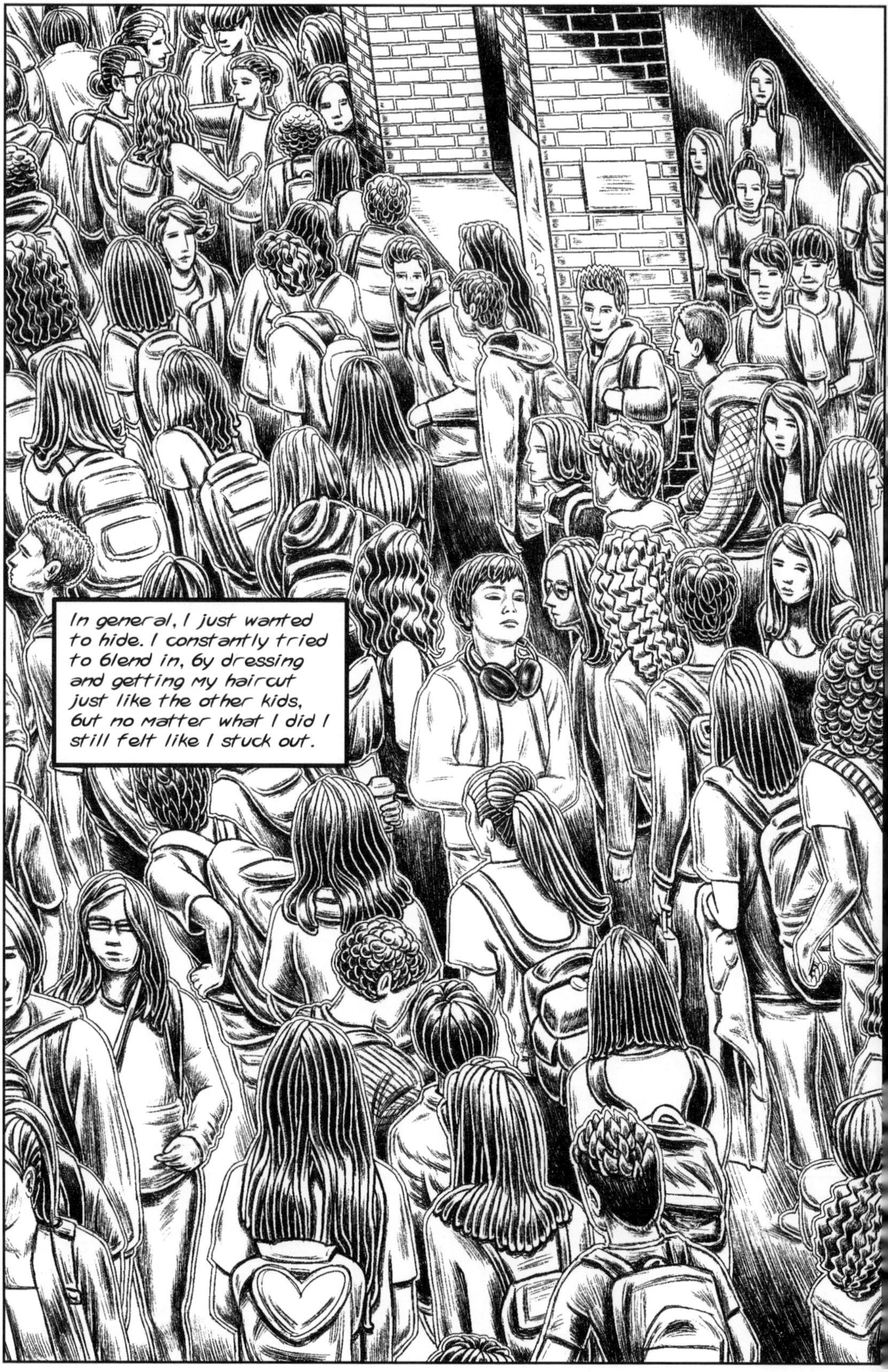
In general, I just wanted to hide. I constantly tried to blend in, by dressing and getting my haircut just like the other kids, but no matter what I did I still felt like I stuck out.

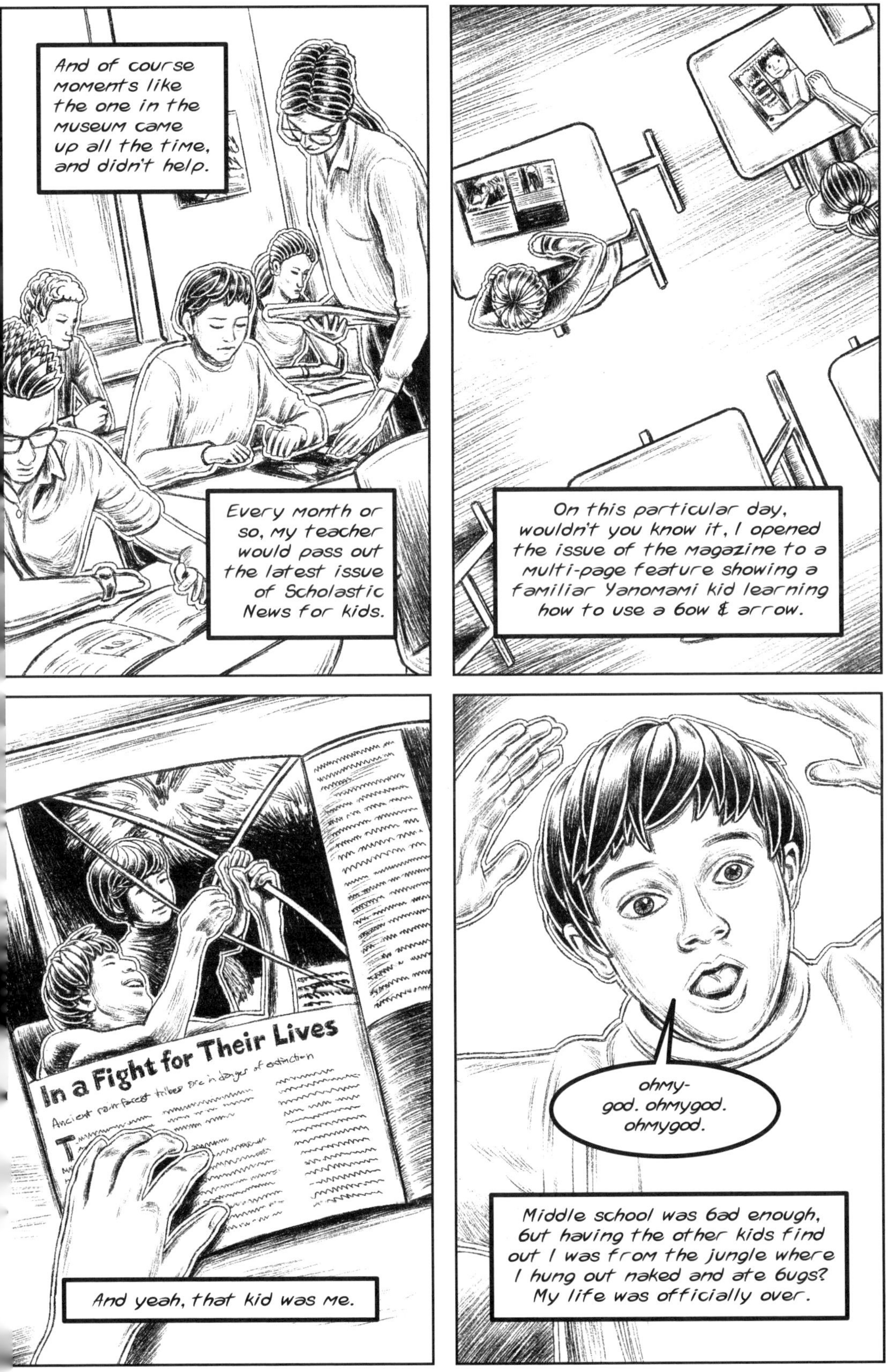
And of course moments like the one in the museum came up all the time, and didn't help.
Every month or so, my teacher would pass out the latest issue of Scholastic News for kids.
On this particular day, wouldn't you know it, I opened the issue of the magazine to a multi-page feature showing a familiar Yanomami kid learning how to use a bow & arrow.
In a Fight for Their Lives
Ancient rain forest tribes are in danger of extinction
And yeah, that kid was me.
ohmy-god. ohmygod. ohmygod.
Middle school was bad enough, but having the other kids find out I was from the jungle where I hung out naked and ate bugs? My life was officially over.

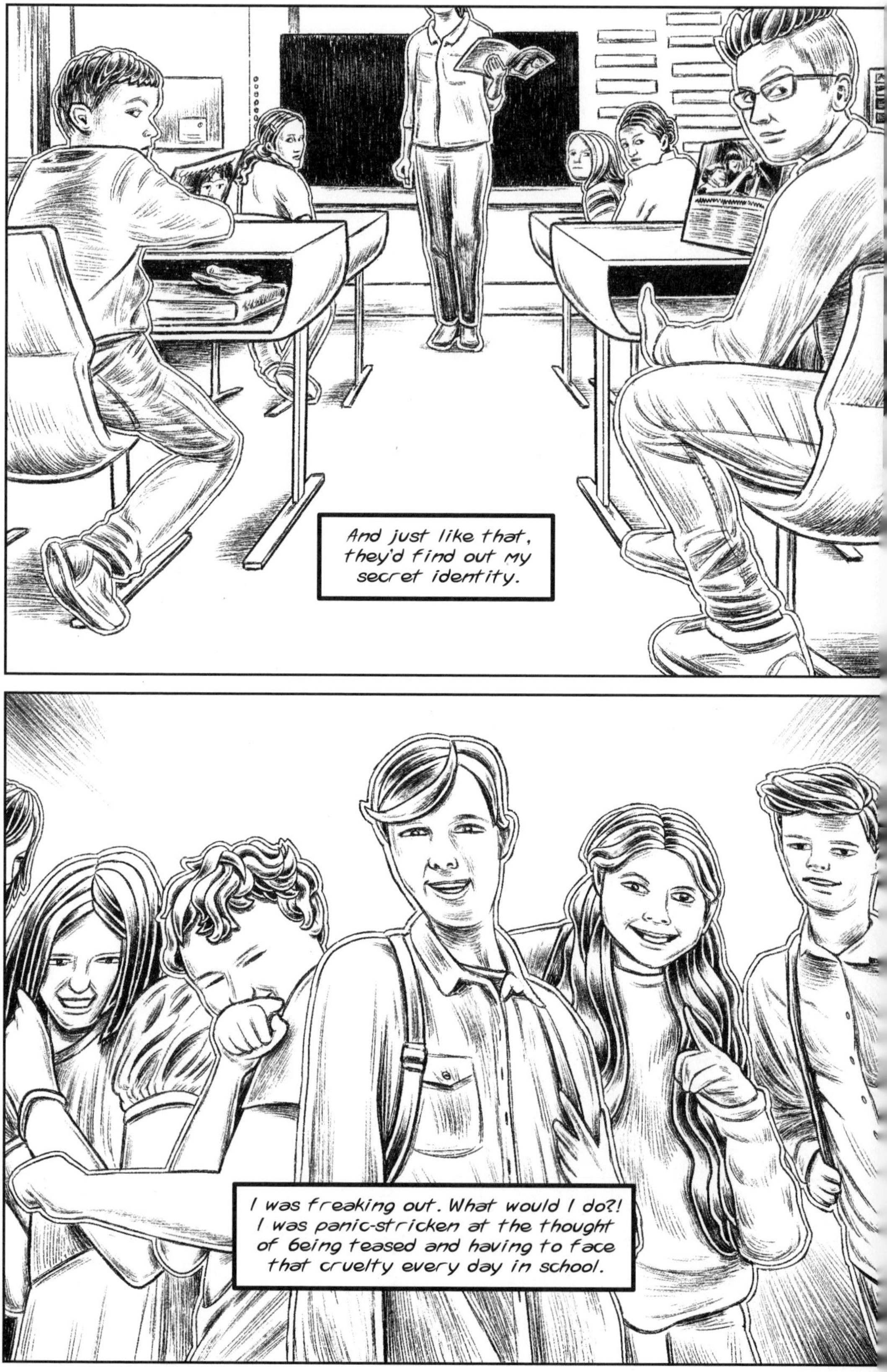
And just like that, they'd find out my secret identity.
I was freaking out. What would I do?! I was panic-stricken at the thought of being teased and having to face that cruelty every day in school.

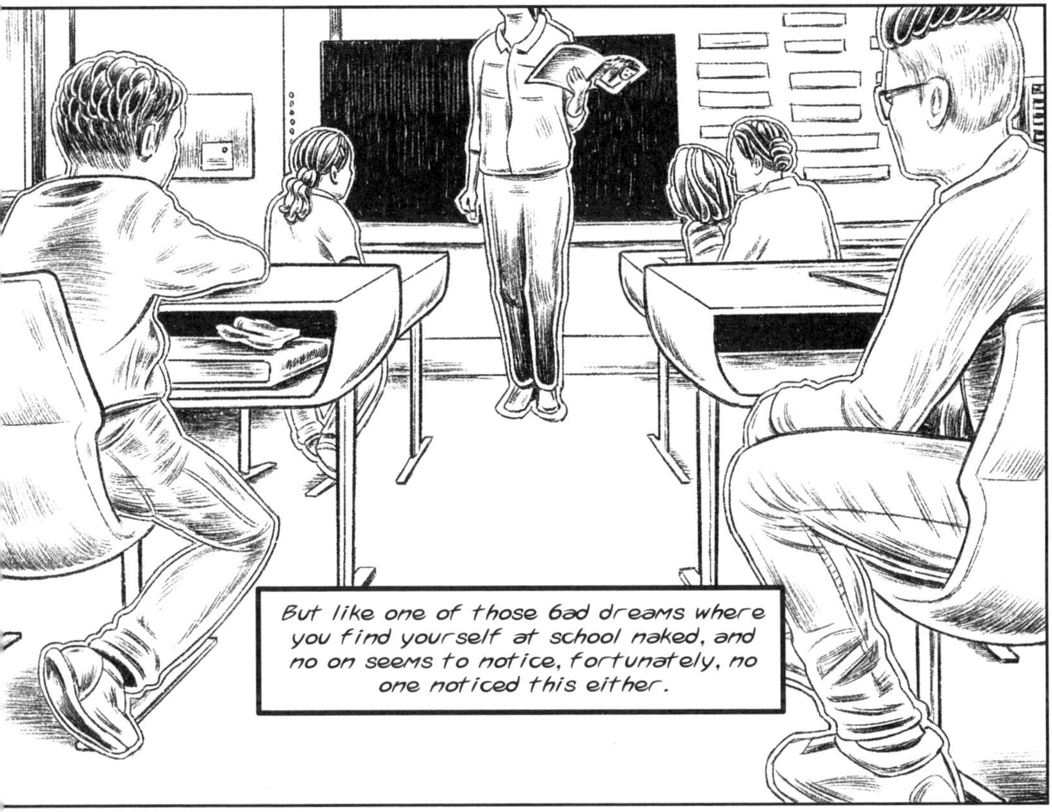
But like one of those bad dreams where you find yourself at school naked, and no on seems to notice, fortunately, no one noticed this either.

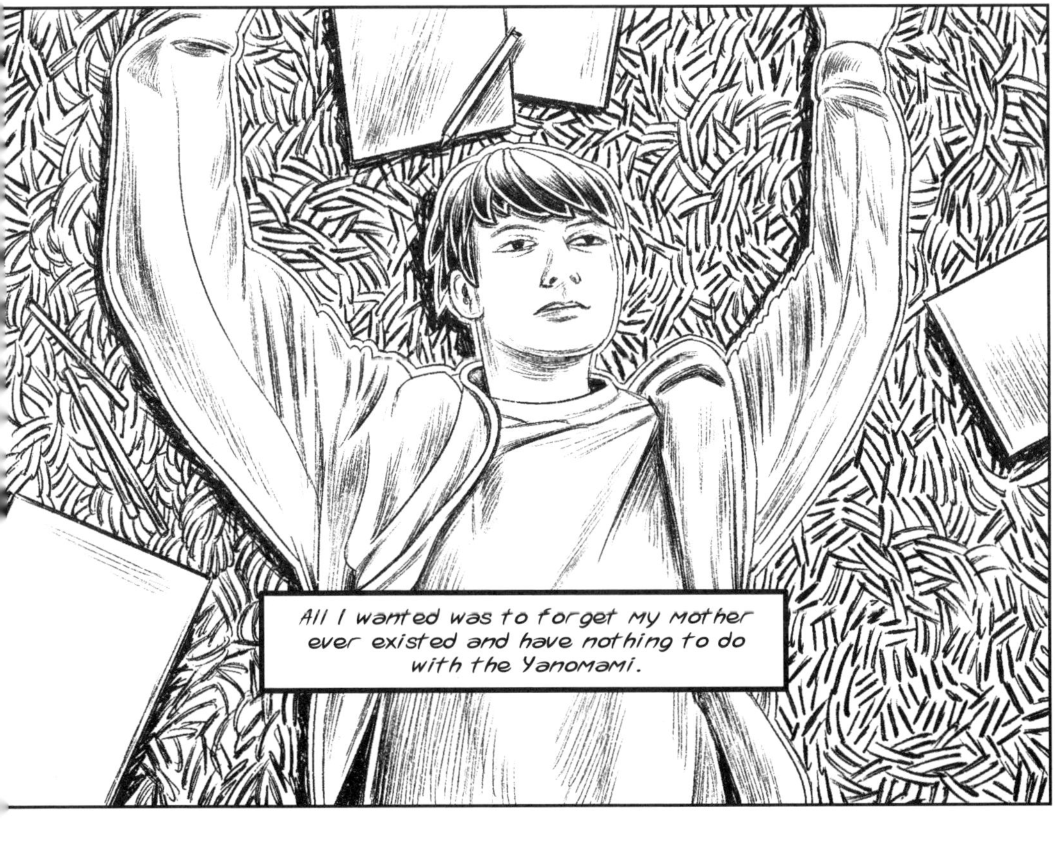
All I wanted was to forget my mother ever existed and have nothing to do with the Yanomami.

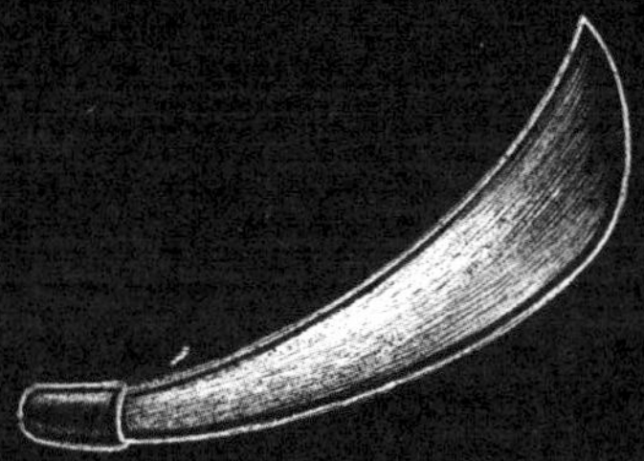

chapter 5

STICKS + STONES

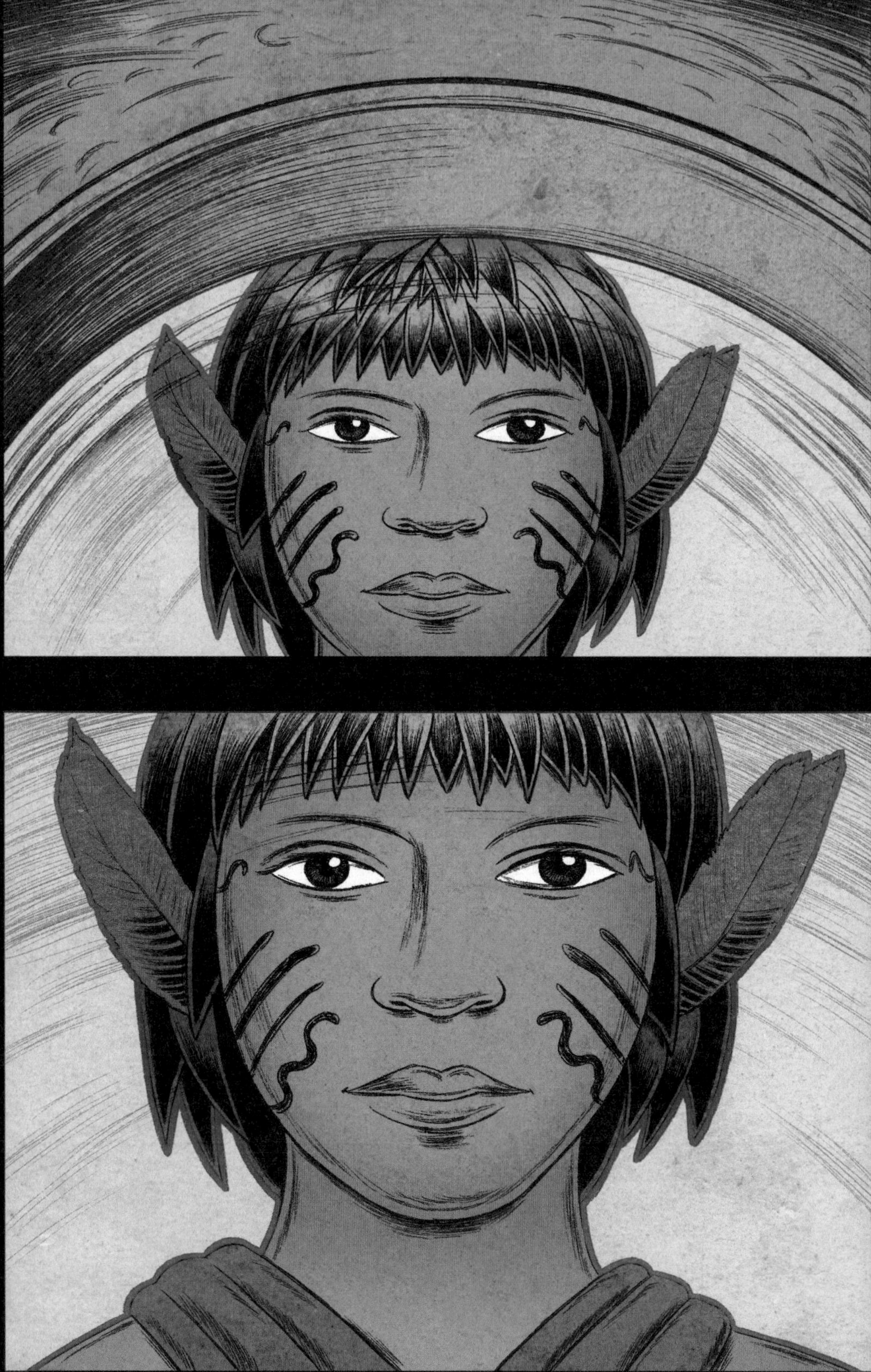

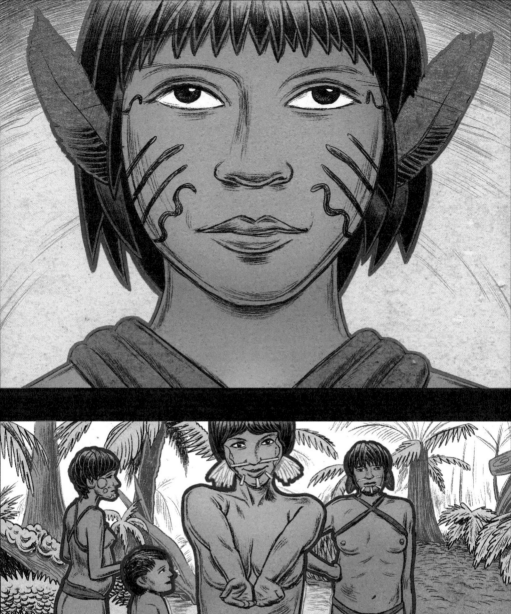

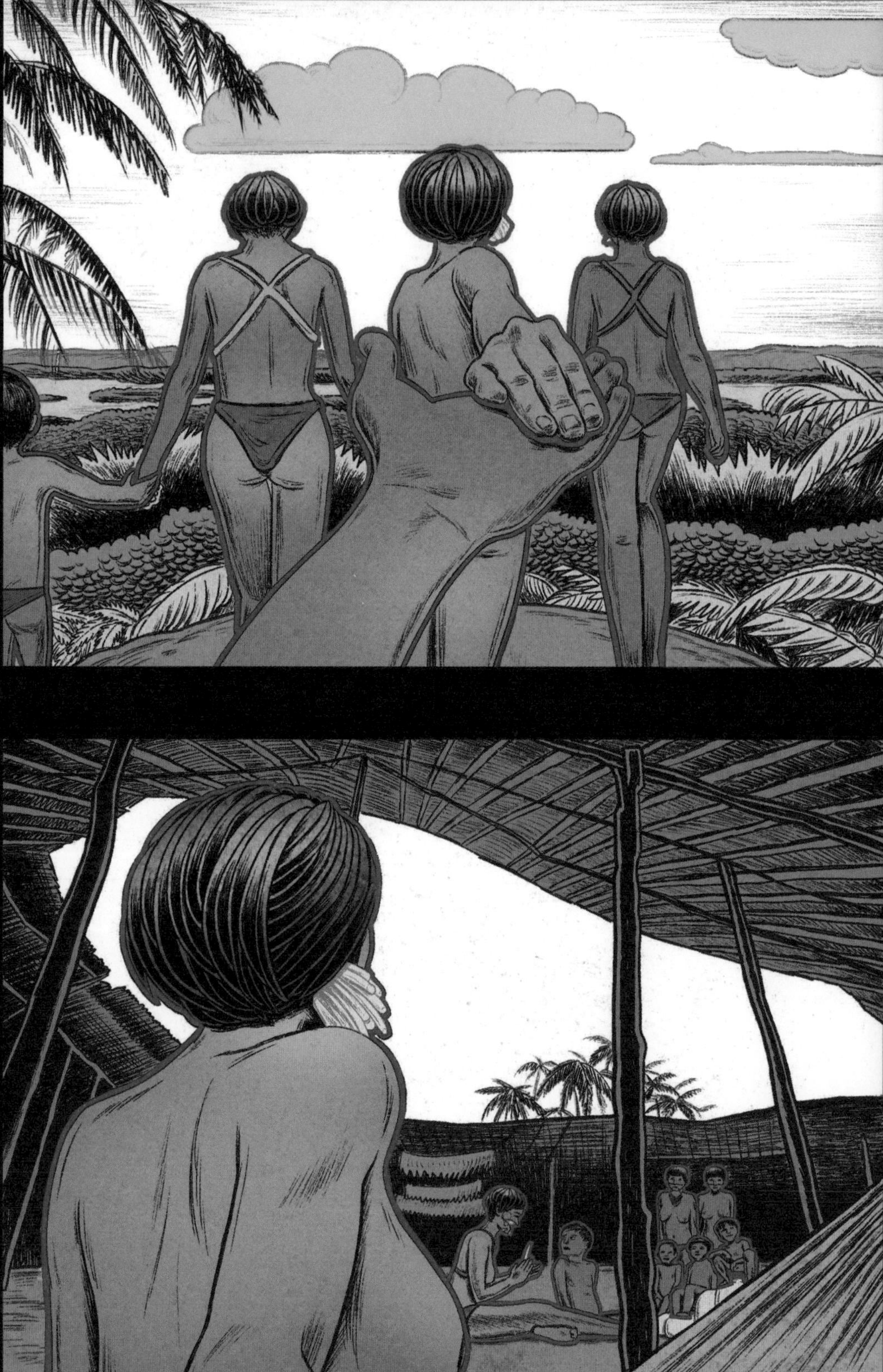

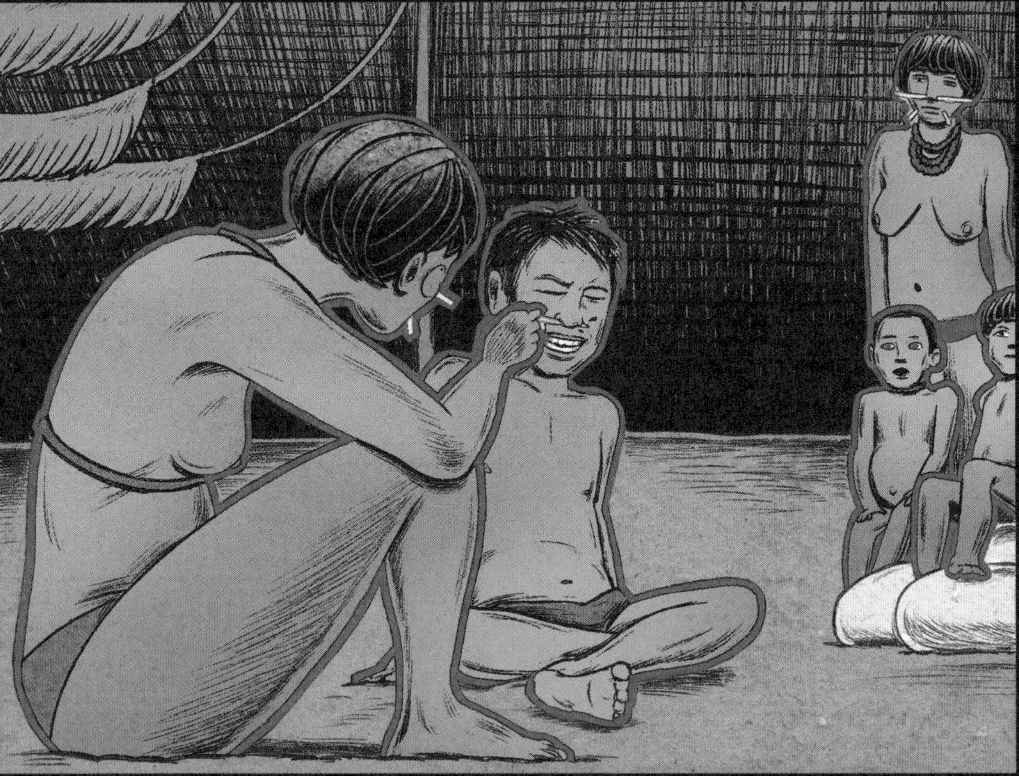
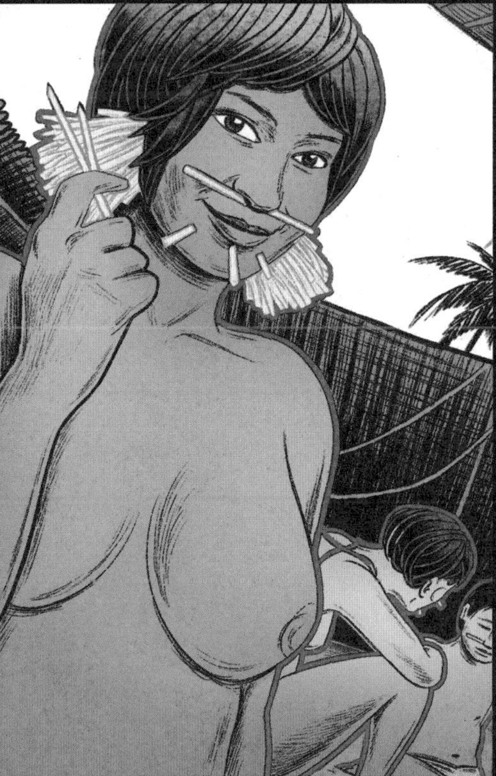
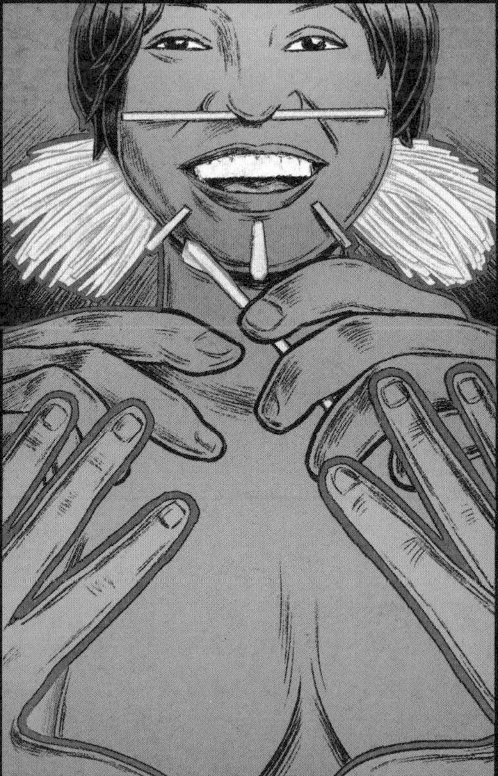

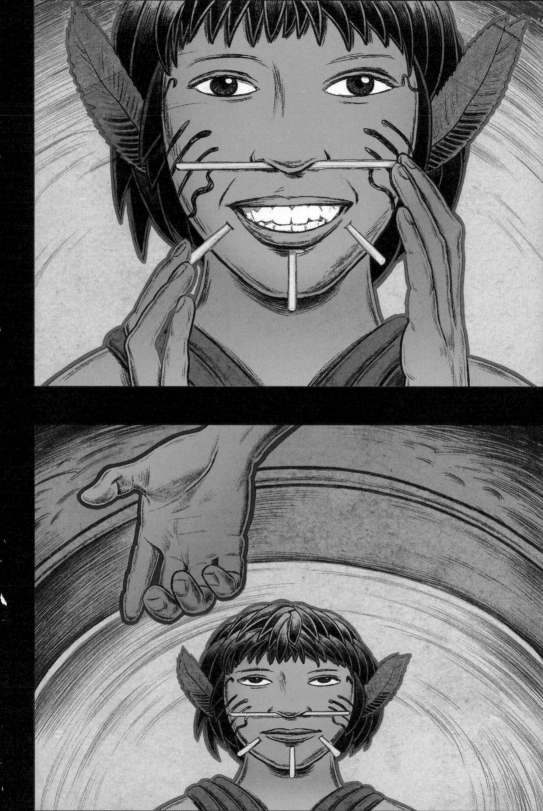

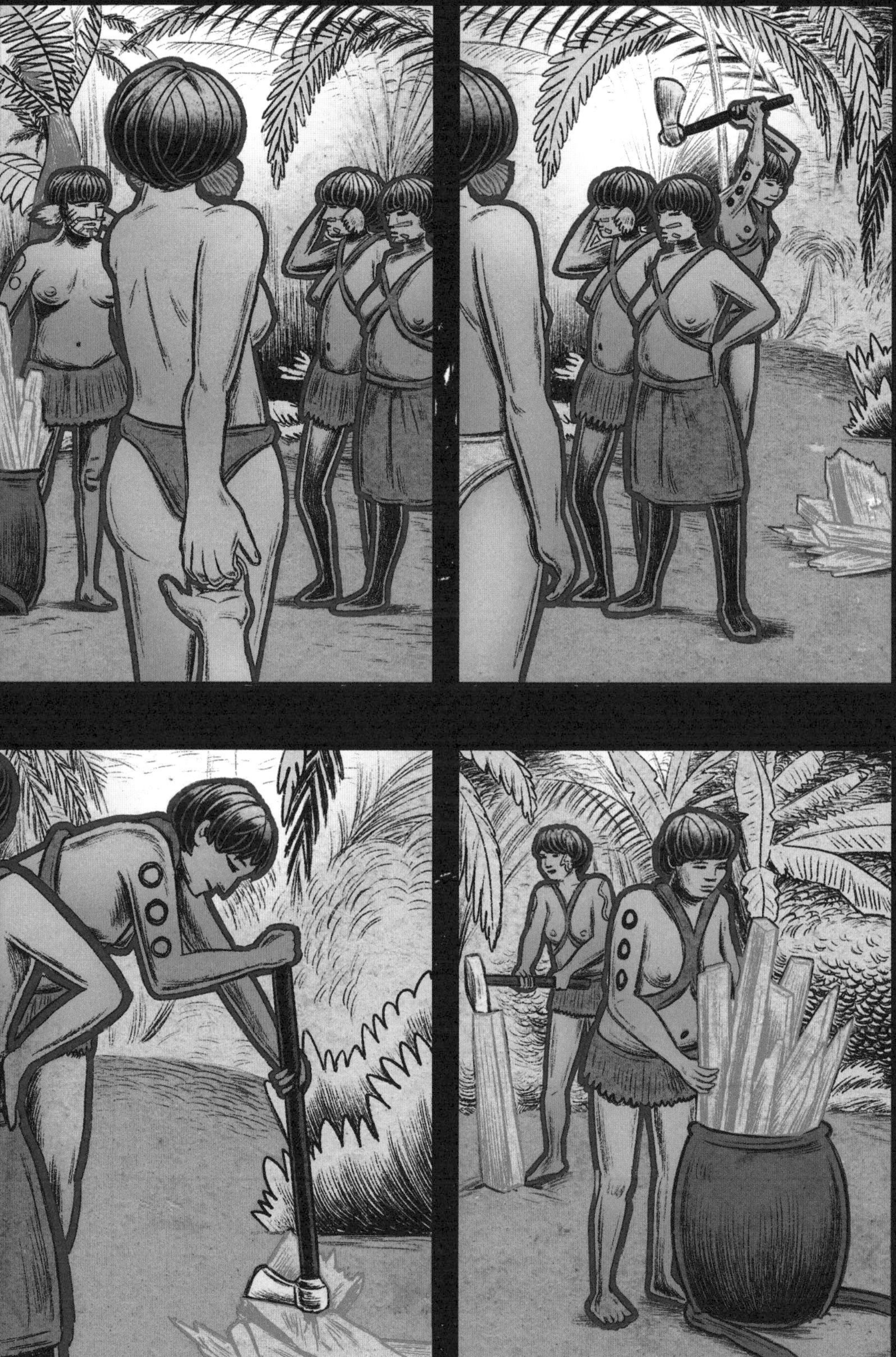

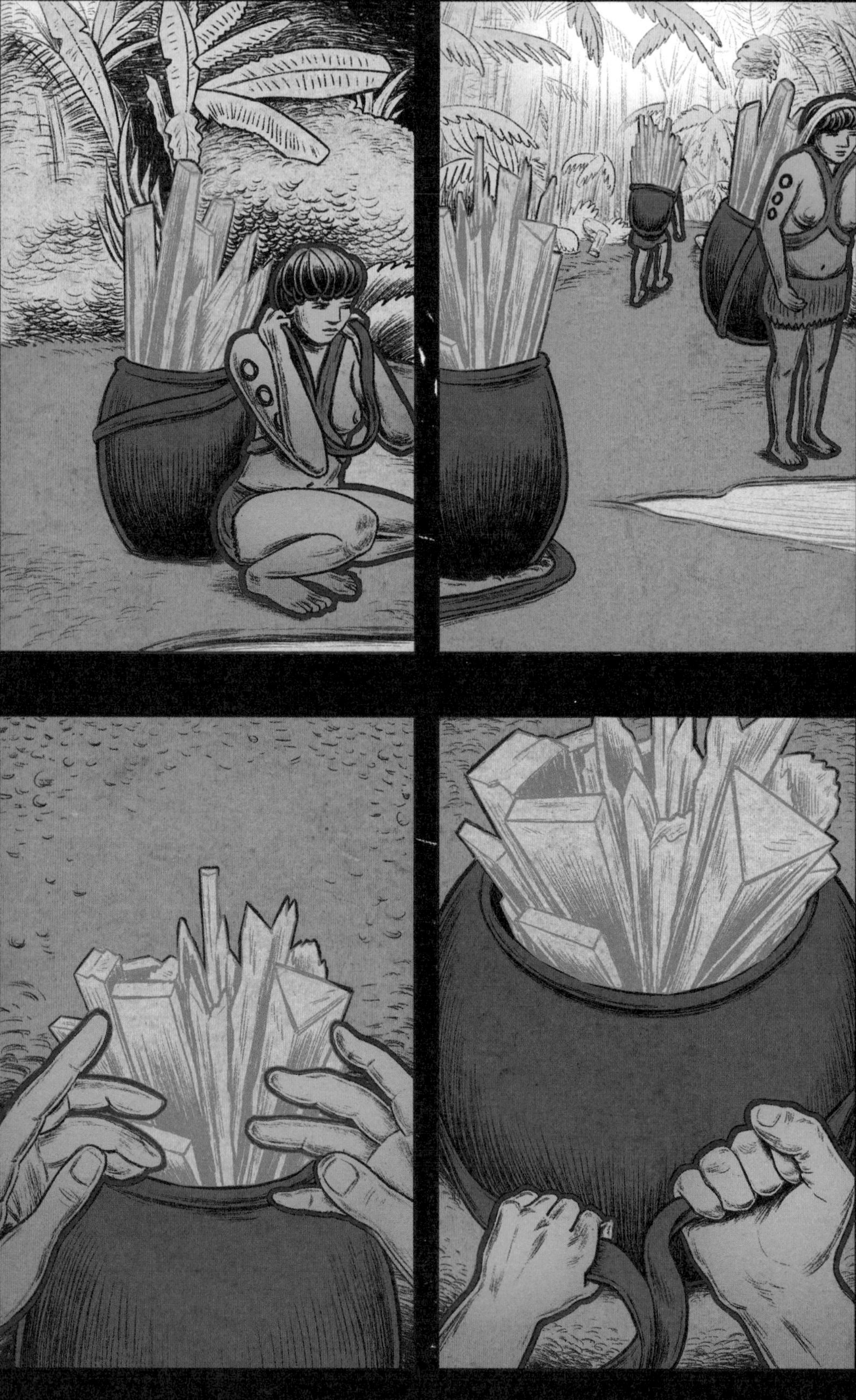

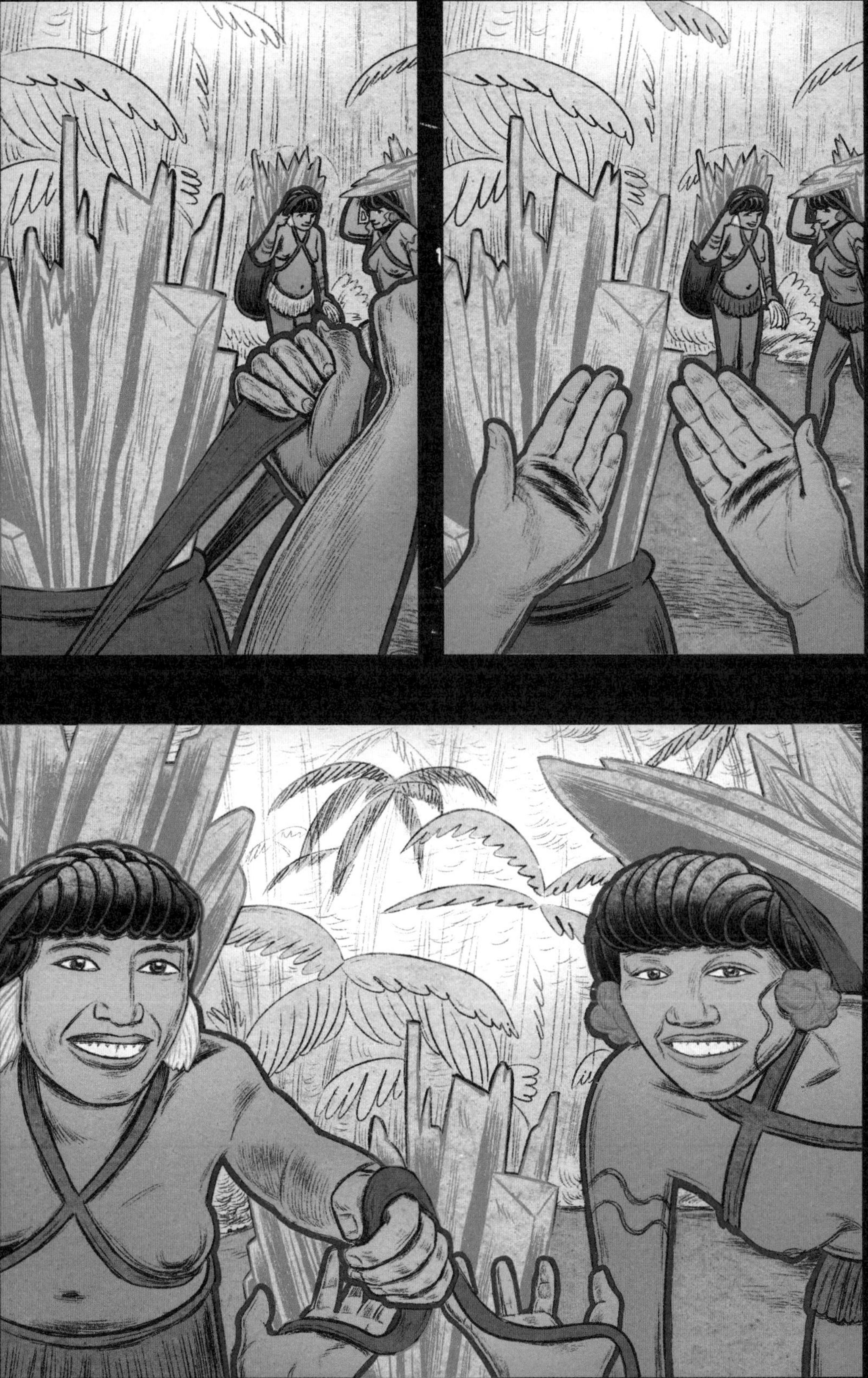

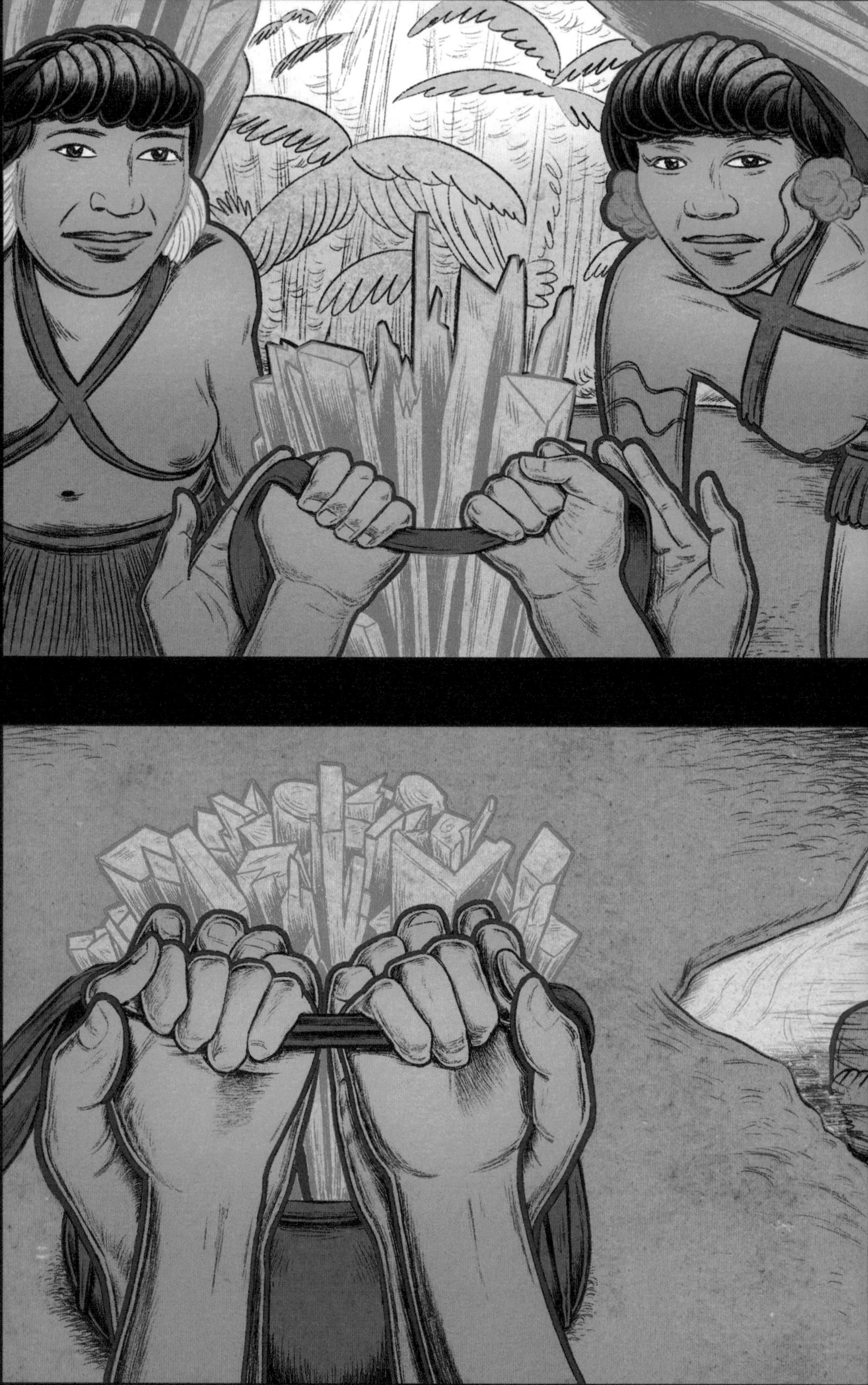

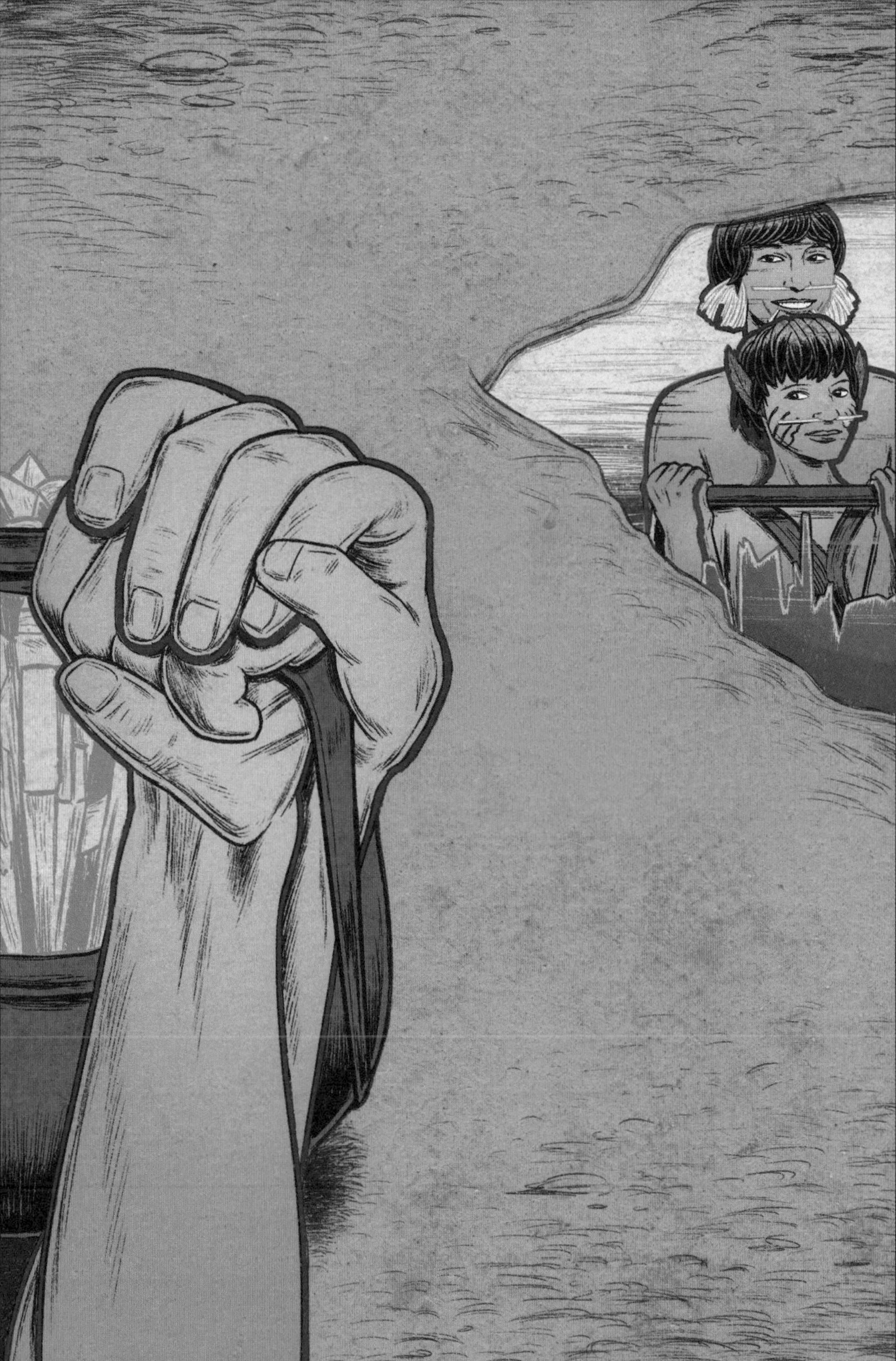

chapter 6

HIDE + SEEK

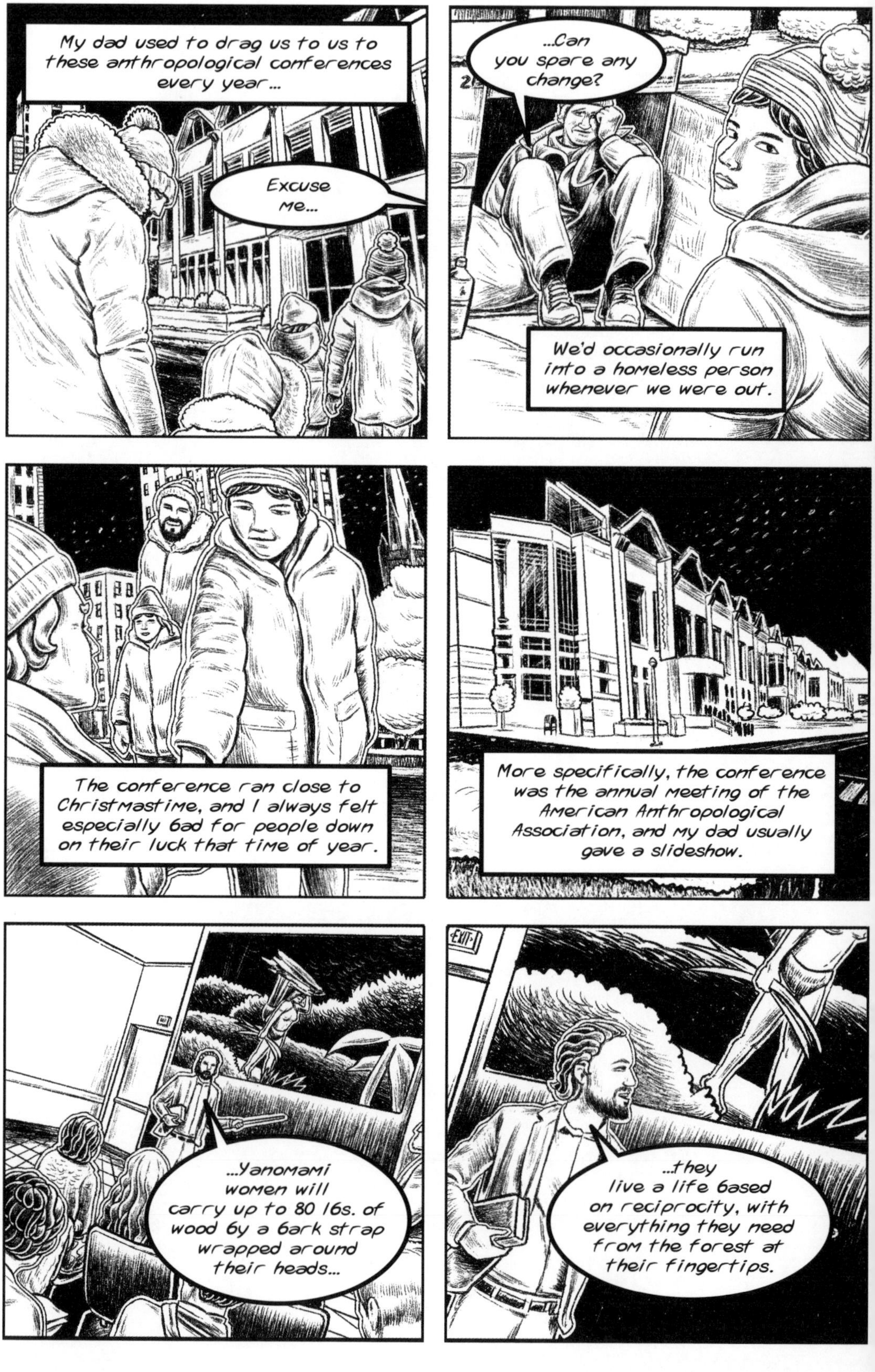

My dad used to drag us to us to these anthropological conferences every year...
Excuse me...
...Can you spare any change?
We'd occasionally run into a homeless person whenever we were out.
The conference ran close to Christmastime, and I always felt especially bad for people down on their luck that time of year.
More specifically, the conference was the annual meeting of the American Anthropological Association, and my dad usually gave a slideshow.
...Yanomami women will carry up to 80 lbs. of wood by a bark strap wrapped around their heads...
...they live a life based on reciprocity, with everything they need from the forest at their fingertips.

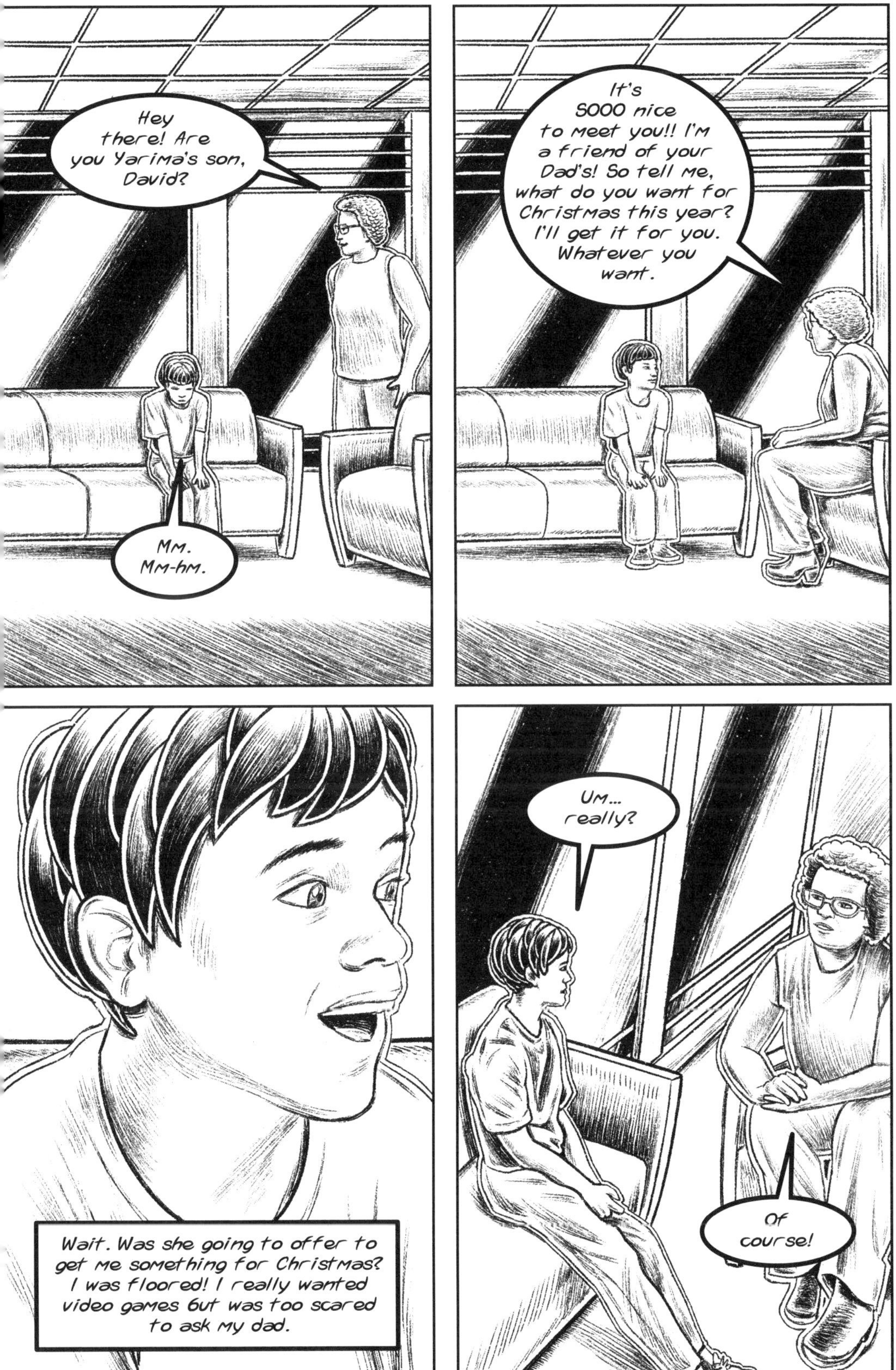
Hey there! Are you Yarima's son, David?
Mm. Mm-hm.
It's SOOO nice to meet you!! I'm a friend of your Dad's! So tell me, what do you want for Christmas this year? I'll get it for you. Whatever you want.
Wait. Was she going to offer to get me something for Christmas? I was floored! I really wanted video games but was too scared to ask my dad.
Um... really?
Of course!

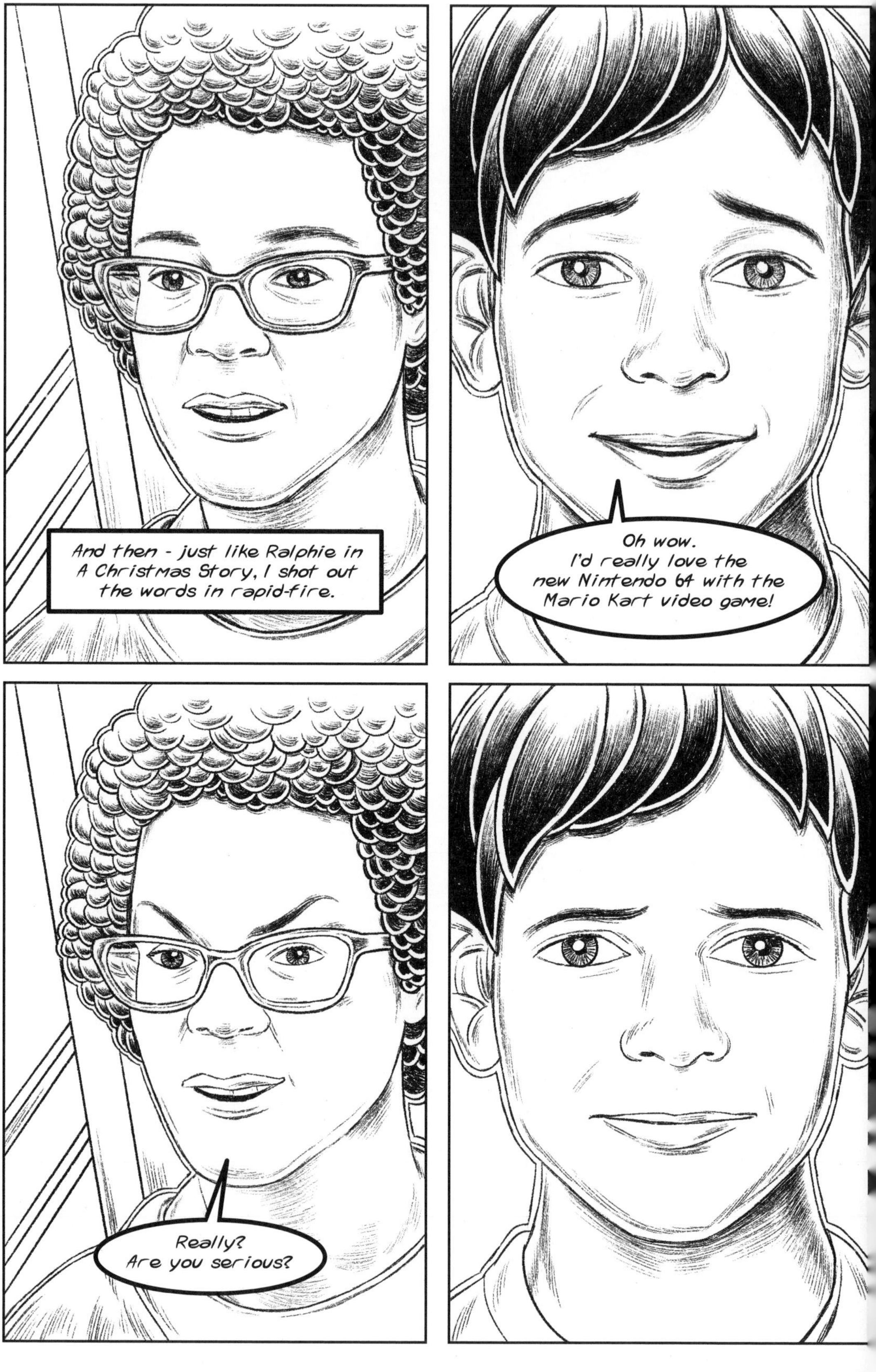
And then - just like Ralphie in A Christmas Story, I shot out the words in rapid-fire.
Oh wow. I'd really love the new Nintendo 64 with the Mario Kart video game!
Really? Are you serious?

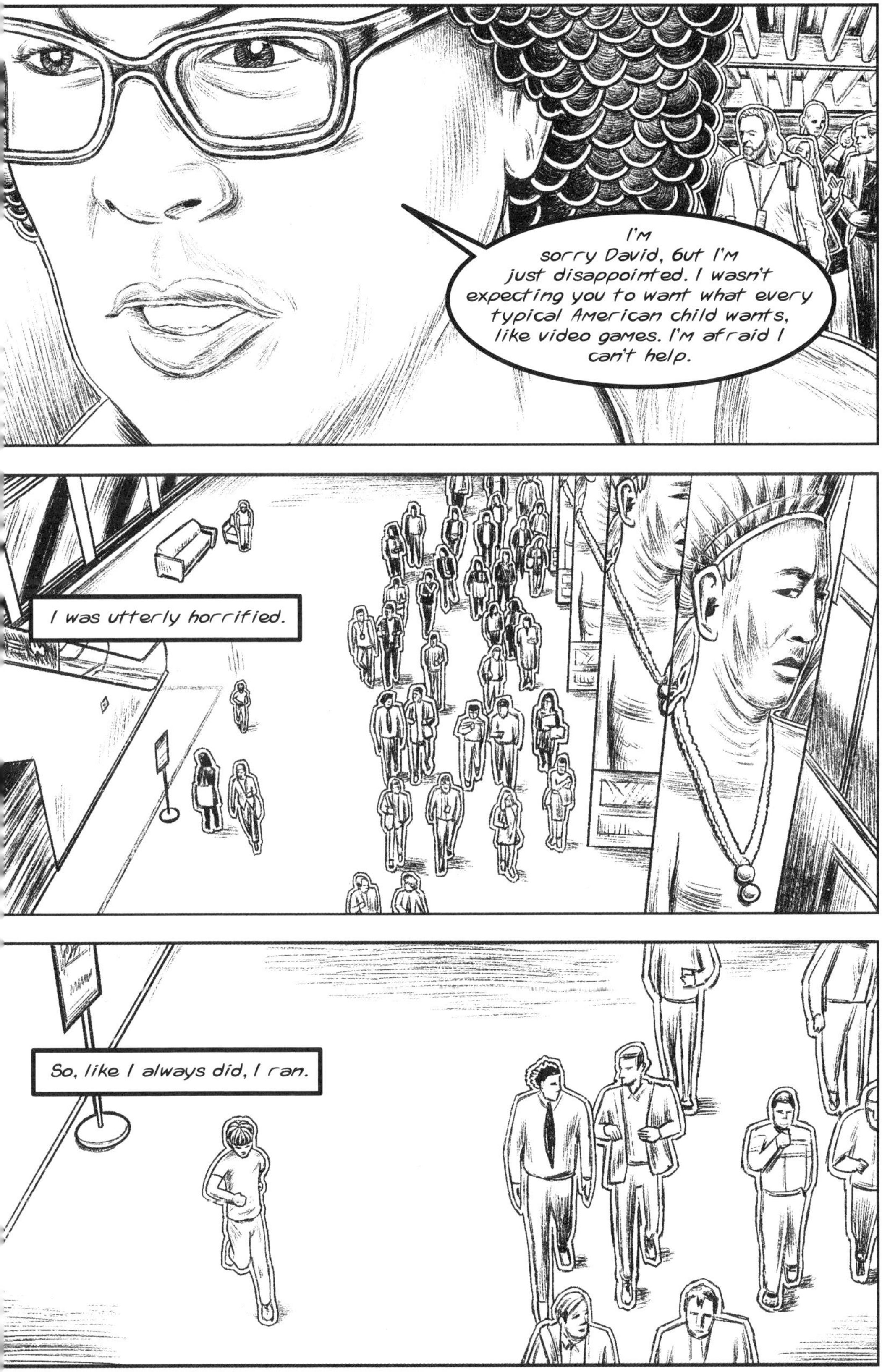
I'm sorry David, but I'm just disappointed. I wasn't expecting you to want what every typical American child wants, like video games. I'm afraid I can't help.
I was utterly horrified.
So, like I always did, I ran.

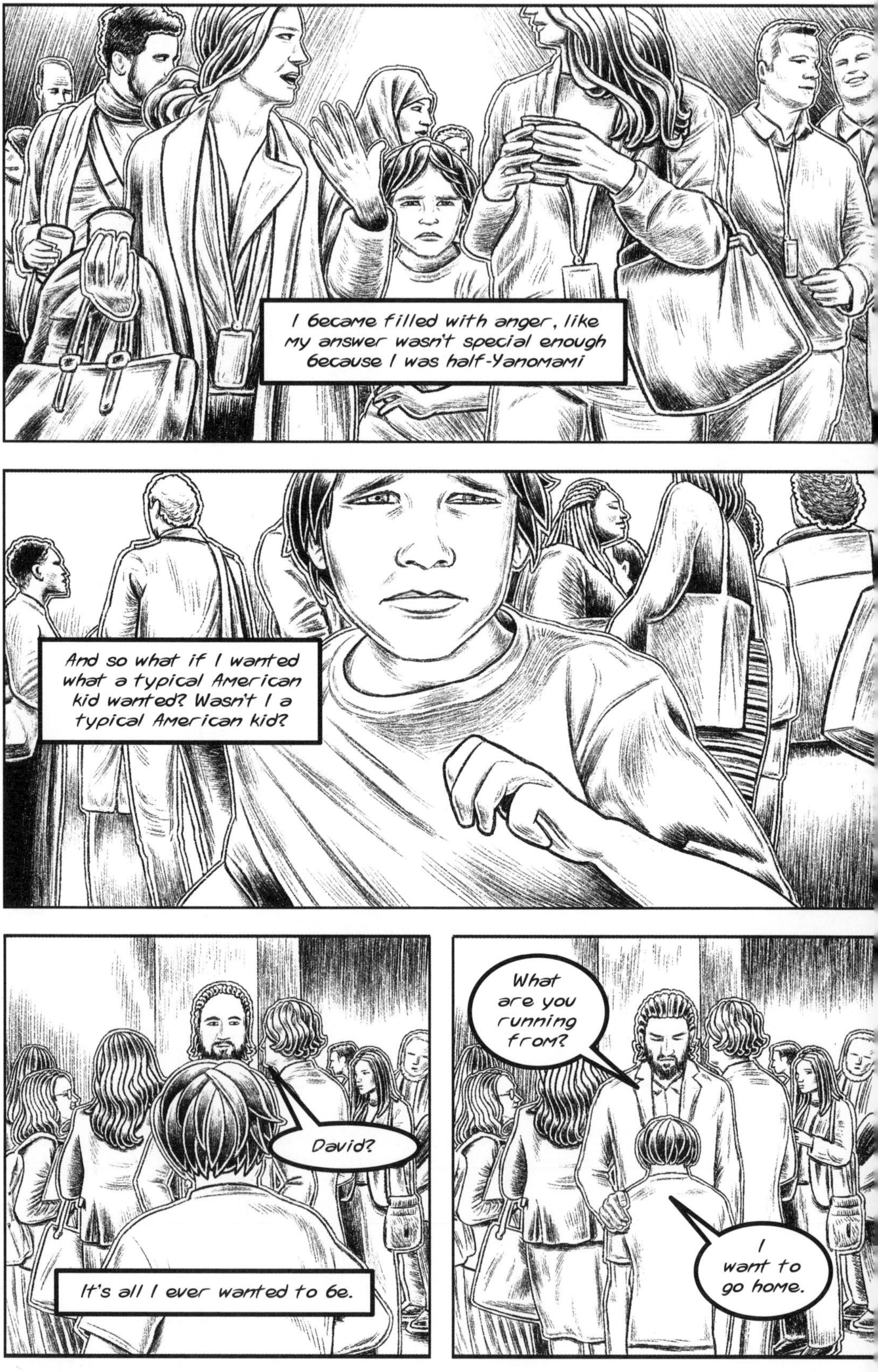
I became filled with anger, like my answer wasn't special enough because I was half-Yanomami
And so what if I wanted what a typical American kid wanted? Wasn't I a typical American kid?
David?
It's all I ever wanted to be.
What are you running from?
I want to go home.

When I was 12 we moved to the su6ur6s of Easton, Pennsylvania.

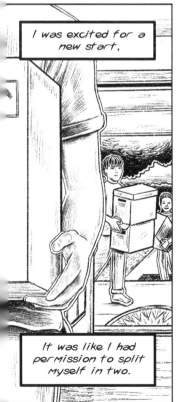

I was excited for a new start,

It was like I had permission to split myself in two.

At home I could 6e that kid with no mother who was half-Yanomami.

But in pu6lic I could 6e normal and cool, like everyone else.

I could even re-write my origin story.

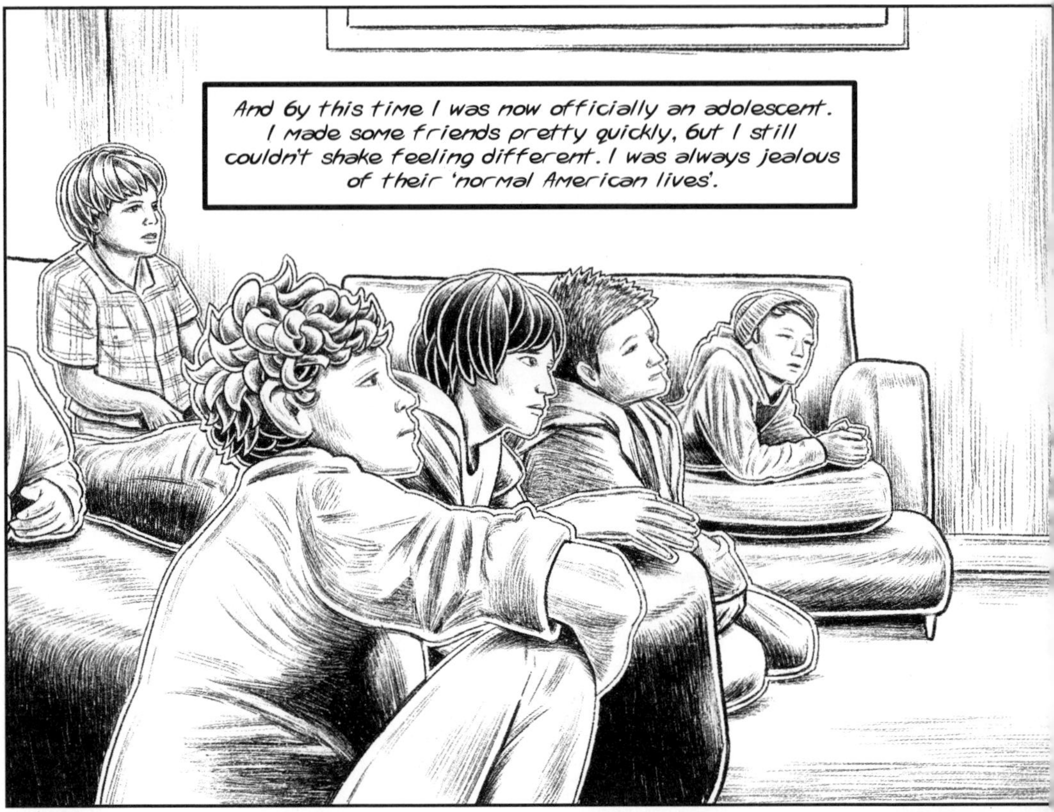
And by this time I was now officially an adolescent. I made some friends pretty quickly, but I still couldn't shake feeling different. I was always jealous of their 'normal American lives'.

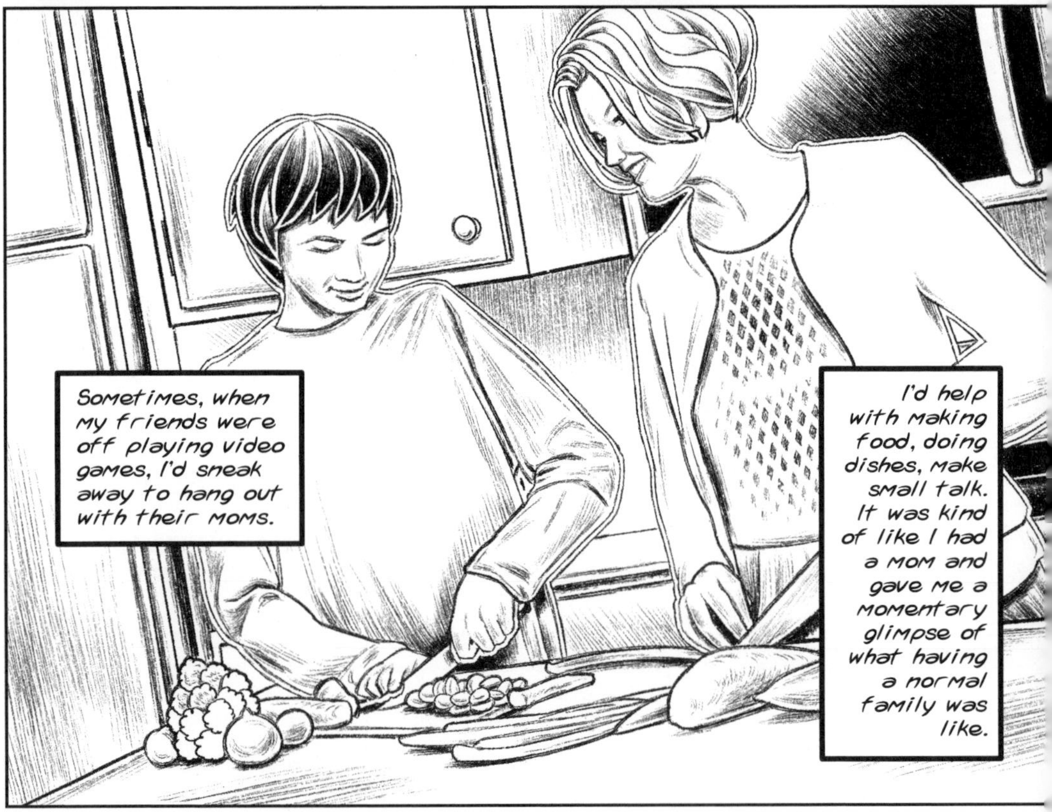
Sometimes, when my friends were off playing video games, I'd sneak away to hang out with their moms.
I'd help with making food, doing dishes, make small talk. It was kind of like I had a mom and gave me a momentary glimpse of what having a normal family was like.

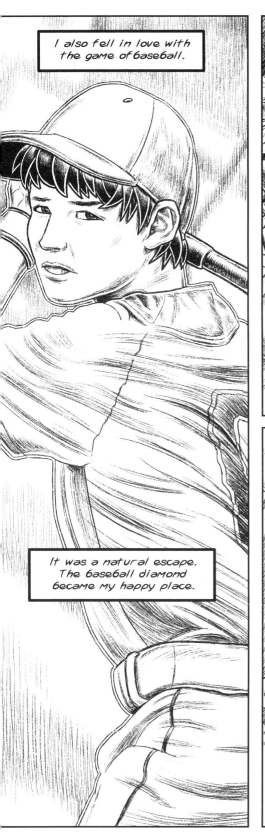

I also fell in love with the game of 6ase6all.

It was a natural escape. The 6ase6all diamond 6ecame my happy place.

I'd 6een playing since I was 5, so 6y this time I'd gotten really good at it.

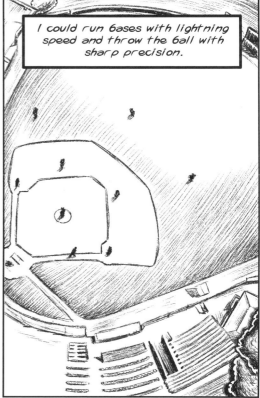

I could run 6ases with lightning speed and throw the 6all with sharp precision.

I felt an overwhelming sense of peace out on the field. It was my haven, a temporary break from the inner turmoil over my identity.

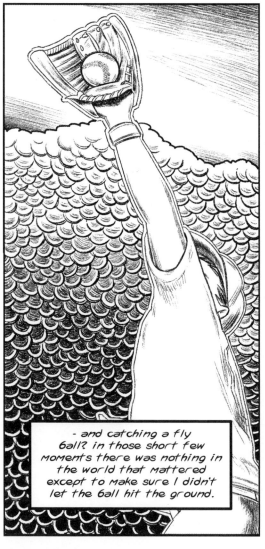

- and catching a fly ball? in those short few moments there was nothing in the world that mattered except to make sure I didn't let the ball hit the ground.

The cheers from my teammates and the fans made me feel an acceptance I never felt otherwise. When I was out there, it didn't matter if I was Yanomami or not. All that mattered was that I played good baseball.

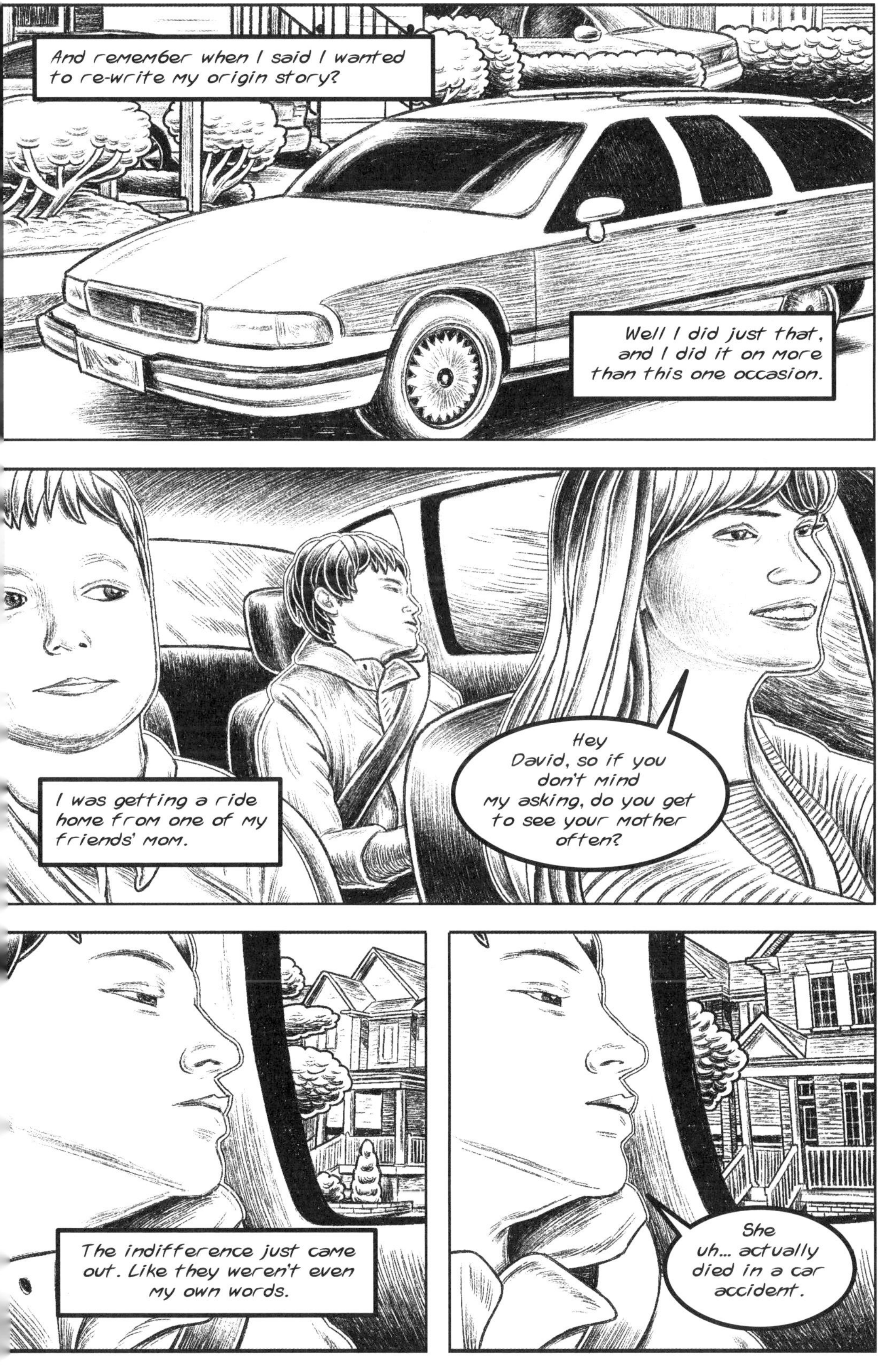

And remember when I said I wanted to re-write my origin story?
Well I did just that, and I did it on more than this one occasion.
I was getting a ride home from one of my friends' mom.
Hey David, so if you don't mind my asking, do you get to see your mother often?
The indifference just came out. Like they weren't even my own words.
She uh... actually died in a car accident.

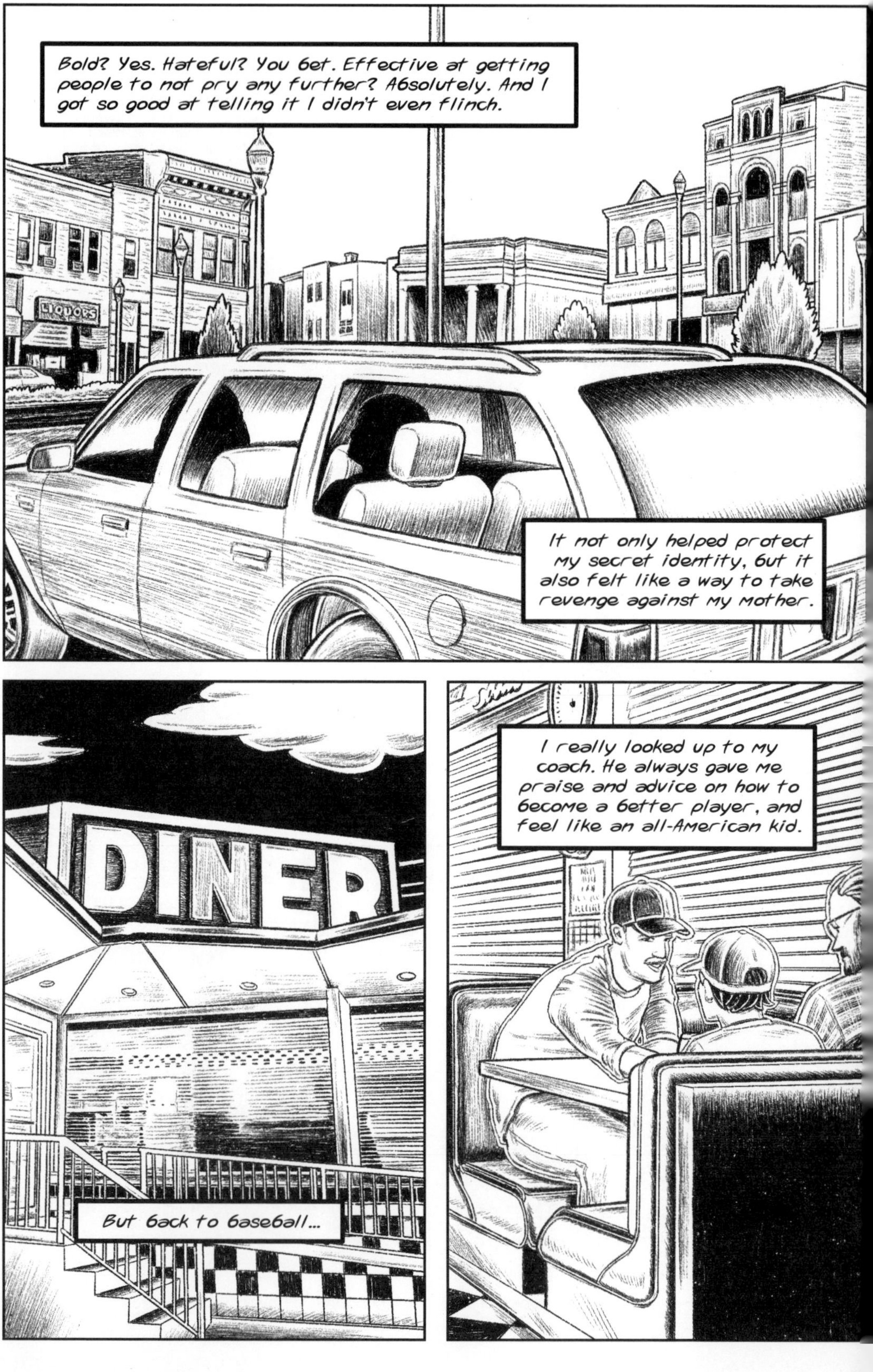
Bold? Yes. Hateful? You bet. Effective at getting people to not pry any further? Absolutely. And I got so good at telling it I didn't even flinch.
LIQUORS
It not only helped protect my secret identity, but it also felt like a way to take revenge against my mother.
DINER
But back to baseball...
I really looked up to my coach. He always gave me praise and advice on how to become a better player, and feel like an all-American kid.

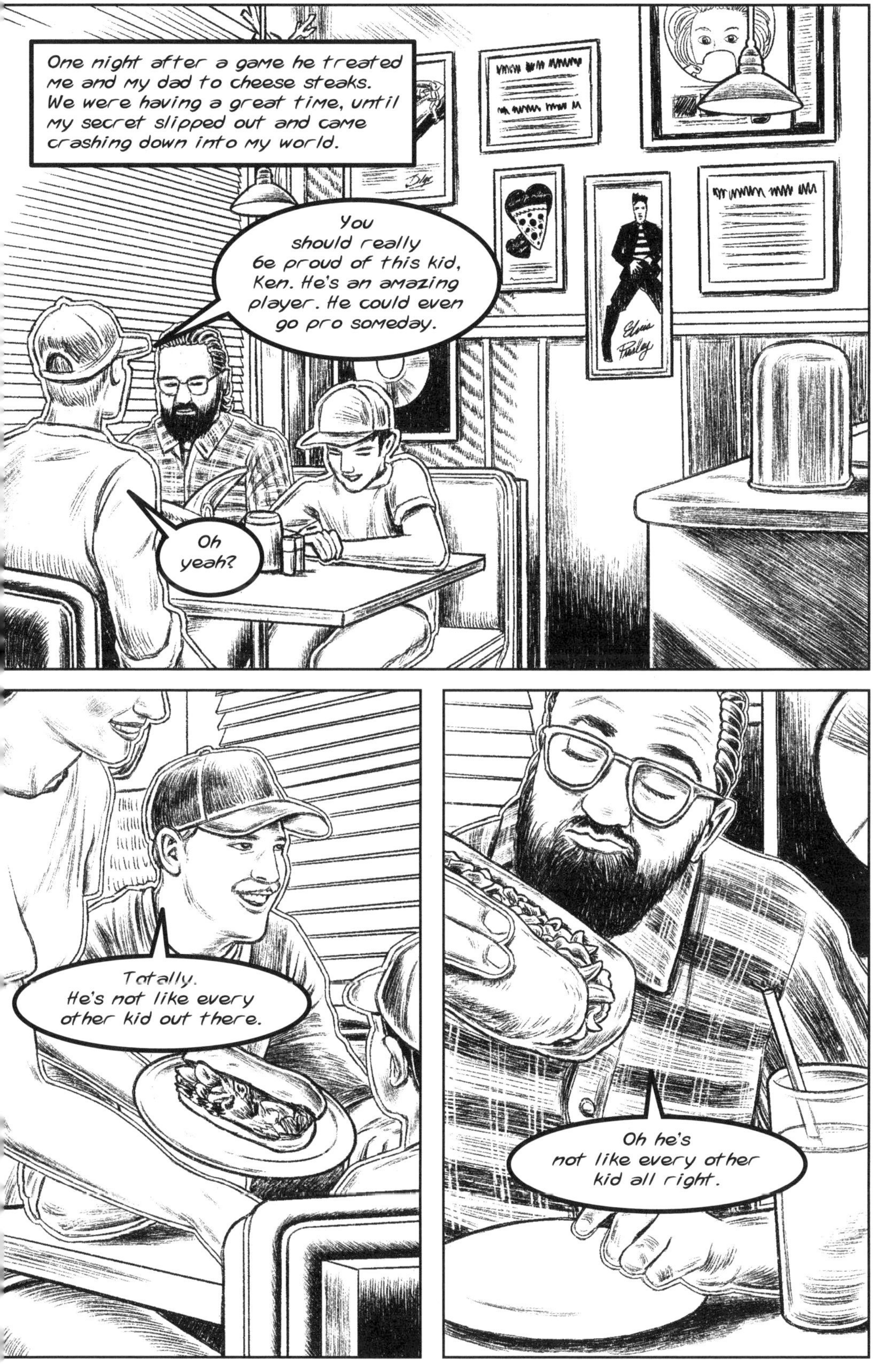
One night after a game he treated me and my dad to cheese steaks. We were having a great time, until my secret slipped out and came crashing down into my world.
You should really be proud of this kid, Ken. He's an amazing player. He could even go pro someday.
Oh yeah?
Totally. He's not like every other kid out there.
Oh he's not like every other kid all right.

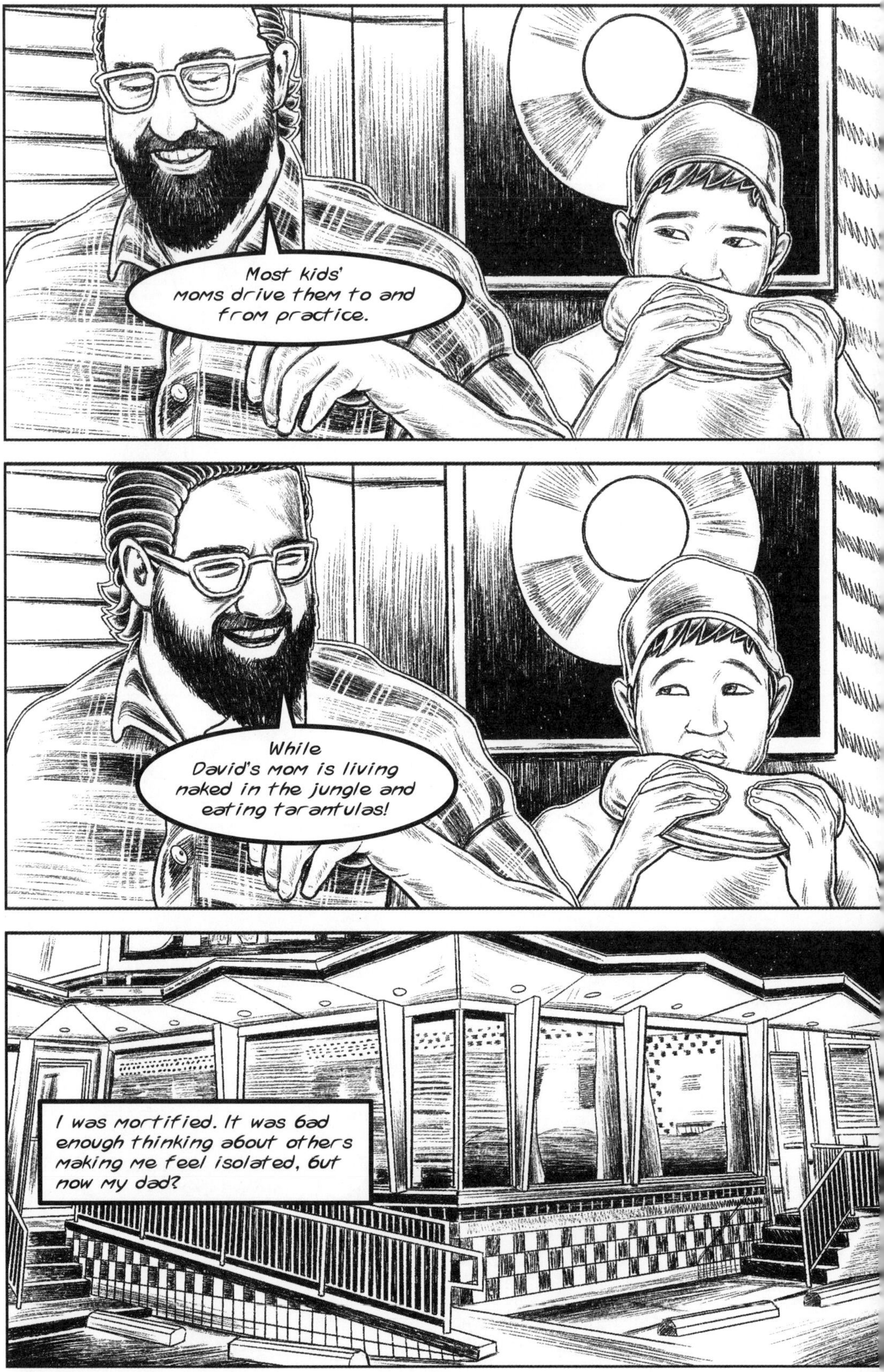
Most kids' moms drive them to and from practice.
While David's mom is living naked in the jungle and eating tarantulas!
I was mortified. It was bad enough thinking about others making me feel isolated, but now my dad?

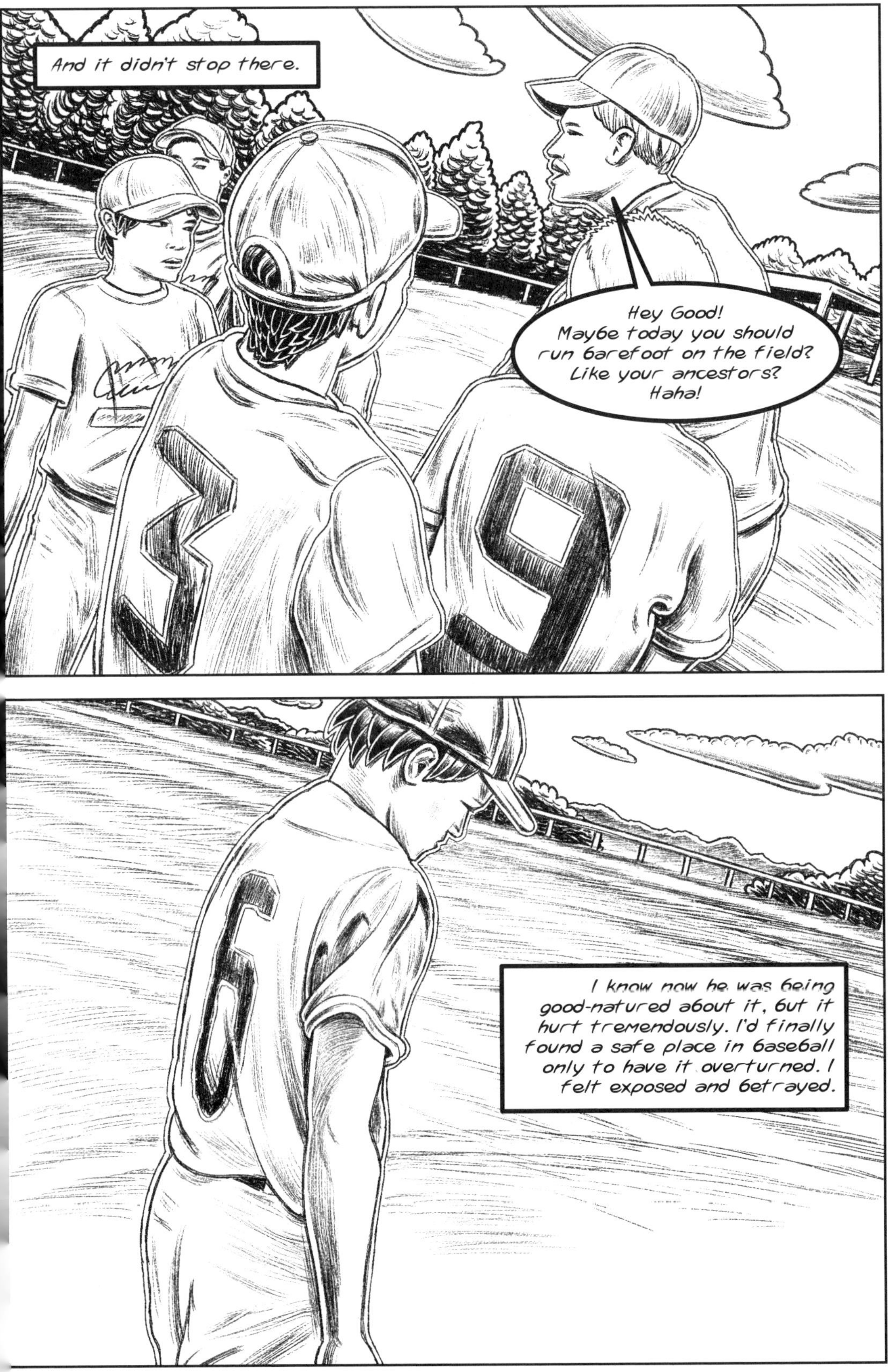
And it didn't stop there.
Hey Good! Maybe today you should run barefoot on the field? Like your ancestors? Haha!
I know now he was being good-natured about it, but it hurt tremendously. I'd finally found a safe place in baseball only to have it overturned. I felt exposed and betrayed.

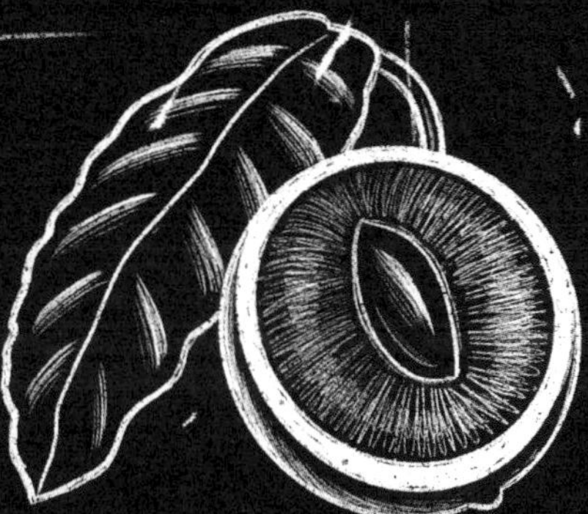

chapter 7

EARTH MOTHER

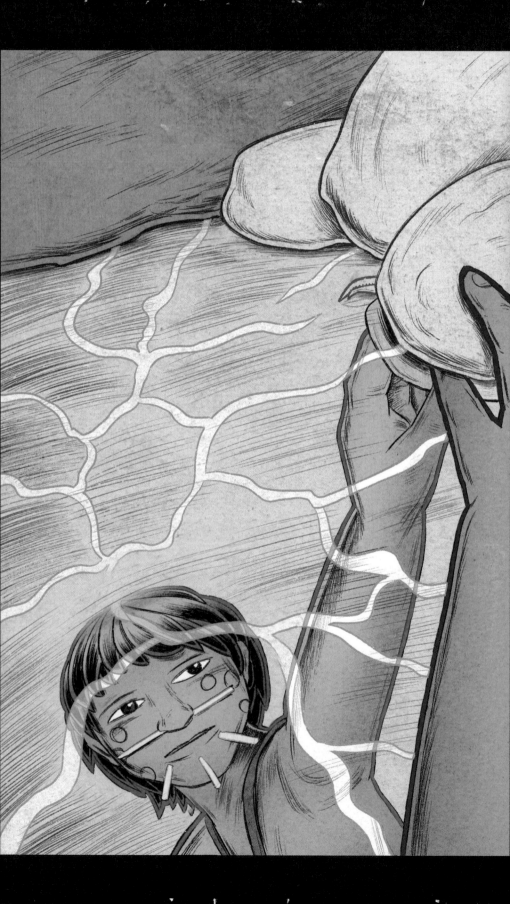

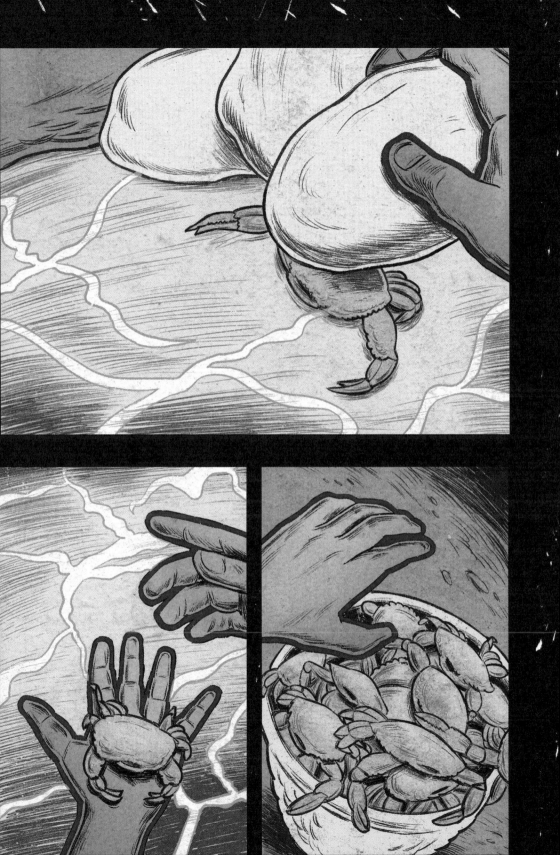

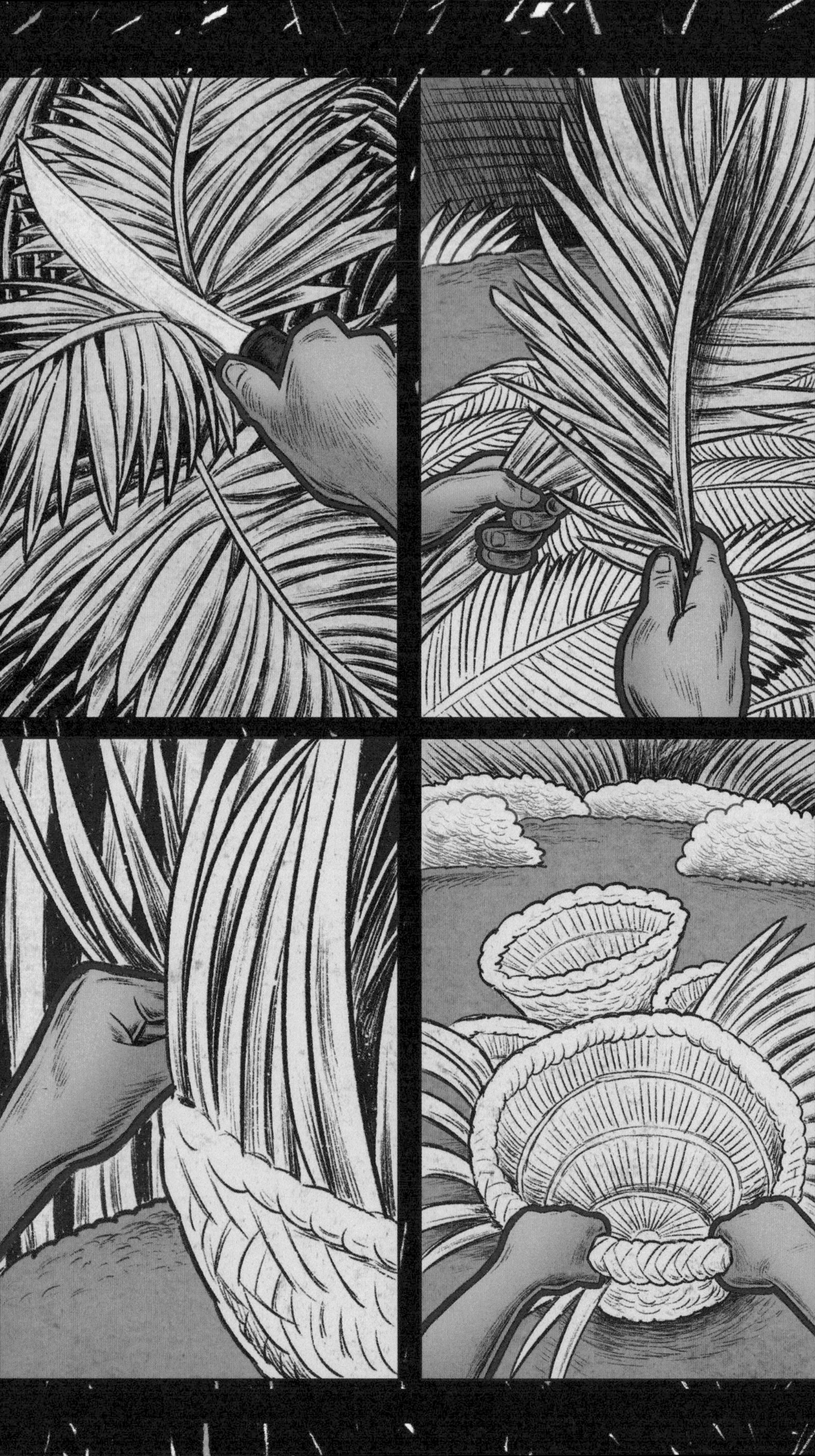

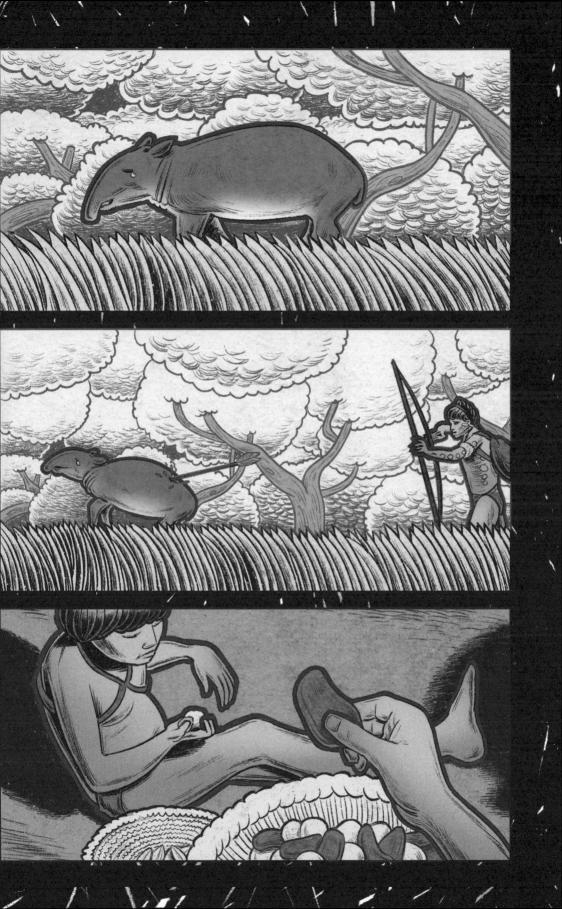

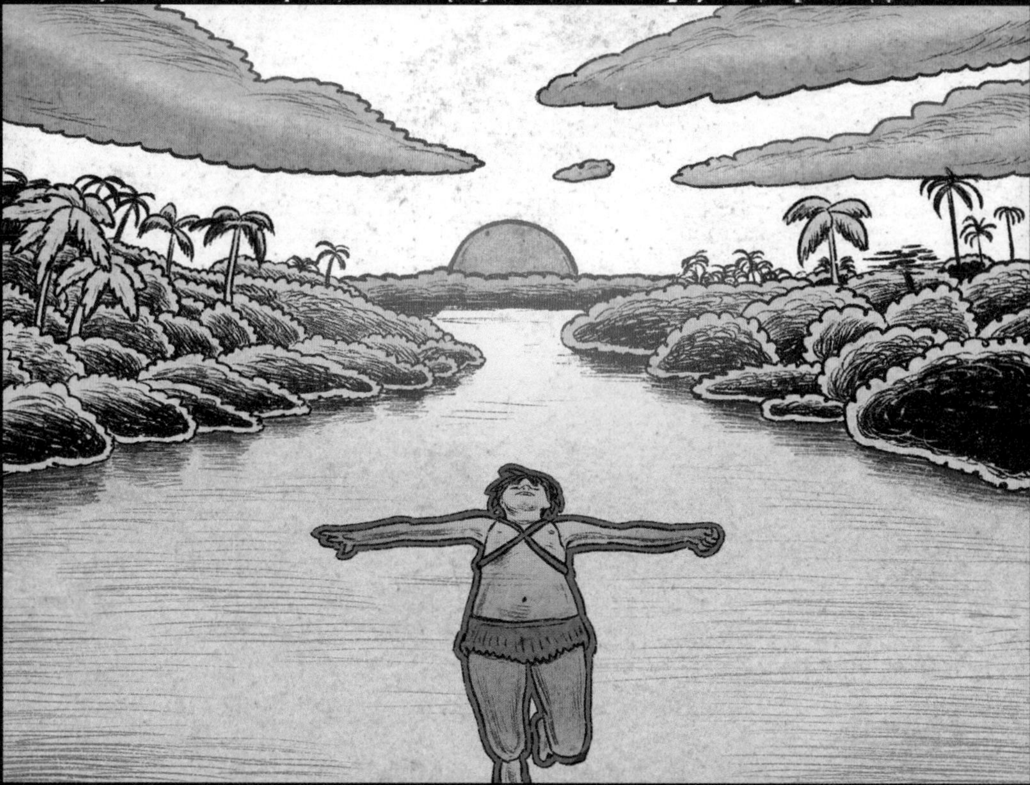

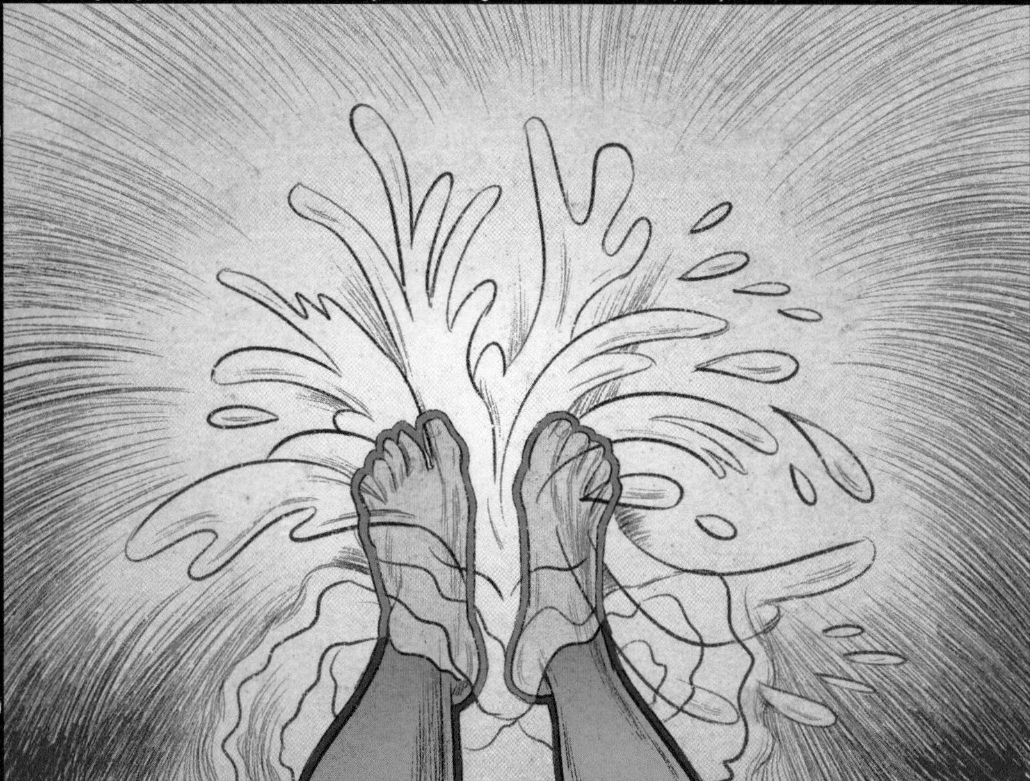

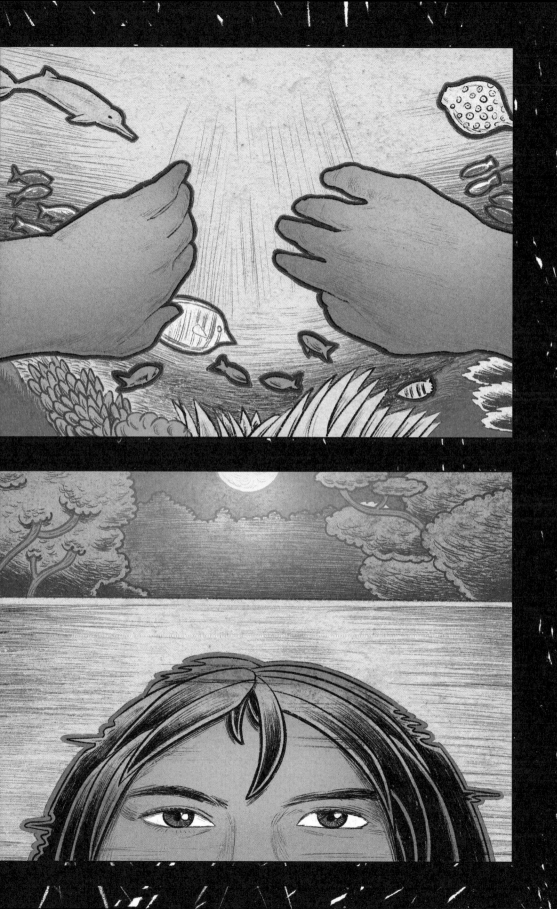

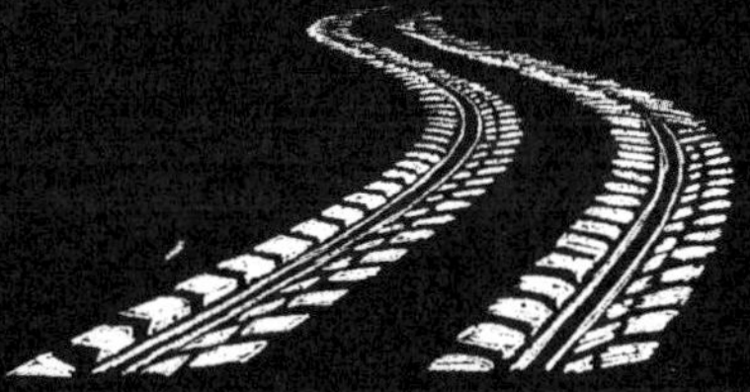

chapter 8

TREK

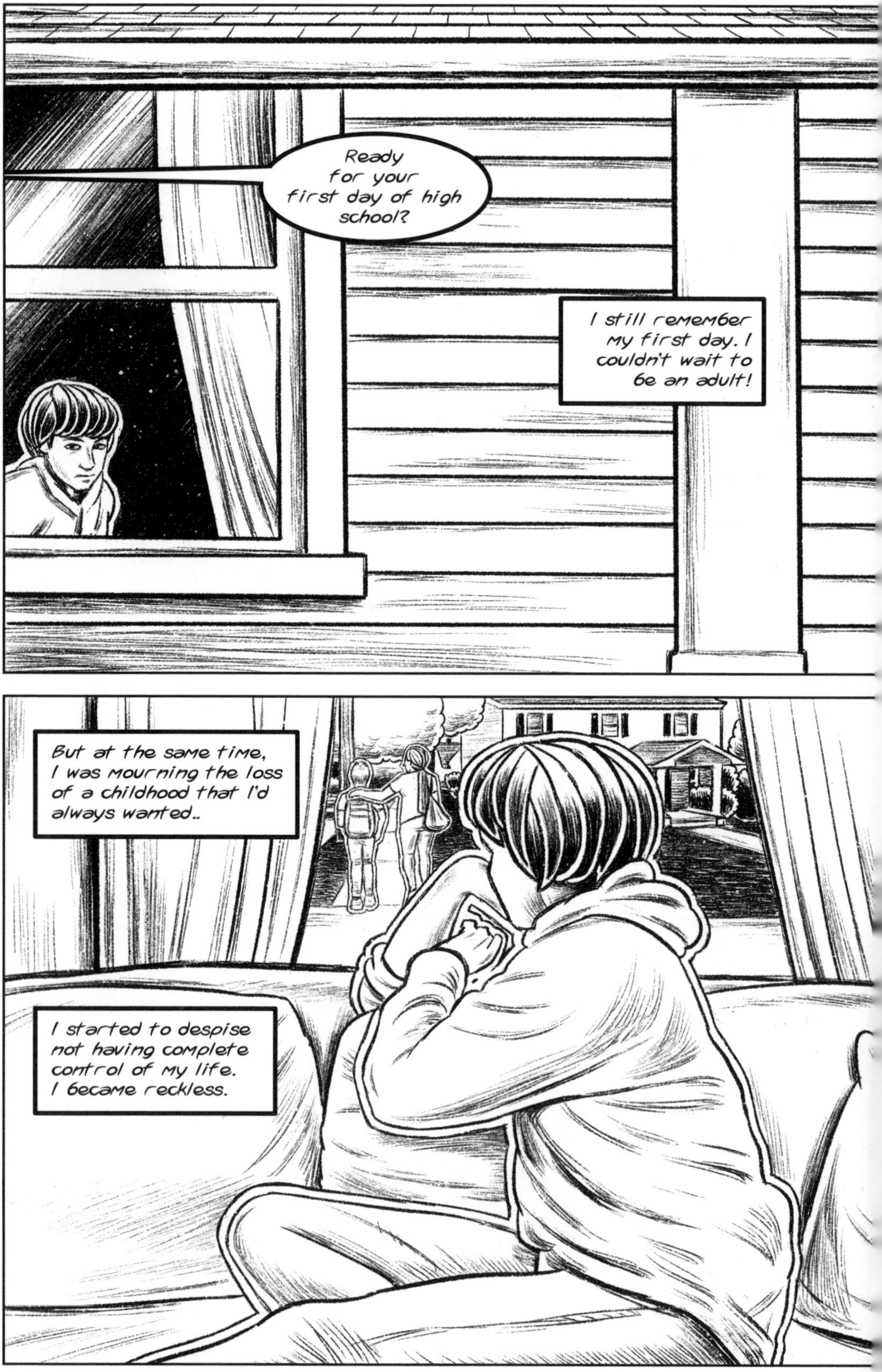
Ready for your first day of high school?
I still remember my first day. I couldn't wait to be an adult!
But at the same time, I was mourning the loss of a childhood that I'd always wanted..
I started to despise not having complete control of my life. I became reckless.

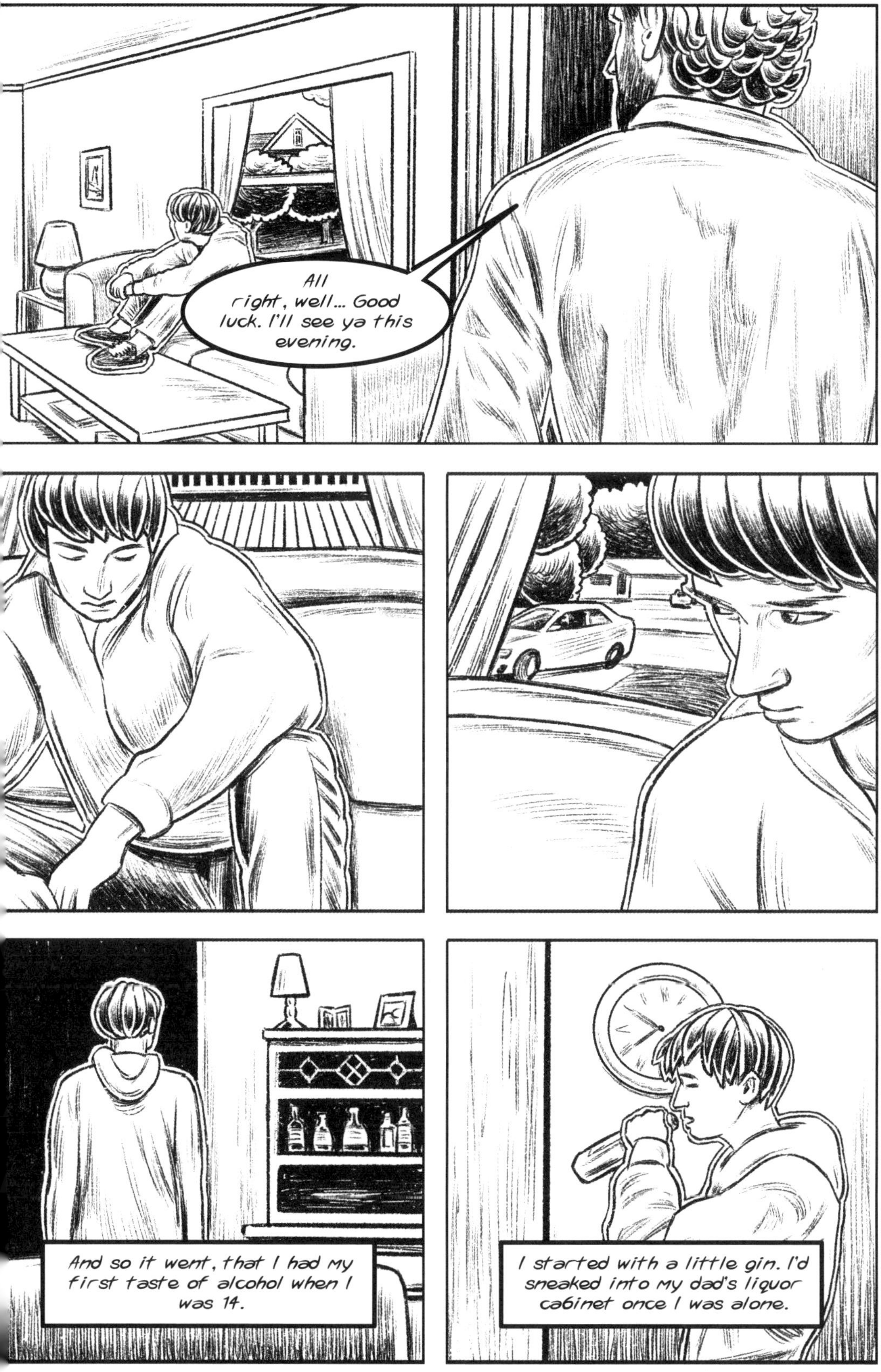
All right, well... Good luck. I'll see ya this evening.
And so it went, that I had my first taste of alcohol when I was 14.
I started with a little gin. I'd sneaked into my dad's liquor cabinet once I was alone.

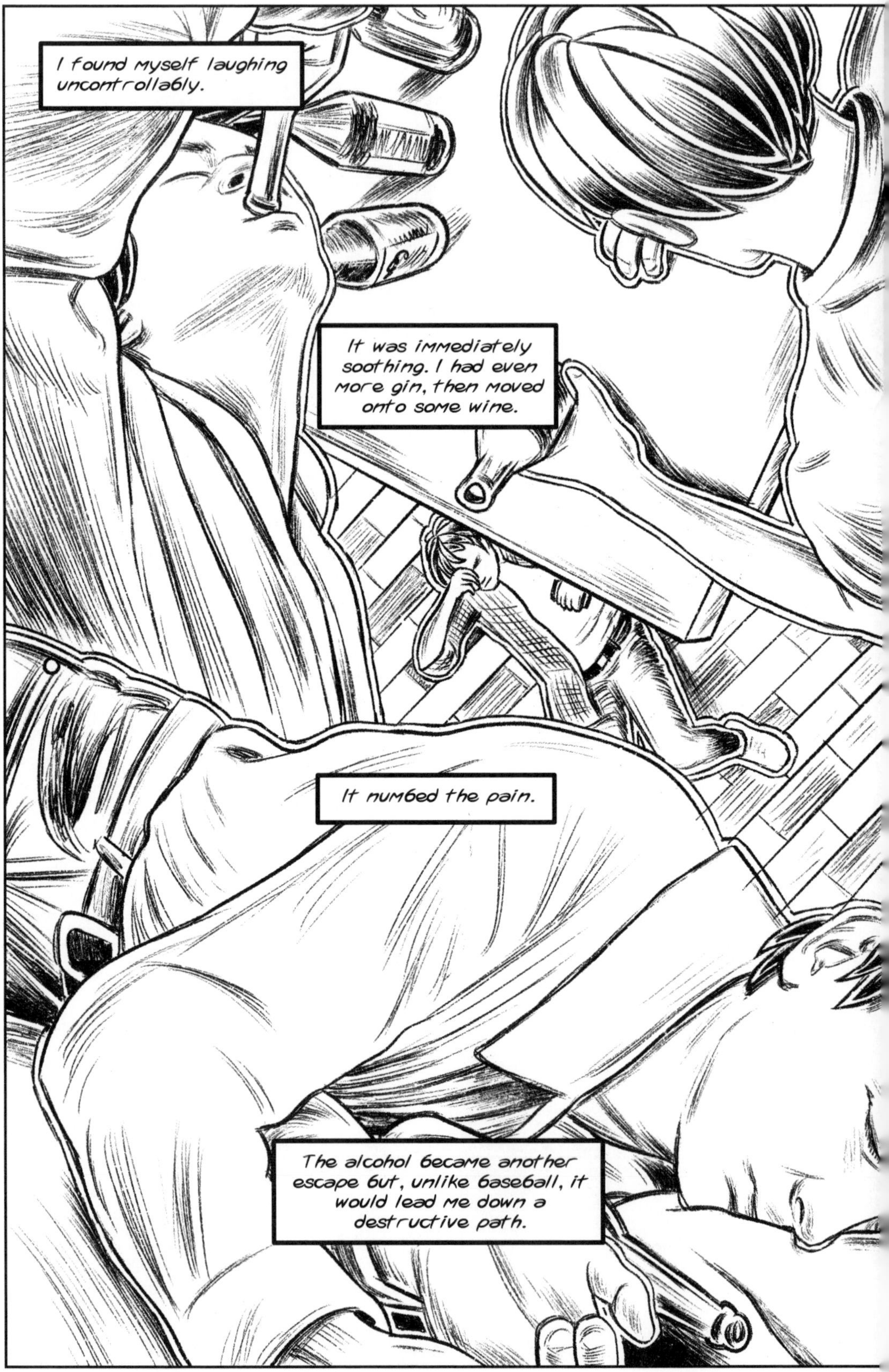
I found myself laughing uncontrollably.
It was immediately soothing. I had even more gin, then moved onto some wine.
It numbed the pain.
The alcohol became another escape but, unlike baseball, it would lead me down a destructive path.

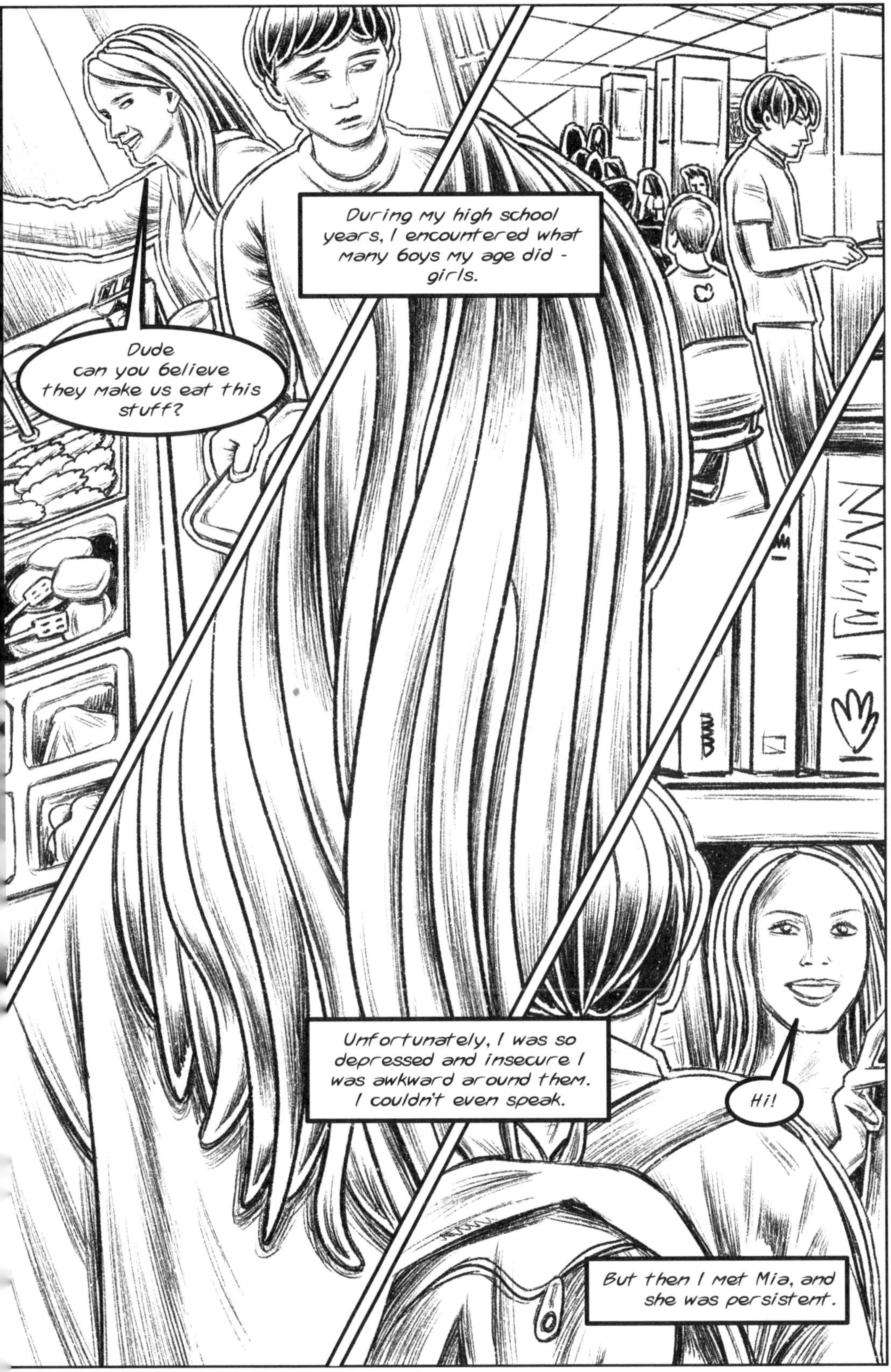
During my high school years, I encountered what many boys my age did - girls.
Dude can you believe they make us eat this stuff?
Unfortunately, I was so depressed and insecure I was awkward around them. I couldn't even speak.
Hi!
But then I met Mia, and she was persistent.

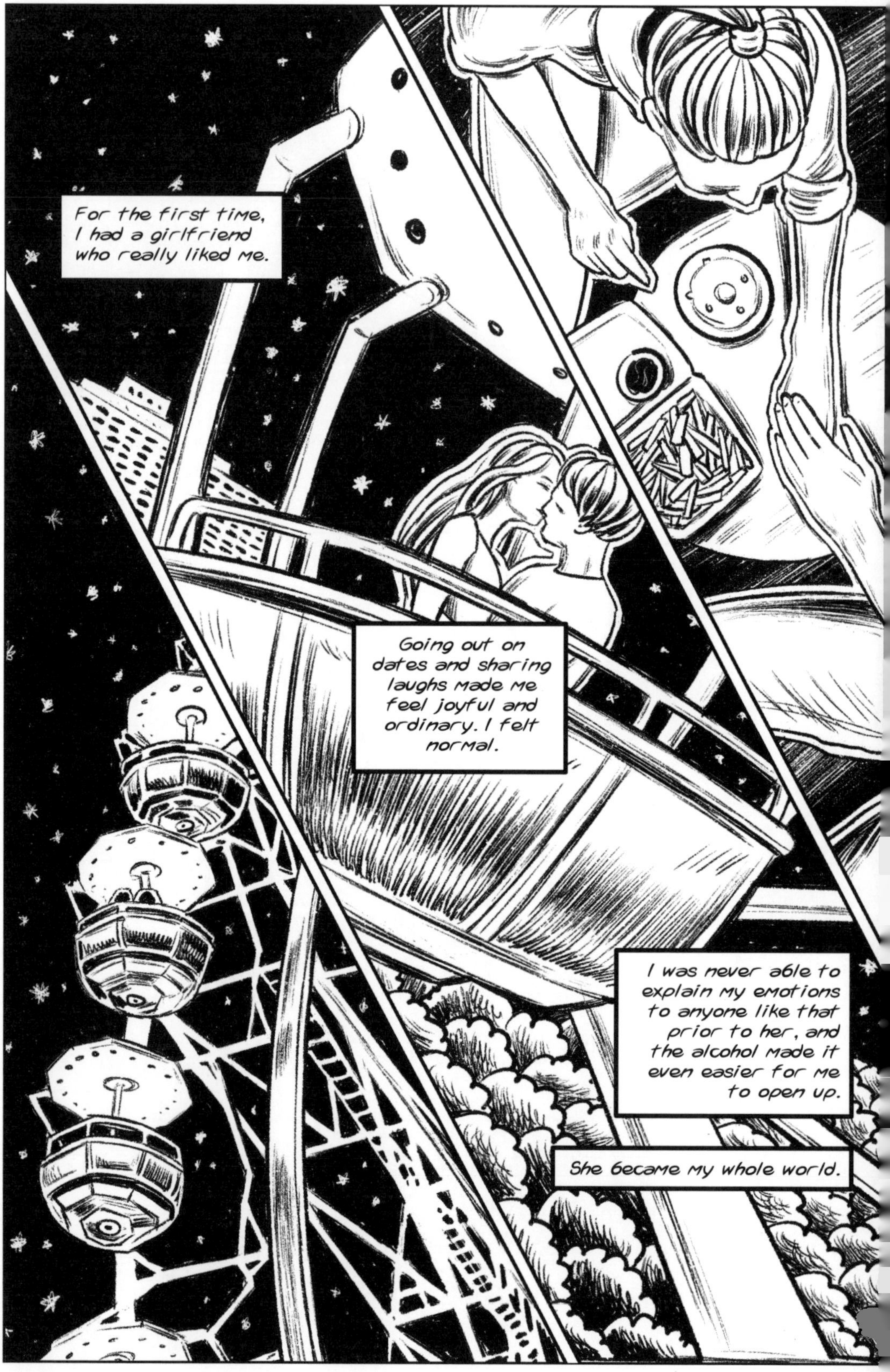
For the first time, I had a girlfriend who really liked me.
Going out on dates and sharing laughs made me feel joyful and ordinary. I felt normal.
I was never able to explain my emotions to anyone like that prior to her, and the alcohol made it even easier for me to open up.
She became my whole world.

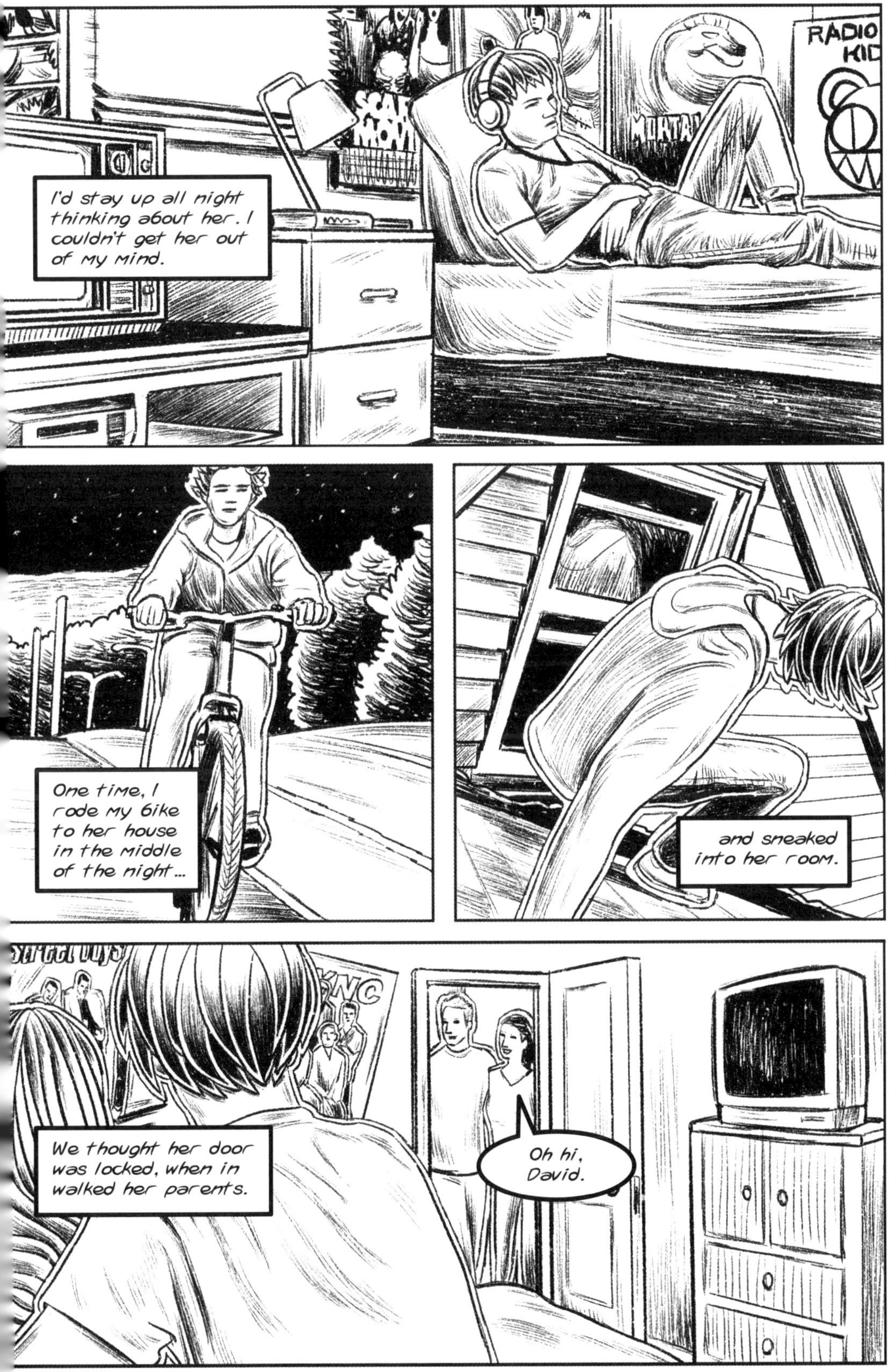
RADIO KID
I'd stay up all night thinking about her. I couldn't get her out of my mind.
One time, I rode my bike to her house in the middle of the night...
and sneaked into her room.
We thought her door was locked, when in walked her parents.
Oh hi, David.

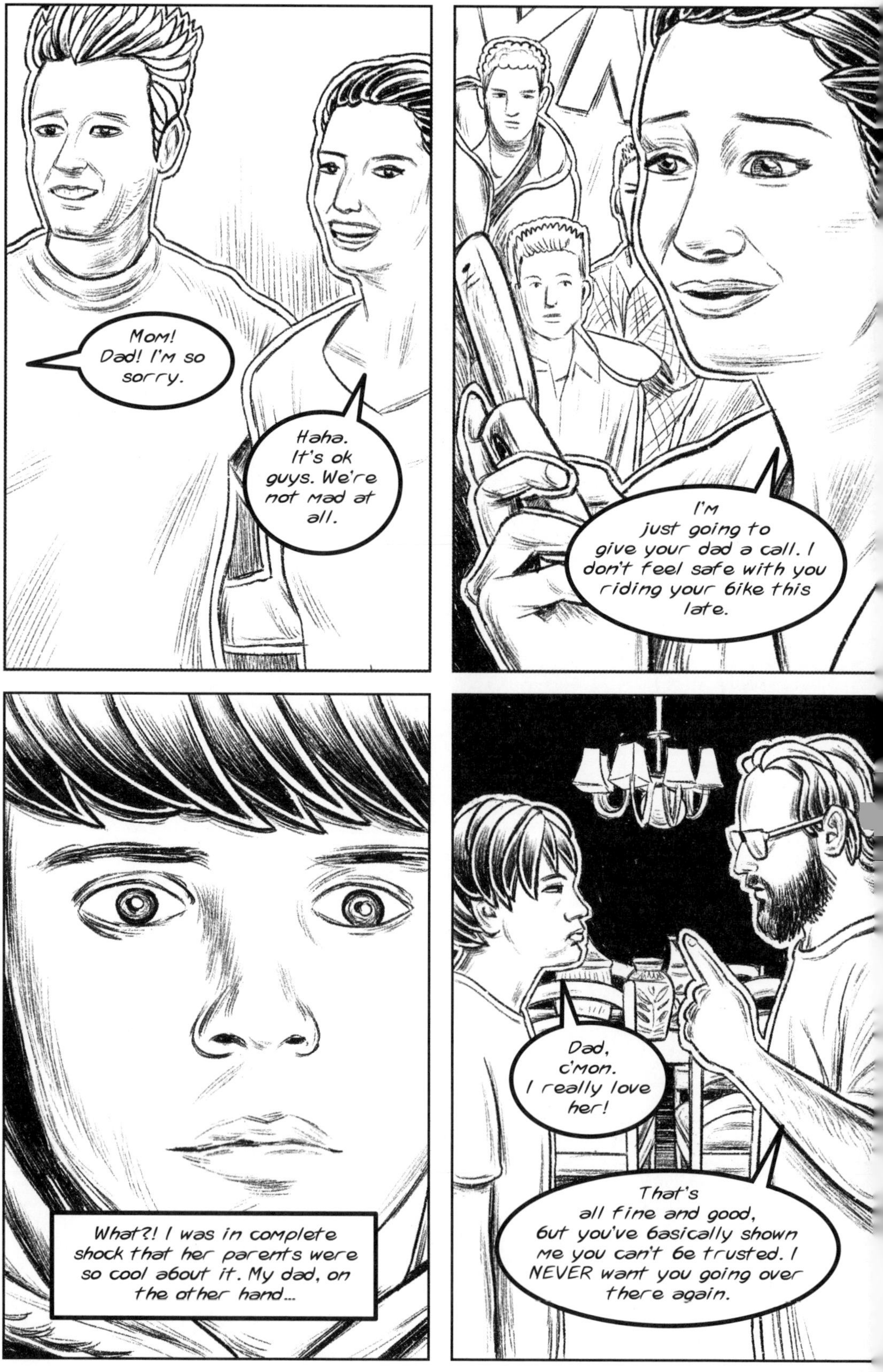
Mom! Dad! I'm so sorry.
Haha. It's ok guys. We're not mad at all.
I'm just going to give your dad a call. I don't feel safe with you riding your bike this late.
What?! I was in complete shock that her parents were so cool about it. My dad, on the other hand...
Dad, c'mon. I really love her!
That's all fine and good, but you've basically shown me you can't be trusted. I NEVER want you going over there again.

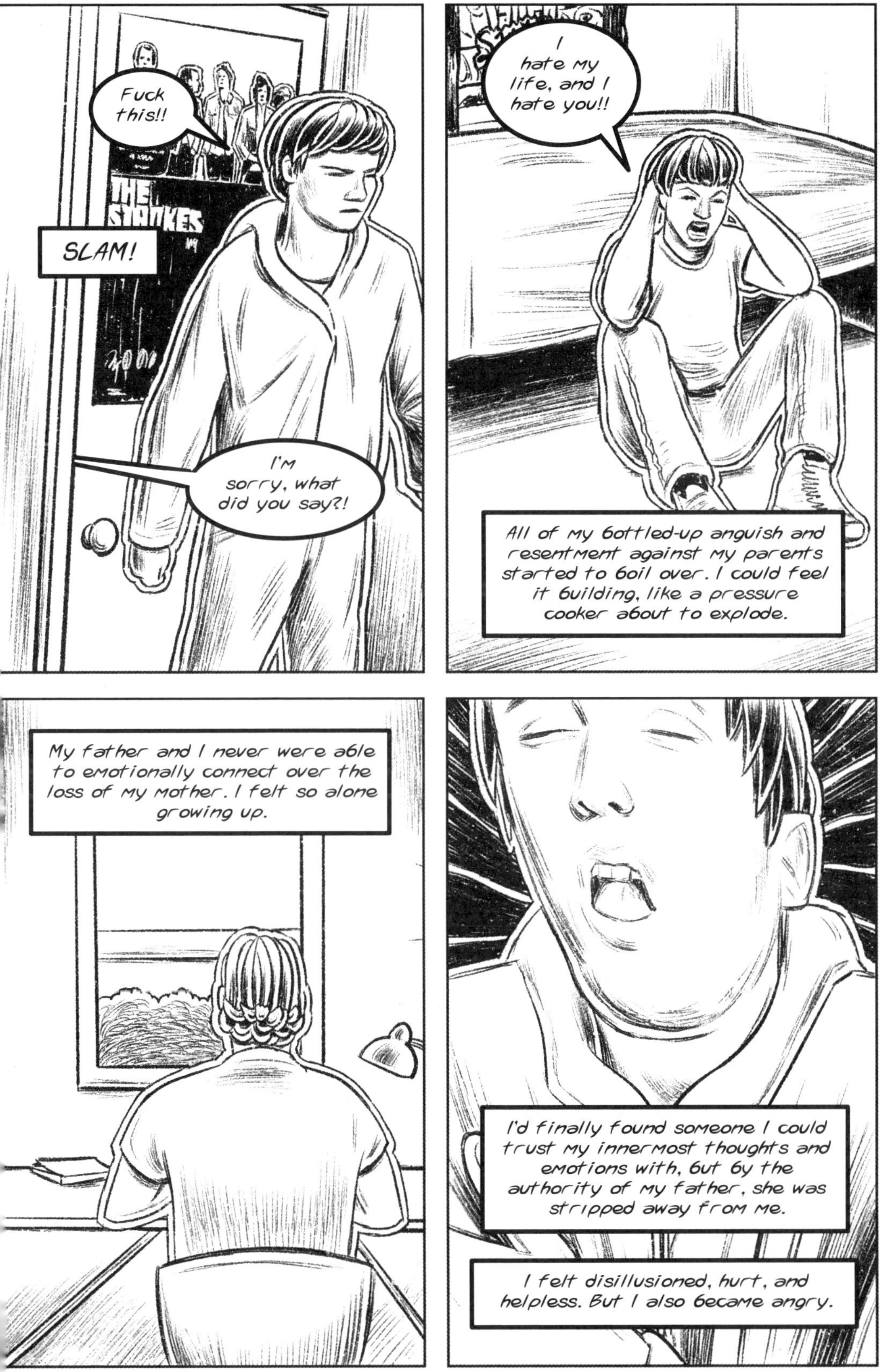
Fuck this!!
THE STROKES
SLAM!
I'm sorry, what did you say?!
I hate my life, and I hate you!!
All of my bottled-up anguish and resentment against my parents started to boil over. I could feel it building, like a pressure cooker about to explode.
My father and I never were able to emotionally connect over the loss of my mother. I felt so alone growing up.
I'd finally found someone I could trust my innermost thoughts and emotions with, but by the authority of my father, she was stripped away from me.
I felt disillusioned, hurt, and helpless. But I also became angry.

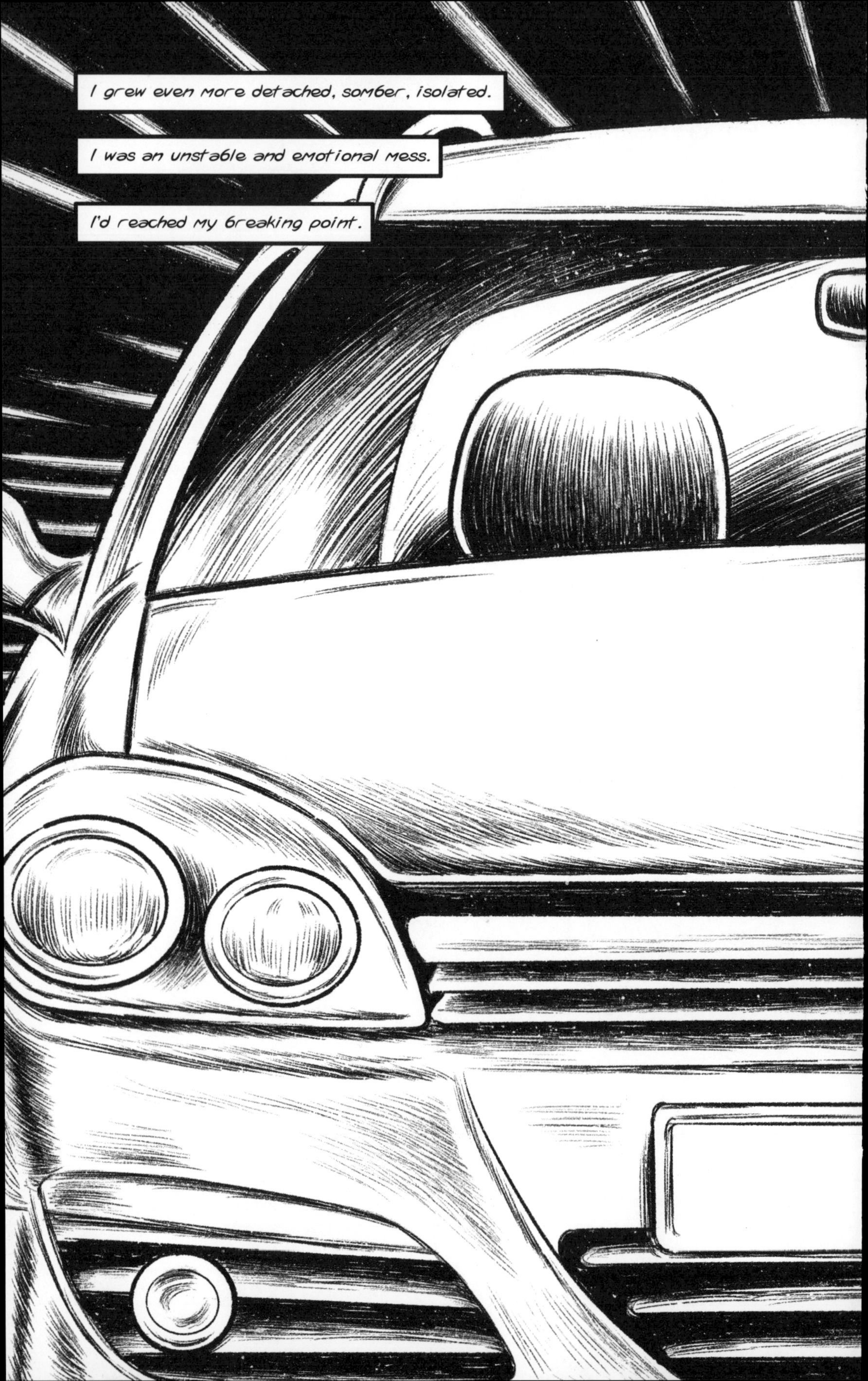
I grew even more detached, somber, isolated.
I was an unstable and emotional mess.
I'd reached my breaking point.

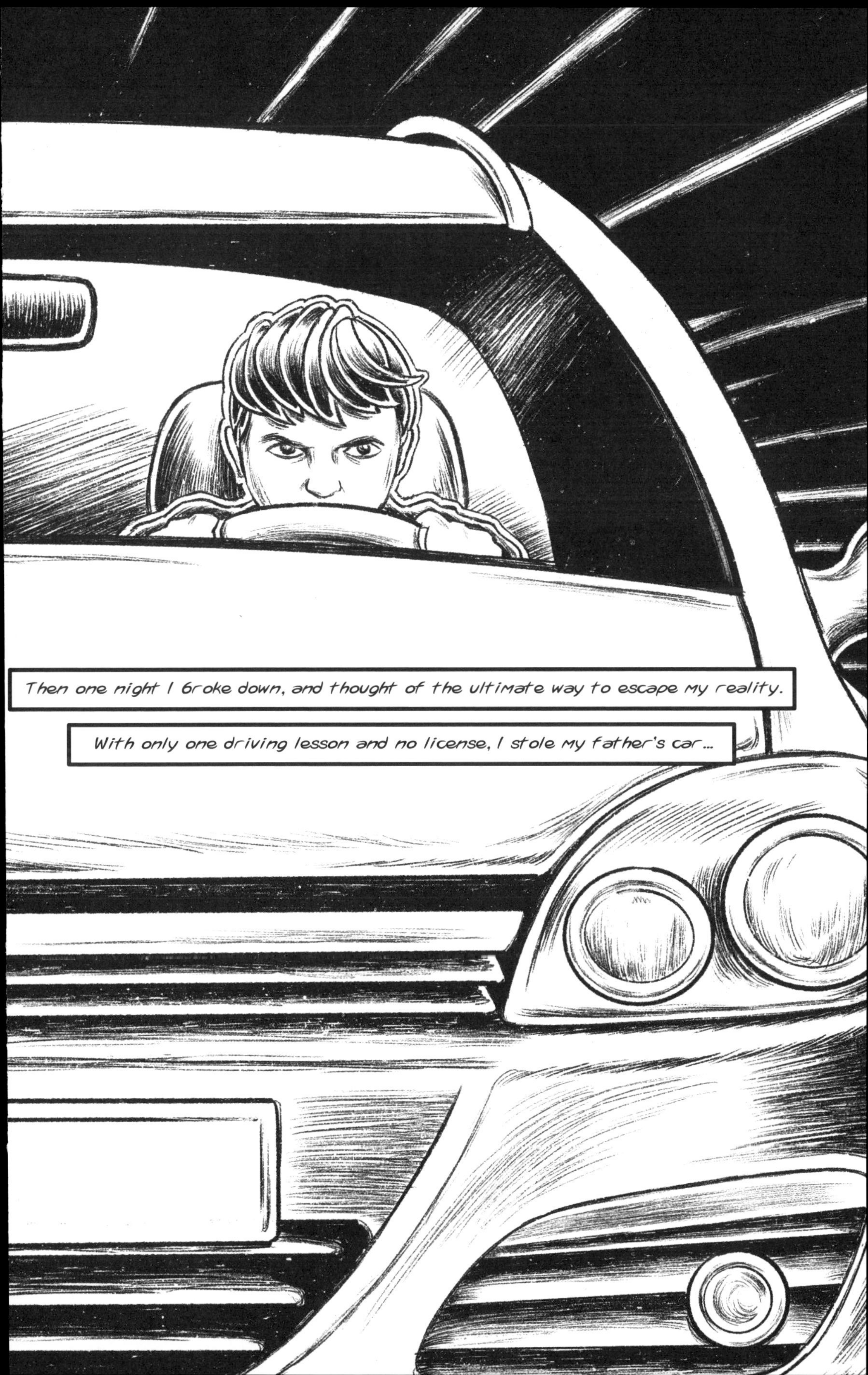
Then one night I broke down, and thought of the ultimate way to escape my reality.
With only one driving lesson and no license, I stole my father's car...

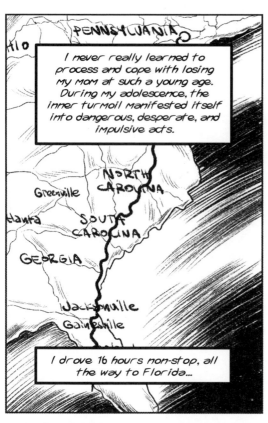

PENNSYLVANIA

I never really learned to process and cope with losing my mom at such a young age. During my adolescence, the inner turmoil manifested itself into dangerous, desperate, and impulsive acts.

NORTH CAROLINA

Greenville

SOUTH CAROLINA

GEORGIA

Jacksonville
Gainesville

I drove 16 hours non-stop, all the way to Florida...

...and cried half of the way there.

I called Mia from a rest stop pay phone when I got there.

Yeah, the police came here... after you left. They asked a lot of questions.

No, I didn't say anything. Yeah, I actually know somebody in Tampa. She's a social worker.

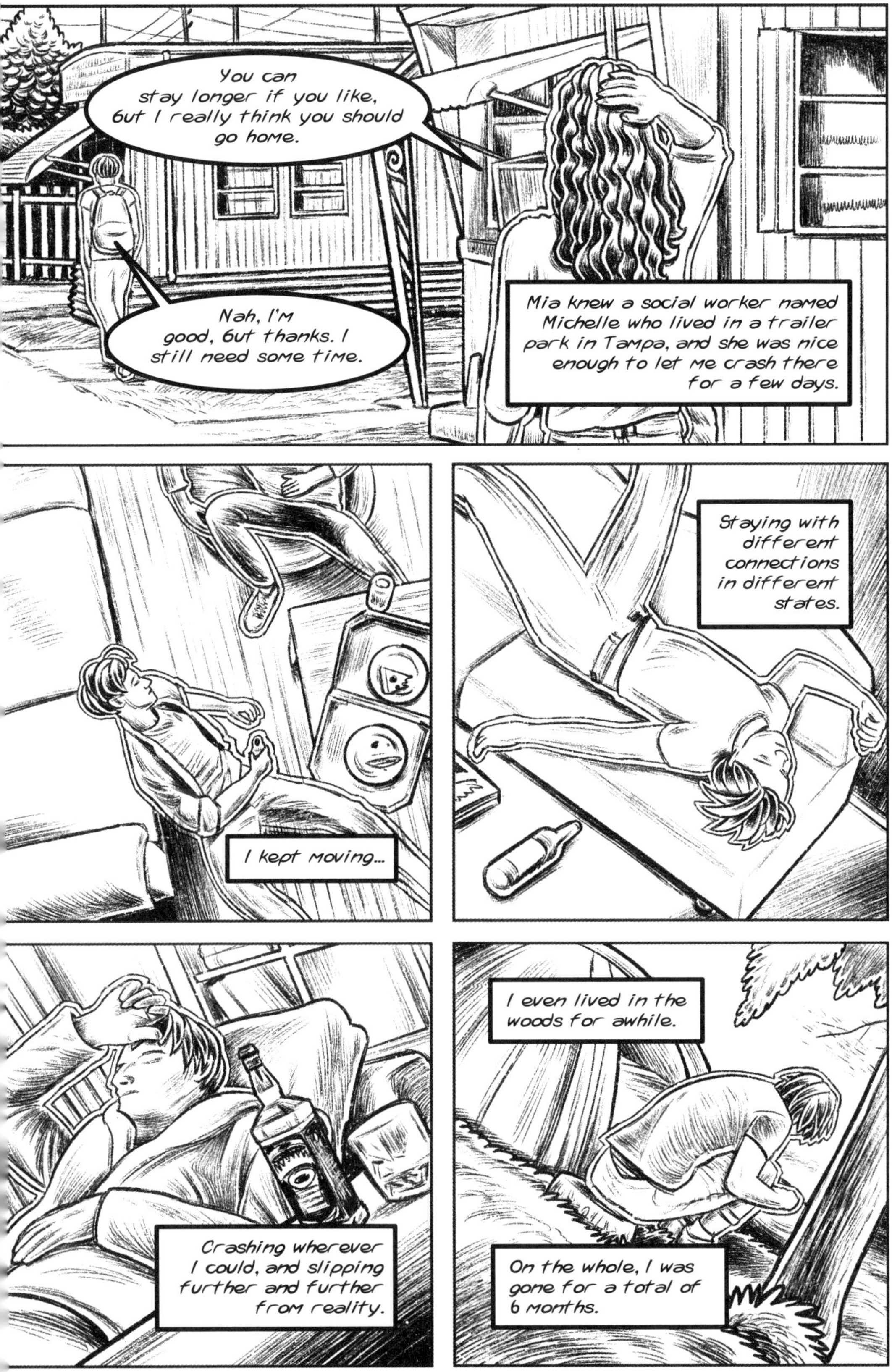
You can stay longer if you like, but I really think you should go home.
Nah, I'm good, but thanks. I still need some time.
Mia knew a social worker named Michelle who lived in a trailer park in Tampa, and she was nice enough to let me crash there for a few days.
I kept moving...
Staying with different connections in different states.
Crashing wherever I could, and slipping further and further from reality.
I even lived in the woods for awhile.
On the whole, I was gone for a total of 6 months.

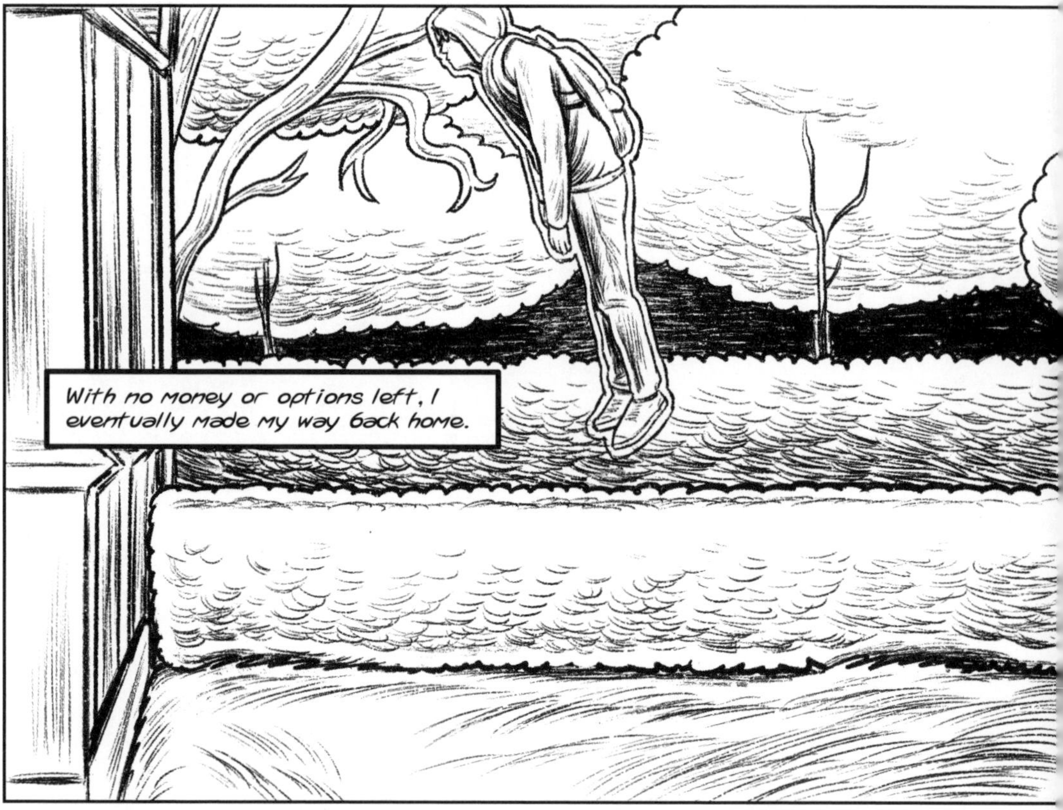
With no money or options left, I eventually made my way back home.

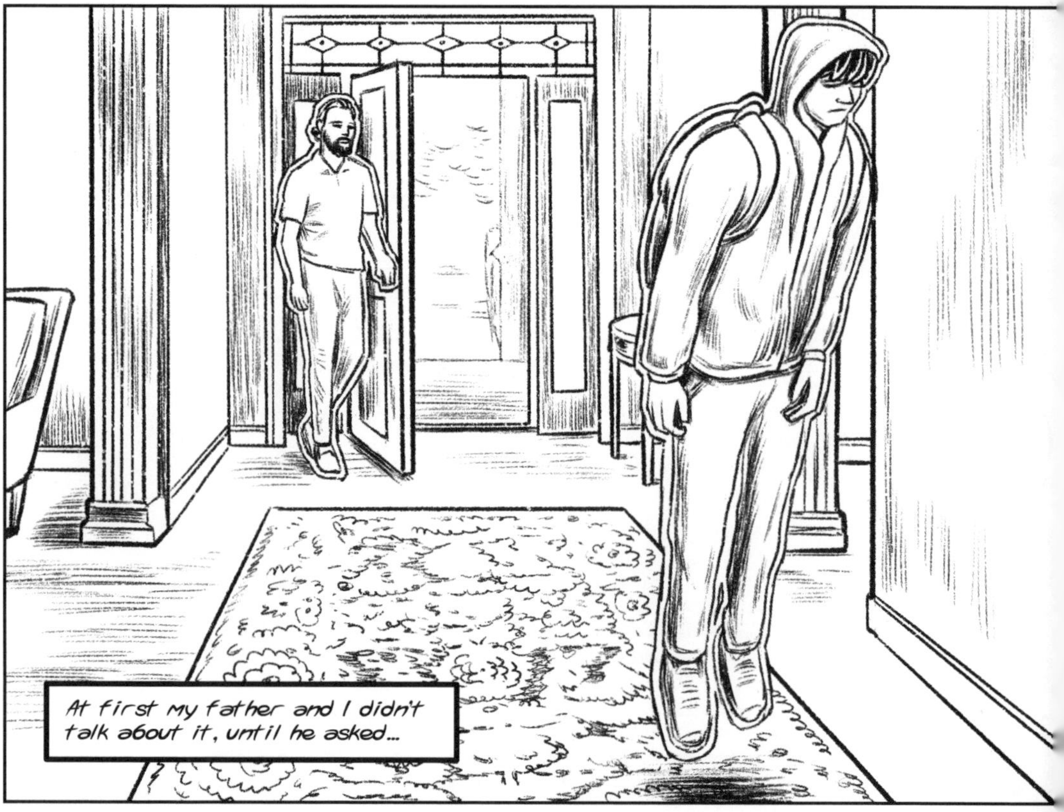
At first my father and I didn't talk about it, until he asked...

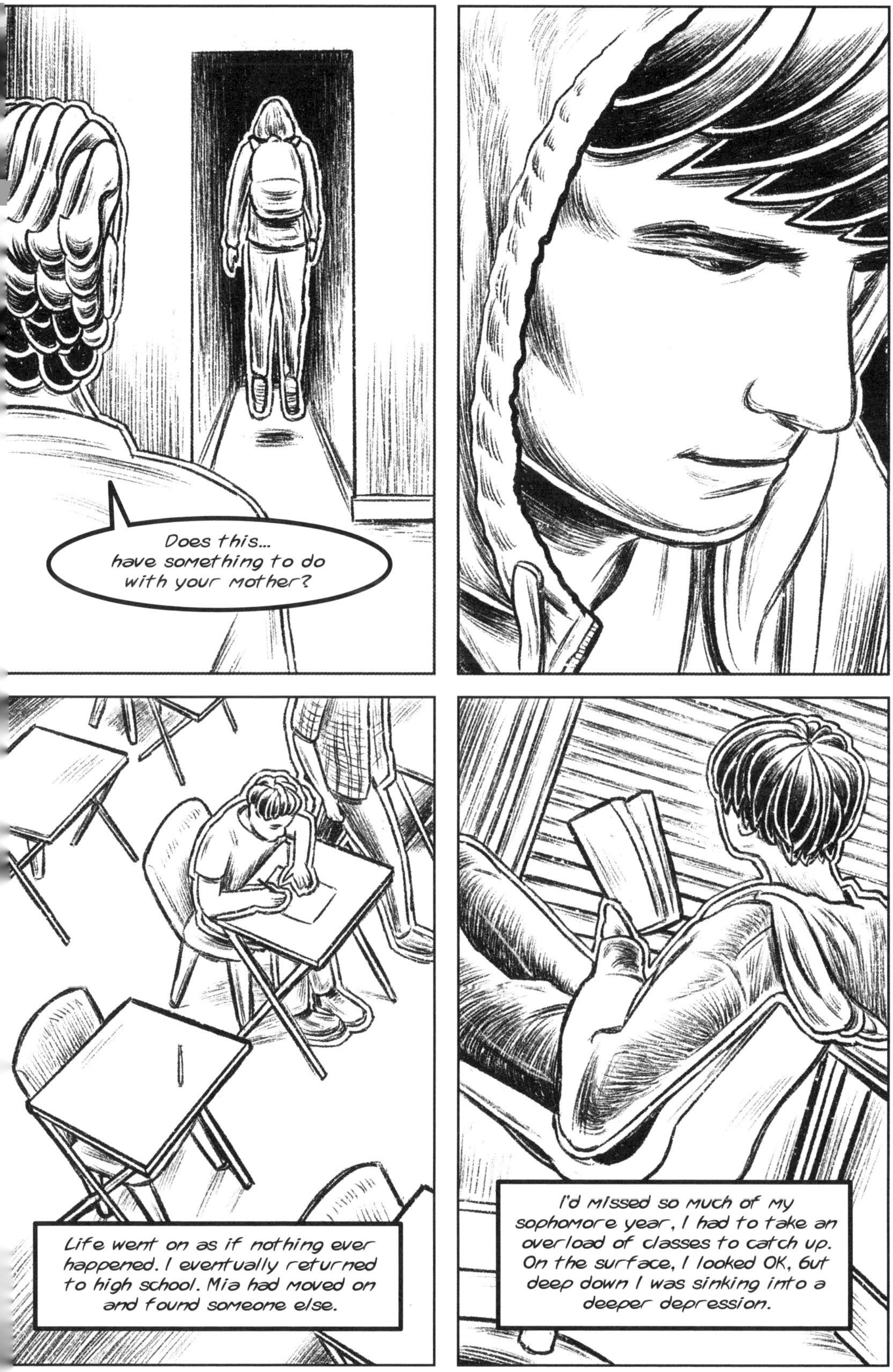
Does this... have something to do with your mother?
Life went on as if nothing ever happened. I eventually returned to high school. Mia had moved on and found someone else.
I'd missed so much of my sophomore year, I had to take an overload of classes to catch up. On the surface, I looked OK, but deep down I was sinking into a deeper depression.

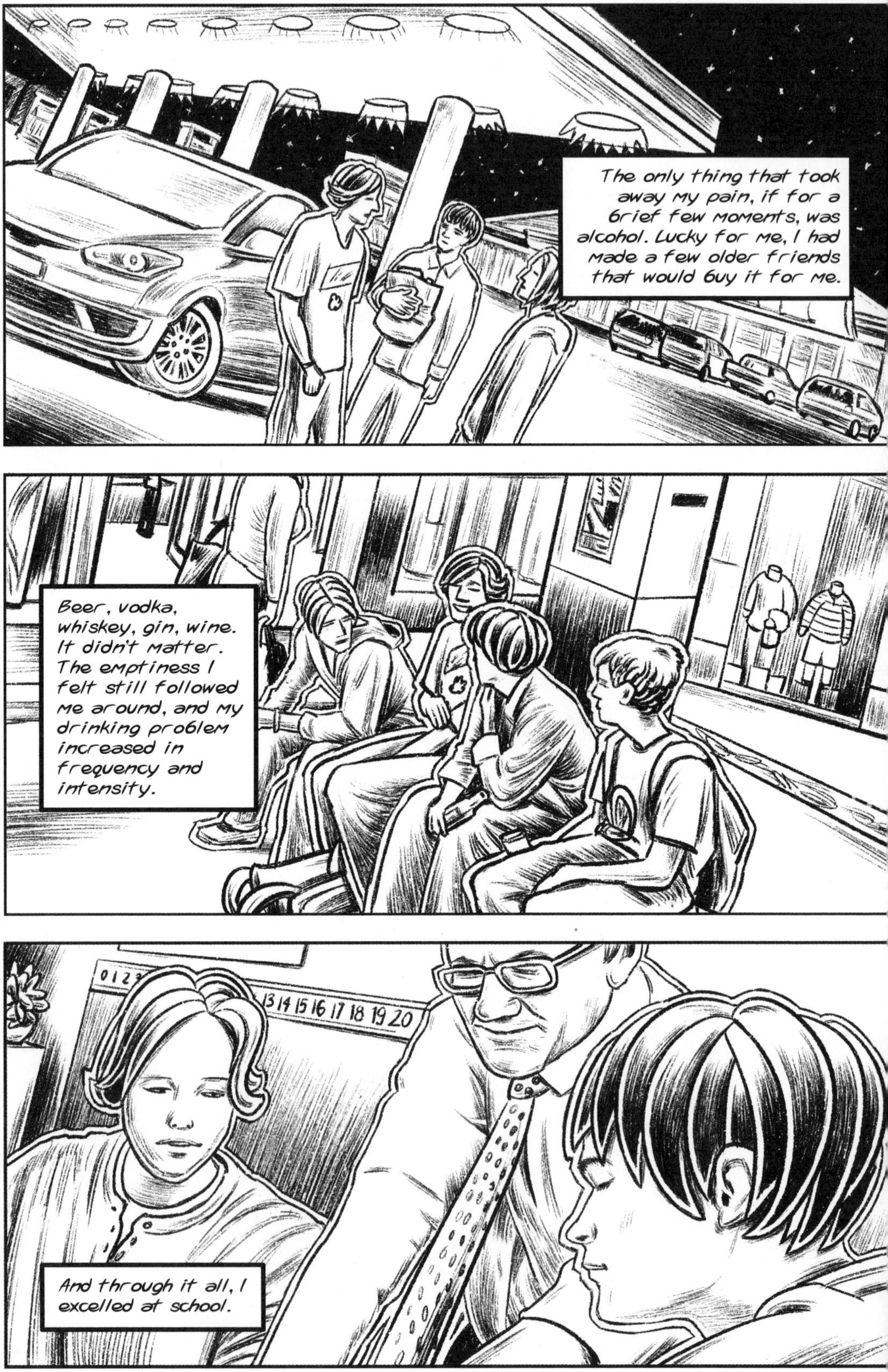
The only thing that took away my pain, if for a brief few moments, was alcohol. Lucky for me, I had made a few older friends that would buy it for me.
Beer, vodka, whiskey, gin, wine. It didn't matter. The emptiness I felt still followed me around, and my drinking problem increased in frequency and intensity.
0123
13 14 15 16 17 18 19 20
And through it all, I excelled at school.

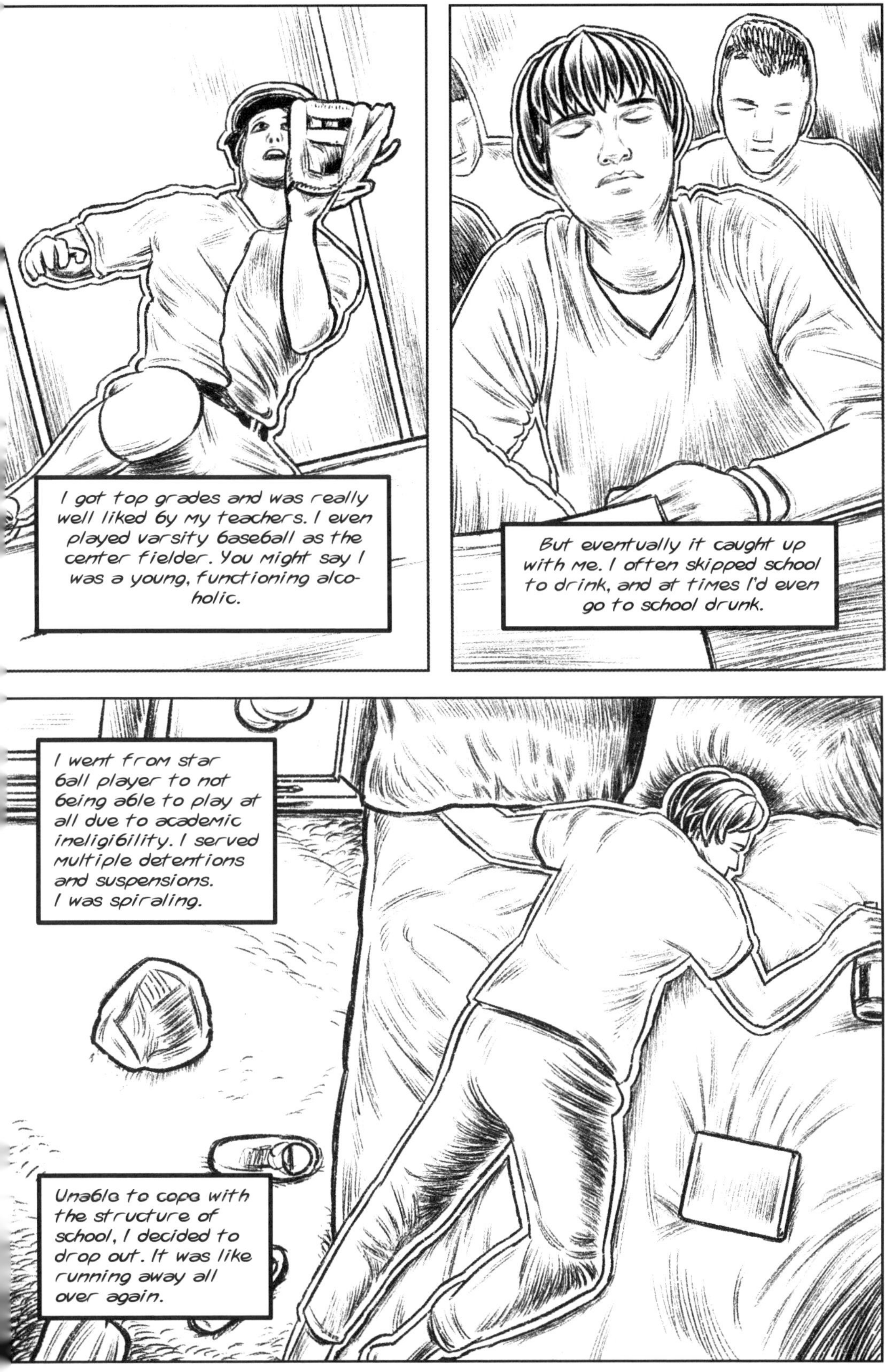
I got top grades and was really well liked by my teachers. I even played varsity baseball as the center fielder. You might say I was a young, functioning alco-holic.
But eventually it caught up with me. I often skipped school to drink, and at times I'd even go to school drunk.
I went from star ball player to not being able to play at all due to academic ineligibility. I served multiple detentions and suspensions. I was spiraling.
Unable to cope with the structure of school, I decided to drop out. It was like running away all over again.

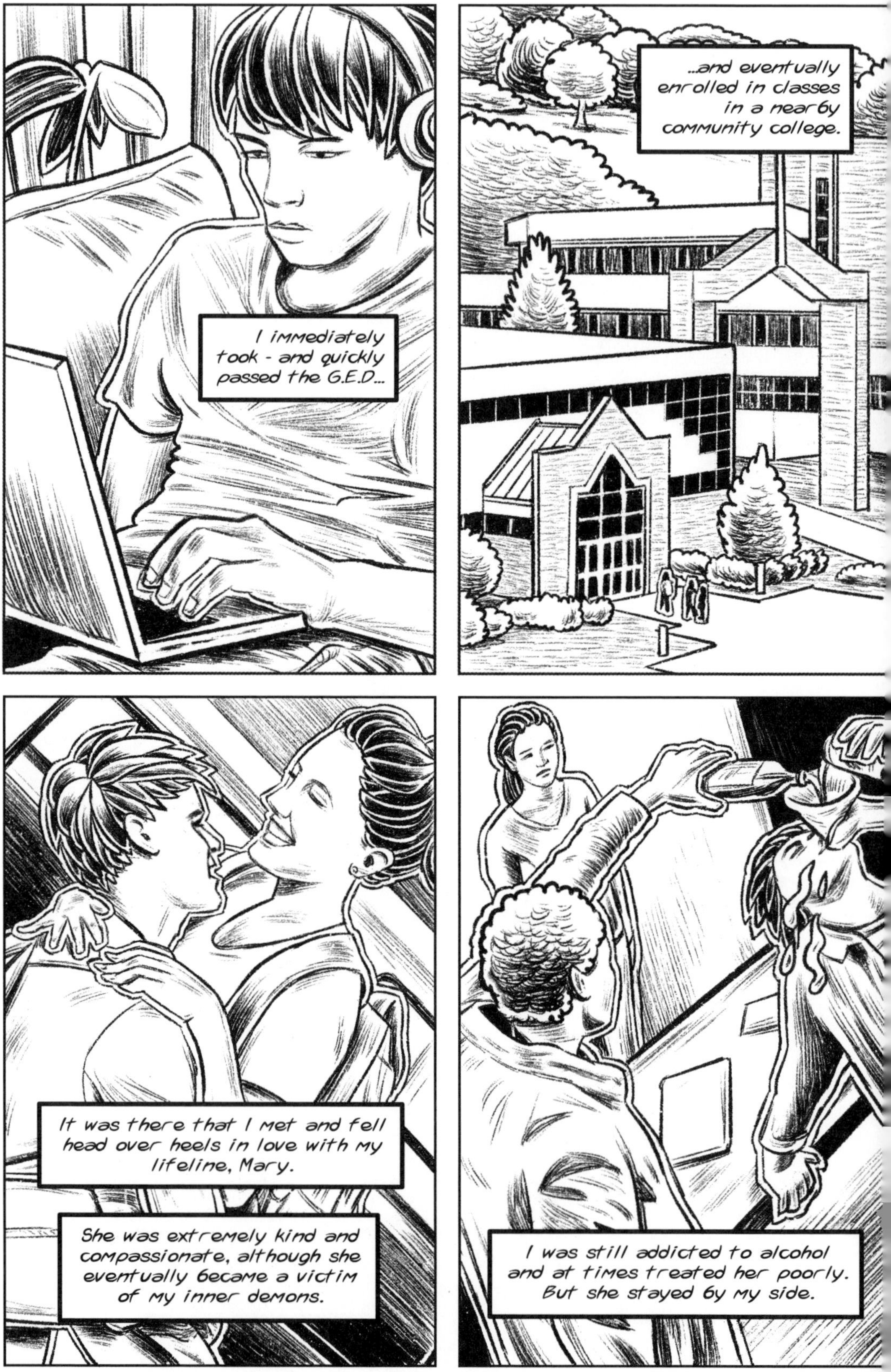
I immediately took - and quickly passed the G.E.D...
...and eventually enrolled in classes in a nearby community college.
It was there that I met and fell head over heels in love with my lifeline, Mary.
She was extremely kind and compassionate, although she eventually became a victim of my inner demons.
I was still addicted to alcohol and at times treated her poorly. But she stayed by my side.

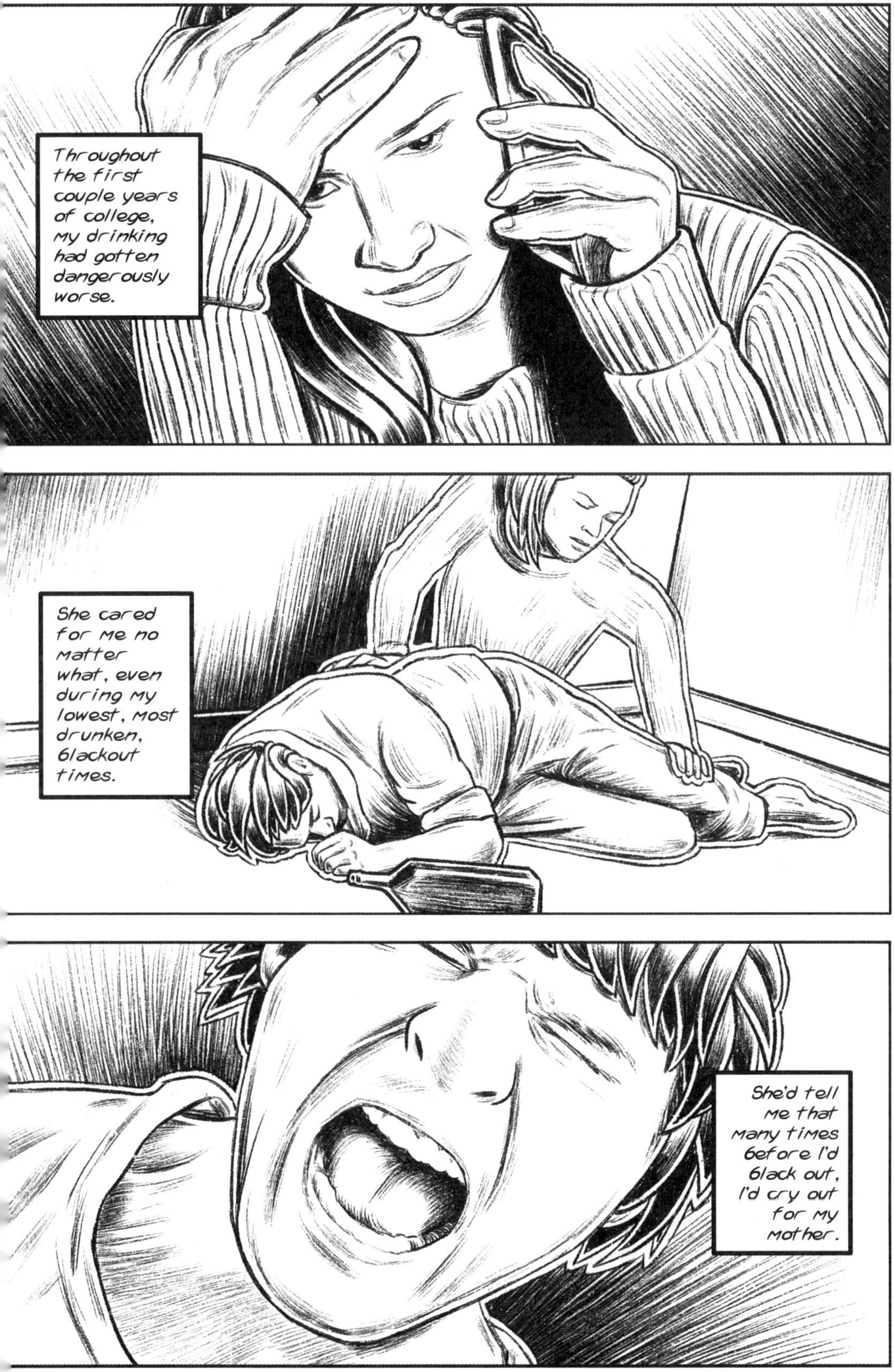
Throughout the first couple years of college, my drinking had gotten dangerously worse.
She cared for me no matter what, even during my lowest, most drunken, blackout times.
She'd tell me that many times before I'd black out, I'd cry out for my mother.

chapter 9

FIRE

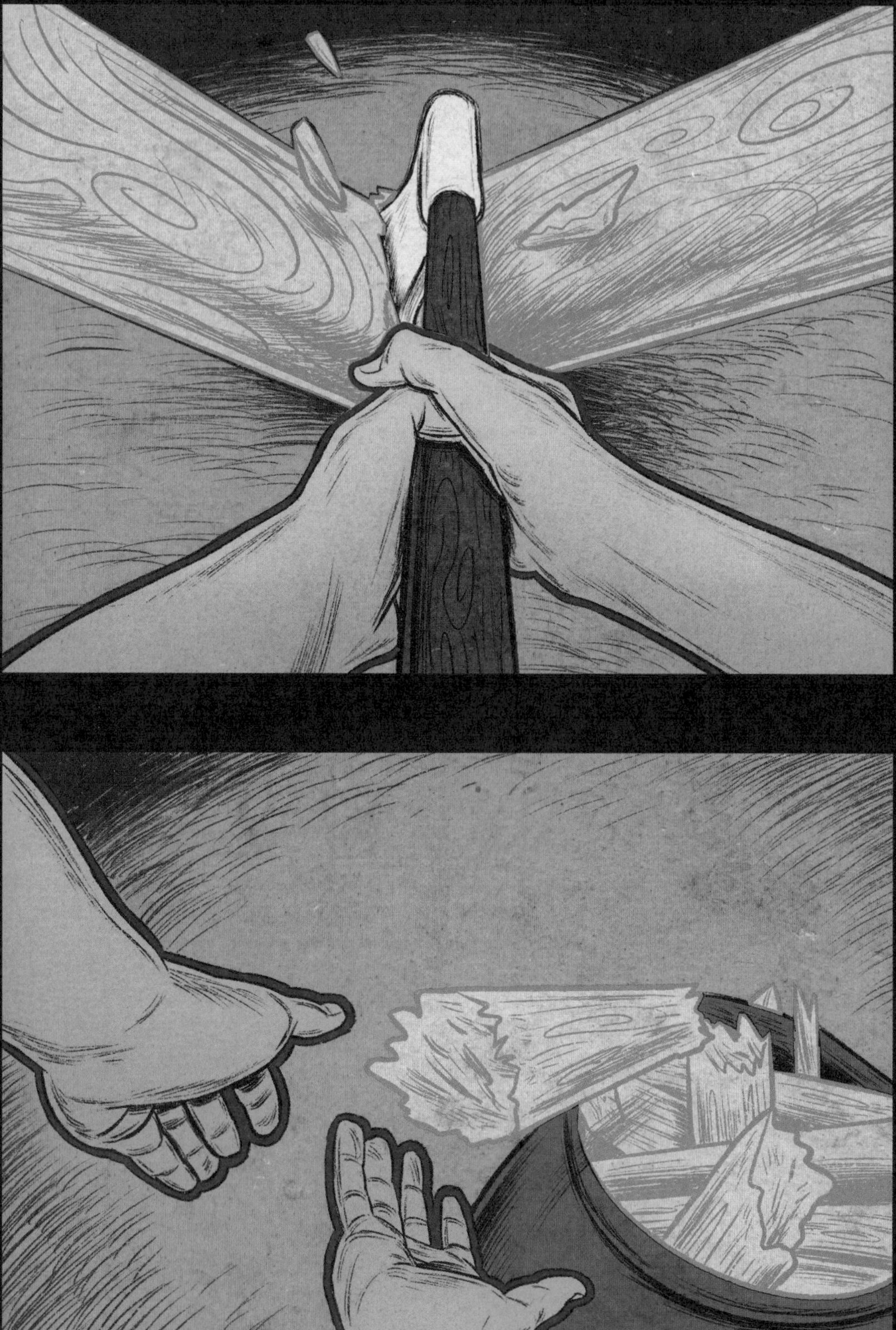

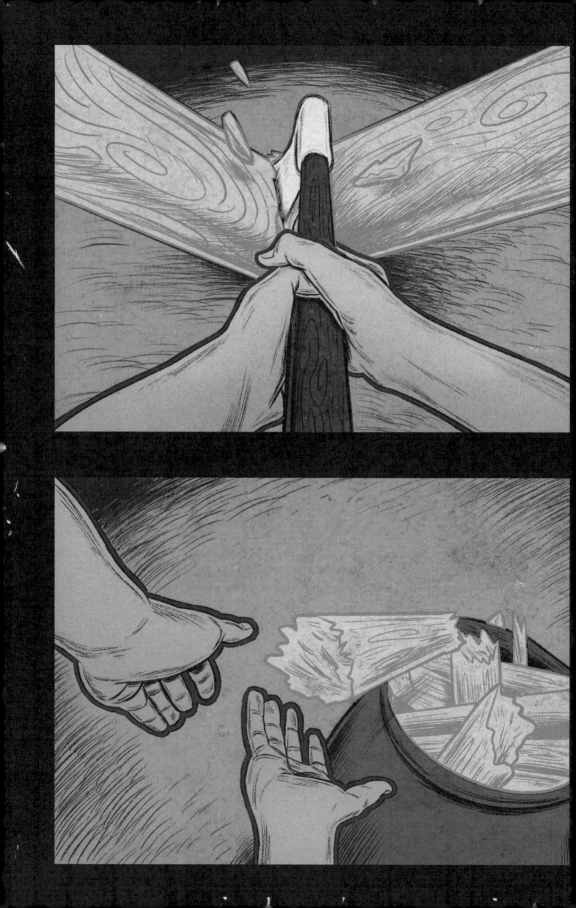

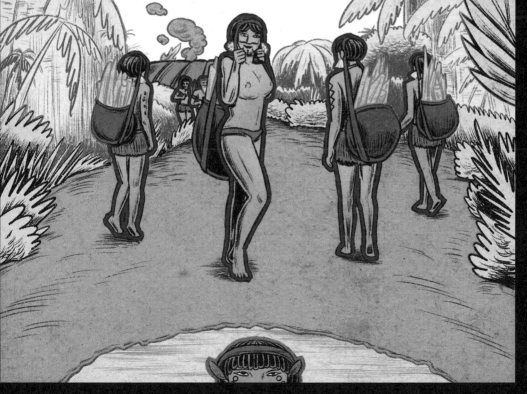

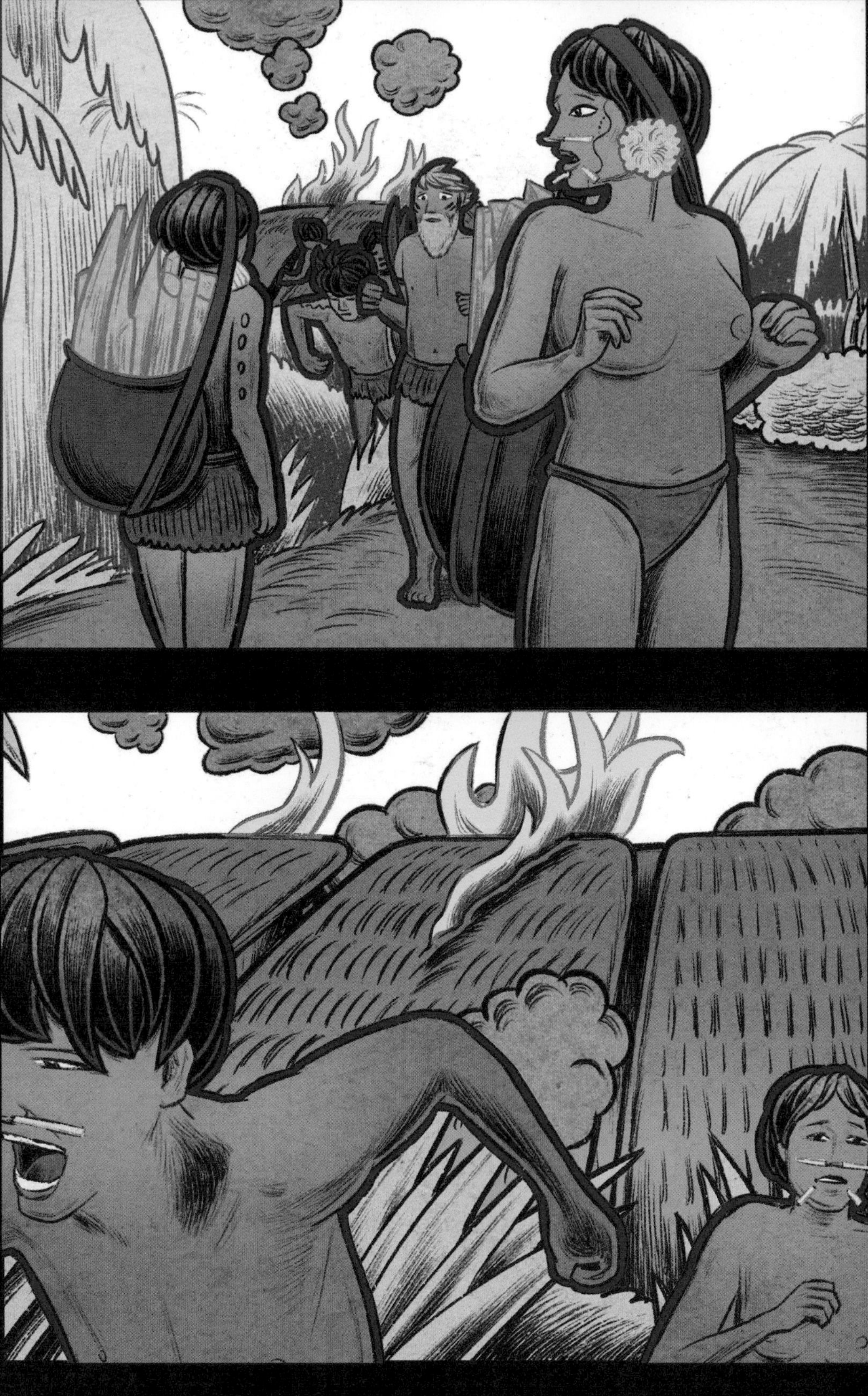

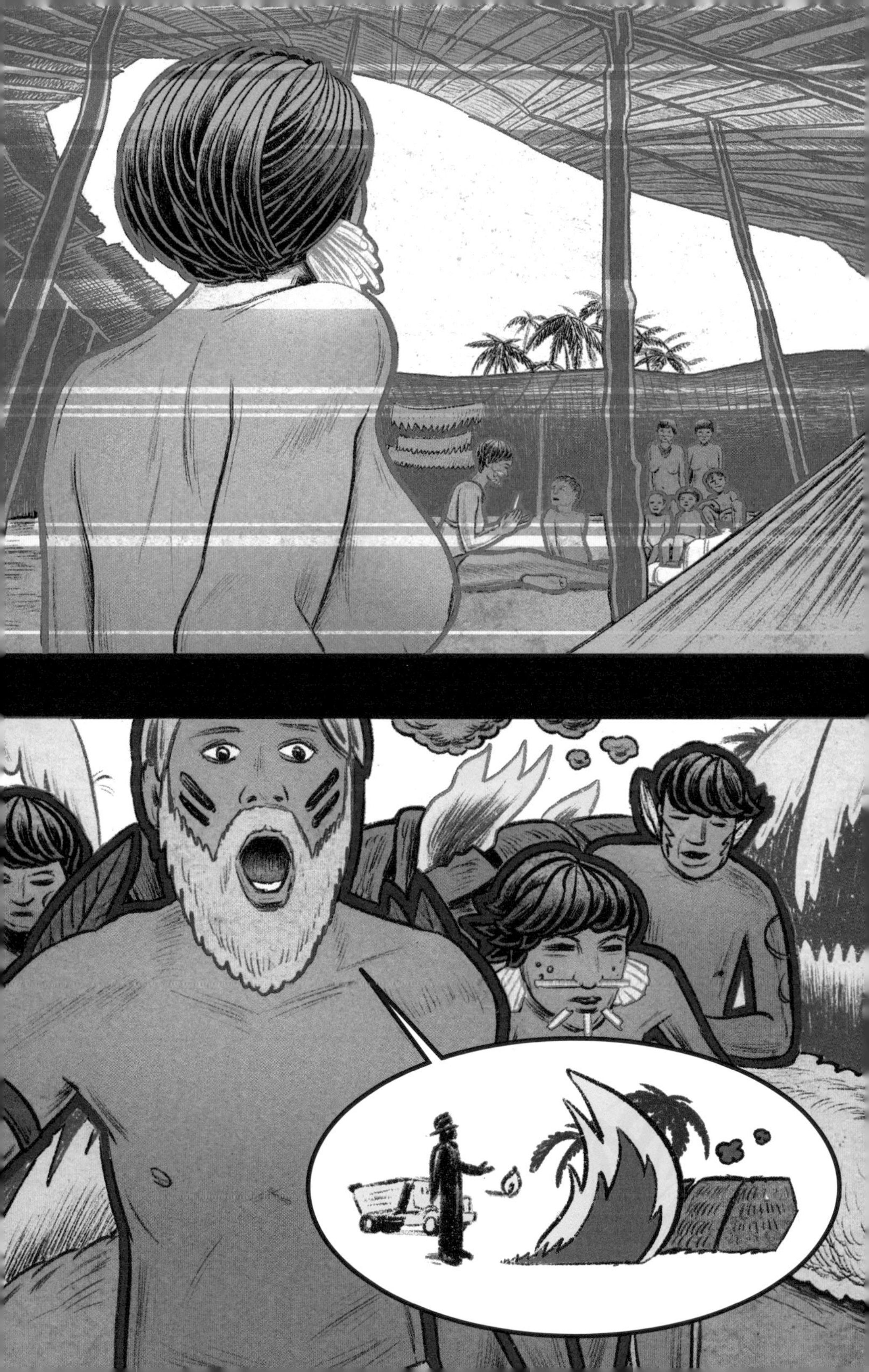

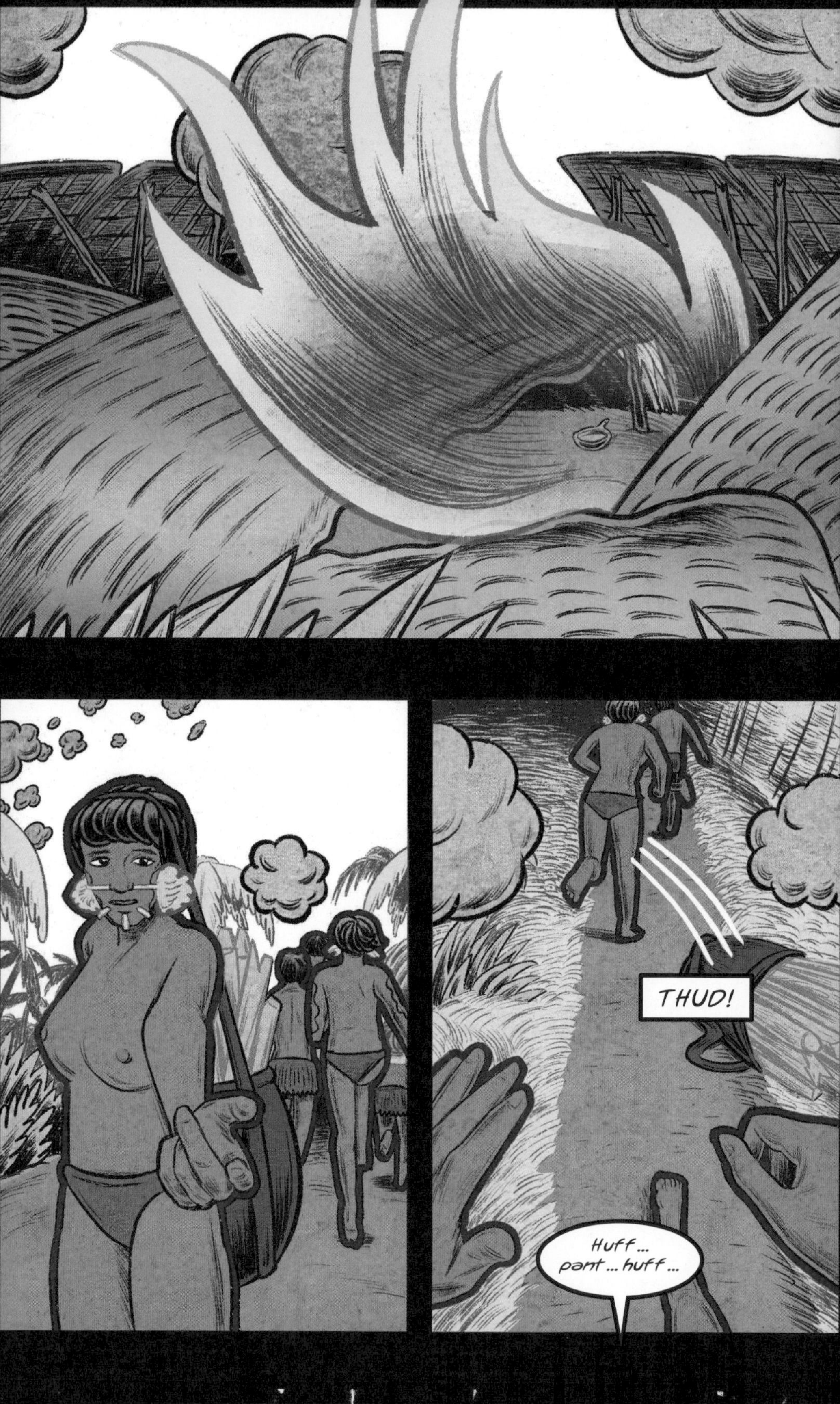
THUD!
Huff...
pant... huff...

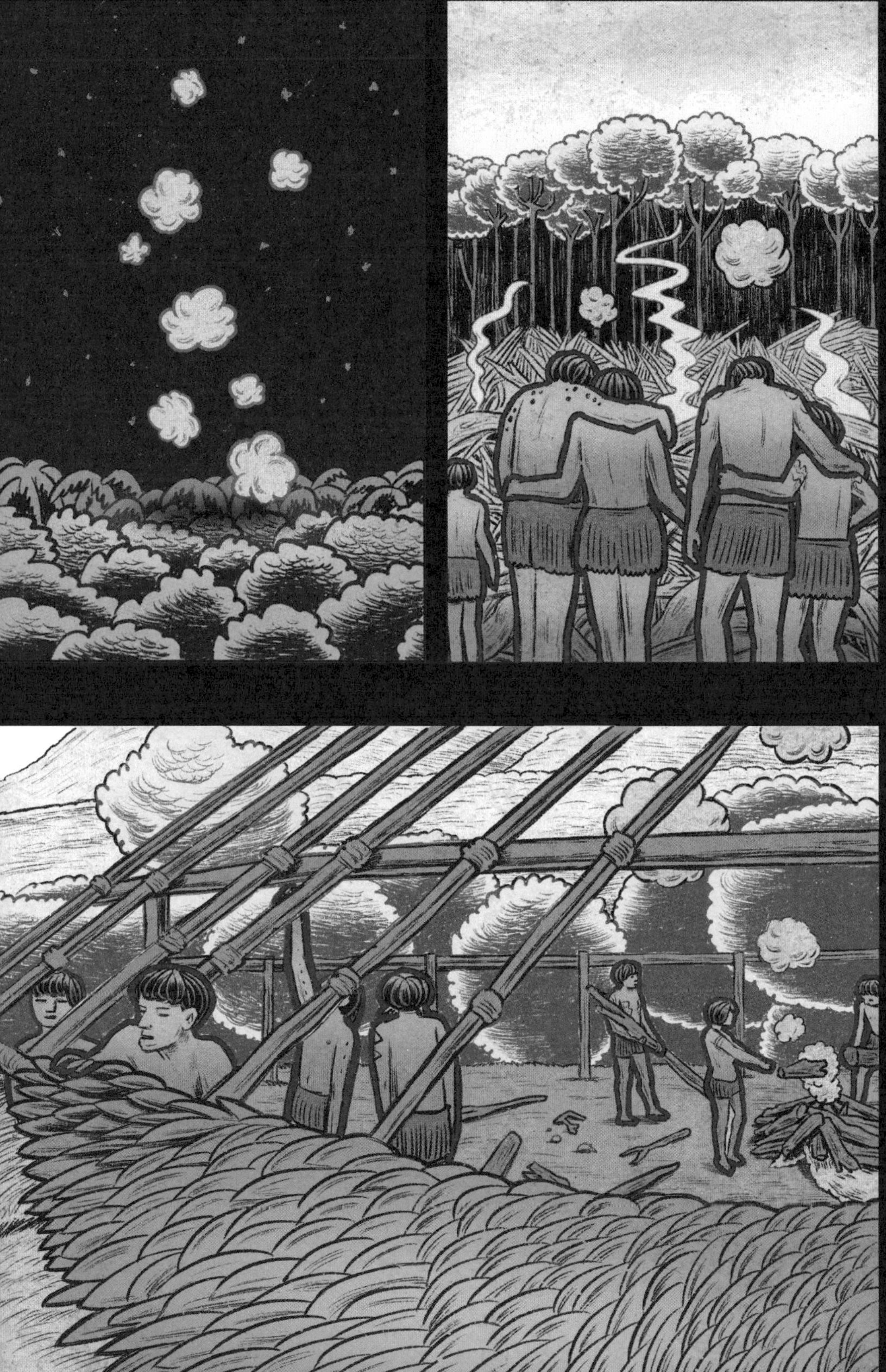

chapter 10

ABANDON

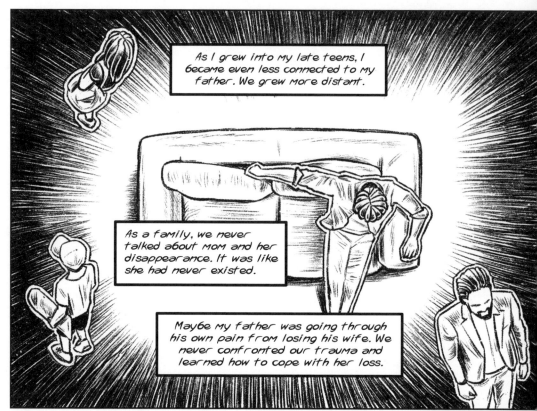

As I grew into my late teens, I became even less connected to my father. We grew more distant.

As a family, we never talked about mom and her disappearance. It was like she had never existed.

Maybe my father was going through his own pain from losing his wife. We never confronted our trauma and learned how to cope with her loss.

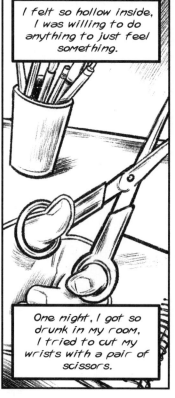

I felt so hollow inside, I was willing to do anything to just feel something.

One night, I got so drunk in my room, I tried to cut my wrists with a pair of scissors.

It wasn't enough to cause any serious damage. I had no real intention of killing myself. But I wanted to get close to it.

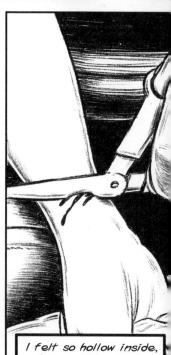

I felt so hollow inside, I was willing to do anything to just feel something.

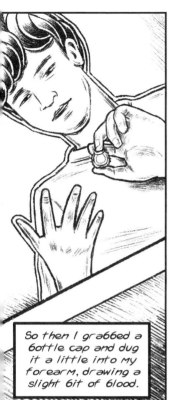

So then I gra66ed a 6ottle cap and dug it a little into my forearm, drawing a slight 6it of 6lood.

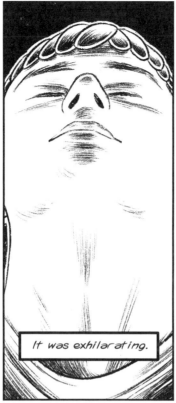

It was exhilarating.

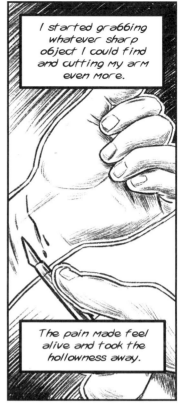

I started gra66ing whatever sharp o6ject I could find and cutting my arm even more.

The pain made feel alive and took the hollowness away.

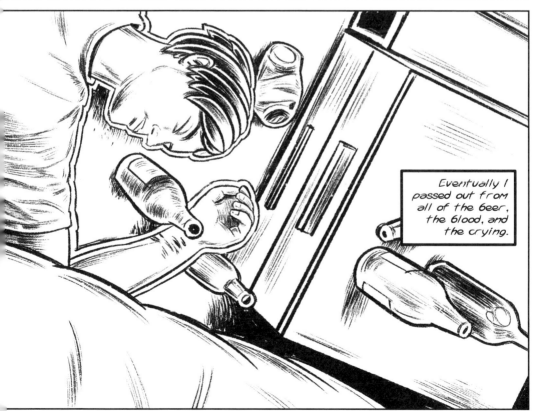

Eventually I passed out from all of the 6eer, the 6lood, and the crying.

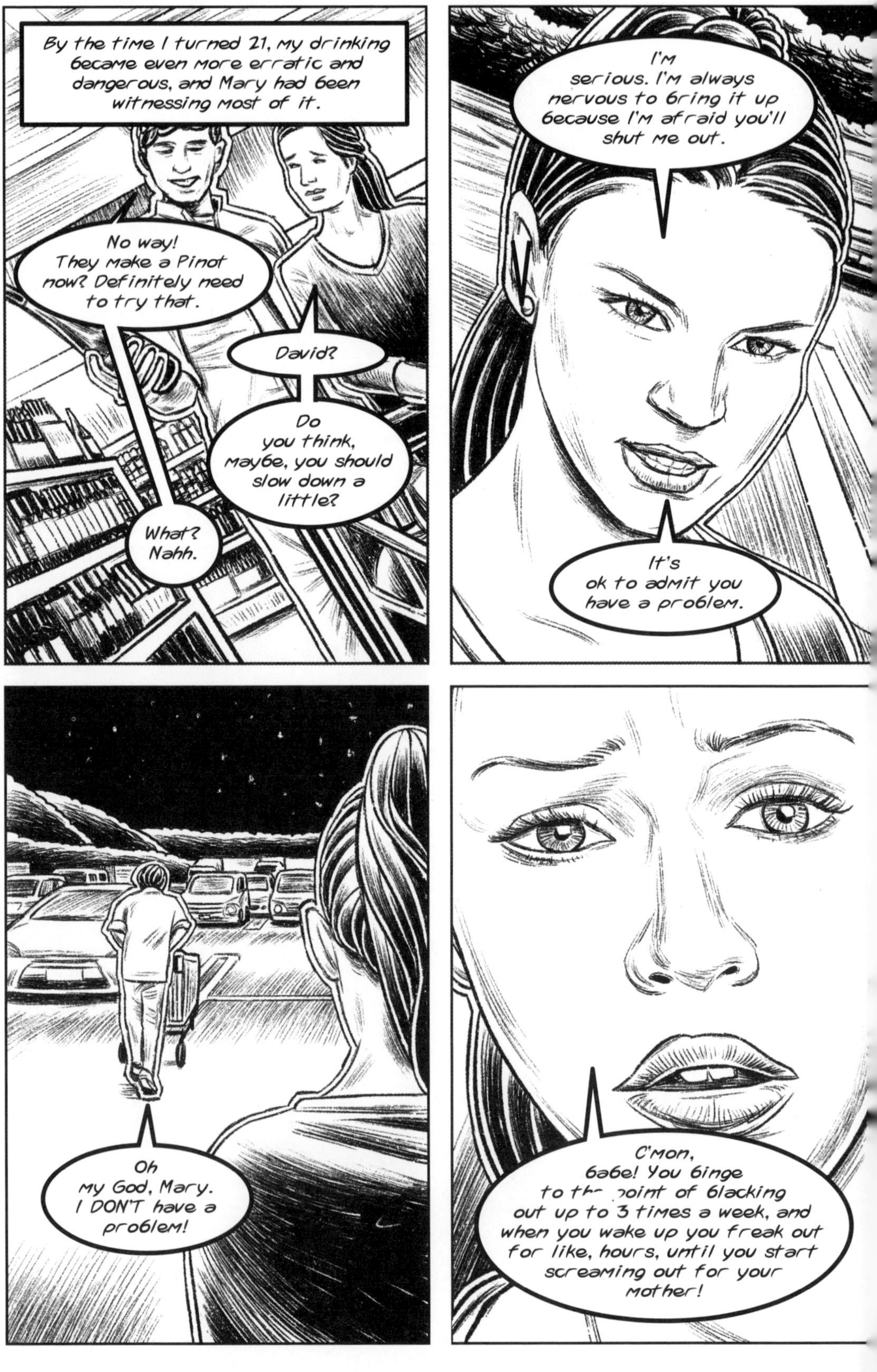

By the time I turned 21, my drinking became even more erratic and dangerous, and Mary had been witnessing most of it.
No way! They make a Pinot now? Definitely need to try that.
David?
Do you think, maybe, you should slow down a little?
What? Nahh.
I'm serious. I'm always nervous to bring it up because I'm afraid you'll shut me out.
It's ok to admit you have a problem.
Oh my God, Mary. I DON'T have a problem!
C'mon, babe! You binge to the point of blacking out up to 3 times a week, and when you wake up you freak out for like, hours, until you start screaming out for your mother!

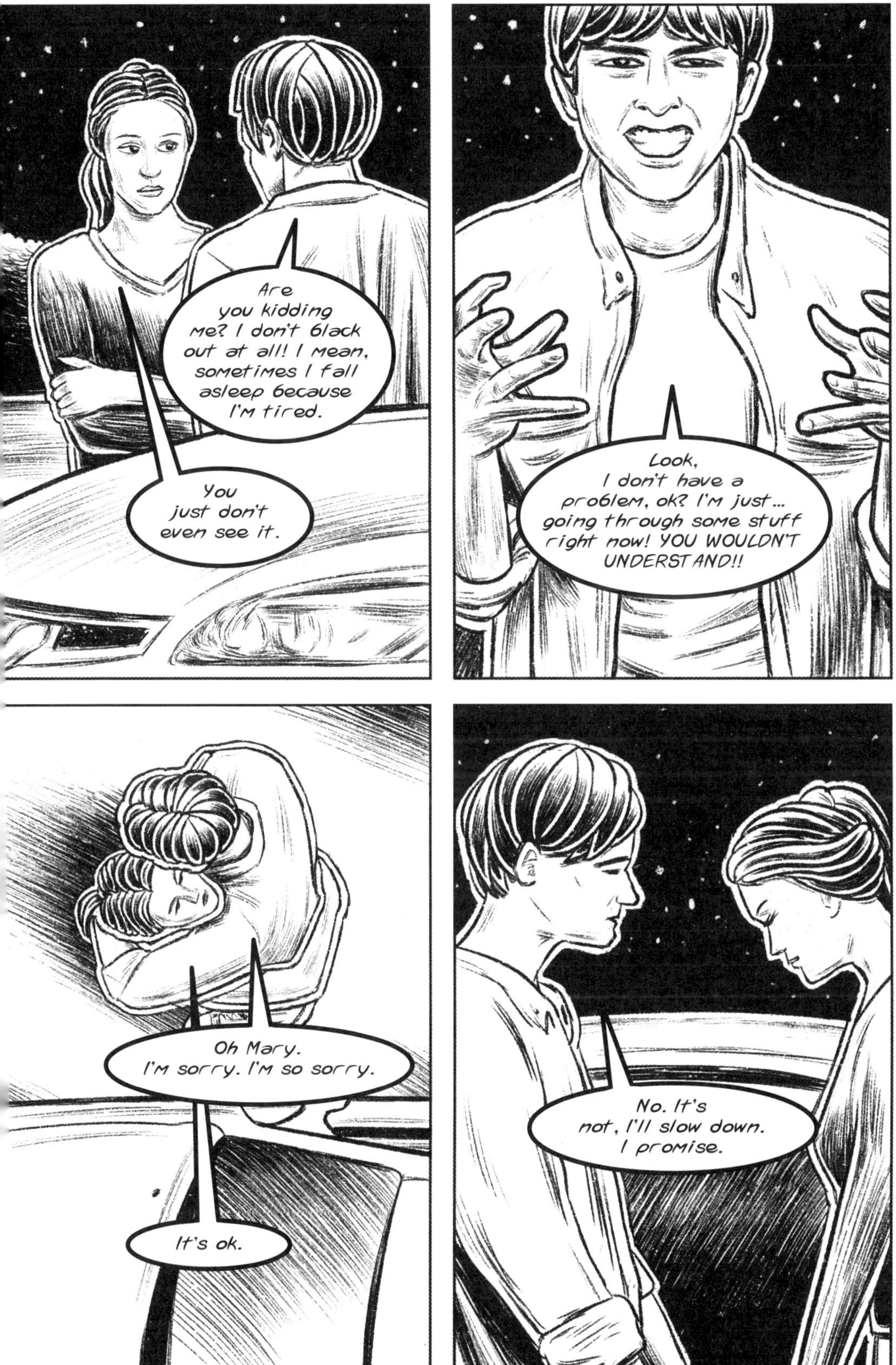
Are you kidding me? I don't black out at all! I mean, sometimes I fall asleep because I'm tired.
You just don't even see it.
Look, I don't have a problem, ok? I'm just... going through some stuff right now! YOU WOULDN'T UNDERSTAND!!
Oh Mary. I'm sorry. I'm so sorry.
It's ok.
No. It's not, I'll slow down. I promise.

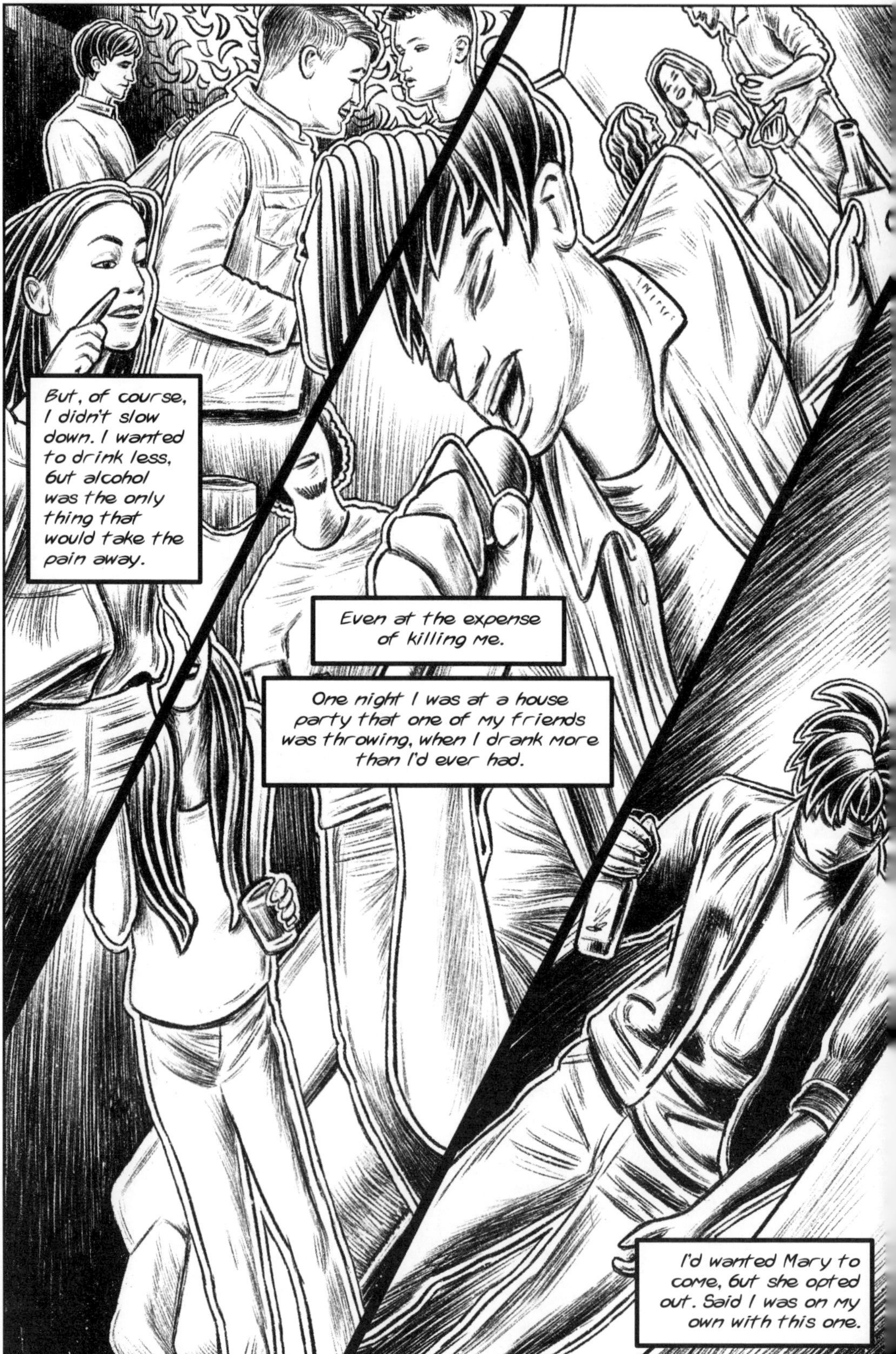

But, of course, I didn't slow down. I wanted to drink less, but alcohol was the only thing that would take the pain away.
Even at the expense of killing me.
One night I was at a house party that one of my friends was throwing, when I drank more than I'd ever had.
I'd wanted Mary to come, but she opted out. Said I was on my own with this one.

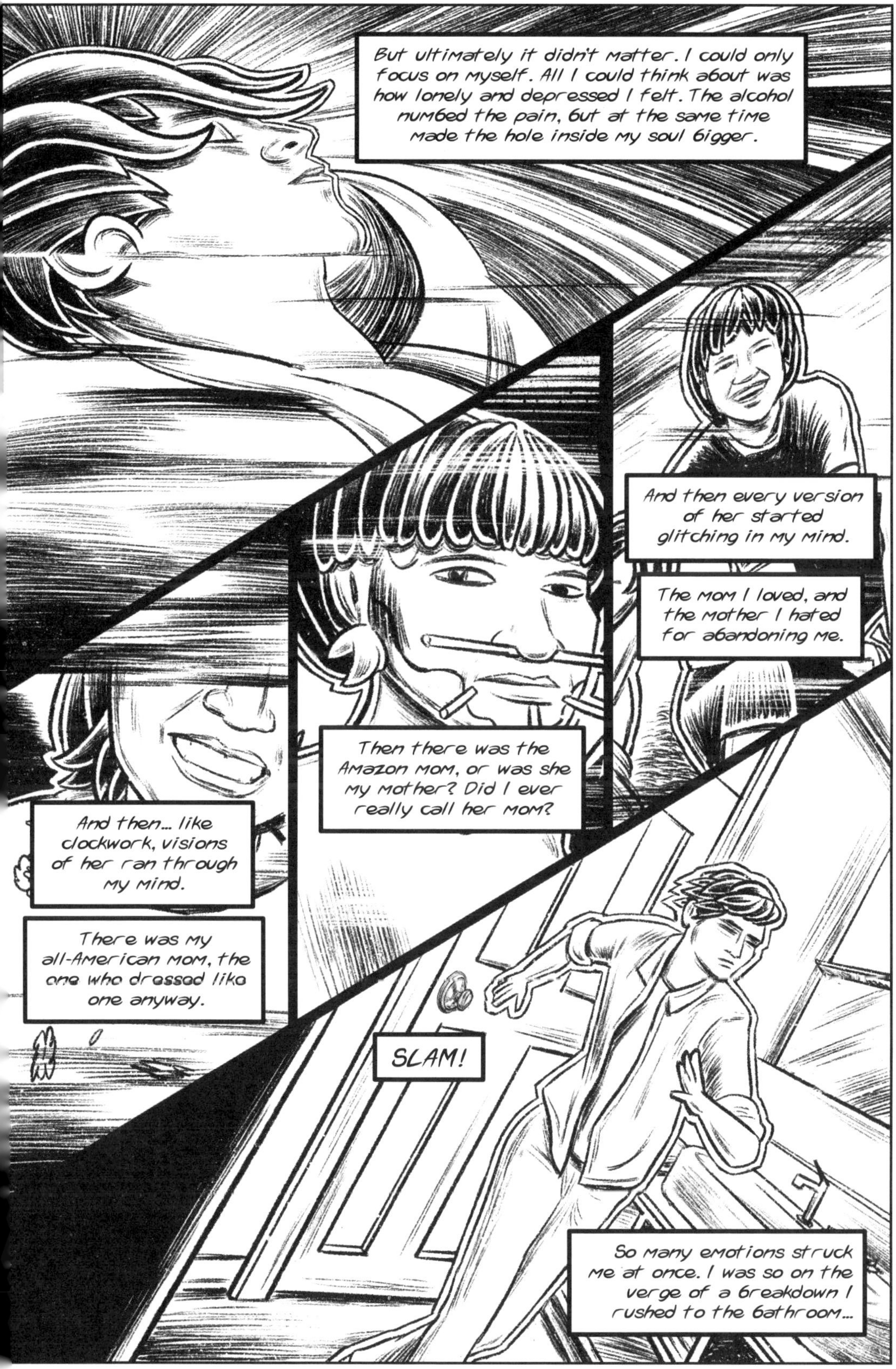

But ultimately it didn't matter. I could only focus on myself. All I could think about was how lonely and depressed I felt. The alcohol numbed the pain, but at the same time made the hole inside my soul bigger.
And then every version of her started glitching in my mind.
The mom I loved, and the mother I hated for abandoning me.
Then there was the Amazon mom, or was she my mother? Did I ever really call her mom?
And then... like clockwork, visions of her ran through my mind.
There was my all-American mom, the one who dressed like one anyway.
SLAM!
So many emotions struck me at once. I was so on the verge of a breakdown I rushed to the bathroom...

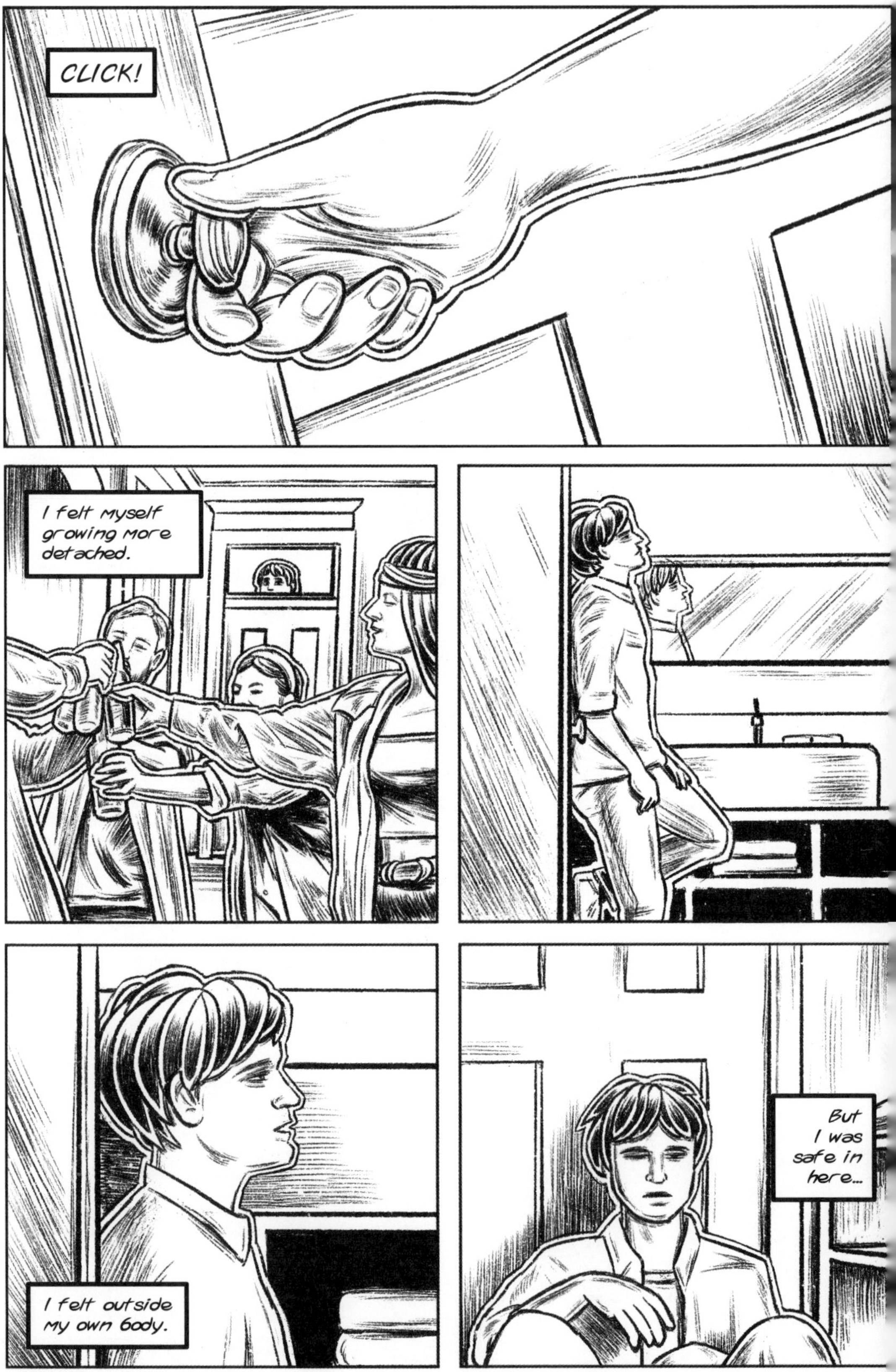
CLICK!
I felt myself growing more detached.
I felt outside my own body.
But I was safe in here...

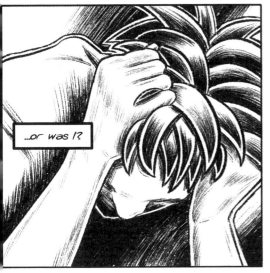

...or was I?

My body quivered. Cold sweats came from every part of me at once.

I was terrified.

Mom. Why?

Why did you LEAVE?!!

After who-knows-how-long of lying there, I crawled my way up and looked at myself in the mirror.

I looked beyond terrible and felt insane. It hit me that I hadn't slept in 24 hours

And I was so ashamed. I had to get out of there but didn't want anybody to see me.

I got a few scratches, but with sloth-like movements I sort of slid my way out of the window.

Honestly. What the hell was i thinking? Did I actually think I was going to be able to drive?

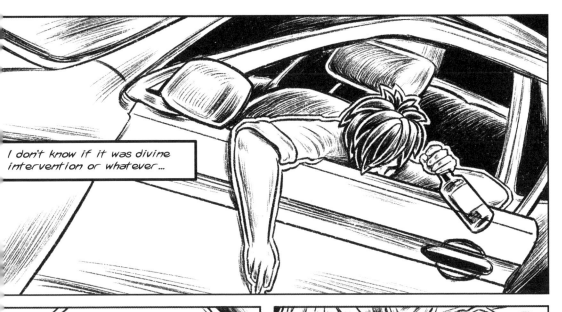

I don't know if it was divine intervention or whatever...

...but somehow I strapped myself in,

got the car started,

and made my way. All I wanted to do was go home, crawl into bed, and forget this ever happened.

I remembered this back road. I was pretty sure it led to the main highway?

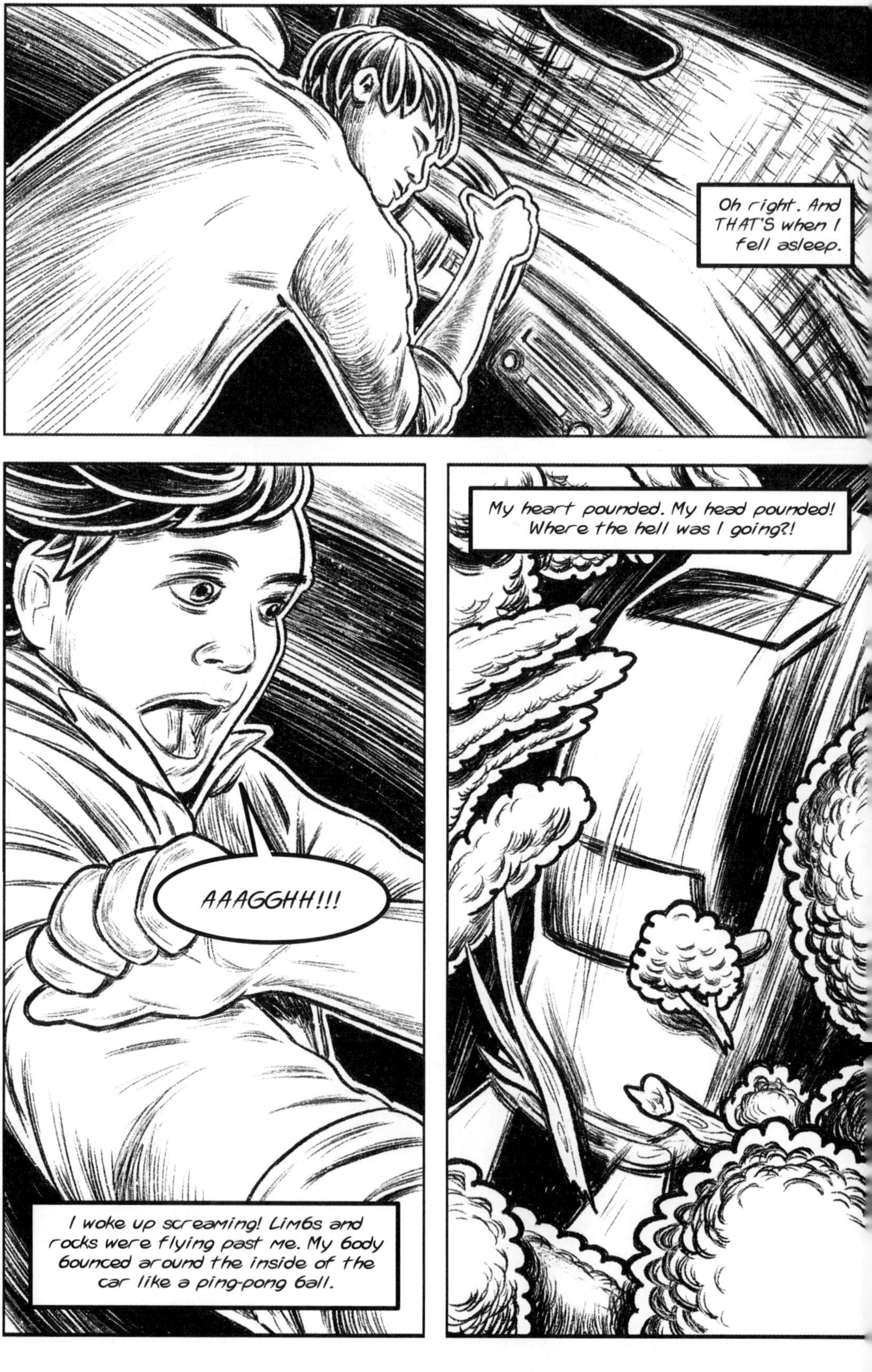
Oh right. And THAT'S when I fell asleep.
AAAGGHH!!!
I woke up screaming! Limbs and rocks were flying past me. My body bounced around the inside of the car like a ping-pong ball.
My heart pounded. My head pounded! Where the hell was I going?!

I remember I just kept hurtling for what felt like an eternity.

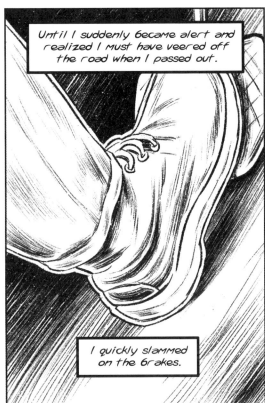

Until I suddenly became alert and realized I must have veered off the road when I passed out.

I quickly slammed on the brakes.

My whole body jerked forward as I landed in a ditch. The windshield shattered completely, and the airbags deployed.

The car had tipped onto its right side.

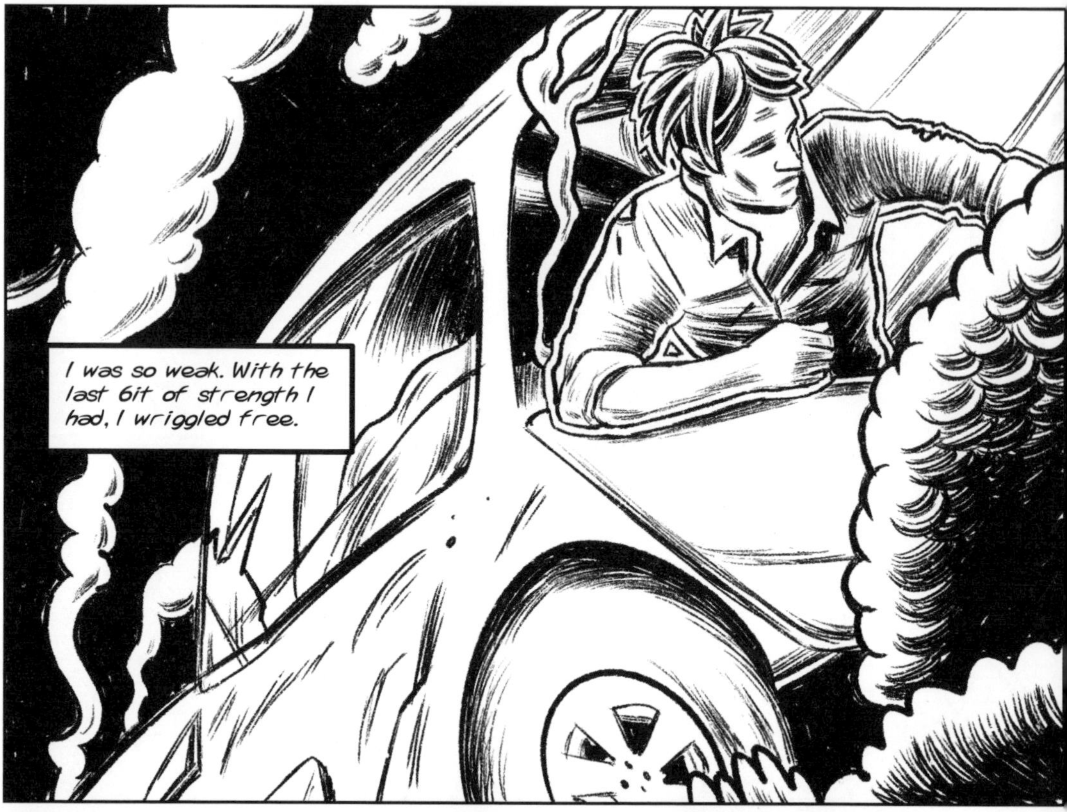
I was so weak. With the last bit of strength I had, I wriggled free.

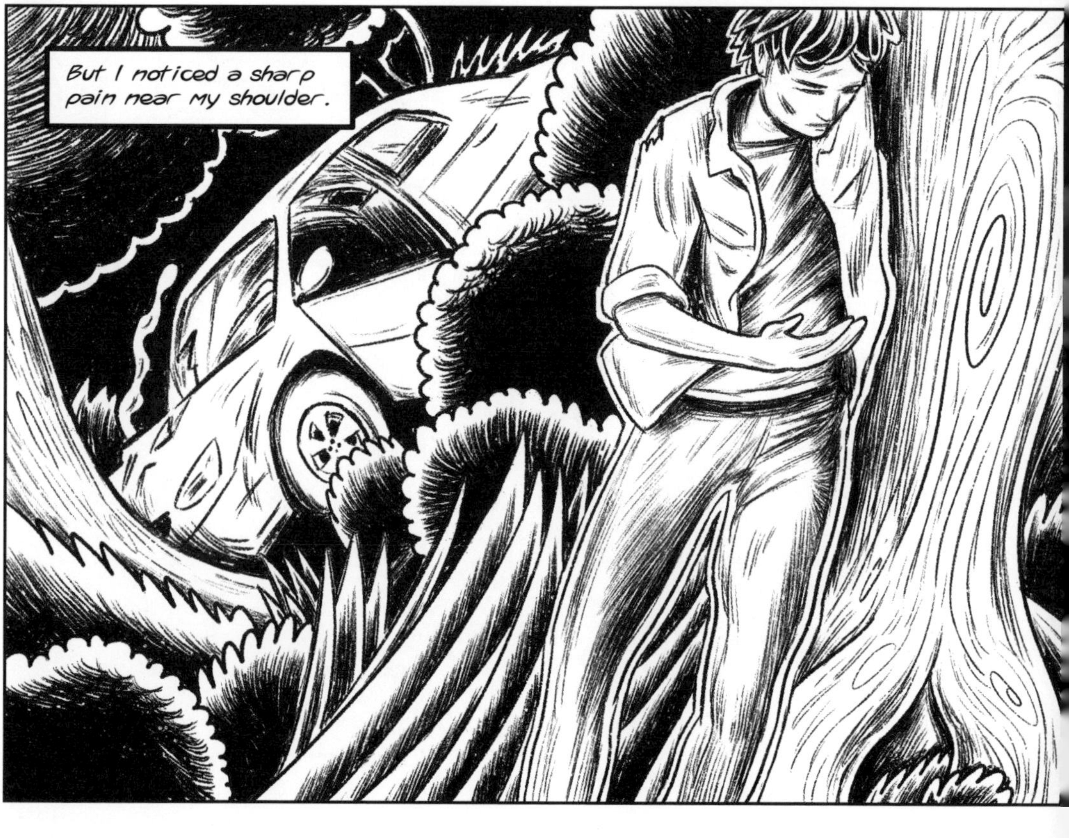
But I noticed a sharp pain near my shoulder.

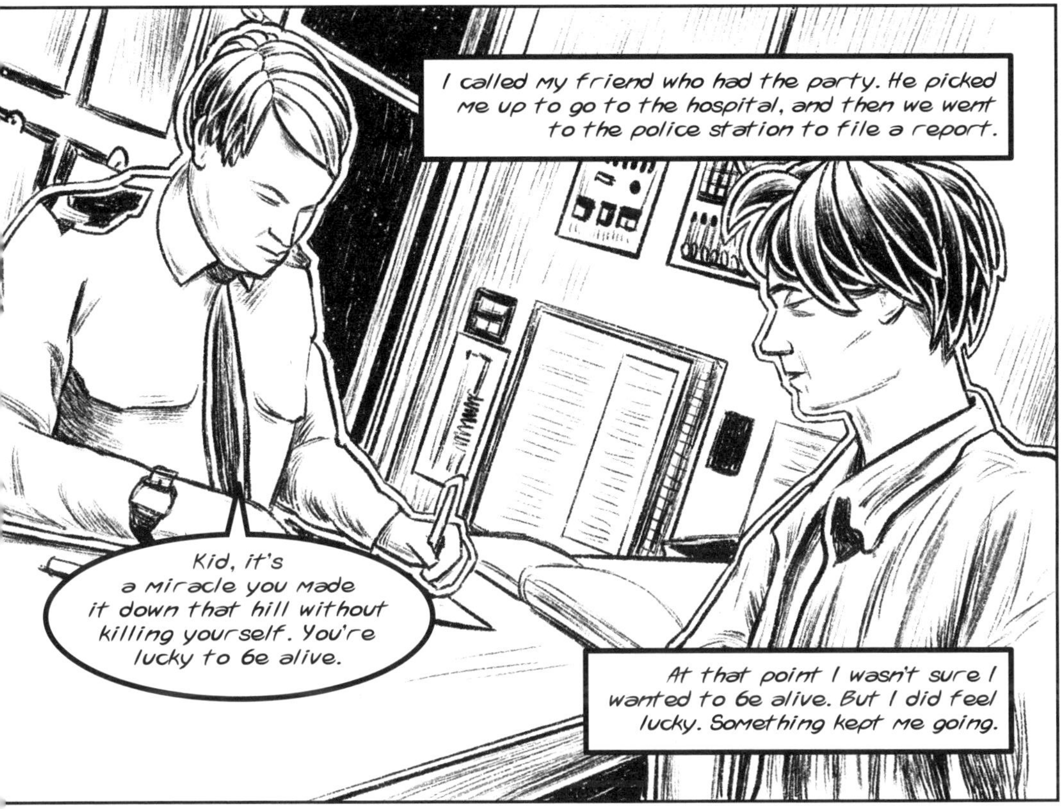
I called my friend who had the party. He picked me up to go to the hospital, and then we went to the police station to file a report.
Kid, it's a miracle you made it down that hill without killing yourself. You're lucky to be alive.
At that point I wasn't sure I wanted to be alive. But I did feel lucky. Something kept me going.

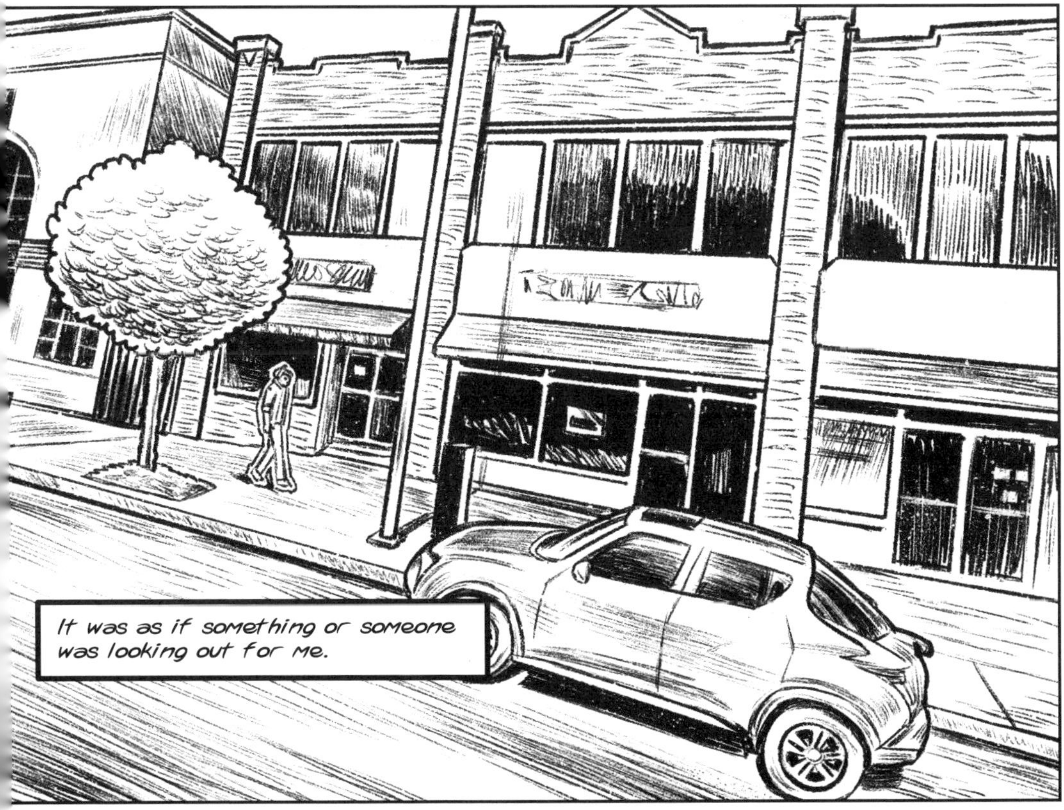
It was as if something or someone was looking out for me.

chapter 11

DRIFT

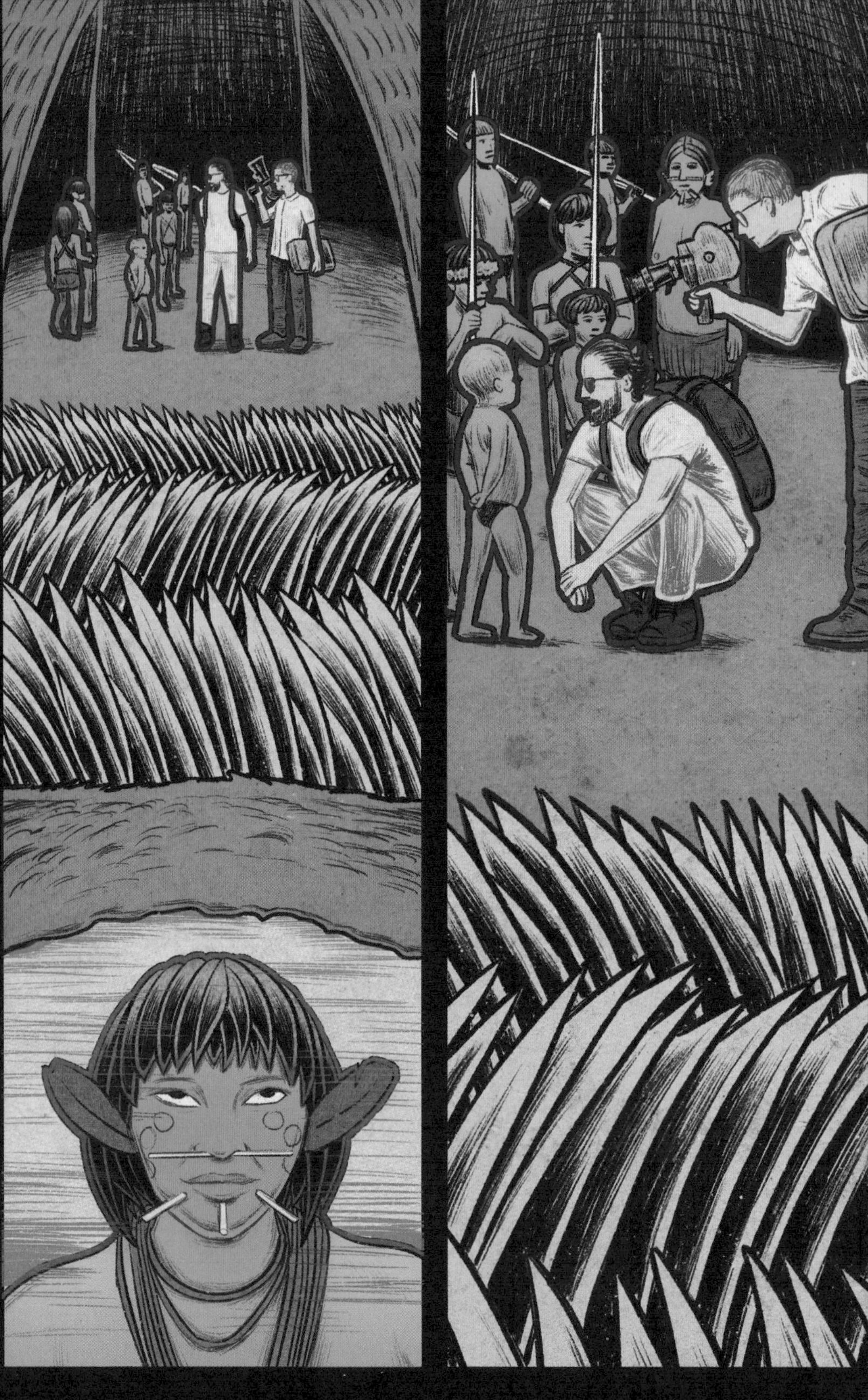

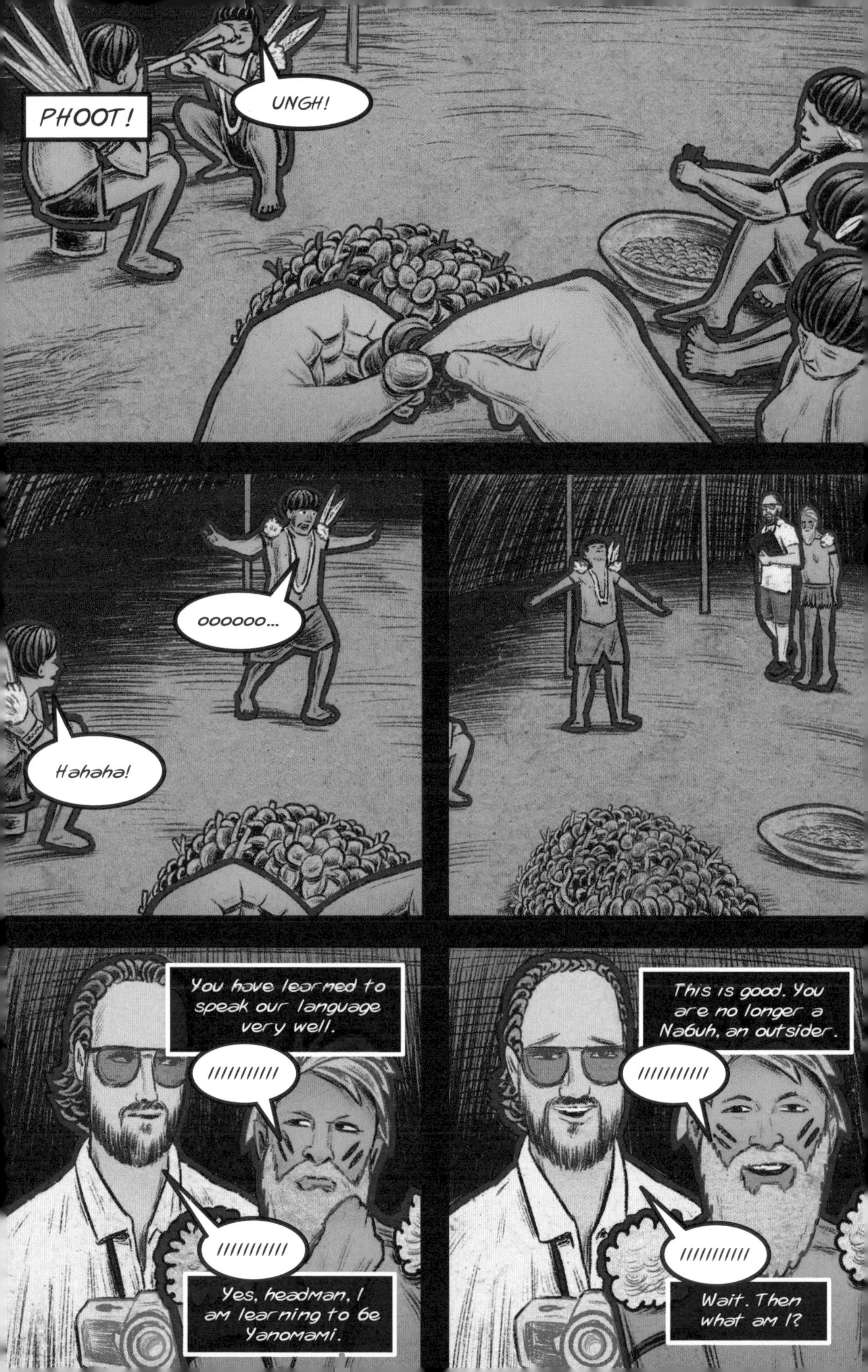
PHOOT!
UNGH!
OOOOOO...
Hahaha!
You have learned to speak our language very well.
//////////
//////////
Yes, headman, I am learning to be Yanomami.
This is good. You are no longer a Nabuh, an outsider.
//////////
//////////
Wait. Then what am I?

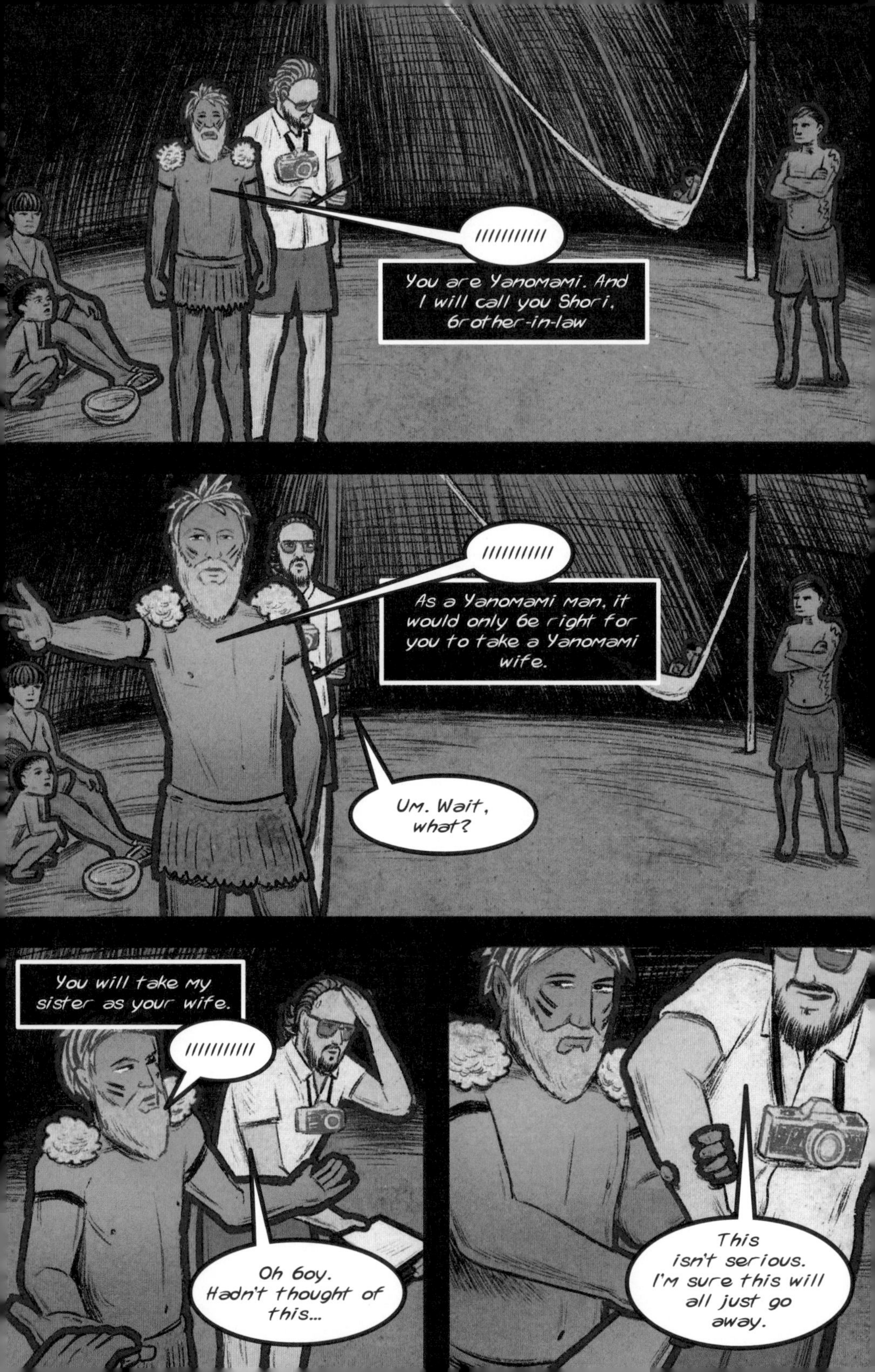

IIIIIIIIIII
You are Yanomami. And I will call you Shori, brother-in-law
IIIIIIIIIII
As a Yanomami man, it would only be right for you to take a Yanomami wife.
Um. Wait, what?
You will take my sister as your wife.
IIIIIIIIIII
Oh boy. Hadn't thought of this...
This isn't serious. I'm sure this will all just go away.

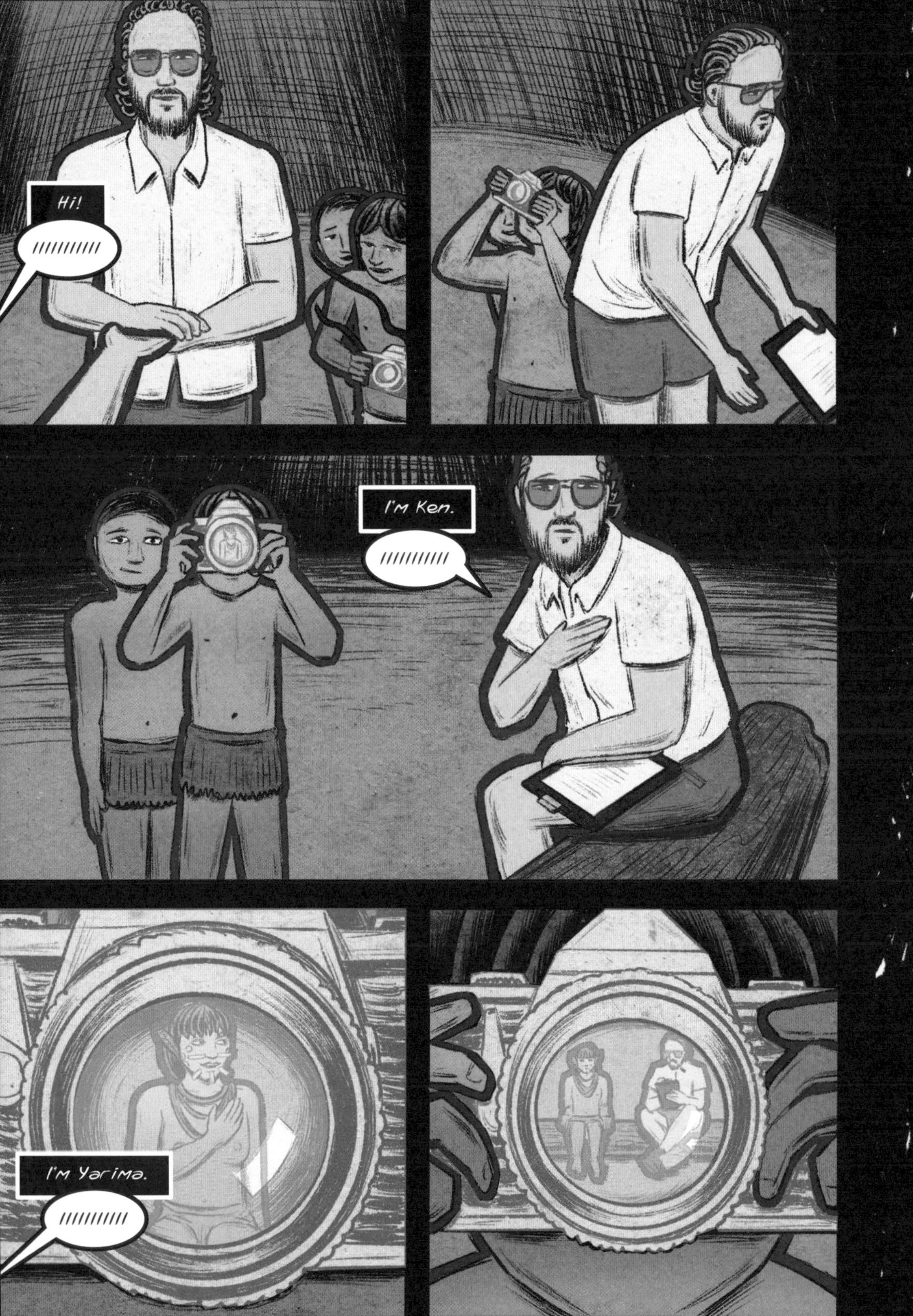
Hi!
//////////
I'm Ken.
//////////
I'm Yarima.
//////////

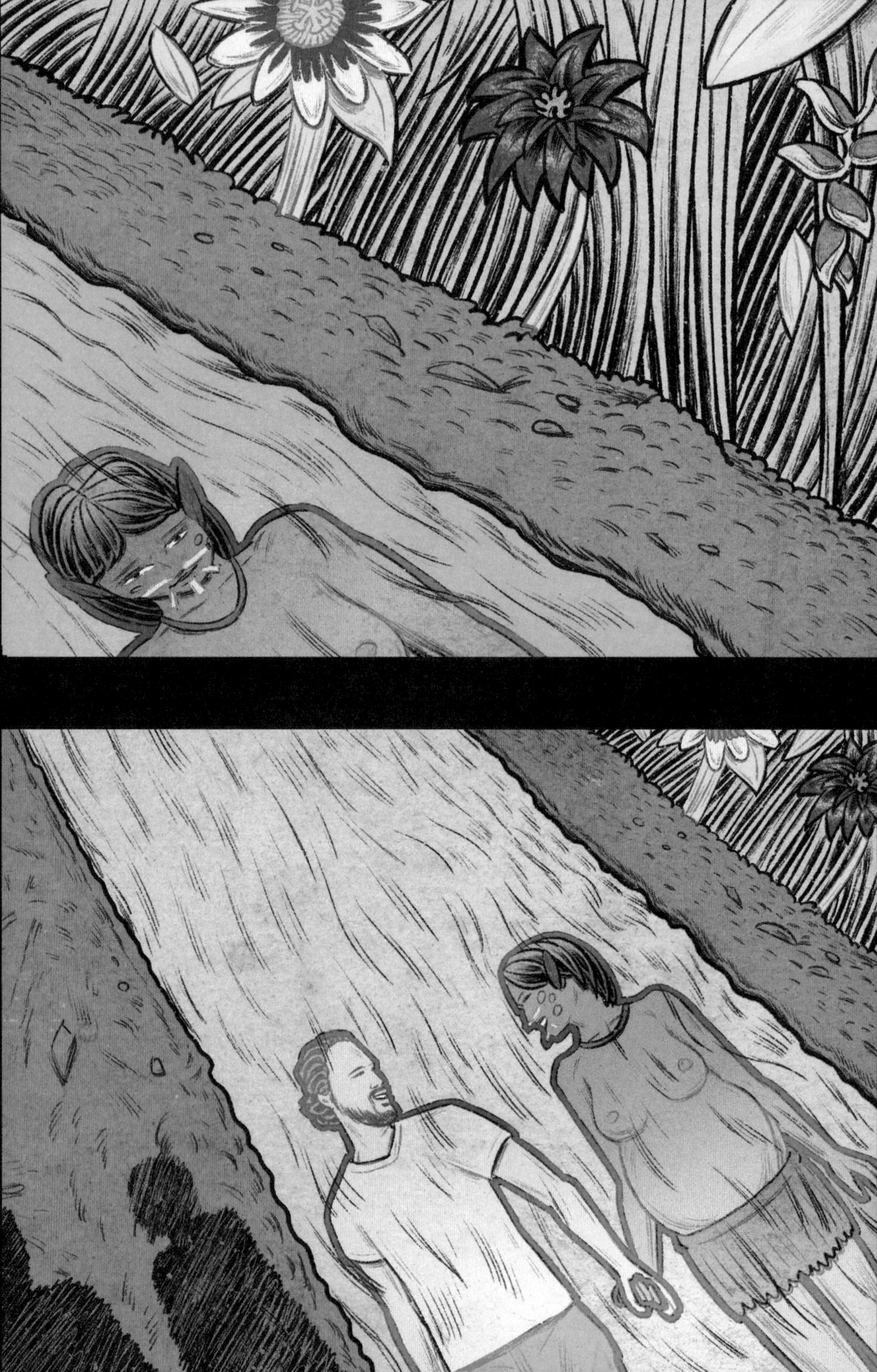

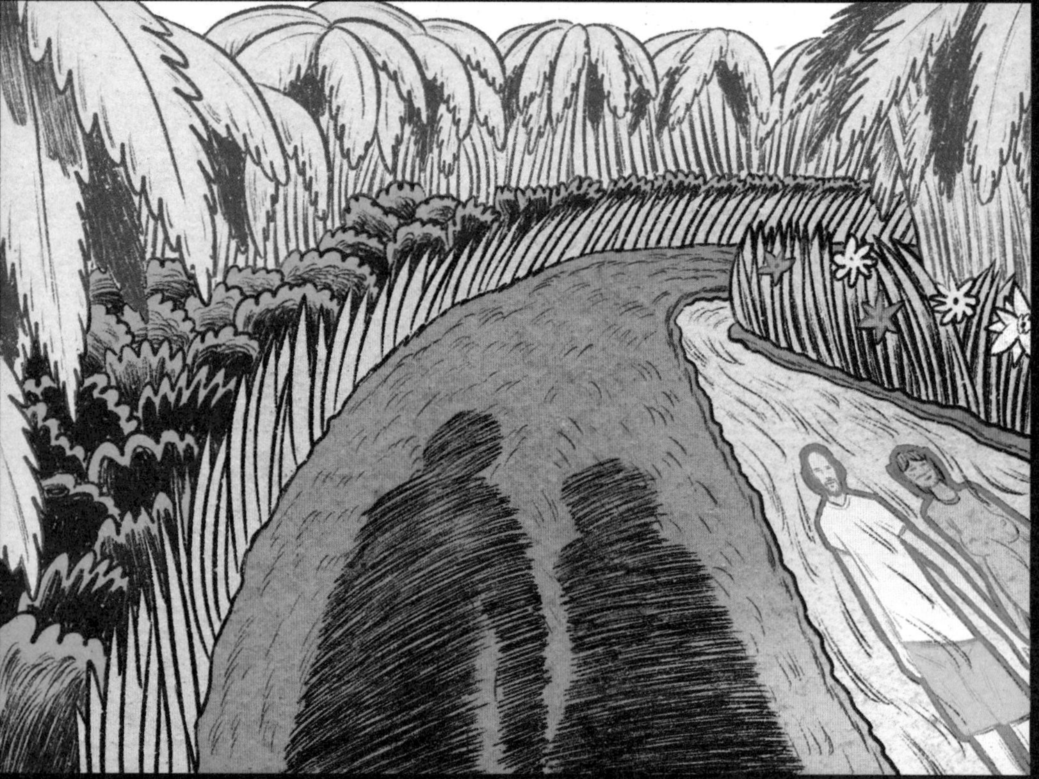

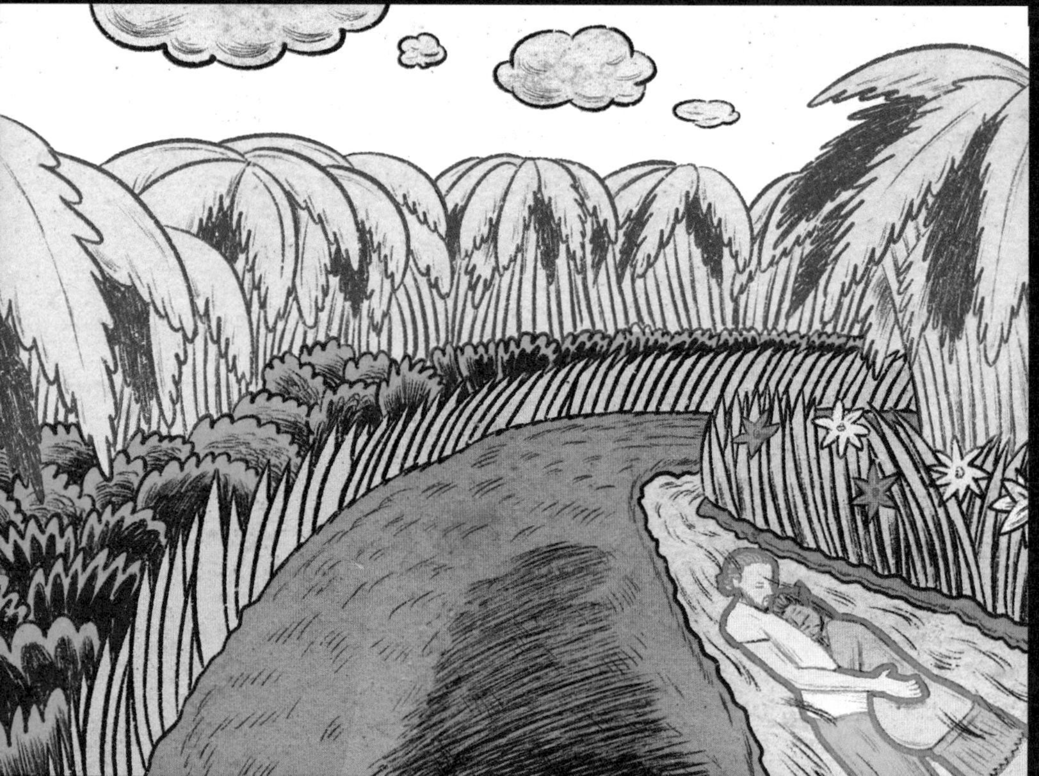

chapter12

WAYUMI

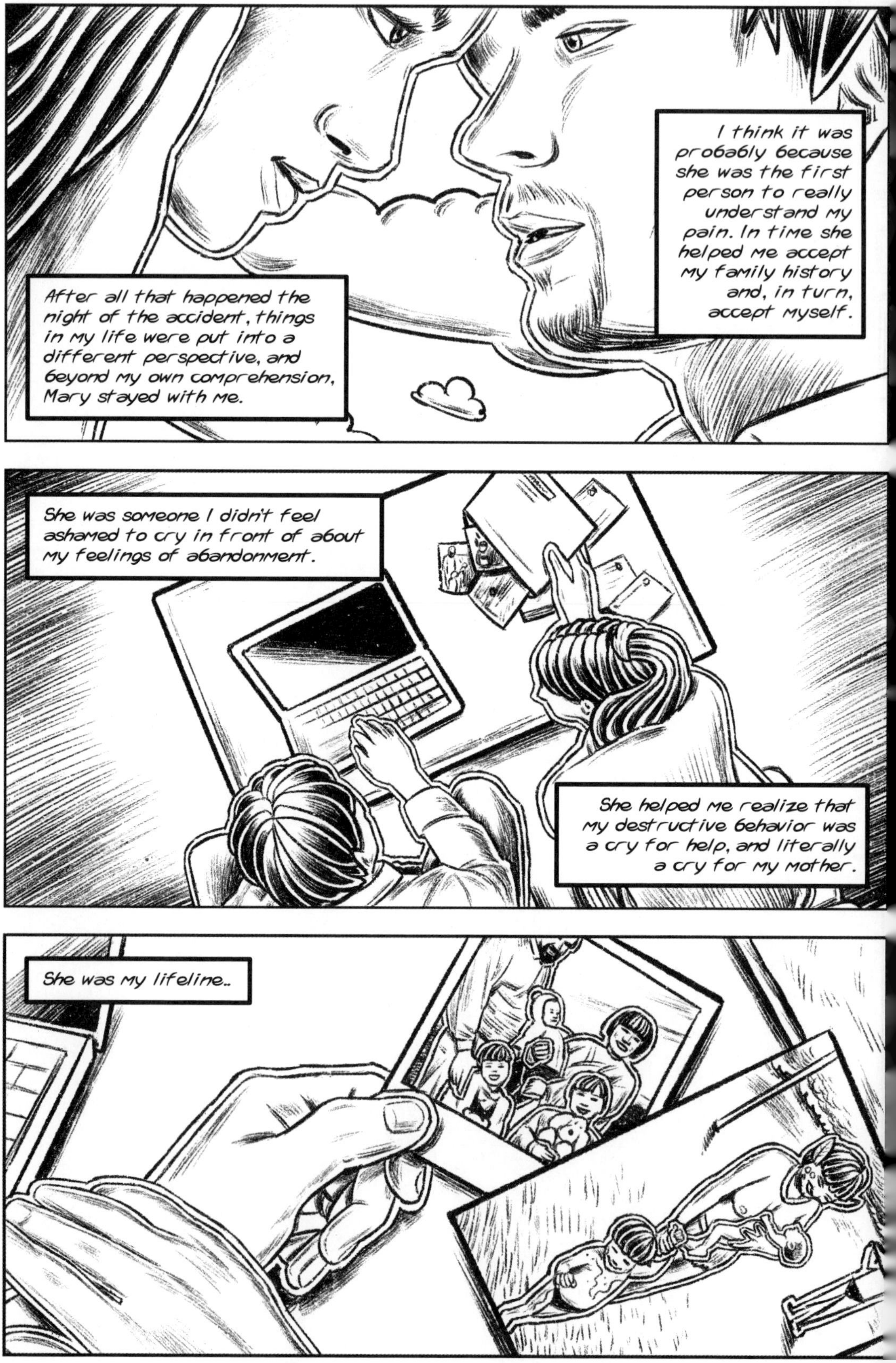
After all that happened the night of the accident, things in my life were put into a different perspective, and beyond my own comprehension, Mary stayed with me.
I think it was probably because she was the first person to really understand my pain. In time she helped me accept my family history and, in turn, accept myself.
She was someone I didn't feel ashamed to cry in front of about my feelings of abandonment.
She helped me realize that my destructive behavior was a cry for help, and literally a cry for my mother.
She was my lifeline..

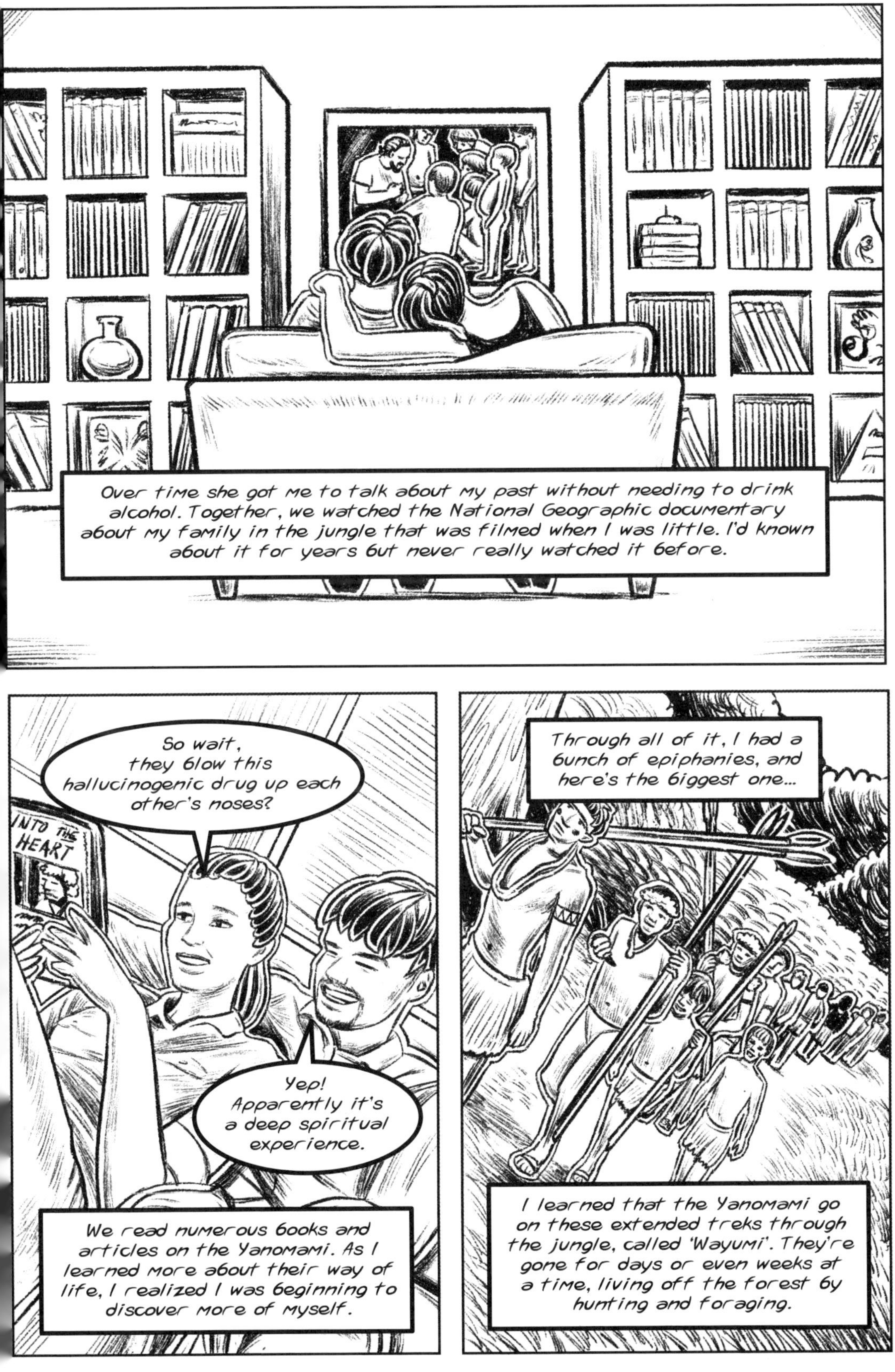
Over time she got me to talk about my past without needing to drink alcohol. Together, we watched the National Geographic documentary about my family in the jungle that was filmed when I was little. I'd known about it for years but never really watched it before.
So wait, they blow this hallucinogenic drug up each other's noses?
INTO THE HEART
Yep! Apparently it's a deep spiritual experience.
We read numerous books and articles on the Yanomami. As I learned more about their way of life, I realized I was beginning to discover more of myself.
Through all of it, I had a bunch of epiphanies, and here's the biggest one...
I learned that the Yanomami go on these extended treks through the jungle, called 'Wayumi'. They're gone for days or even weeks at a time, living off the forest by hunting and foraging.

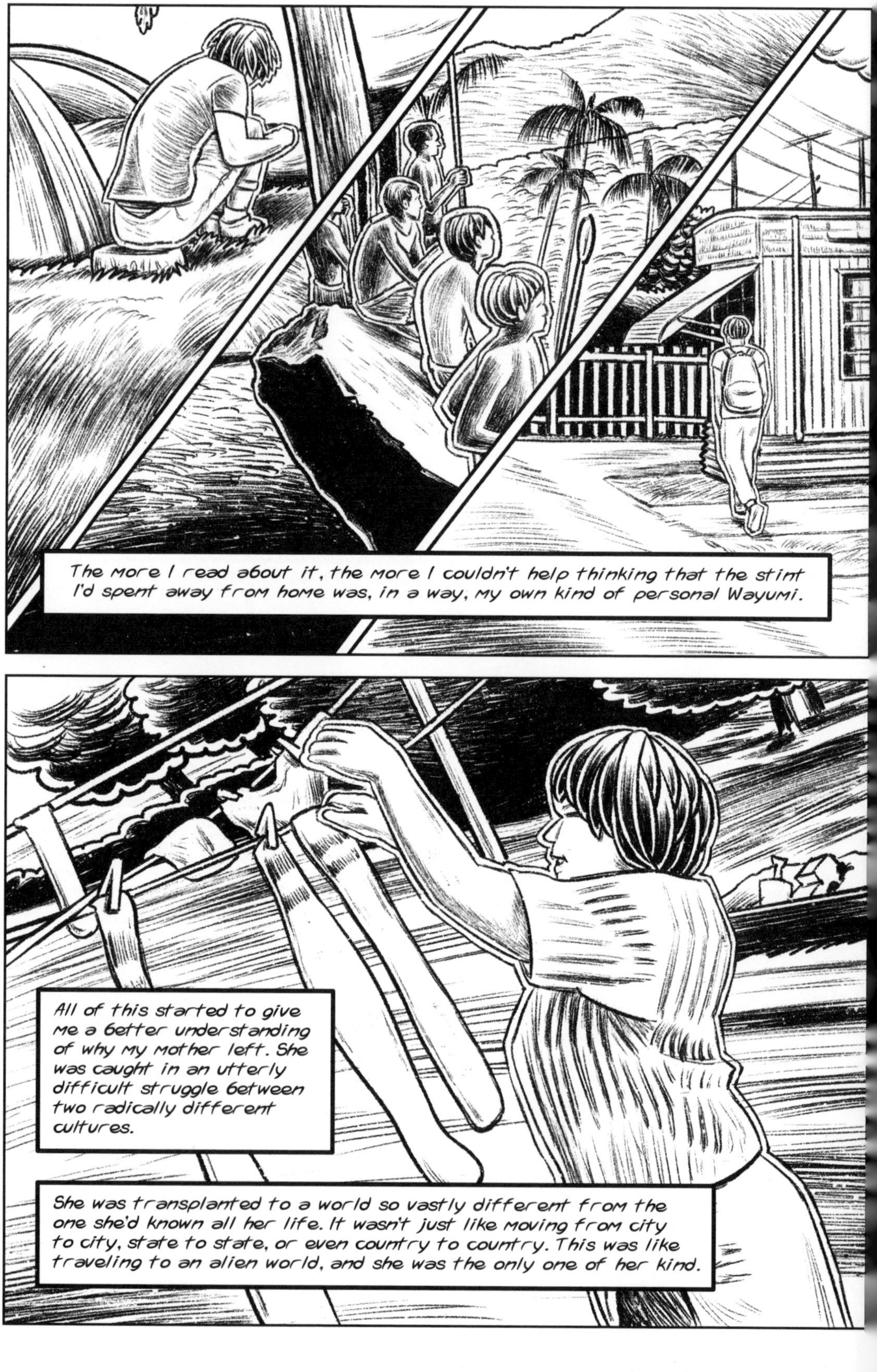
The more I read about it, the more I couldn't help thinking that the stint I'd spent away from home was, in a way, my own kind of personal Wayumi.
All of this started to give me a better understanding of why my mother left. She was caught in an utterly difficult struggle between two radically different cultures.
She was transplanted to a world so vastly different from the one she'd known all her life. It wasn't just like moving from city to city, state to state, or even country to country. This was like traveling to an alien world, and she was the only one of her kind.

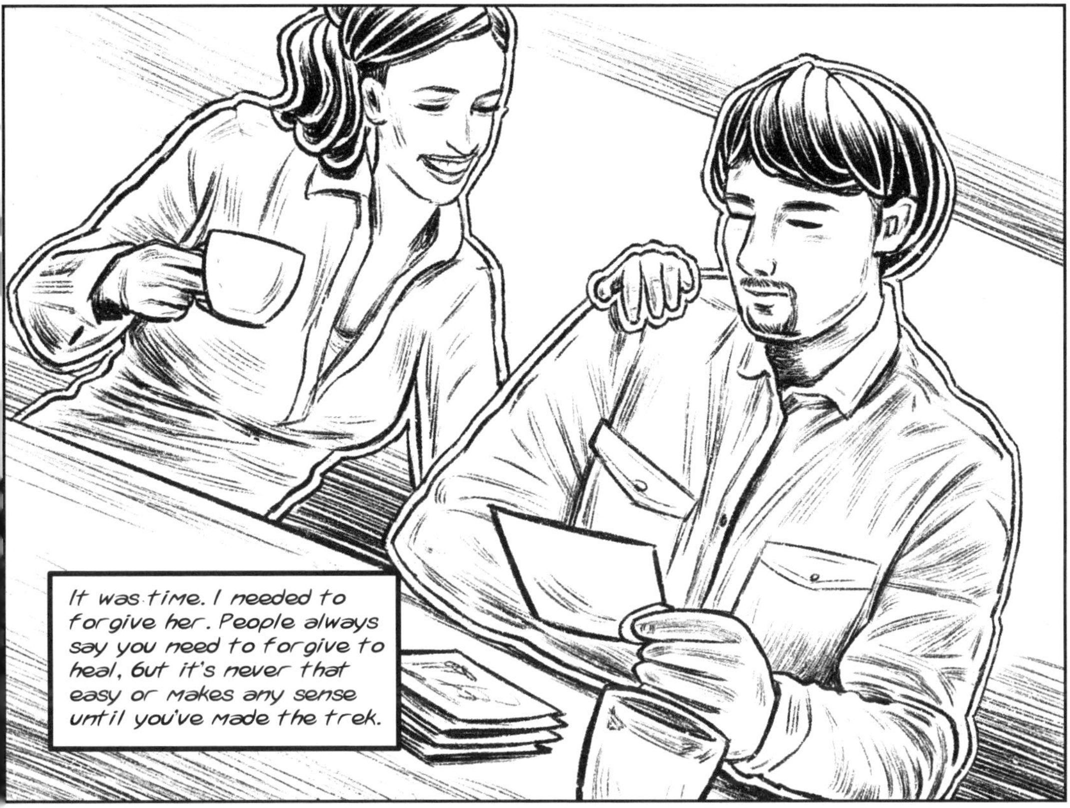
It was time. I needed to forgive her. People always say you need to forgive to heal, but it's never that easy or makes any sense until you've made the trek.

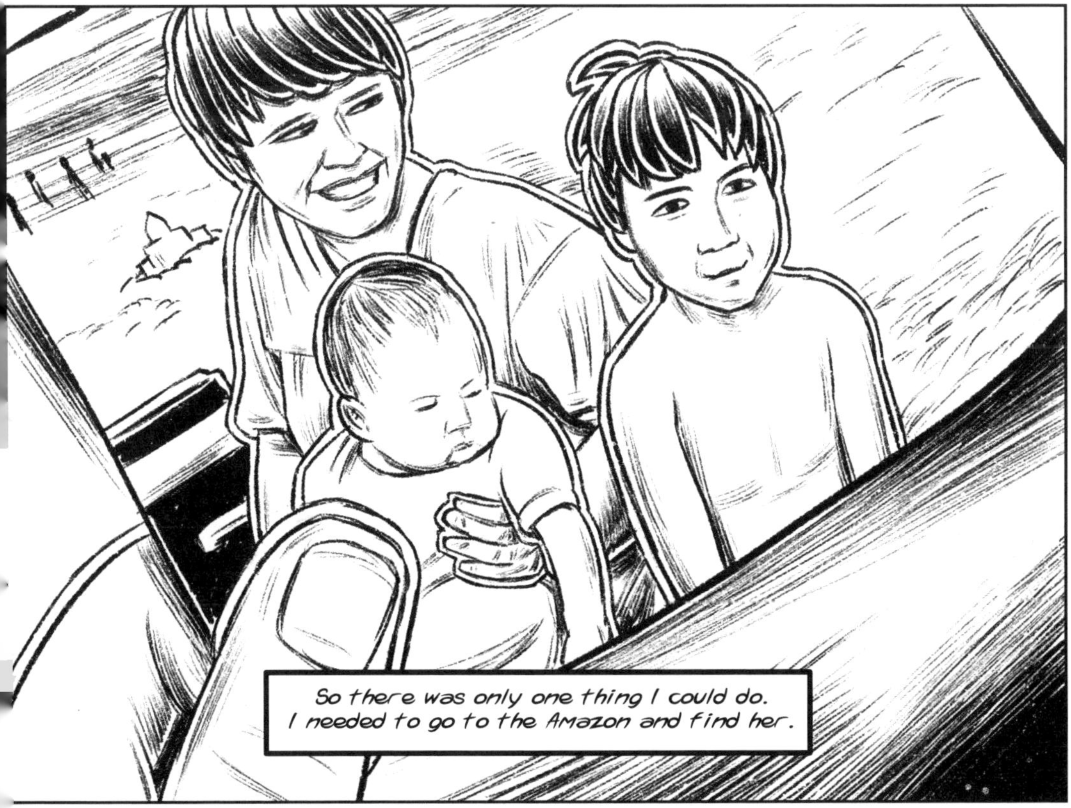
So there was only one thing I could do. I needed to go to the Amazon and find her.

chapter 13

UPROOTED

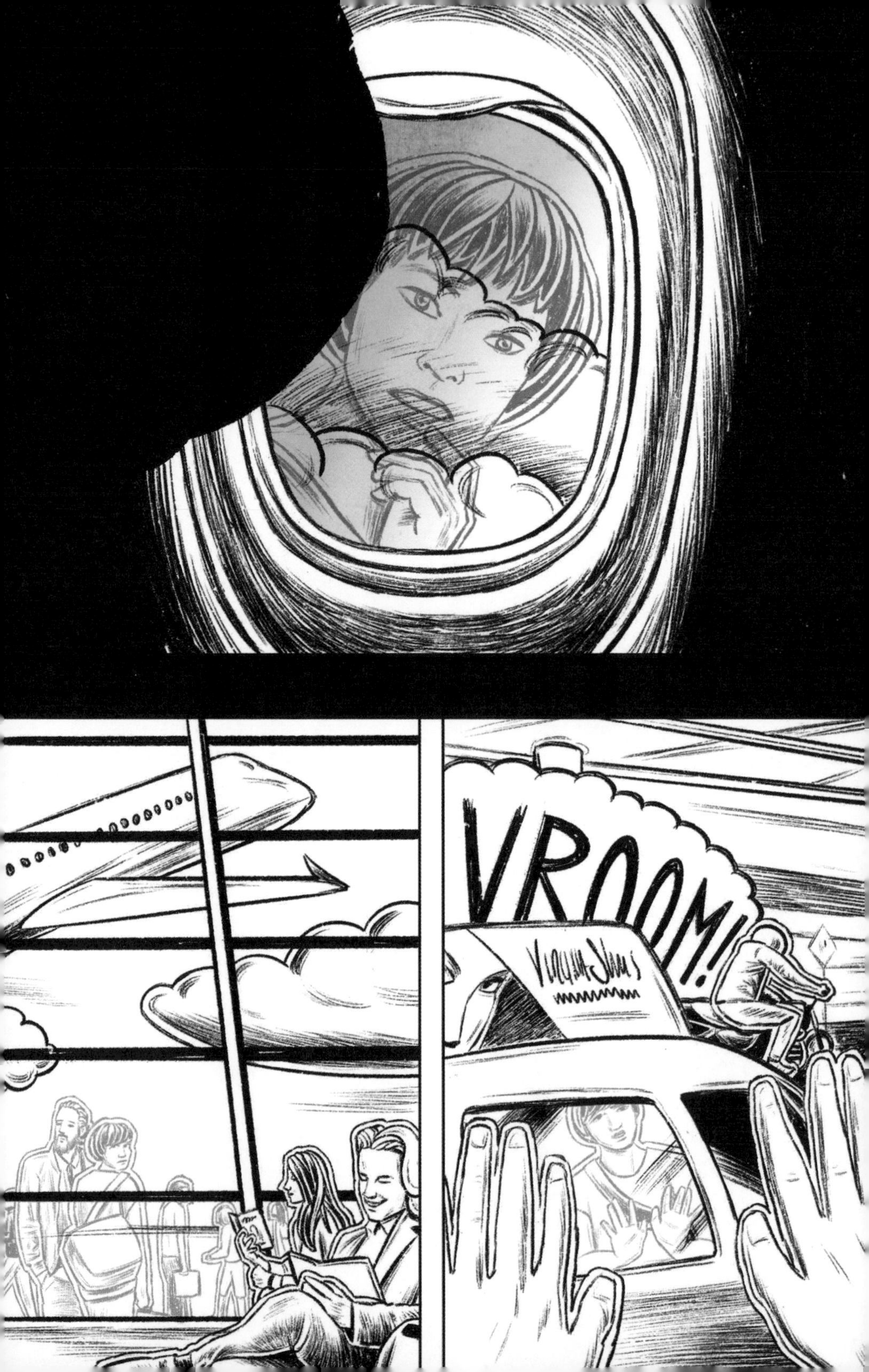
VROOM!

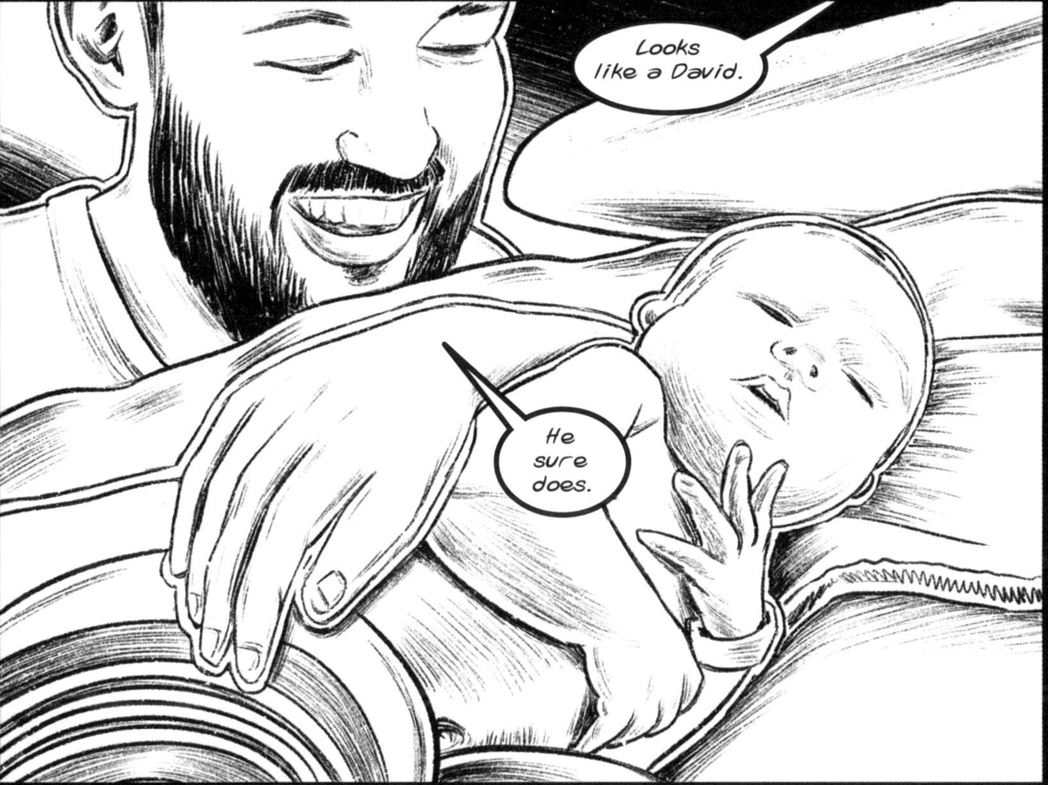
Looks like a David.
He sure does.

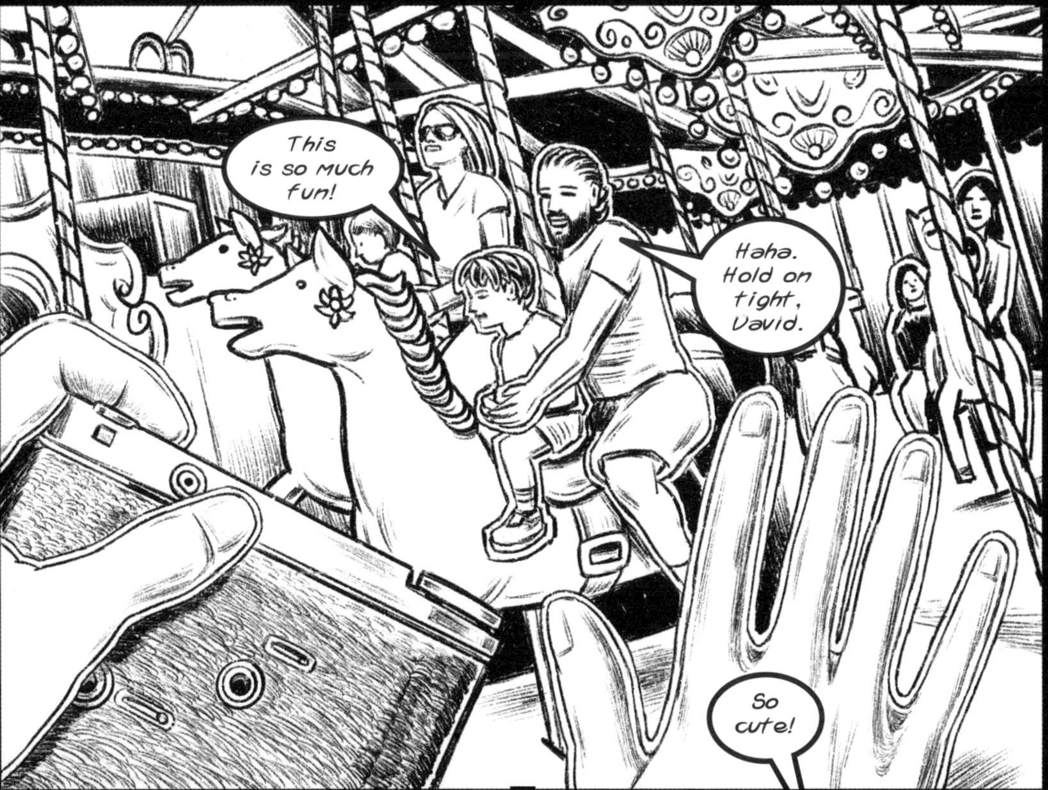
This is so much fun!
Haha. Hold on tight, David.
So cute!

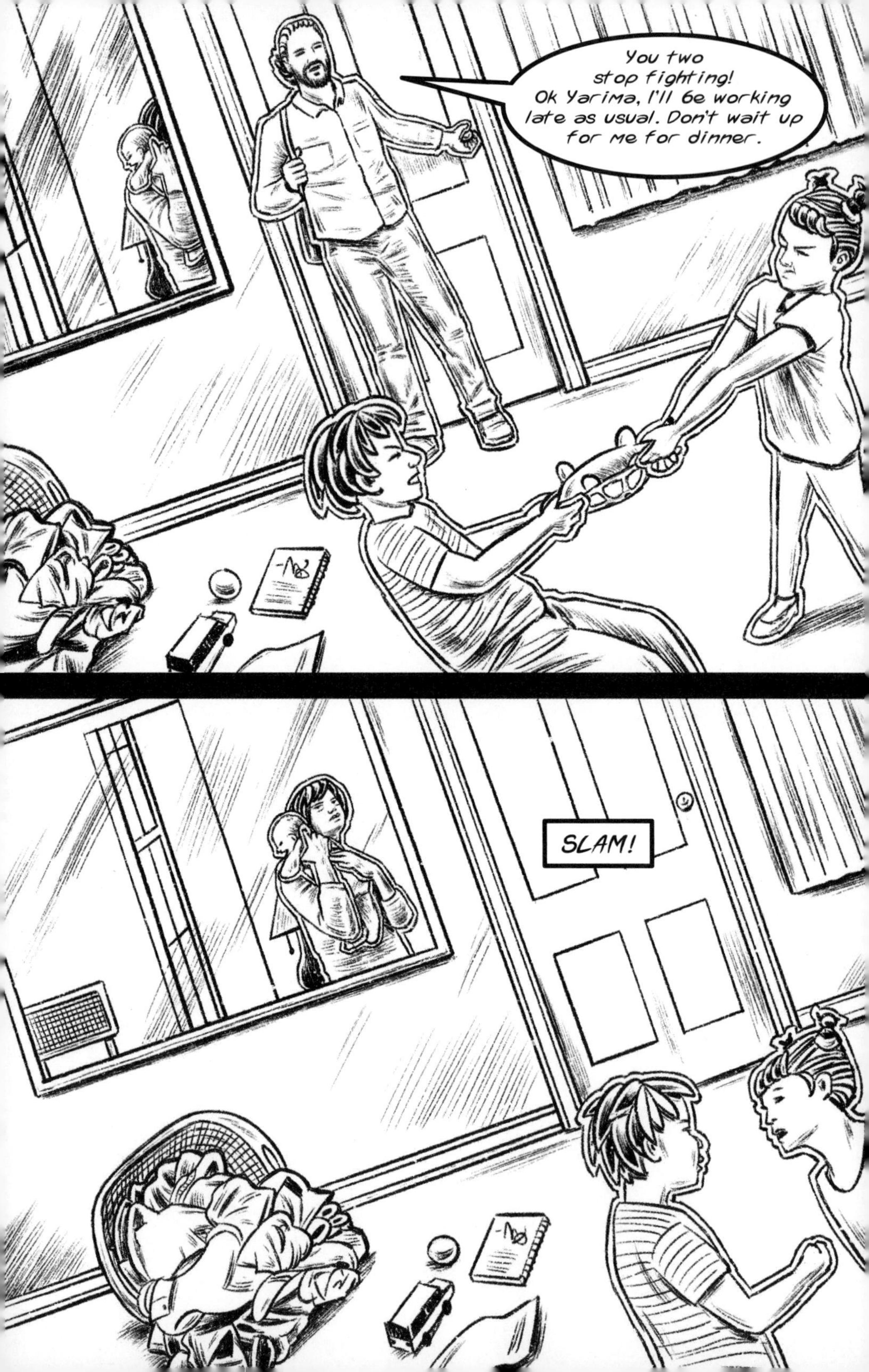
You two stop fighting! Ok Yarima, I'll 6e working late as usual. Don't wait up for me for dinner.
SLAM!

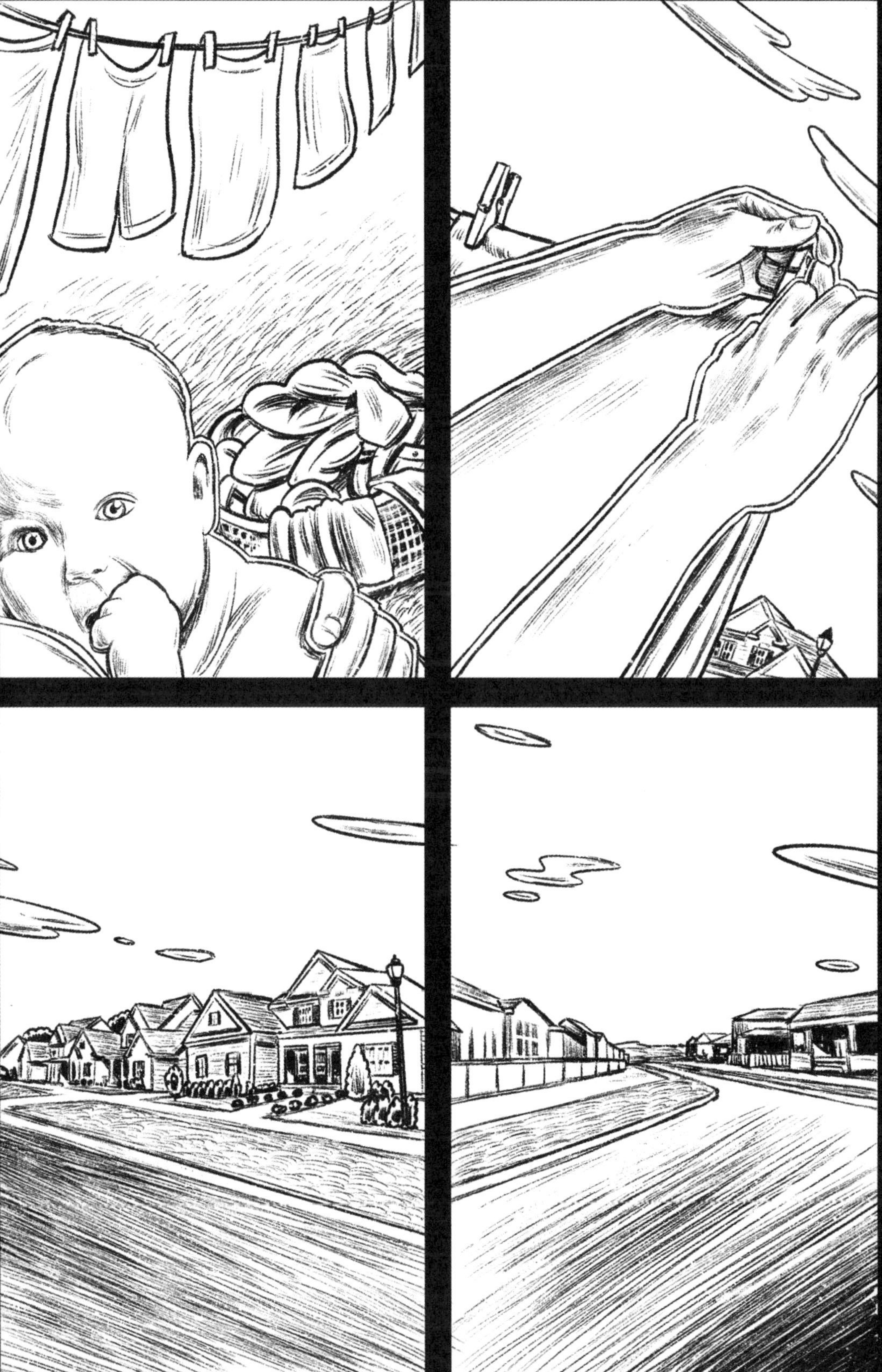

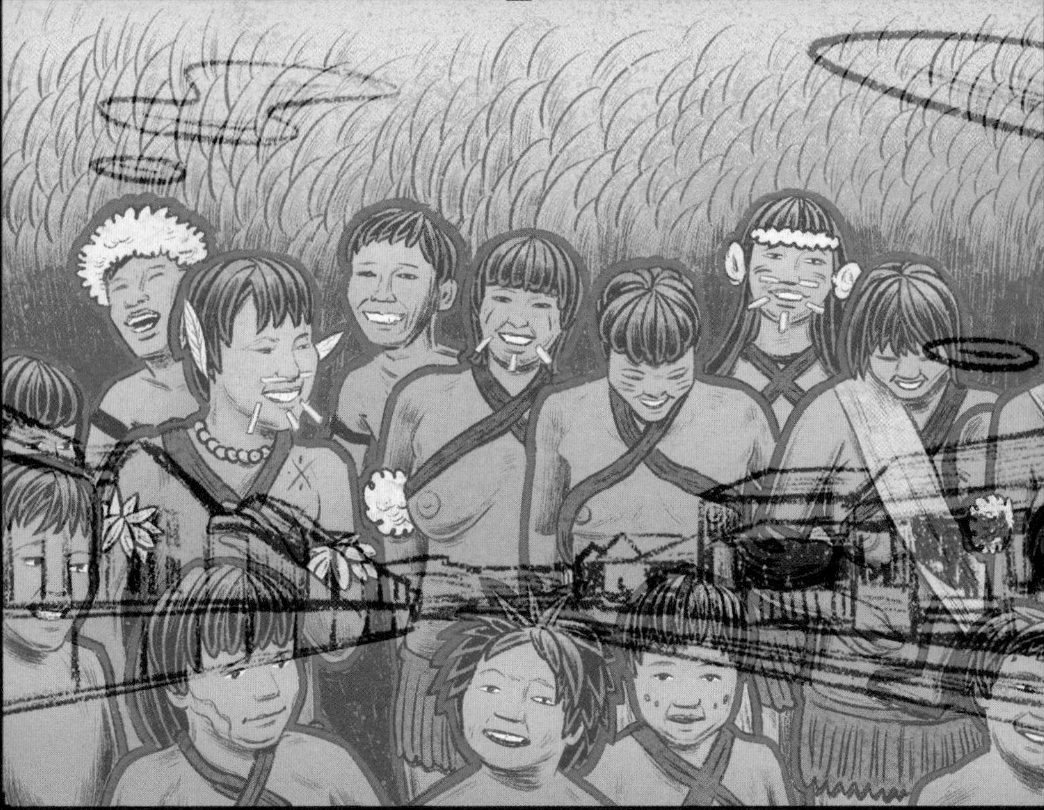
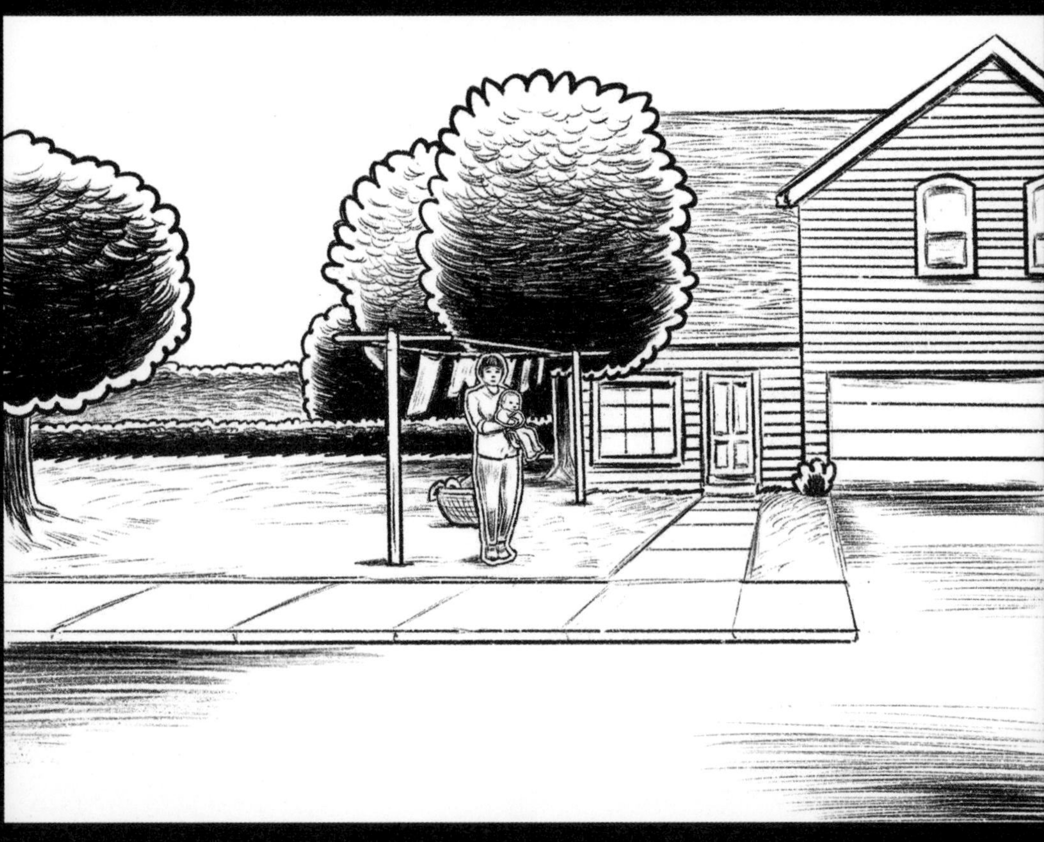

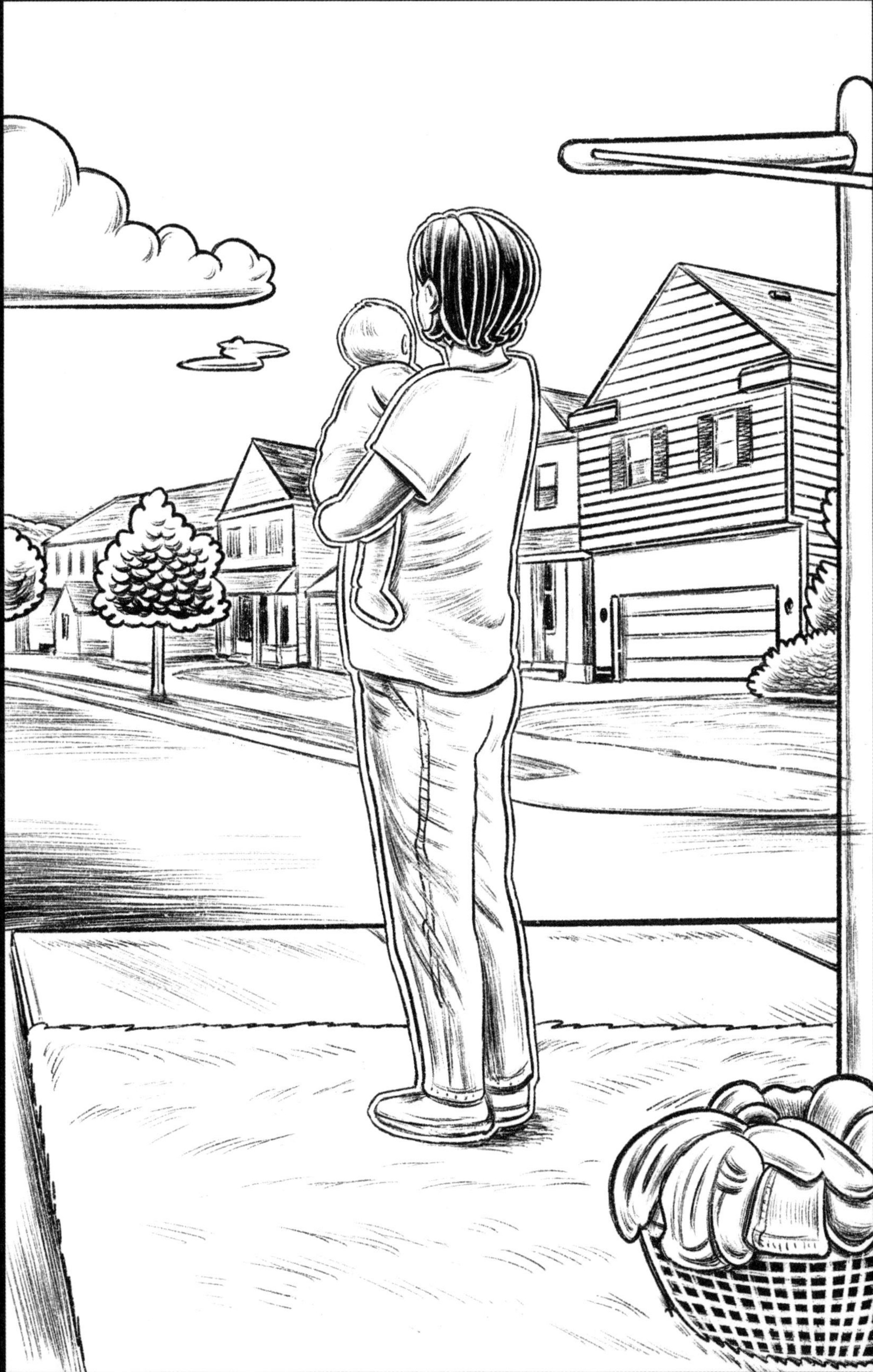

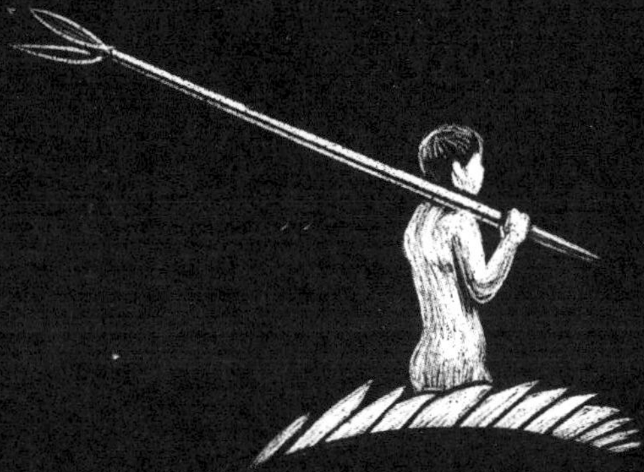

chapter 14

CONTACT

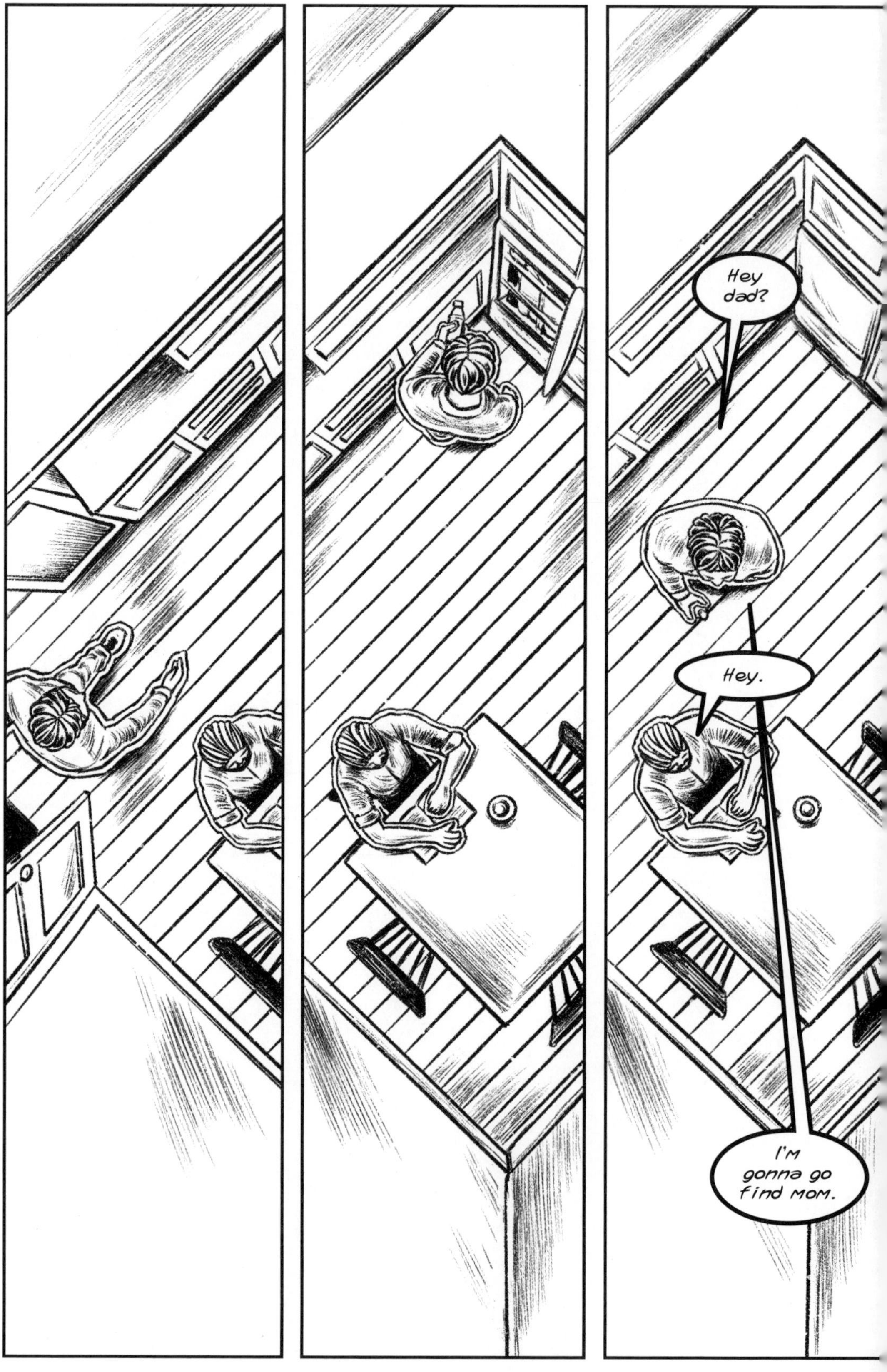
Hey dad?
Hey.
I'm gonna go find MOM.

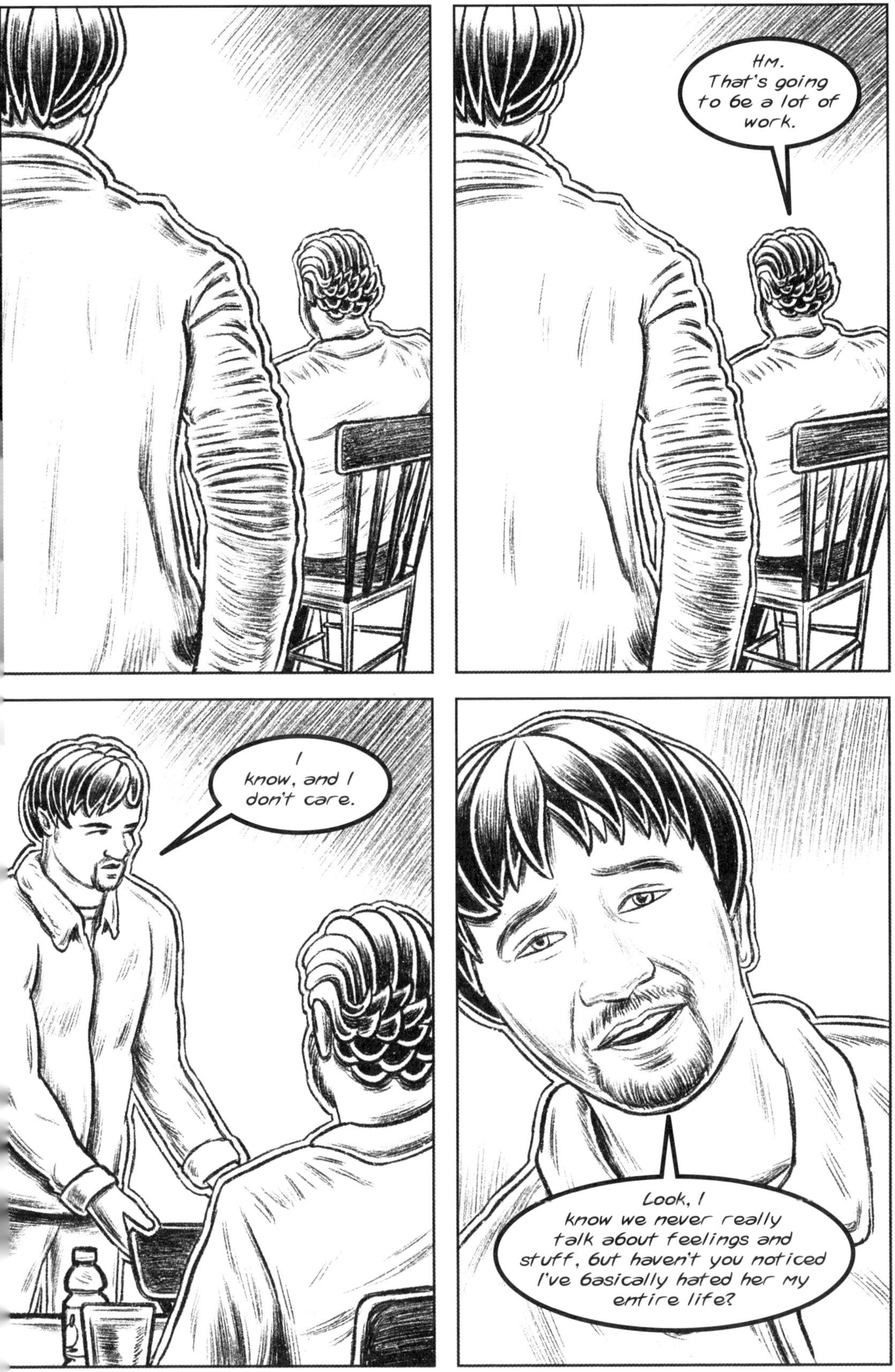
HM. That's going to be a lot of work.
I know, and I don't care.
Look, I know we never really talk about feelings and stuff, but haven't you noticed I've basically hated her my entire life?

Wait. Didn't you just say you wanted to go see her? Now I'm confused.

C'mon Dad, I'm serious.

Okay I know you've had a rough past couple of years. I figured it had something to do with it, but I had no idea you hated her.

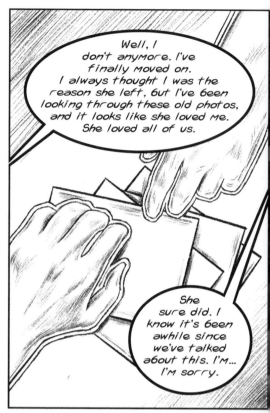

Well, I don't anymore. I've finally moved on. I always thought I was the reason she left, but I've been looking through these old photos, and it looks like she loved me. She loved all of us.

She sure did. I know it's been awhile since we've talked about this. I'm... I'm sorry.

Her name means 'wind'.

Her own mother died when she was very young, and she was raised by her aunt. So in a way you share a similar loss.

It was many years before she and I even started really showing affection for each other.

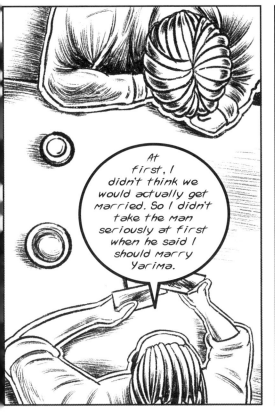

At first, I didn't think we would actually get married. So I didn't take the man seriously at first when he said I should marry Yarima.

But in time, she and I did fall in love.

And when you and the other kids came along, I felt that we could live with a foot in both worlds. Your mother kept biding her time and thought we'd eventually move back to the jungle permanently.

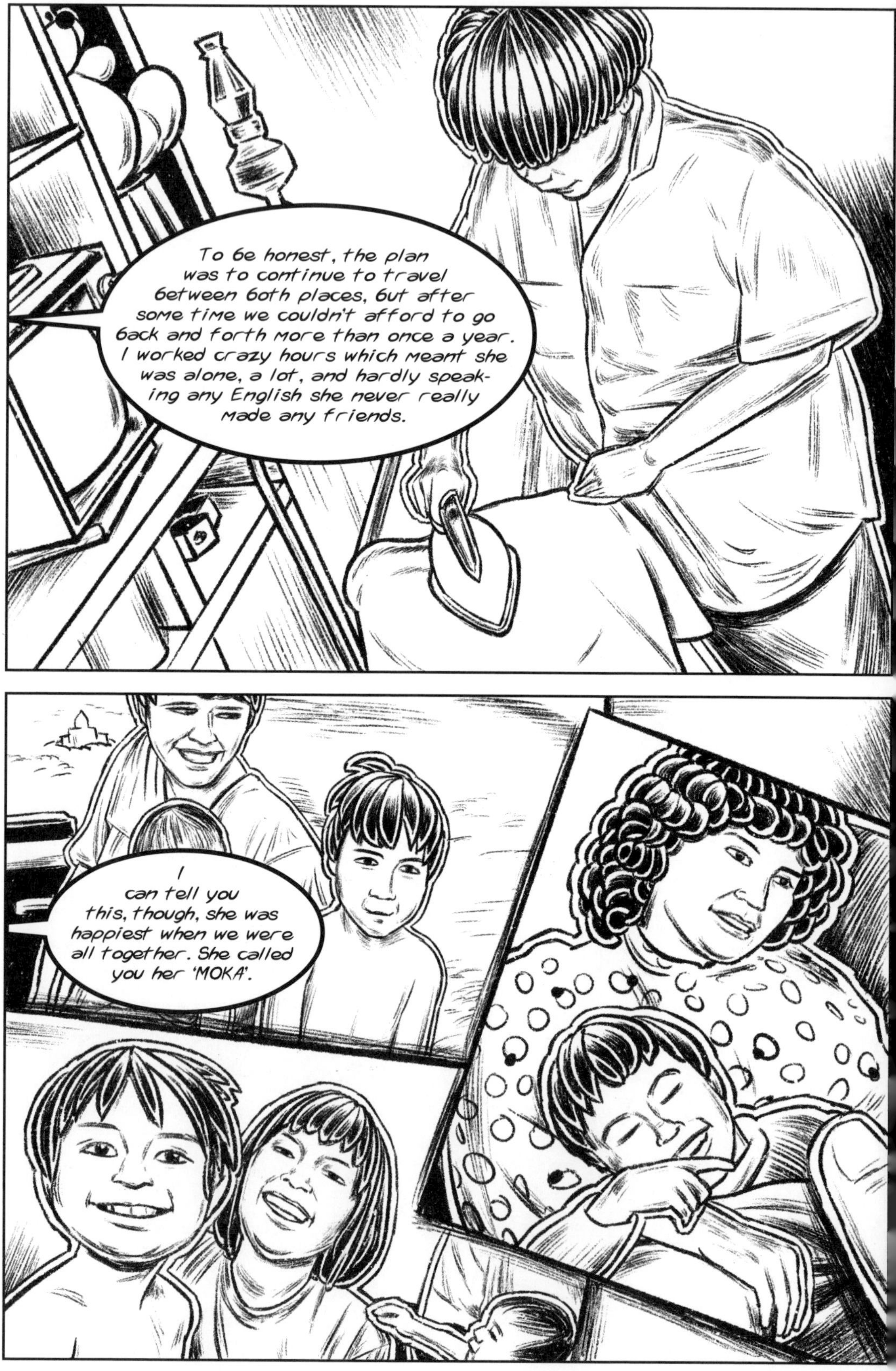
To 6e honest, the plan was to continue to travel 6etween 6oth places, 6ut after some time we couldn't afford to go 6ack and forth more than once a year. I worked crazy hours which meant she was alone, a lot, and hardly speak-ing any English she never really made any friends.
I can tell you this, though, she was happiest when we were all together. She called you her 'MOKA'.

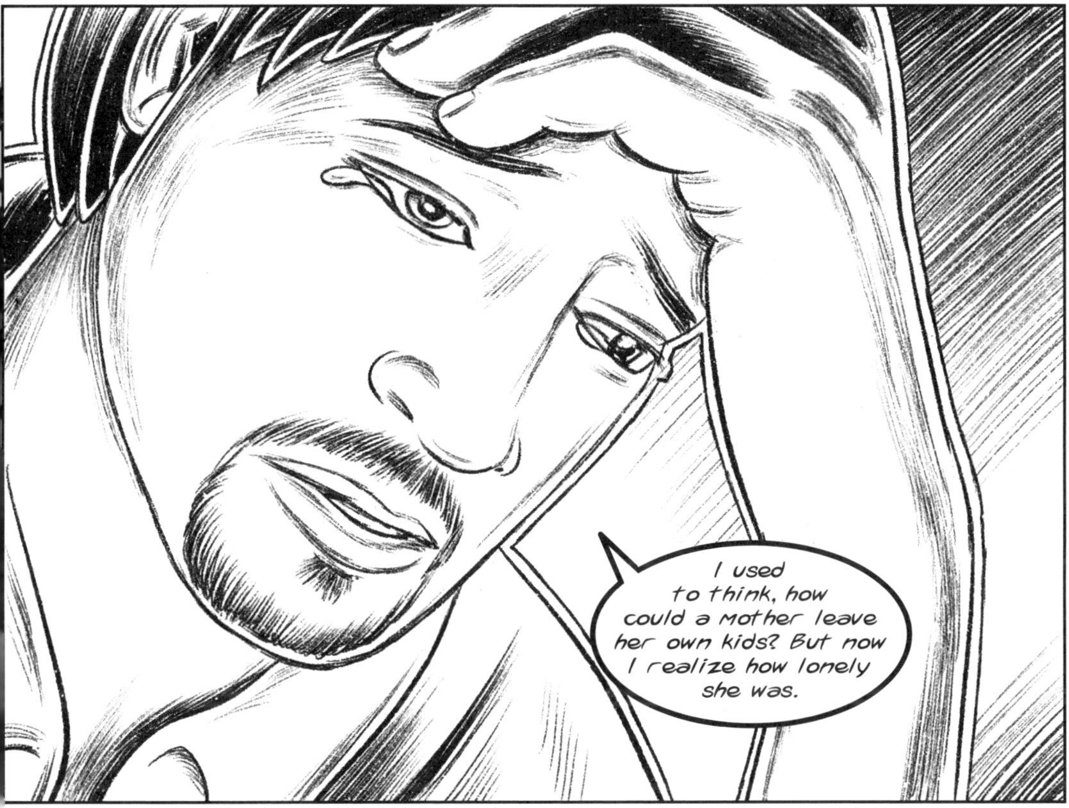
I used to think, how could a mother leave her own kids? But now I realize how lonely she was.

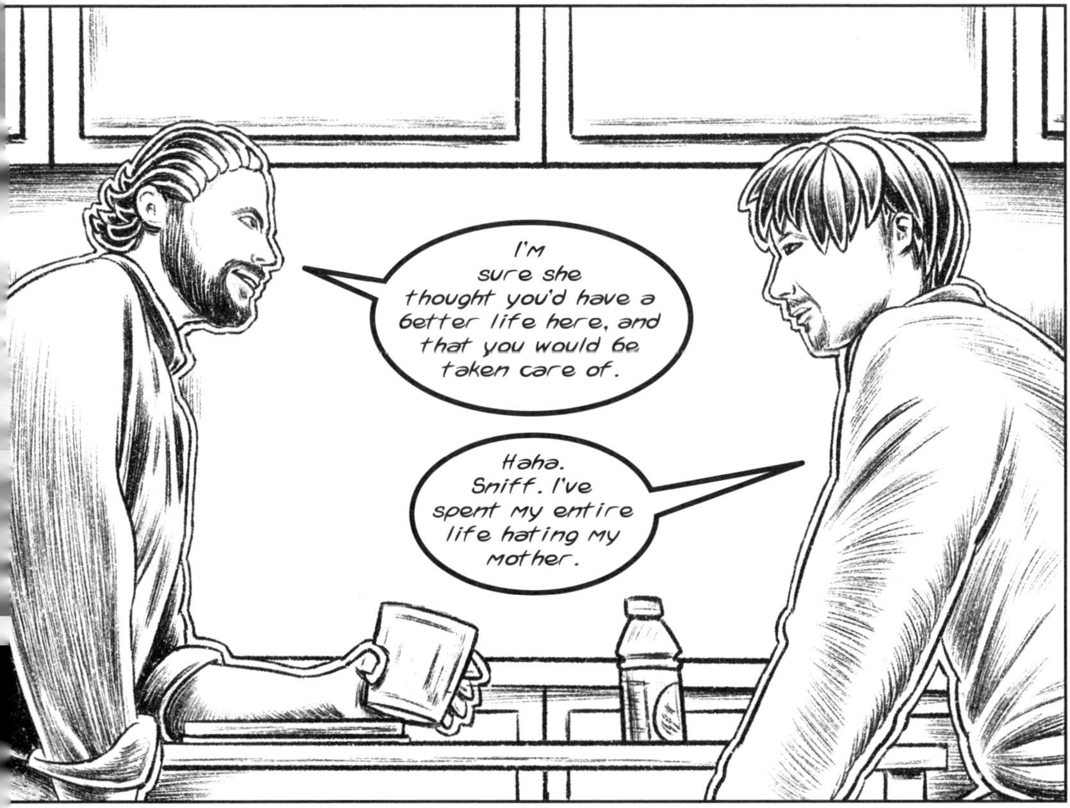
I'm sure she thought you'd have a better life here, and that you would be taken care of.
Haha. Sniff. I've spent my entire life hating my mother.

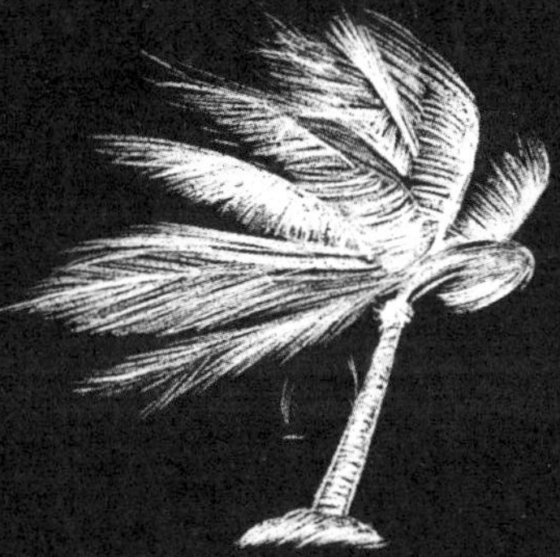

chapter 15

WIND

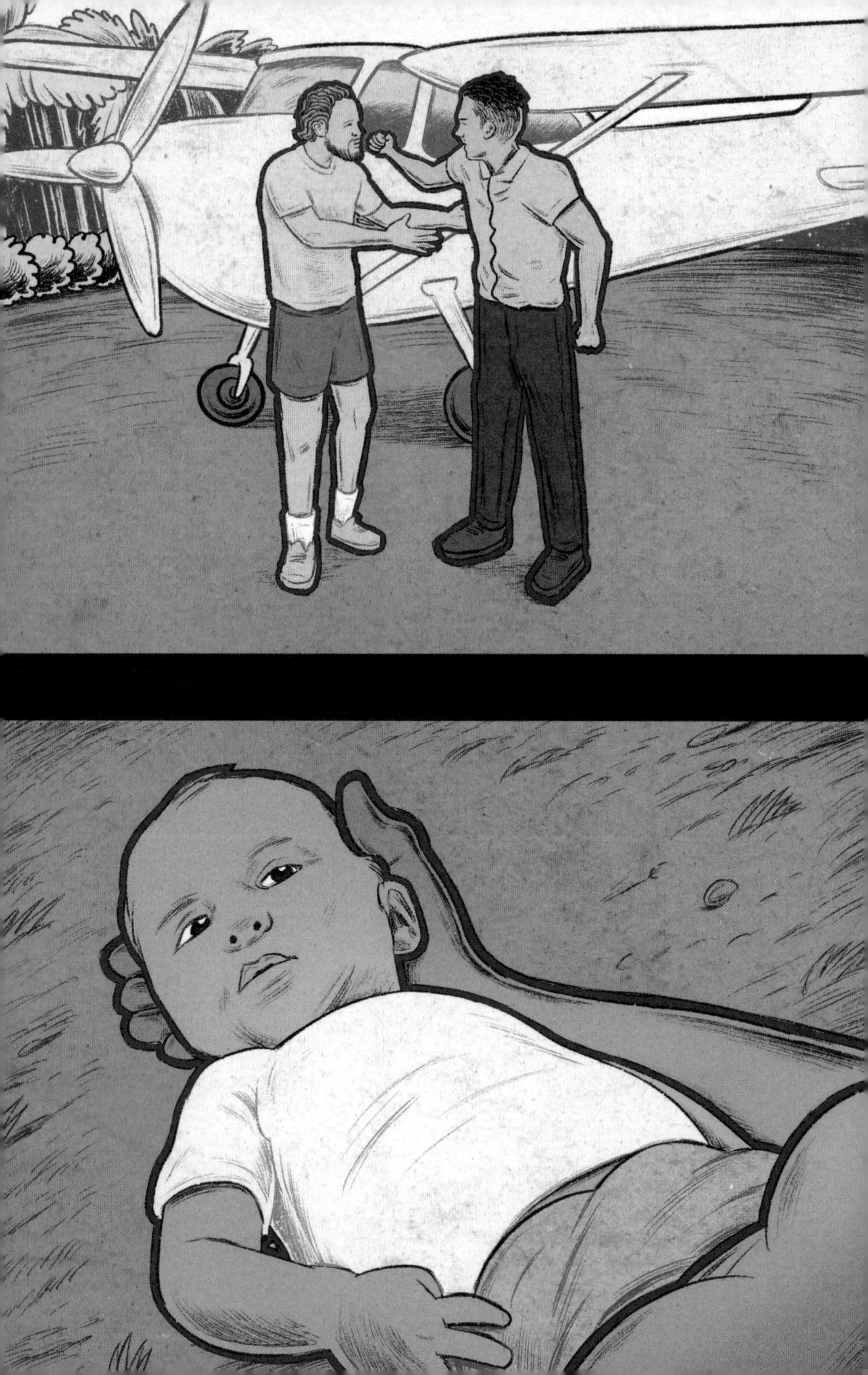

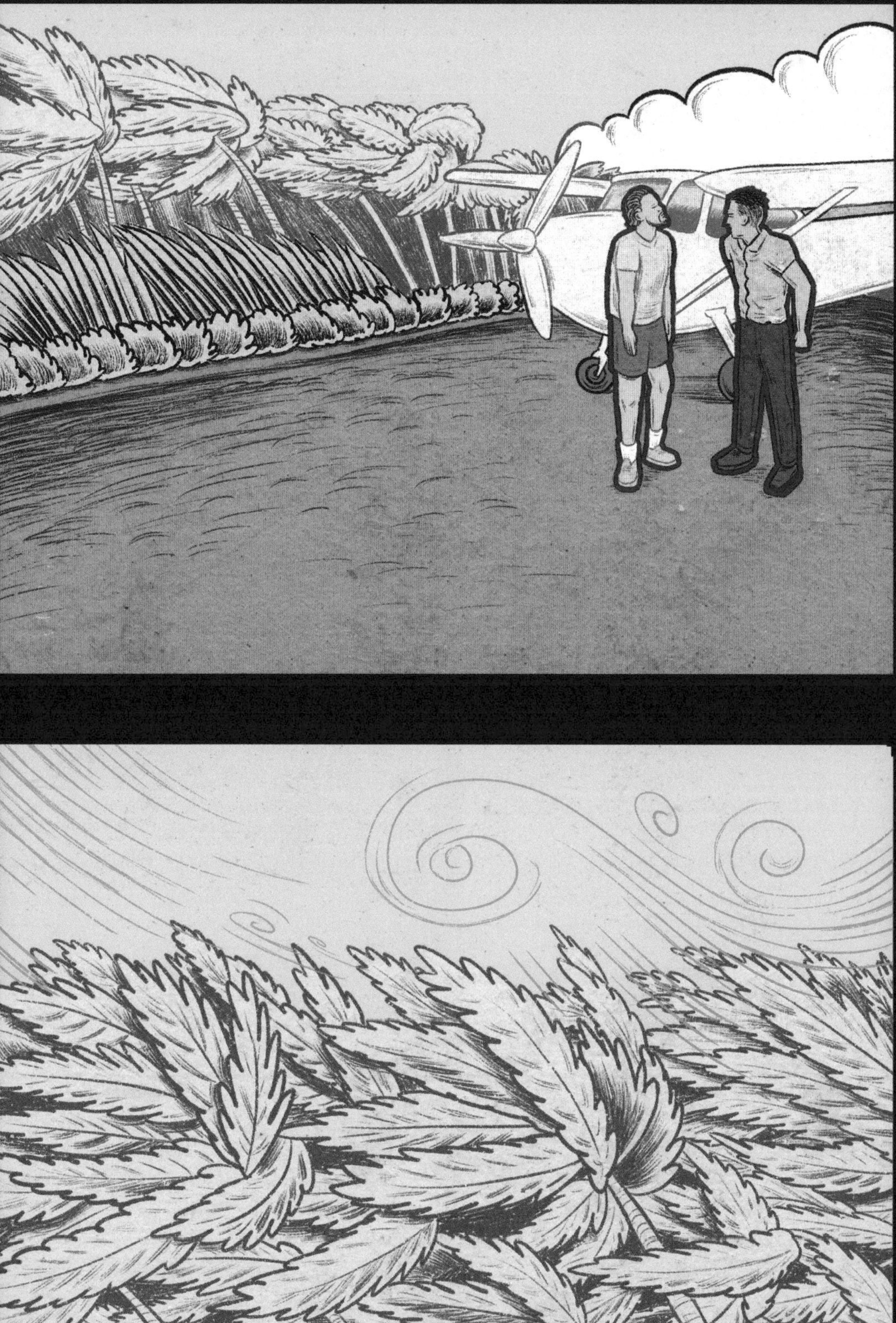

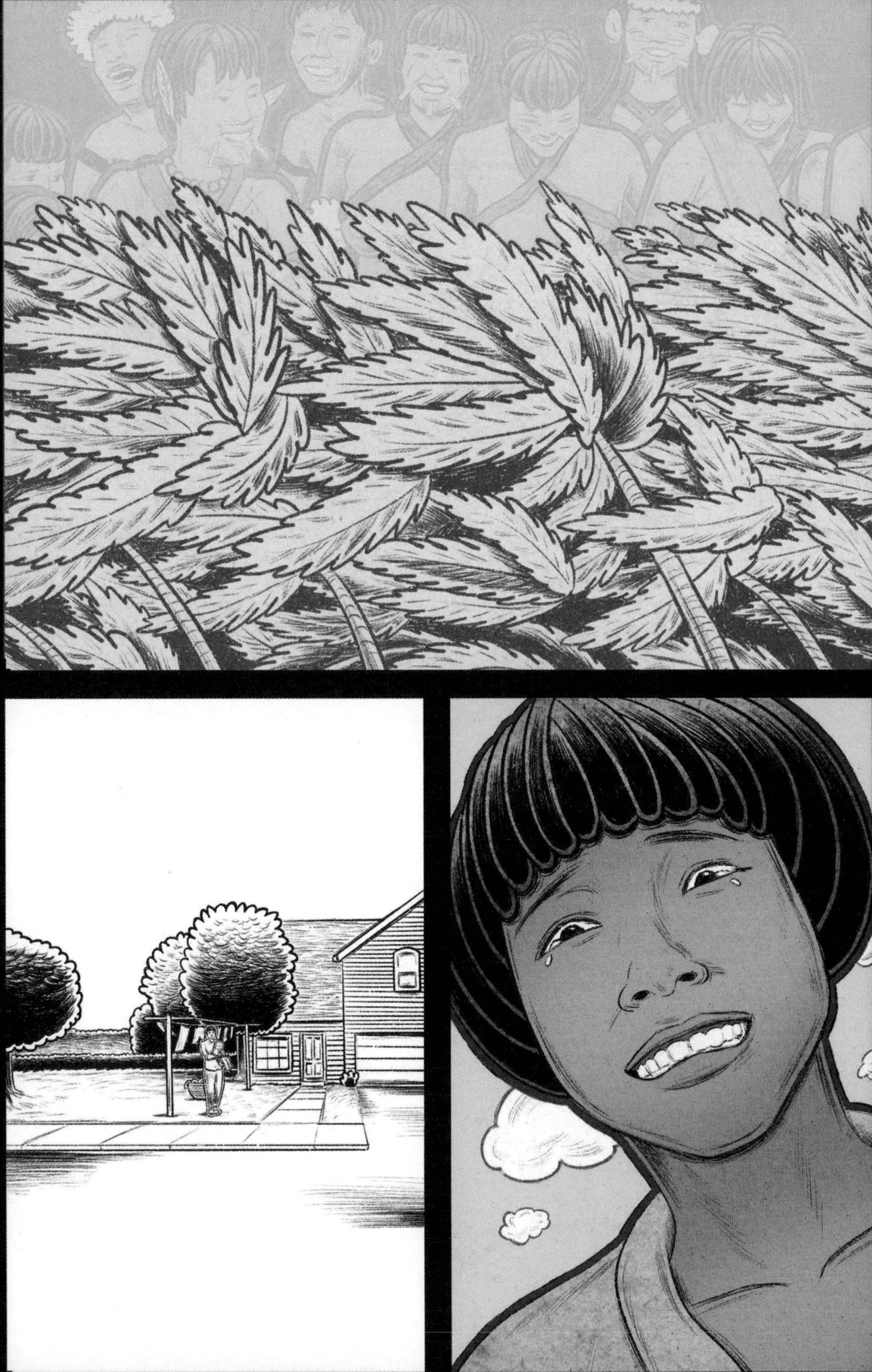

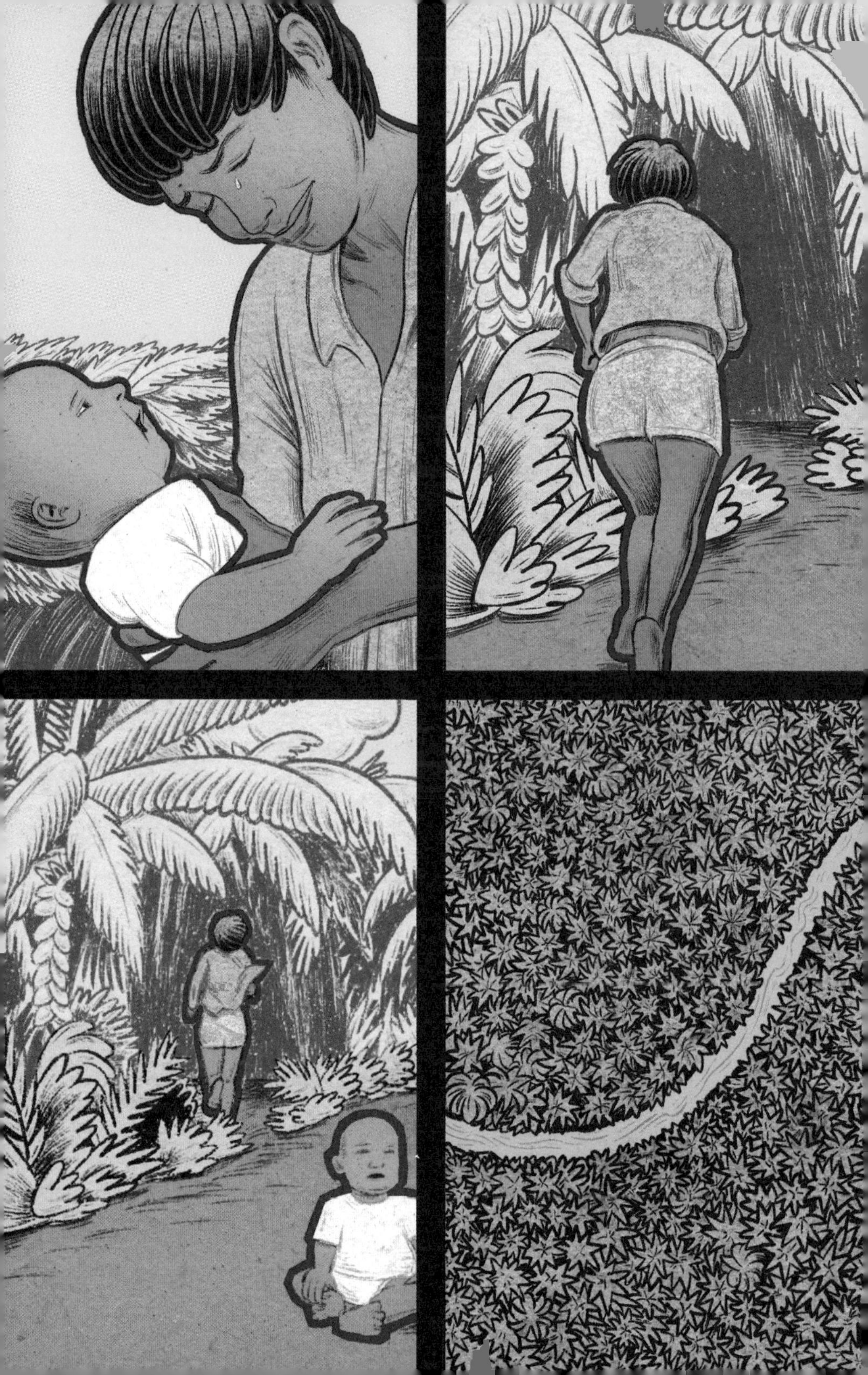

chapter 16

TRIBE

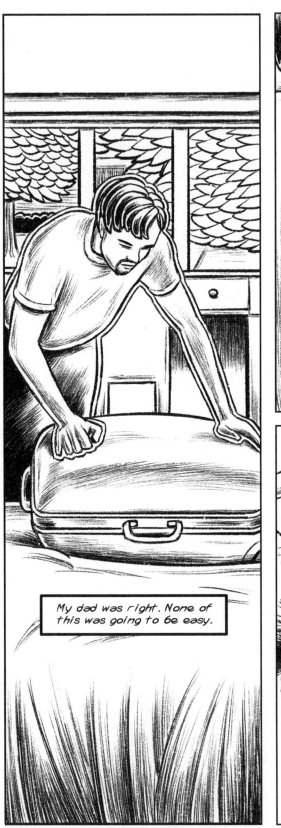

My dad was right. None of this was going to be easy.

But I was suddenly filled with a strong and fulfilling purpose. I was both extremely excited and nervous to meet her.

I was also lucky enough to track down and connect with a Caracas-based anthropologist who had worked with the Yanomami for over 20 years.

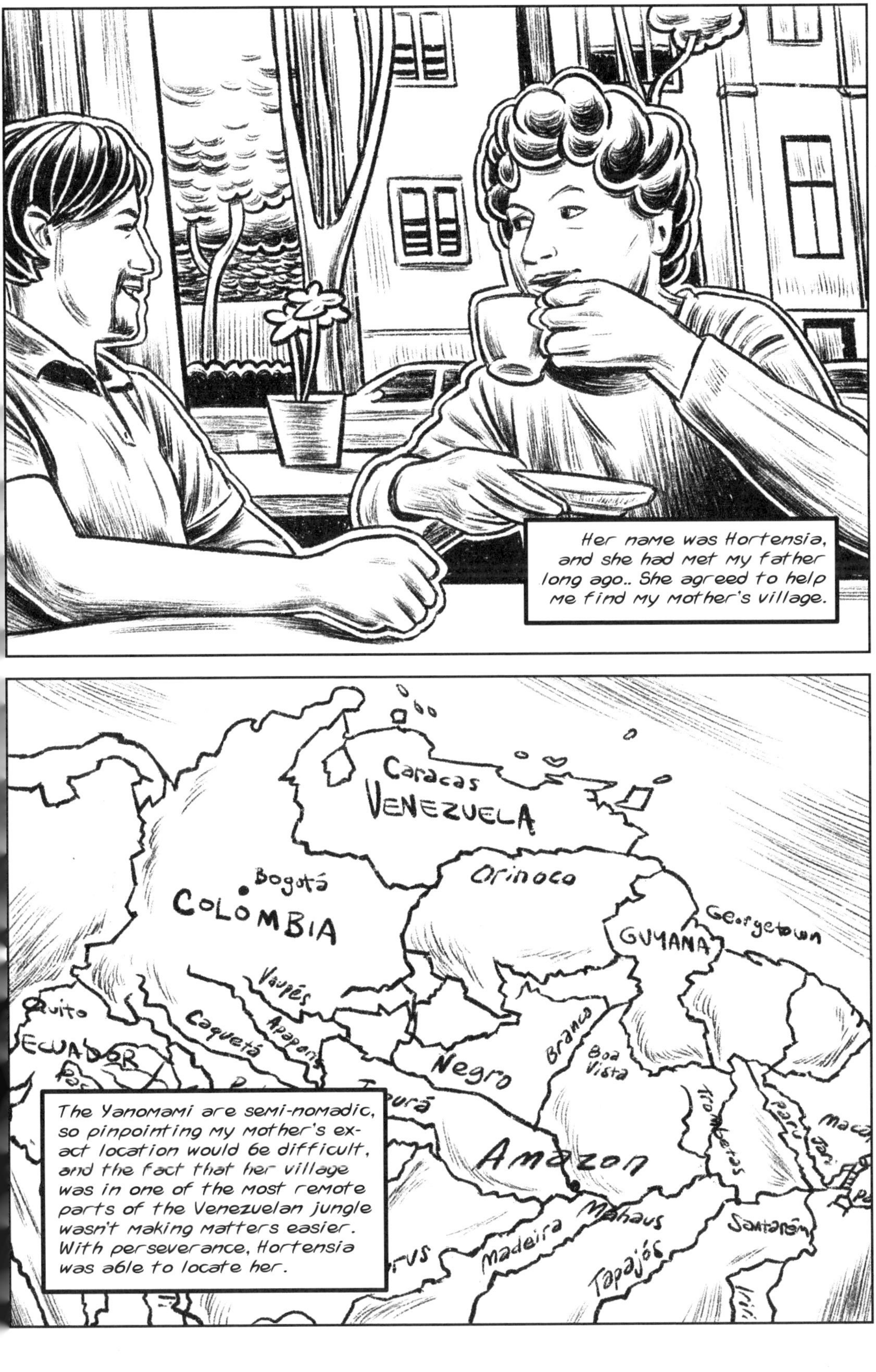
Her name was Hortensia, and she had met my father long ago.. She agreed to help me find my mother's village.
Caracas
VENEZUELA
Bogotá
COLOMBIA
Orinoco
Georgetown
GUYANA
Vaupés
Quito
Caquetá
Apaporis
ECUADOR
Negro
Branco
Boa Vista
Amazon
Trombetas
Manaus
Santarém
Madeira
Tapajós
The Yanomami are semi-nomadic, so pinpointing my mother's exact location would be difficult, and the fact that her village was in one of the most remote parts of the Venezuelan jungle wasn't making matters easier. With perseverance, Hortensia was able to locate her.

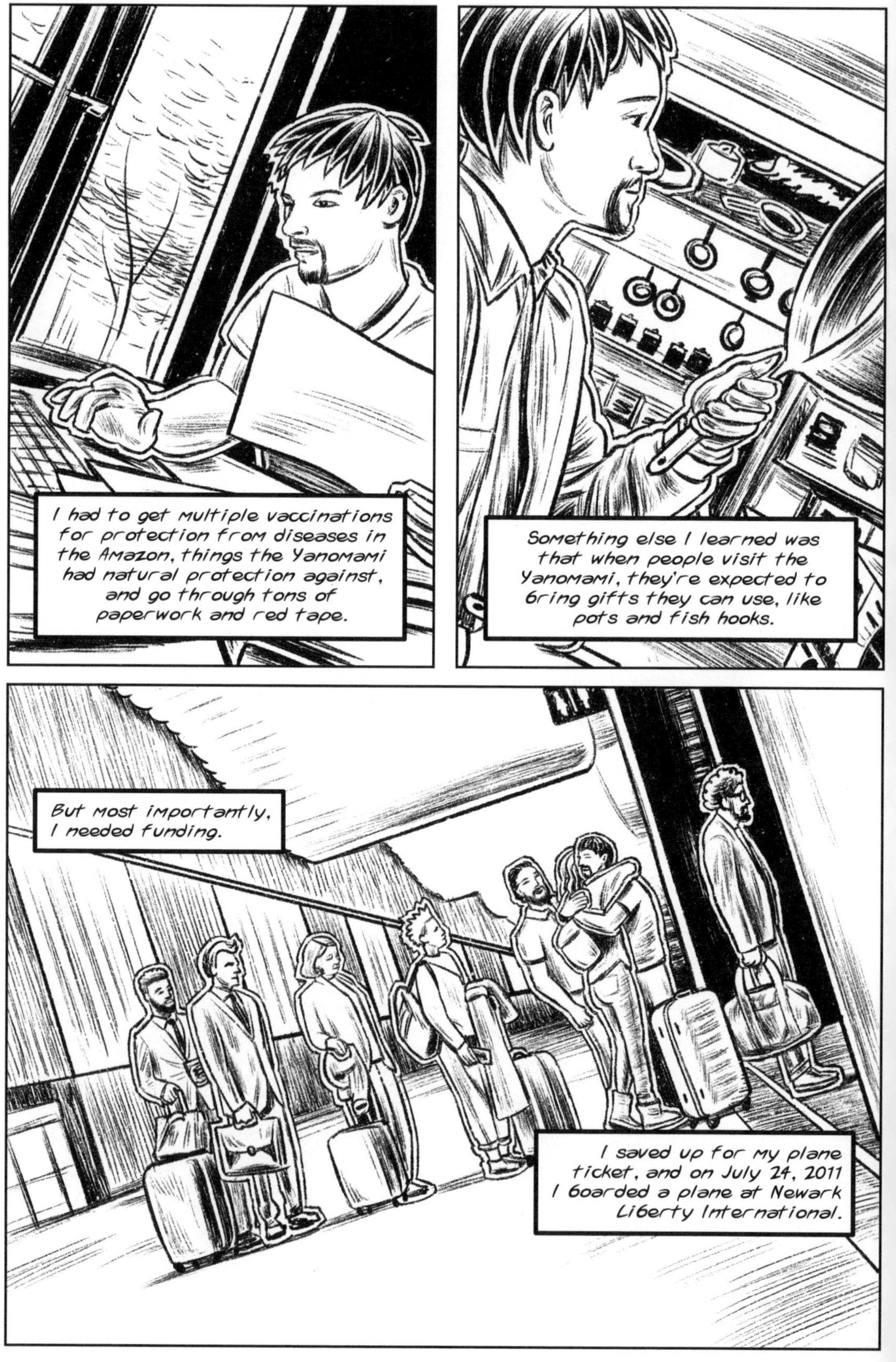
I had to get multiple vaccinations for protection from diseases in the Amazon, things the Yanomami had natural protection against, and go through tons of paperwork and red tape.
Something else I learned was that when people visit the Yanomami, they're expected to bring gifts they can use, like pots and fish hooks.
But most importantly, I needed funding.
I saved up for my plane ticket, and on July 24, 2011 I boarded a plane at Newark Liberty International.

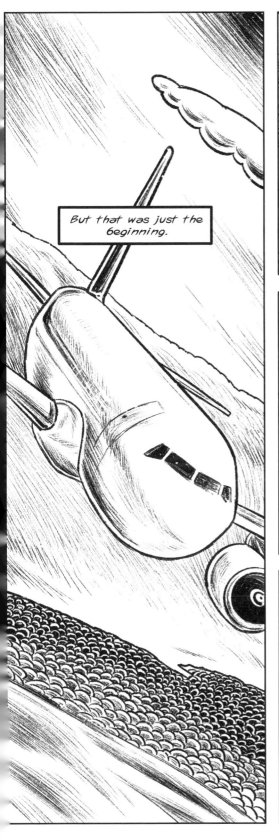

But that was just the beginning.

Once in the hot and busy city of Caracas, Venezuela, I met with Hortensia.

We then took a short plane ride to Puerto Ayacucho, the capital of the Amazonas state.

We then took a bus to Samariapo, a small port town on the Orinoco river.

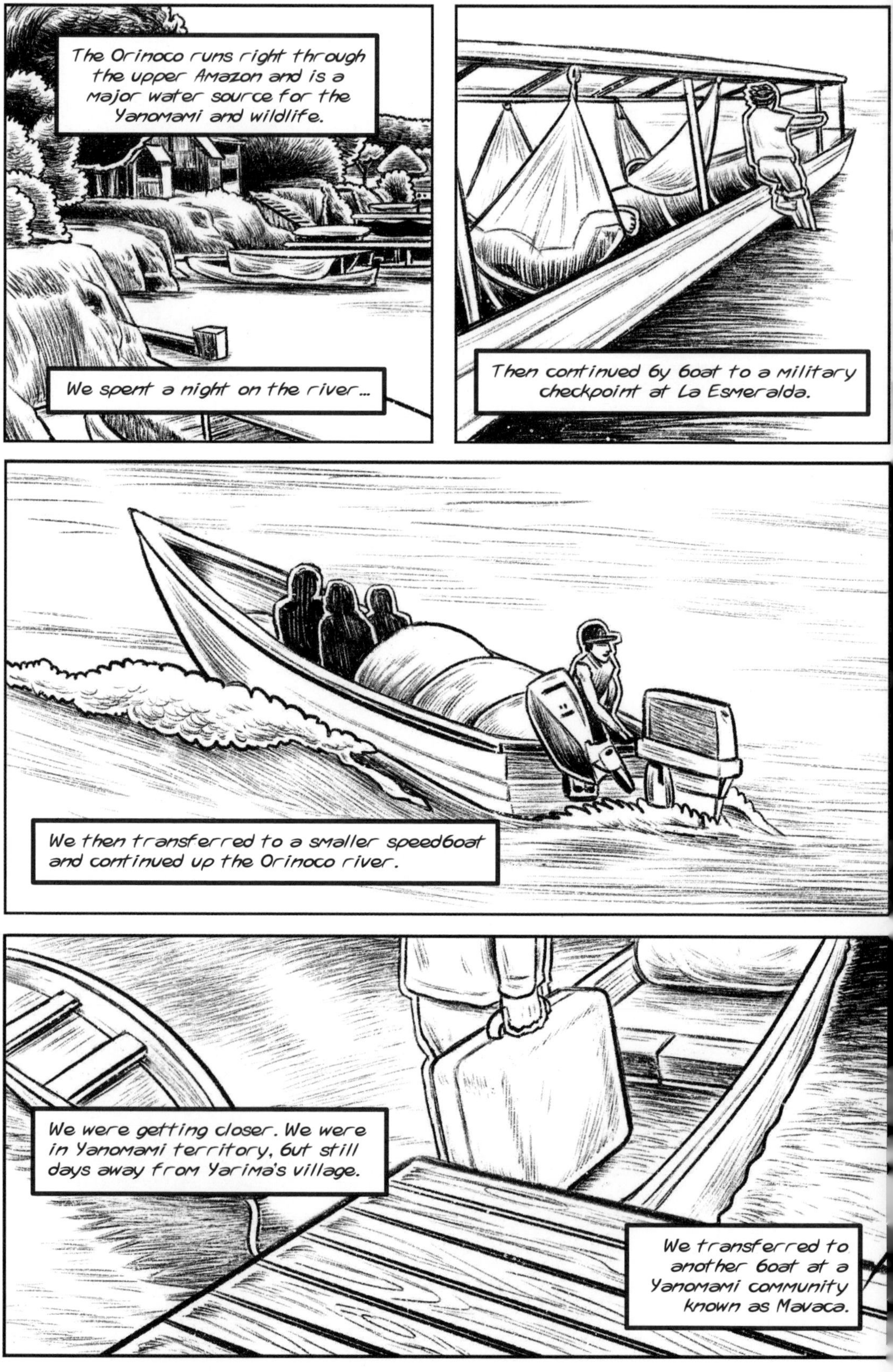
The Orinoco runs right through the upper Amazon and is a major water source for the Yanomami and wildlife.
We spent a night on the river...
Then continued by boat to a military checkpoint at La Esmeralda.
We then transferred to a smaller speedboat and continued up the Orinoco river.
We were getting closer. We were in Yanomami territory, but still days away from Yarima's village.
We transferred to another boat at a Yanomami community known as Mavaca.

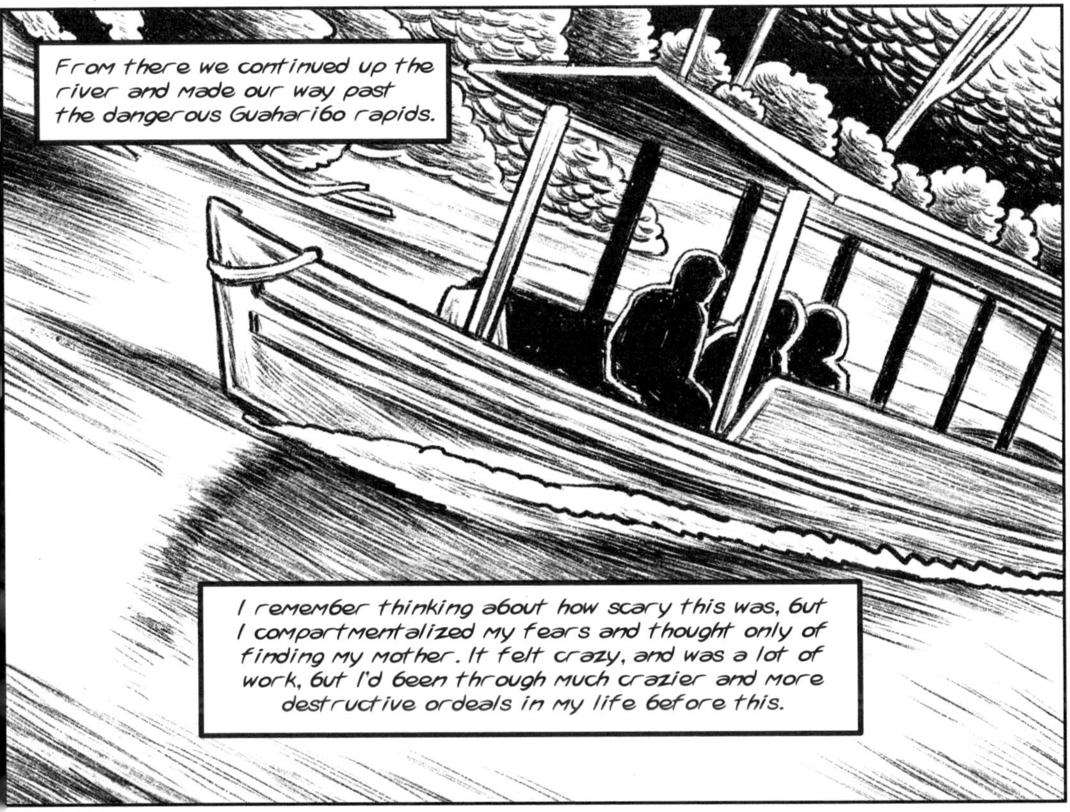
From there we continued up the river and made our way past the dangerous Guaharibo rapids.
I remember thinking about how scary this was, but I compartmentalized my fears and thought only of finding my mother. It felt crazy, and was a lot of work, but I'd been through much crazier and more destructive ordeals in my life before this.

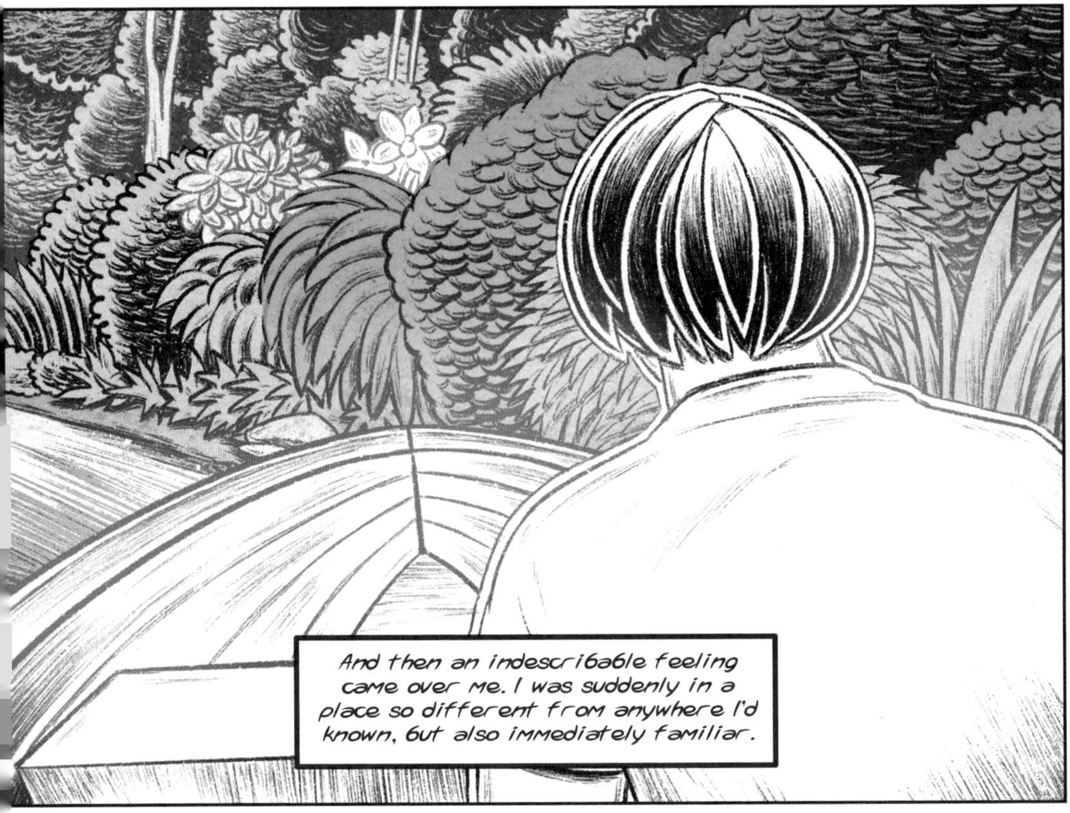
And then an indescribable feeling came over me. I was suddenly in a place so different from anywhere I'd known, but also immediately familiar.

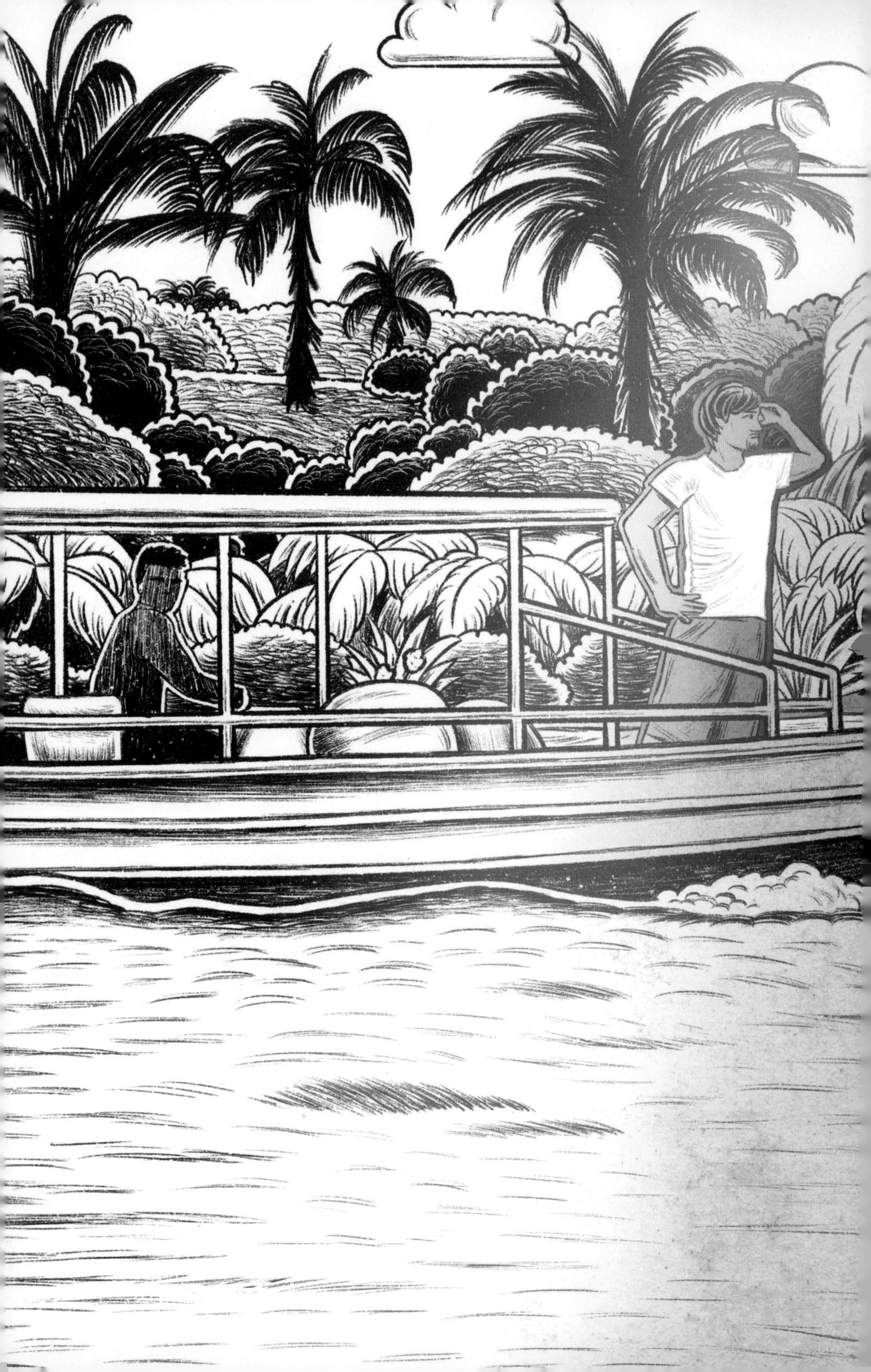

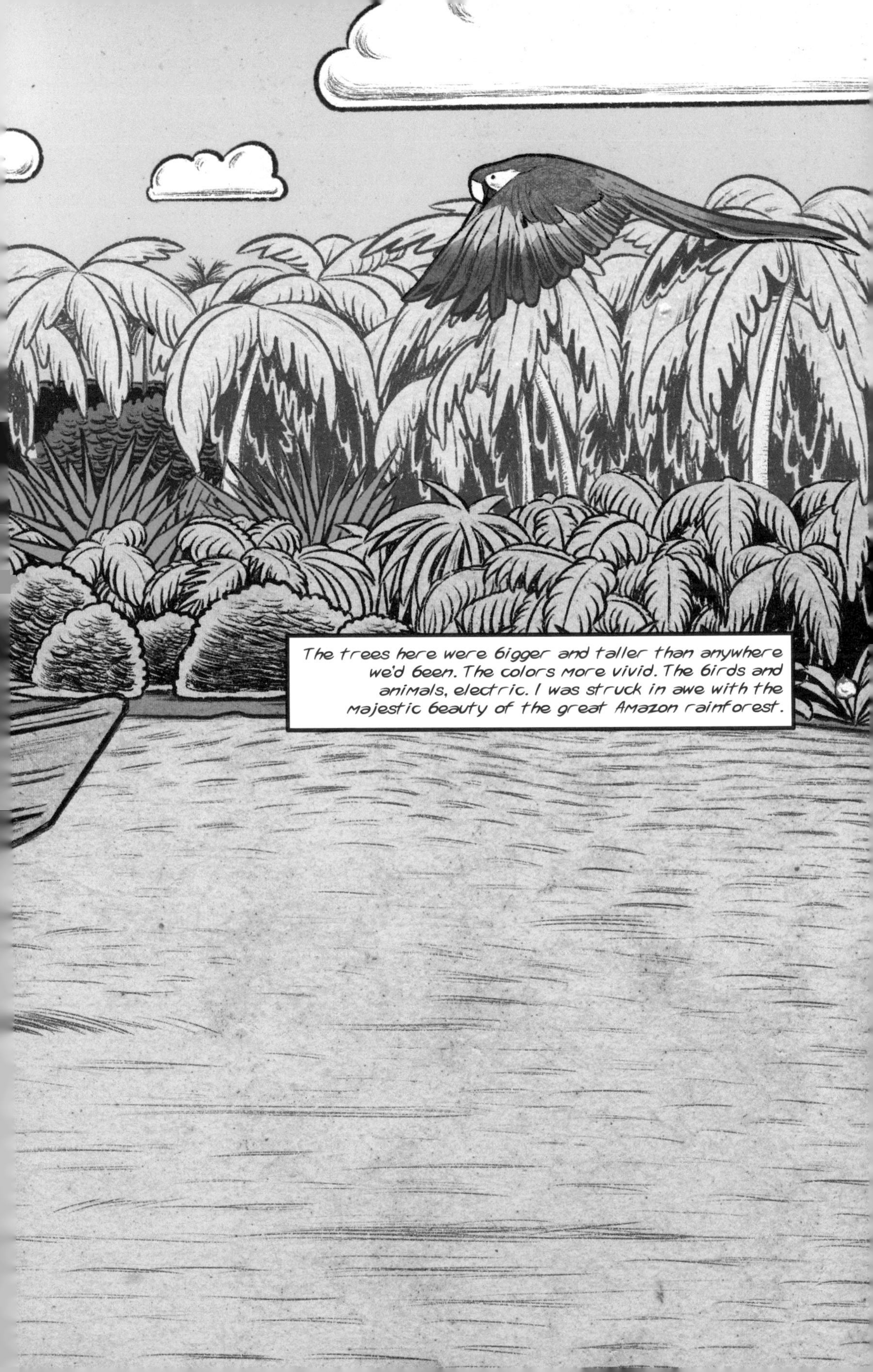
The trees here were bigger and taller than anywhere we'd been. The colors more vivid. The birds and animals, electric. I was struck in awe with the majestic beauty of the great Amazon rainforest.

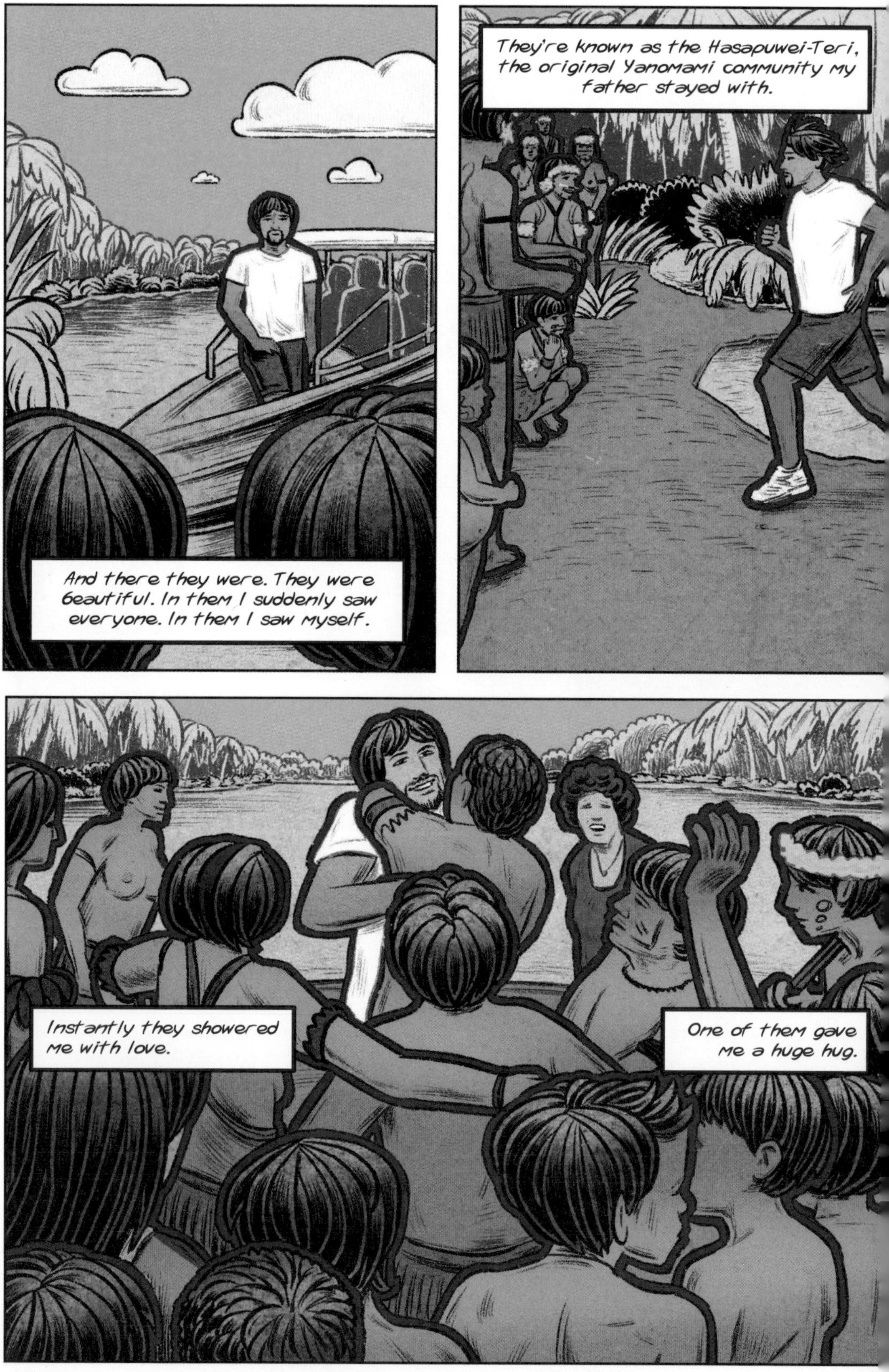
And there they were. They were beautiful. In them I suddenly saw everyone. In them I saw myself.
They're known as the Hasapuwei-Teri, the original Yanomami community my father stayed with.
Instantly they showered me with love.
One of them gave me a huge hug.

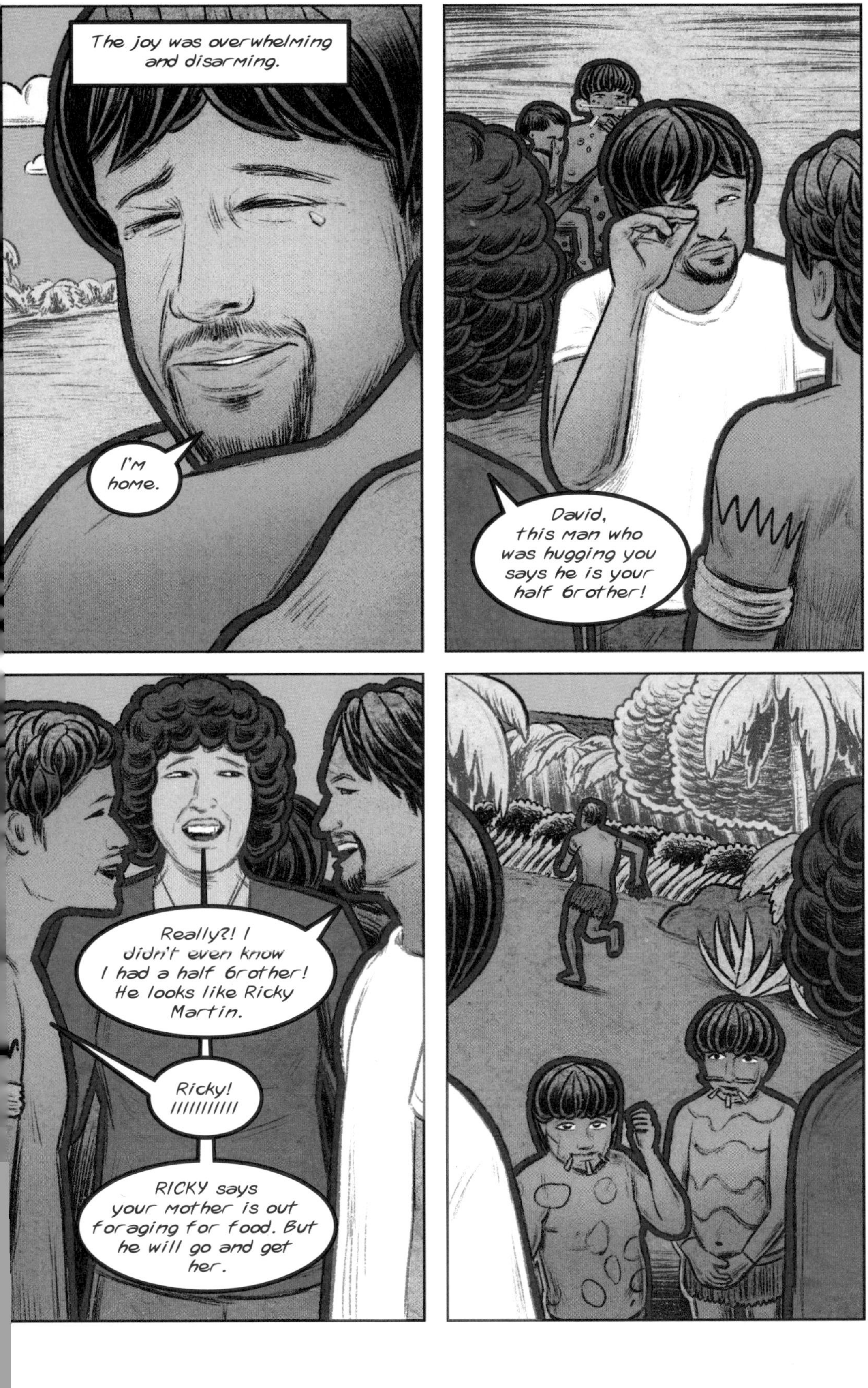
The joy was overwhelming and disarming.
I'm home.
David, this man who was hugging you says he is your half 6rother!
Really?! I didn't even know I had a half 6rother! He looks like Ricky Martin.
Ricky! IIIIIIIIIII
RICKY says your mother is out foraging for food. But he will go and get her.

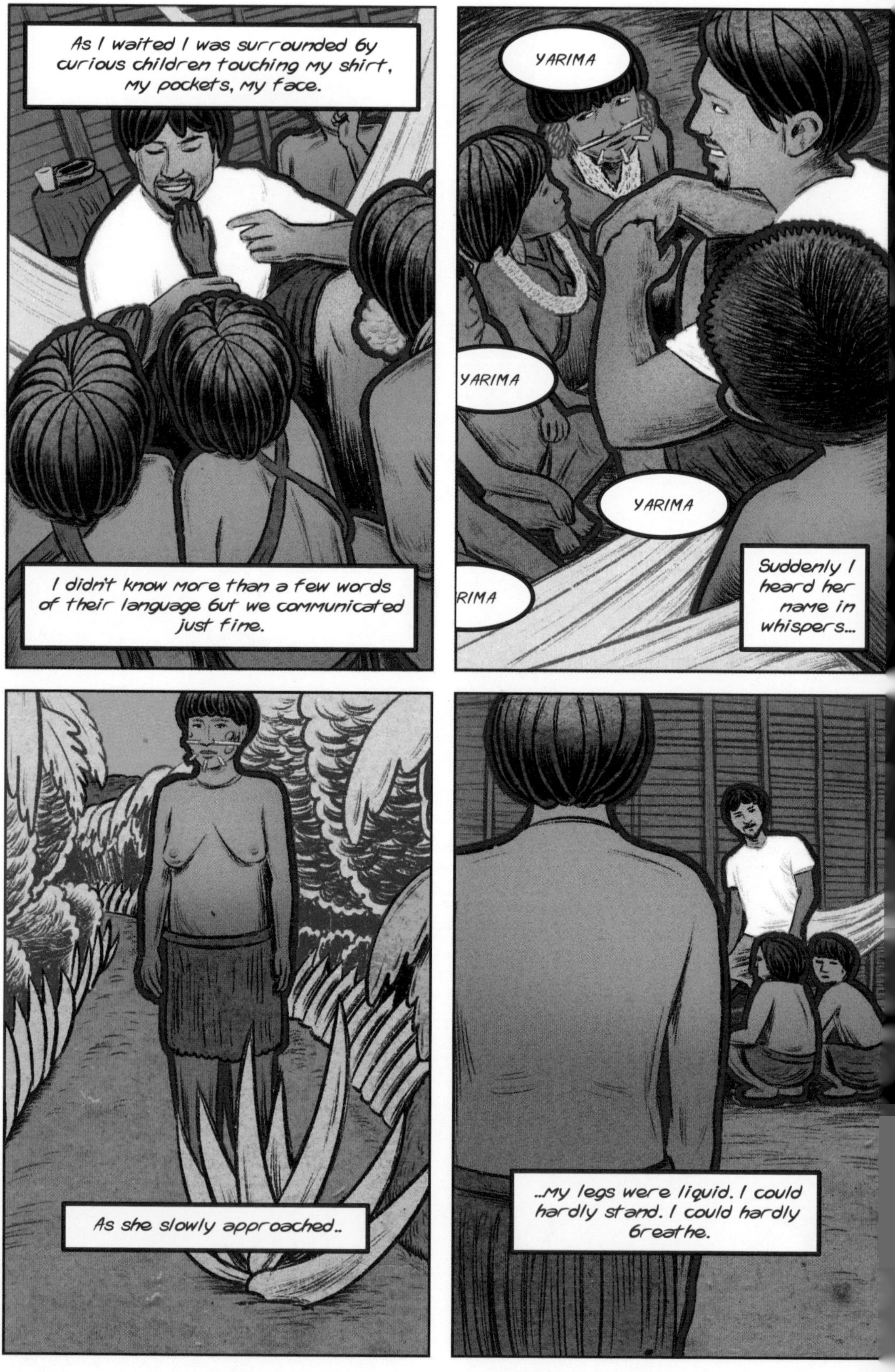
As I waited I was surrounded by curious children touching my shirt, my pockets, my face.
I didn't know more than a few words of their language but we communicated just fine.
YARIMA
YARIMA
YARIMA
RIMA
Suddenly I heard her name in whispers...
As she slowly approached..
..My legs were liquid. I could hardly stand. I could hardly breathe.

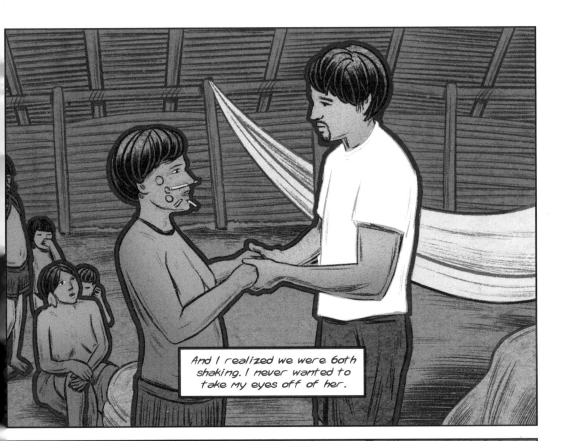

And I realized we were both shaking. I never wanted to take my eyes off of her.

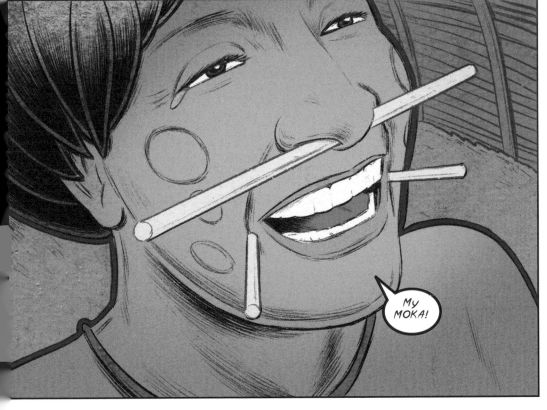

MY MOKA!

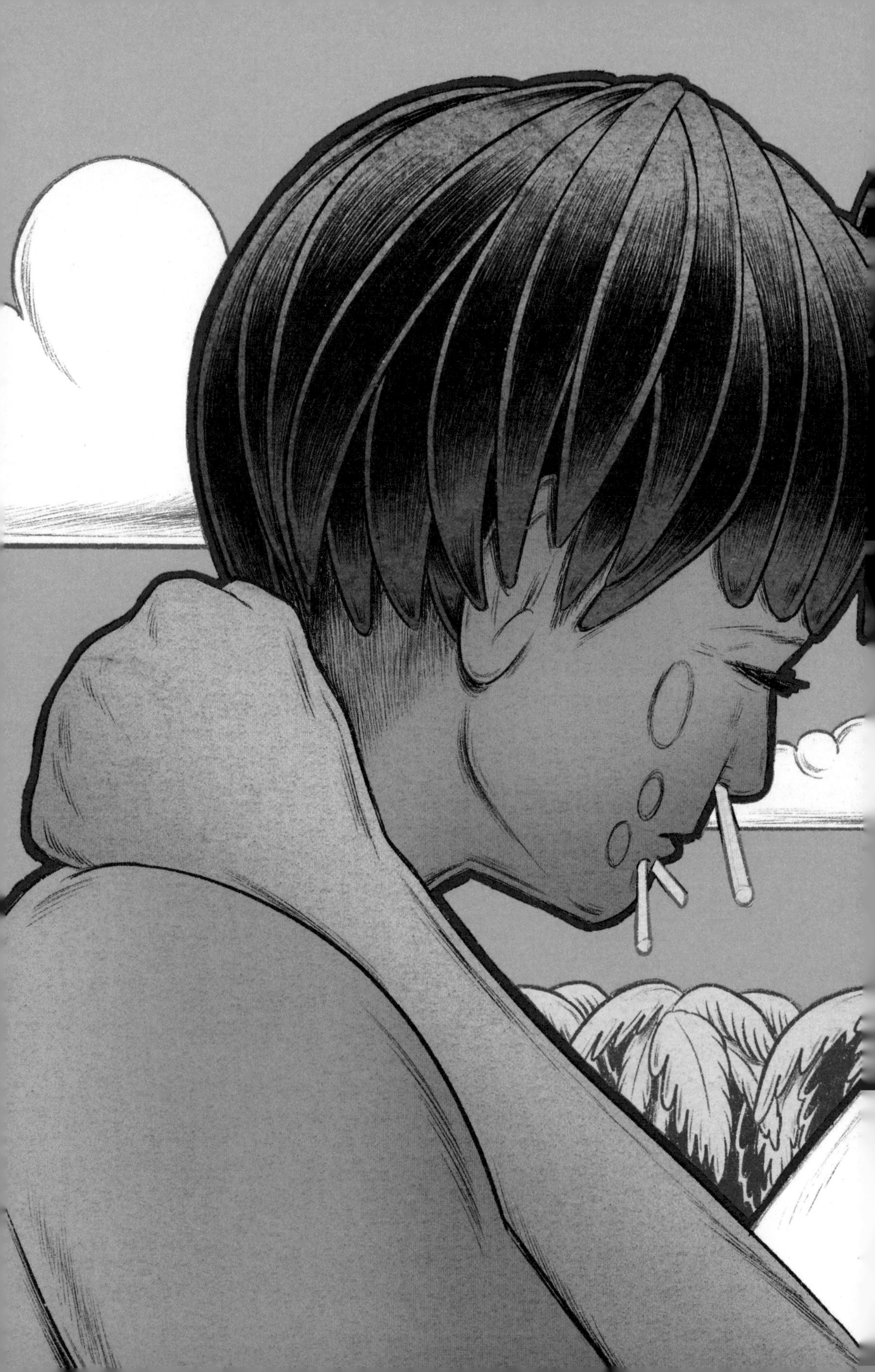

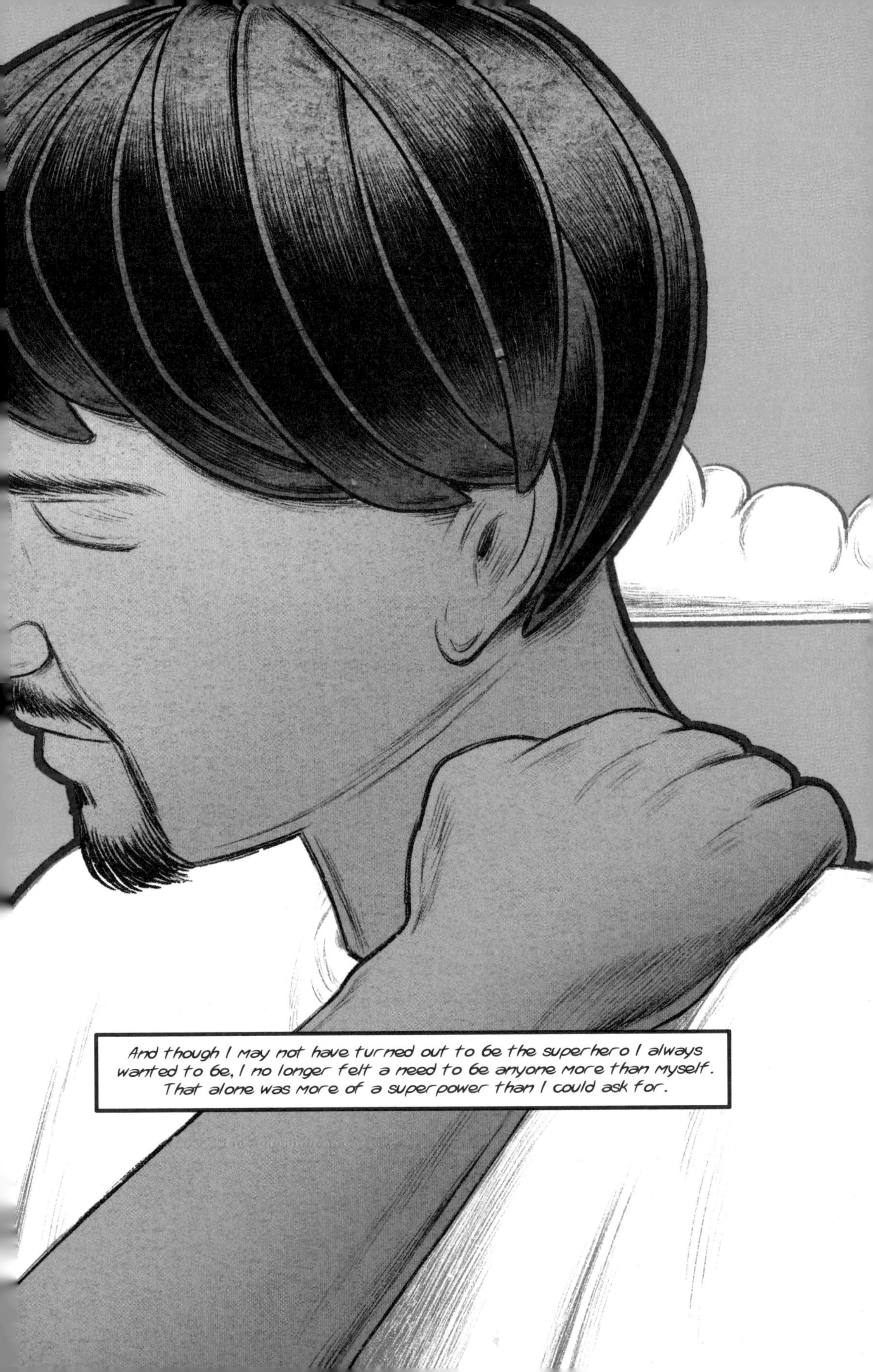
And though I may not have turned out to be the superhero I always wanted to be, I no longer felt a need to be anyone more than myself. That alone was more of a superpower than I could ask for.

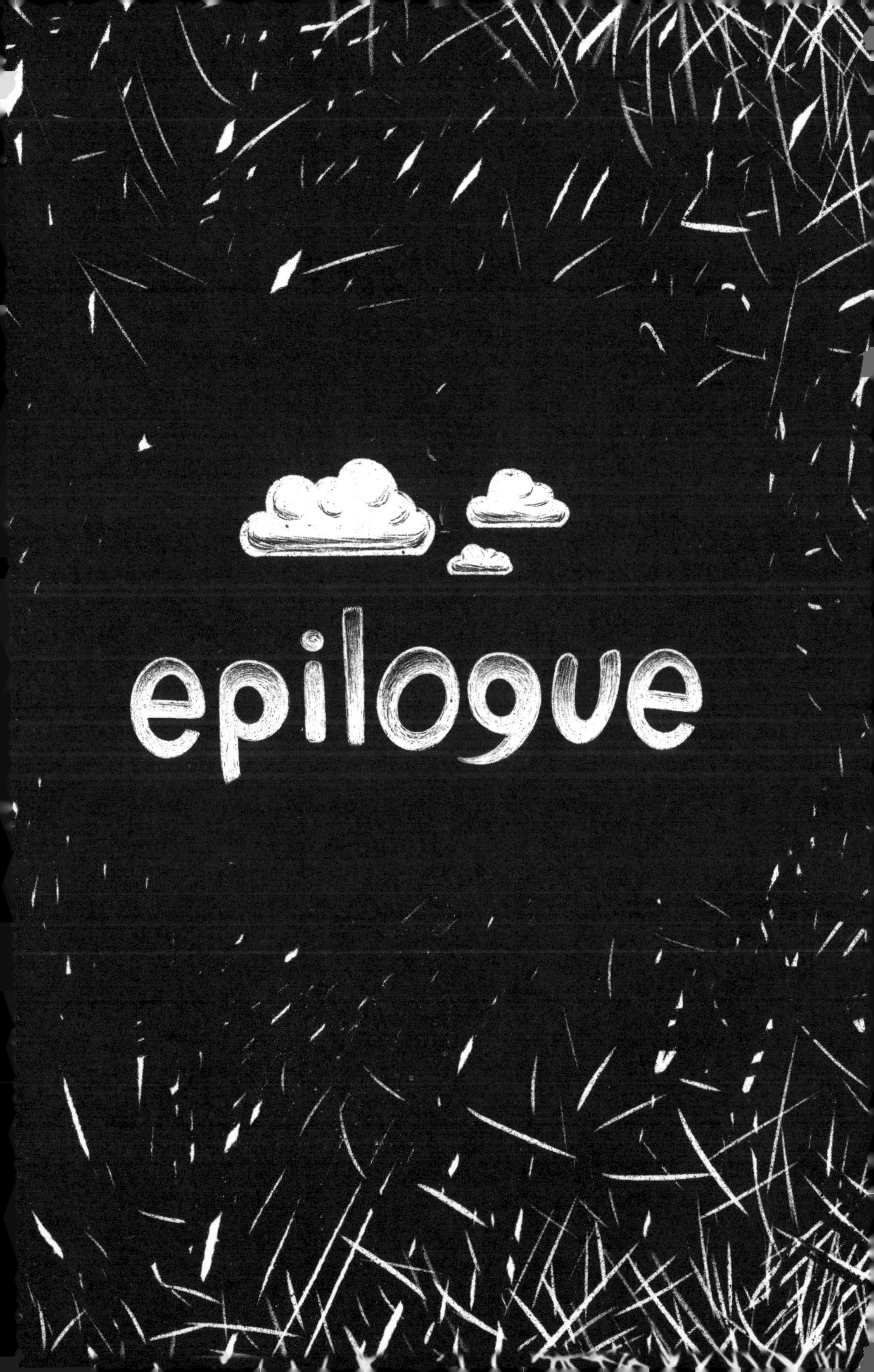
epilogue

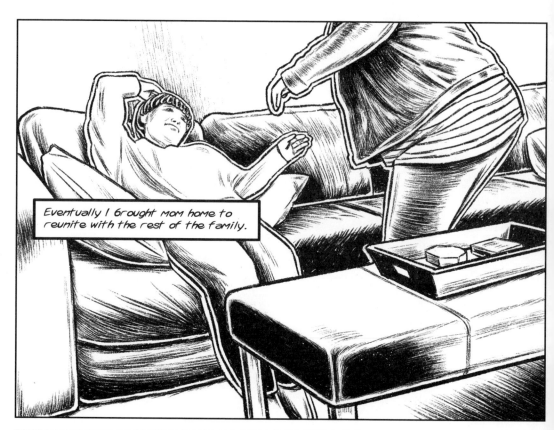

Eventually I brought mom home to reunite with the rest of the family.

My sister,

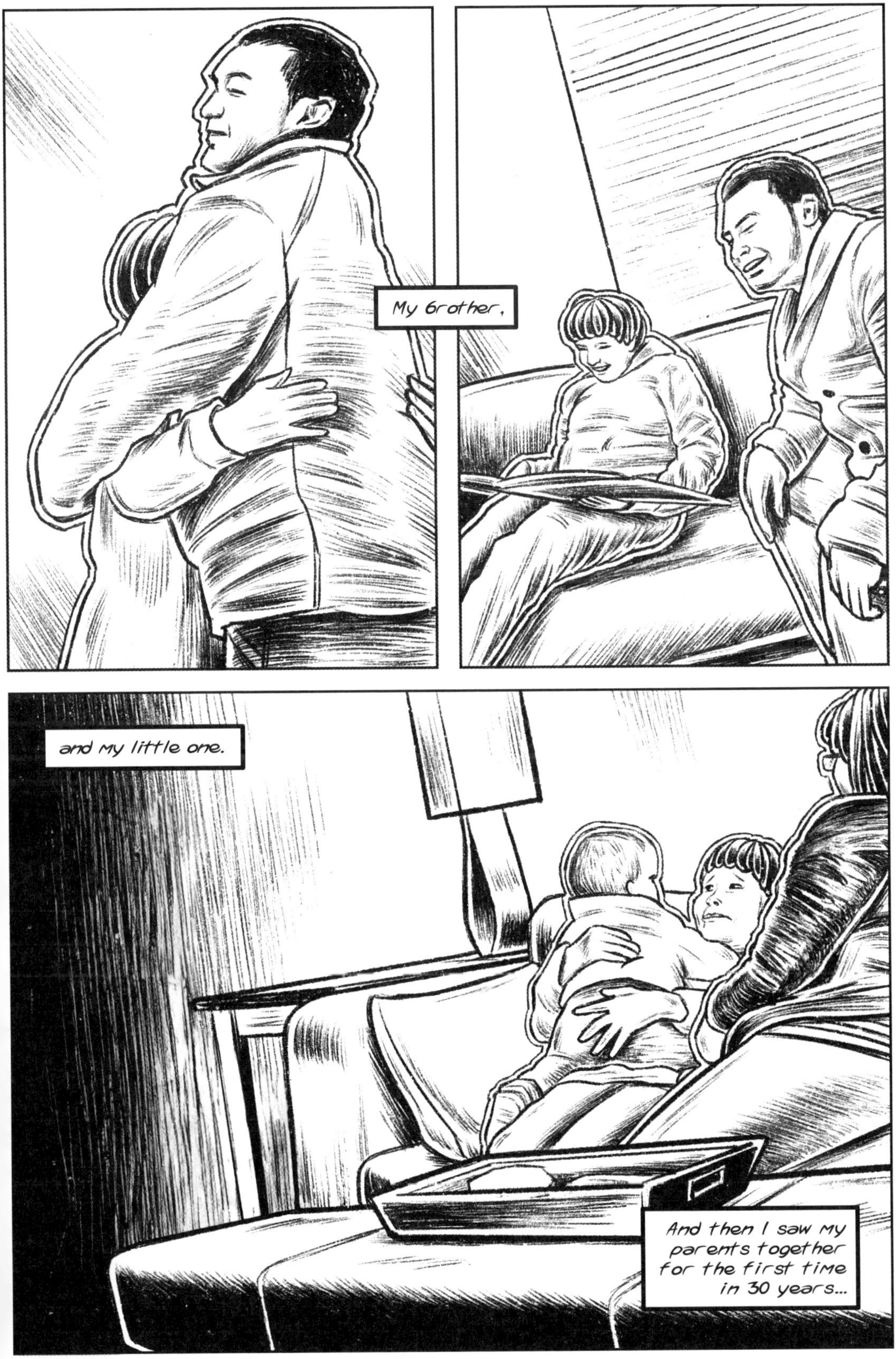
My brother,
and my little one.
And then I saw my parents together for the first time in 30 years...

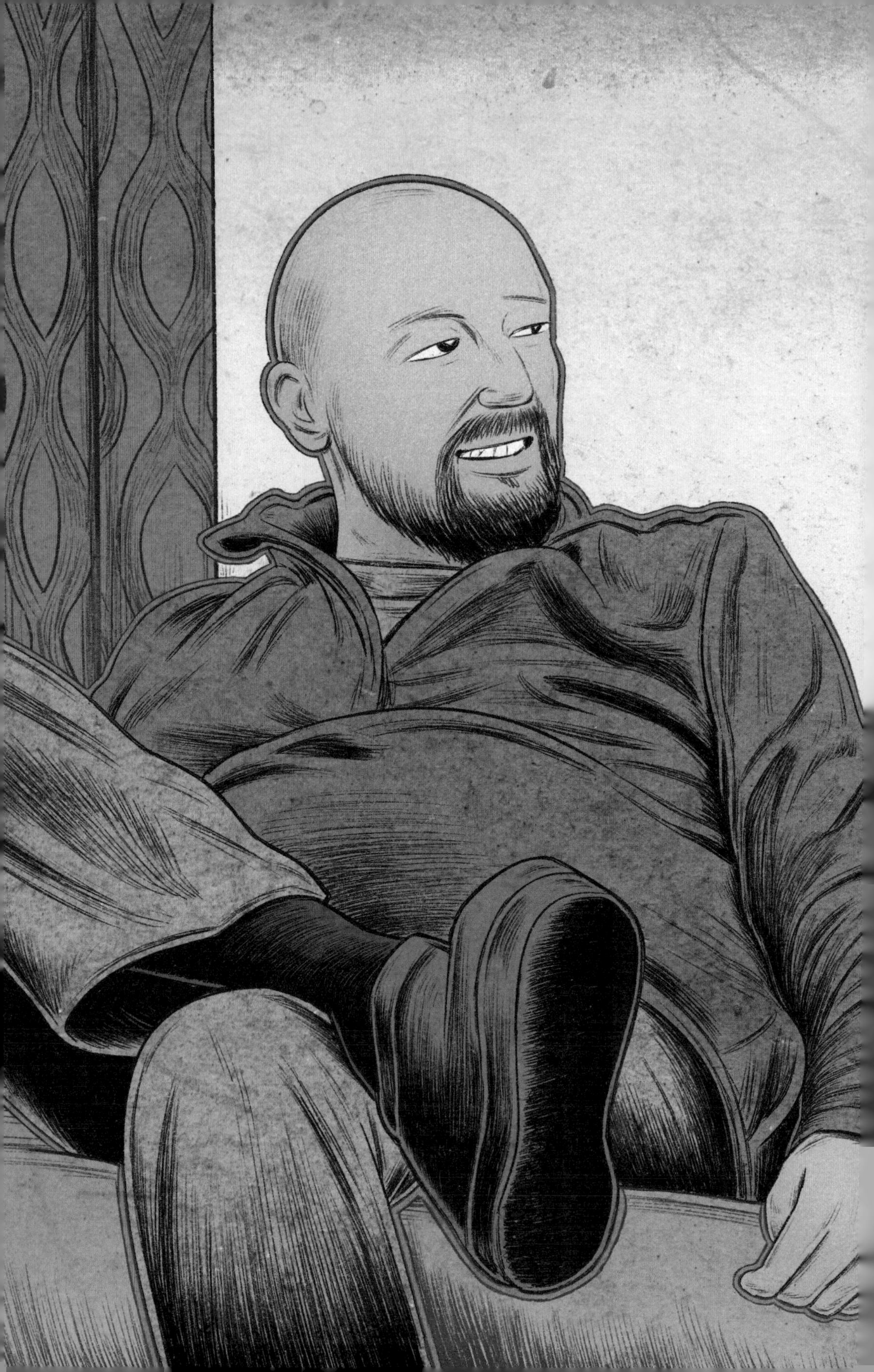

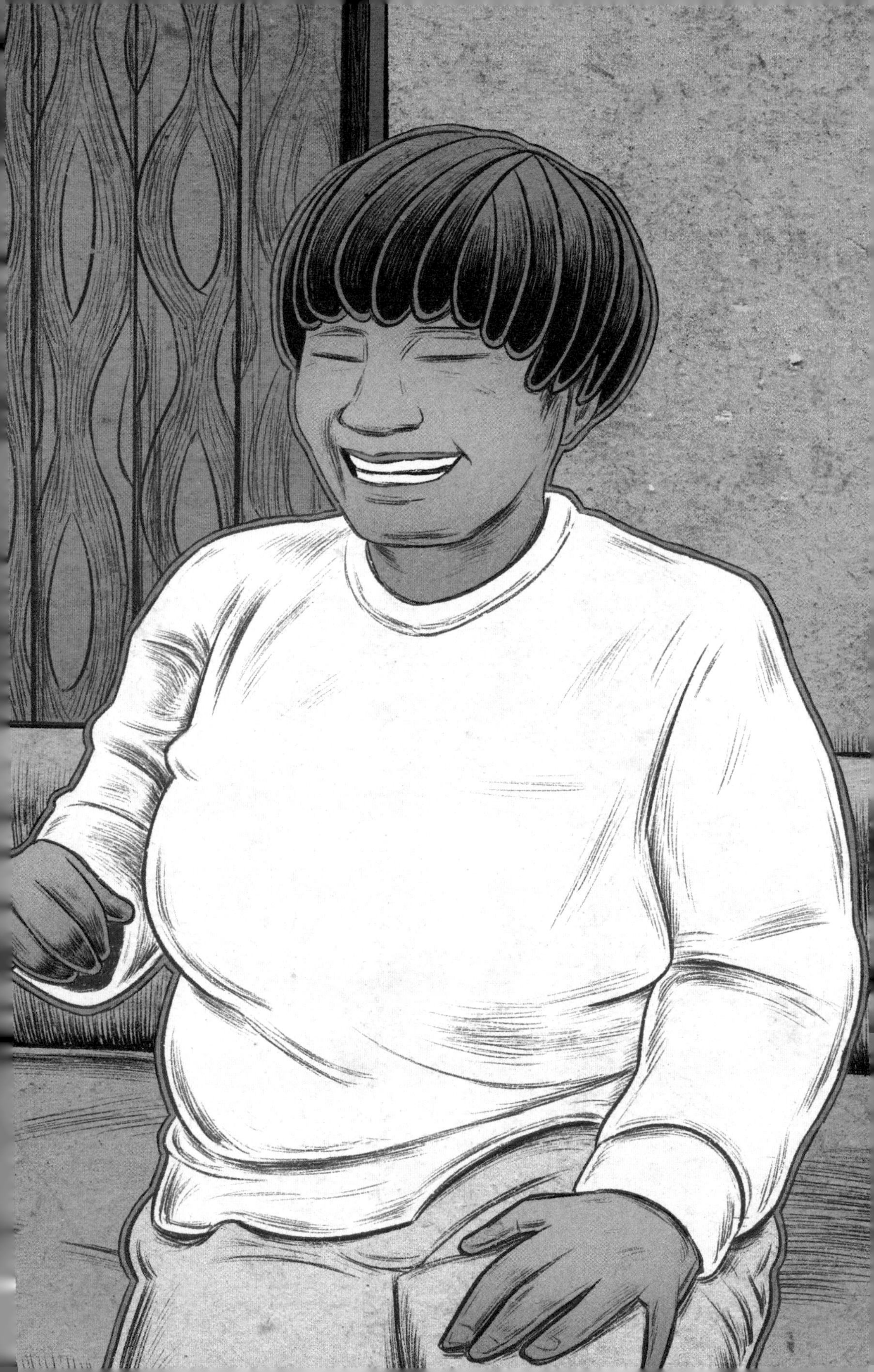

David Good is a member of the Yanomami tribe, author, explorer, filmmaker, and founder of the Yanomami Foundation. He is currently a PhD candidate in microbiology at the University of Guelph, Ontario. His research focuses on the gut microbiome of Yanomami communities still living a traditional lifestyle of hunting-gathering and gardening.

A member of the Explorer's Club, he coordinates expeditions to Yanomami territory to support programs in health, biocultural research, education, and cultural preservation. His unique ancestry and scientific training provide a rare opportunity to advance our understanding of the human microbiome, while building global awareness on the importance of protecting these few remaining isolated indigenous societies.

Multi-award-winning contemporary artist FLuX is a practitioner of contemporary classical realism and illustration. FLuX's work has been exhibited globally and is included in collections with notable artists such as Andy Warhol and Jeff Koons.

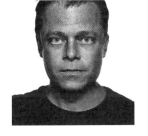

With a self-taught background in illustration and design, FLuX has worked with commercial clients including Apple, Swatch and others. He is also an author of graphic novels. He has received numerous awards, including Creativity International, Communication Arts, and Society of Illustrators, and has been featured in The Big Book of Illustration and Spectrum.

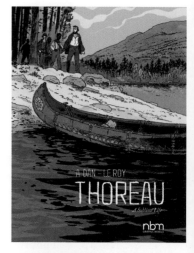
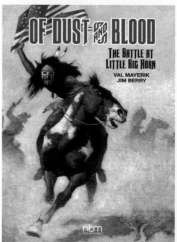
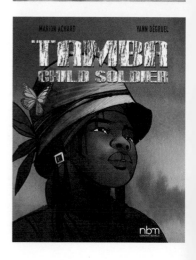

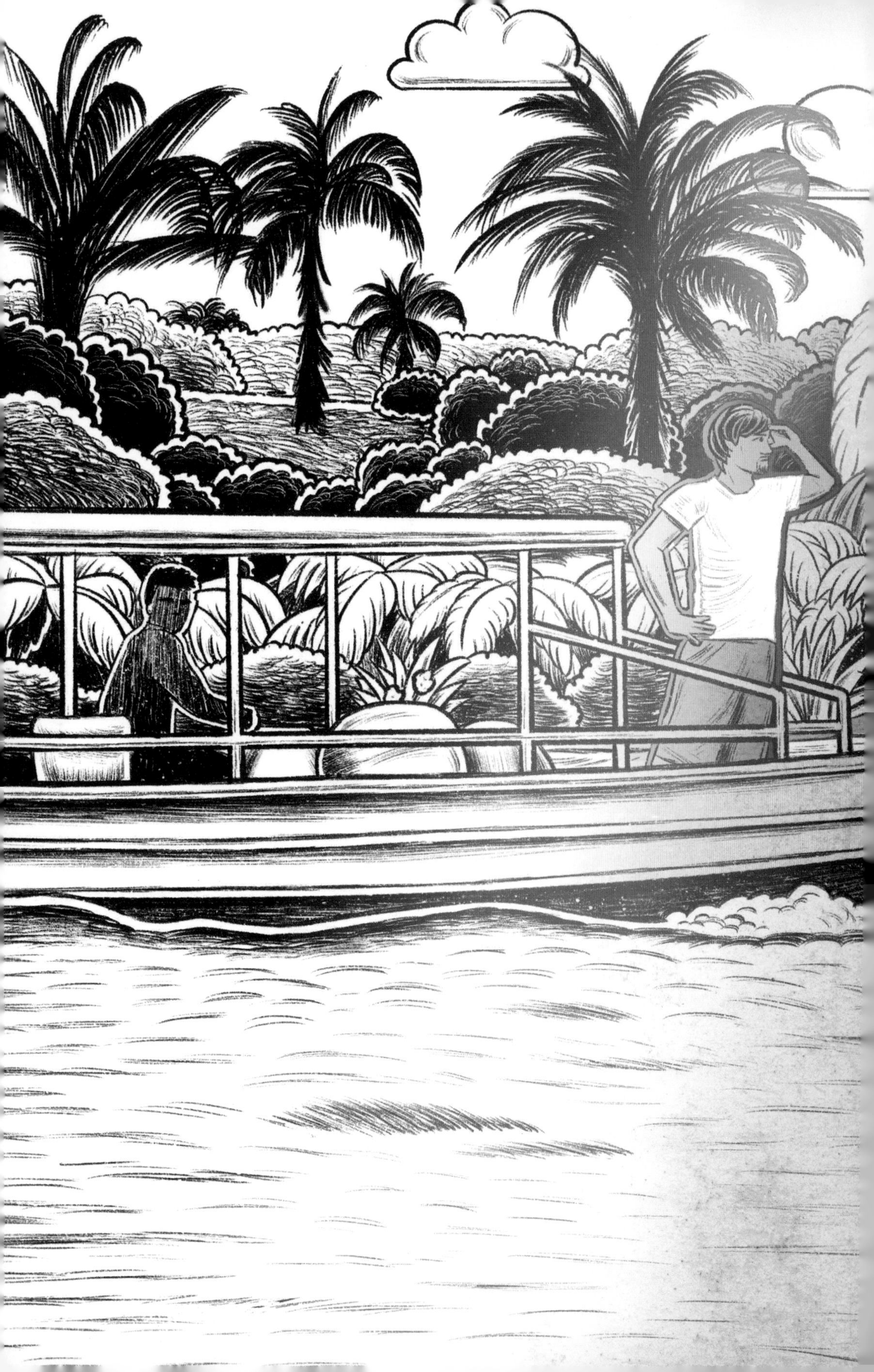